Veer Savarkar

Praise for the Book

The authors present several new facets of Savarkar which are unknown to the country. They effectively bring out how Savarkar presented the first-ever robust defence and diplomacy doctrine for independent India. This book is a must-read for every Indian who cares for the nation and dreams of India as a great nation in the years to come.

—**Rajnath Singh**, Union Defence Minister

This book presents a true account of the tragic story of India's partition and Savarkar's efforts to prevent it. It is based on deep research and offers rare lessons on fighting divisive forces for creating the ideal of united India.

—**Anupam Kher**, Actor

The book is an eye-opener on Savarkar's security vision for India in the spirit of Maharana Pratap and Shivaji Maharaj. Plus, it succinctly brings out how Savarkar was the only leader during the freedom struggle who understood the importance of princely rulers for new India and was proved correct when over 550 rulers merged their states with India without rancour, a unique sacrifice in world history which has not been duly appreciated.

—**Arvind Singh Mewar**, Descendent of Maharana Pratap and heritage hotelier

Veer Savarkar

THE MAN WHO COULD HAVE PREVENTED PARTITION

UDAY MAHURKAR
and **CHIRAYU PANDIT**

Published by
Rupa Publications India Pvt. Ltd 2021
7/16, Ansari Road, Daryaganj
New Delhi 110002

Sales centres:
Allahabad Bengaluru Chennai
Hyderabad Jaipur Kathmandu
Kolkata Mumbai

Copyright © Uday Mahurkar and Chirayu Pandit 2021

All rights reserved.
No part of this publication may be reproduced, transmitted,
or stored in a retrieval system, in any form or by any means,
electronic, mechanical, photocopying, recording or otherwise,
without the prior permission of the publisher.

The views and opinions expressed in this book are
the authors' own and the facts are as reported by them
which have been verified to the extent possible,
and the publishers are not in any way liable for the same.

ISBN: 978-93-5520-048-8

Fourth impression 2022

10 9 8 7 6 5 4

The moral right of the authors has been asserted.

Printed at Parksons Graphics Pvt. Ltd, Mumbai

This book is sold subject to the condition that it shall not,
by way of trade or otherwise, be lent, resold, hired out, or otherwise
circulated, without the publisher's prior consent, in any form of binding
or cover other than that in which it is published.

Dedicated to the future generations of India so that they can build a strong, united and resilient nation as envisioned by Veer Savarkar

CONTENTS

Foreword by Mohan Bhagwat — ix
Preface — xiii
Introduction: Dawn of the Savarkar Era — xxiii

1. Deadlock at Aligarh — 1
2. Congress Surrenders to Muslim Gravamin Politics — 26
3. Understanding Savarkar's Hindutva — 65
4. India Hails the Prophet of Revolution — 91
5. A Nationalist's Battle for a United India — 128
6. Savarkar's Last Stand: The Darkest Hour — 163
7. New Paradigms in National Security and Diplomacy — 218
8. 'Savarkar-Ism': A Vision Reshapes India — 245

V.D. Savarkar: Calendar of Life Events — 286
Bibliography — 290
Index — 293

FOREWORD

It is said that the true measure of an individual's greatness is the length of the shadow he casts over posterity. By this measure, one has to agree that Shri Vinayak Damodar Savarkar was not only a great patriot but also the cornerstone of our national vision, which forms the basis of today's Bharat emerging after 70 years of learning through trials of various alternative policies and conflicting ideologies in conducting the affairs of our nation and society.

The Savarkar family offered everything it had for the attainment of their only goal—an independent, strong and prosperous Bharat. The sacrifices made for the nation by the Savarkar brothers—Babarao, Vinayakrao and Narayanrao—have few parallels in modern history. The elder brothers Babarao and Vinayakrao faced long and extremely harsh prison sentences, back-breaking labour and mind-breaking humiliation for the sake of the nation.

This book does great service to the nation by placing before it Savarkar, the visionary of India's national security and free India rather than Savarkar, the revolutionary. For, the nation knows the latter but not the former, whose vision is much needed today to fight the divisive forces and feeble ideologies caving into appeasement politics and which are almost as active today as they were before Independence, when they managed to force Partition on the country. They are still the impediments to Bharat emerging as one nation. Indeed, *Veer Savarkar: The Man Who Could Have Prevented Partition* is one of those rare books that delves deep into the real reasons behind India's partition and how the nation could have prevented it had it followed Savarkar's repeated warnings against the Congress's appeasement politics.

Unfortunately, Savarkar did not get his due even in free India. Savarkar himself never wished for any favours or returns. He was, in fact, a selfless sage serving the motherland. His recognition along with that of many others who were inadvertently or deliberately ignored or forgotten, would have established an ideal path for generations to follow and would have given some sense of the value of freedom we have earned.

In fact, just the reverse happened in Savarkar's case. He was portrayed as a communal leader and his doctrine of Hindutva as an exclusive, discriminatory and hateful evil. There was a heinous attempt to frame him in the Mahatma Gandhi assassination conspiracy. All this and much more happened in independent Bharat, for which Savarkar had dedicated his all. The political establishment, out of its fear of losing power as well as other unwarranted reasons, along with communists, who are known haters of everything that is national, stooped to do this to him. It is not difficult to find the reasons behind this 'Hate-Savarkar campaign'. For he and his vision remain the bulwark against the forces of separatism, conversion and exclusion and so these divisive forces must do their utmost to put Savarkar down.

The authors of the book, Uday Mahurkar and Chirayu Pandit, both Savarkar admirers but at the same time dispassionate analysts, have indeed done a great job of bringing before the nation the true definition of Hindutva, which is actually unalloyed nationalism or true Nation First, in which everything—religion, caste or regional pride—is secondary to national interest. Thus, they prove that Hindutva isn't discriminatory in nature but inclusive. This the authors have accomplished by unearthing historical facts through extensive research, cutting across lines. They have proved that Savarkar represents the legacy of Maharana Pratap, Chhatrapati Shivaji, Guru Gobind Singh and also patriots such as Brigadier Mohammad Usman MVC—the hero of the 1947 Indo-Pak War, Ashfaqullah Khan and the hero of 1857, Azimullah Khan. The many patriots who are dying for the nation in Kashmir today, including those from the minority community, are also part of this legacy and the nation is indebted to them in the Savarkarian spirit.

The book also effectively brings out how Savarkar was a great 'Bhavishya Vakta', who predicted much ahead of time almost all the national security threats that India would face. Savarkar predicted the Chinese threat—no less than the threat from Pakistan, the fearful happenings in Assam and many other problems that

Bharat has faced on the national security front. In that sense, the authors' observation that Savarkar is the father of Bharat's national security has merit. Their analysis that the nation has been following Savarkar's true Nation First vision on defence, internal security and foreign policy for the past seven years carries weight, as they have done a very good evaluation of Savarkar's national security and foreign policy vision to supplement their viewpoint.

This book can be seen as a guide on how to fight divisive forces and help Bharat emerge as a strong and united nation, which is the prerequisite when it comes to Bharat realizing its goal of becoming a Vishwaguru, or Teacher of the World. The authors appear very dispassionate in their approach and have also critically analysed Savarkar on the touchstone of truth. The book also draws our attention to how Gandhiji, Savarkar, Subhas Chandra Bose and other key leaders of that time had respect for each other despite their ideological differences. It is a feature from which Bharatiya politics of today has much to learn. Another great feature of the book is the authors' analysis as to how there was a similarity between Savarkar's and Babasaheb Ambedkar's national security vision, how they had mutual respect for each other and how Babasaheb helped Savarkar during the most painful period of his life—the Gandhi assassination trial.

Every Bharatiya had, still has and will always have an unshakeable admiration and immense regard for Savarkar in their heart. The generation of his time and the next who have seen him, know and can feel his strong commitment to freedom, equality and fraternity through the doctrine of Hindutva, and his extreme sacrifice for it. They have heard him as an accomplished, fiery orator, and read his dramas and poems, with their masterful language and beautiful expressions. They have read his classics with emotion and when combined with his sacrifice, they have created an everlasting impact on their lives. Savarkar was a great literary figure and, therefore, the use of the term 'classic' is apt here. They know him as a charismatic and prophetic leader and a profound thinker with a philosophy of his own.

However, these leaders are fast leaving the scene or have already left and therefore, the present-day generation is unaware of Savarkar's philosophy and ideals. But the succeeding batches of haters and baiters continue. They continue to malign and demonize Savarkar and his Hindutva philosophy. On the other hand, there are always blind and staunch believers. They worship and eulogize. It takes quite an effort to see the true picture through this mire of criss-crossing opinions and propaganda. If the present generation is to carry the torch forward, it must know the clear, exact, impartial and factual picture of the legacy that we have to bear. Who were the ones who led us? What were their qualities? What were their shortcomings? What were their deeds? What challenges did they face? How did they maintain relations? How did they manage differences? What true impact did they have on society? We must have an understanding of all these factors.

Many insights and projections that Savarkar gave in his days proved to be correct and many are yielding hitherto unknown successes. As expressed in the introduction to this book, Savarkar's era might have arrived and may be here to stay.

All in all, on the basis of extensive research, the authors have brought to light several unknown and lesser-known facts regarding Savarkar's Hindutva, his vision of Hindu Rashtra, clarity and exact evaluation by him of the Muslim problem, the thought process behind his predictions and warnings, and his relations and differences with contemporary leaders such as Gandhiji. Ample clarity has been provided to clear the confusion and to answer detractors. This book kick-starts the process of an impartial study of the background of today's Bharat, and provides a factual narration of our recent history for the present generation.

The authors and the publisher as well as all those who helped this work deserve congratulations, which I extend from my heart.

With my best wishes for the success of this landmark book.

Mohan Bhagwat
Sarsanghchalak, Rashtriya Swayamsevak Sangh (RSS)
1 July 2021

PREFACE

SCENE ONE: FEBRUARY 1947

That India will be partitioned at the point of the Muslim League's loaded gun in the guise of Direct Action is now final. Riots start engulfing various parts of India, killing thousands. However, the worse massacres in Punjab, such as the one in Sheikhpura that took a toll of over 10,000 lives—mostly Sikhs and Hindus—and that resulted in the dishonour of hundreds of women, are yet to happen. A Congress structure, based on the slogan of complete non-violence and Hindu–Muslim unity at any cost is clueless about the Muslim League violence and, therefore, caving in under influence. In this atmosphere of distrust and violence, Vinayak Damodar (V.D.) 'Veer' Savarkar receives a letter from a distraught Dr Syama Prasad (S.P.) Mukherjee. One line in the letter says it all: 'Had the Hindus listened to your call, they wouldn't have remained slaves in the land of their birth.'[1]

SCENE TWO: MAY 1963

While addressing a meeting as the chief guest at the militarization week of the Hindu Mahasabha in Bombay (now Mumbai), General (later Field Marshal) K.M. Cariappa remarks that had the nation listened to Savarkar and adopted the militarization policy propagated by him and prepared itself, it wouldn't have been placed in such a predicament.[2] He was referring to the debacle of

---

[1] Dhananjay Keer, *Veer Savarkar*, Popular Prakashan Pvt. Ltd; Second edition, 2019, p. 379.
[2] Rohit Thakur, 'Hindu Militarisation–regaining the martial spirit, 16 December 2020, *Rising Hindutva*, https://risinghindutva.in/2020/12/16/hindu-militarisation-regaining-the-martial-spirit/. Accessed on 17 August 2021.

the 1962 Indo-China War.[3]

There comes a moment in the history of a nation when it should ponder over its past and indulge in deep introspection, cutting across the various 'isms' to secure its future. Such a moment has arrived for India today. Interestingly, the canvas of history is sometimes very deceptive. On its turf, people who look like eternal heroes in their lifetimes degenerate into pale figures after some decades or after their demise. Inversely, as history unfolds, some who seem unacceptable during their lifetime emerge as heroes and their true character and contribution emerge before the world. In the first category falls Jawaharlal Nehru, who, despite his extraordinary work in institution building, doesn't carry the tag of a hero anymore, except among a small band of Nehru lovers. This is largely owing to a series of blunders he committed on the national security and foreign policy fronts, for which India has paid a huge price. In addition, his cultural disconnect with the core Indian identity and his Muslim-appeasement policies that have kept the country divided have contributed to his loss of face.

In the second category comes Veer Savarkar, one of the longest-surviving revolutionaries on India's canvas. Born in 1883 in Nashik's Bhagur, he participated in both forms of Indian freedom struggle before Independence, revolutionary as well as political. Even though he neither participated in politics nor in apolitical public activism after Independence, very few know that his contribution to India's vision as a nation was very significant during the 19 years that he lived after 1947. In fact, the insights and political recommendations he offered for free India during the last phase of his life were invaluable. Many of his principles and suggestions were, in fact, incorporated in the Constitution.

Despite this, Savarkar's name has been embroiled in artificial controversies, thanks to the machinations of his ideological opponents. He has been constantly painted as an anarchist, while his defenders have relied only on one theme to defend him—his

---

[3] As part of inculcating military culture, the Hindu Mahasabha used to observe a militarization week annually. This occasion was used to spread awareness about military preparedness with the view to implore the youth to join the defence forces.

sacrifices and exploits as a revolutionary. As a result, very little is known to the common Indian about his thoughts for the evolution and development of free India.

Though he was reviled as sectarian in the heady days of the Indian National Congress (INC), before and after Independence, his warnings on national security threats to India, which were made almost nine decades ago, have come true today. Savarkar died on the sidelines in 1966 as an unsung hero. However, today if India has been able to revoke Article 370 and create a strong security structure against the designs of the fissiparous forces, it is Savarkar's vision of no compromise with divisive forces that the Narendra Modi-led government at the Centre is actually implementing.

People might ask here: where does Sardar Vallabhbhai Patel fit in? Though a valid point, the counter to this question is: had Savarkar been in the Congress, would he have allowed the party to pass the 1942 resolution giving provinces the right to self-determination (secession) on the issue of joining the Indian Union? This resolution proved to be the last seed for nurturing Pakistan and made it a foregone conclusion five years before it was granted. Sardar Patel was a signatory to this resolution, notwithstanding his great role later in the integration of the Indian Republic.

History proves that Savarkar's understanding of the psyche and plans of the pan-Islamists was far better than that of the other two heroes of India's struggle for freedom and integration—Sardar Patel and Netaji Subhas Chandra Bose. Incidentally, Bose was one of the members of the committee that truncated 'Vande Mataram' under Islamist pressure. Perhaps the only political leaders who could fully match Savarkar's understanding of the pan-Islamist psyche and strategy were Dr B.R. Ambedkar and Hindu Mahasabha leader, B.S. Munje (better known as Dharamvir Munje).

It is this historical need of the hour that has impelled me and my co-author, Chirayu Pandit, an extremely knowledgeable person on the Savarkarian ideology, to attempt this work. Though a large number of works on Savarkar in the past are surcharged with an emotional narrative, this book represents a broader analysis of Savarkar and his true contribution to the nation, which goes beyond his role as a revolutionary. It analyses Savarkar the thinker and the guarantor of India's security in totality.

Our book proves that even while holding strong views about the Muslim community, Savarkar welcomed those Muslims who didn't demand special concessions for their community, who wanted to remain in the national mainstream and believed in the principle of 'one-person, one-vote', which is the essence of true democracy and nationalism. But it is also true that Savarkar's harsh views on Muslims were proved correct when in the 1945–46 Central Legislative Assembly elections almost 87 per cent of the total Muslim votes polled went to the Muslim League and only 3 per cent to the Congress.[4] This is further acknowledged in Sardar Patel's famous 3 January 1948 public speech in Calcutta (now Kolkata): 'Most of the Muslims who have stayed back in Hindustan, helped in creating Pakistan. Now, I don't understand what has changed in one night that they are asking us not to doubt their loyalty.'[5]

No honest student of history can deny that probably the main basis of Pakistan was the Muslim-appeasement policy of the Congress, which encouraged the Muslim leadership to make more and more special demands before the nation. Its last demand was Pakistan. Of course, the Anglo-Muslim Alliance in which the British encouraged the Muslims' separatist demands also played a significant role. From tracing the history of the phenomenon to showing how allegations aimed at defaming Savarkar to make him unacceptable for the nation's new generation are all wrong, this book uncovers the complete dark side of this disease that has negatively affected the nation's progress. It is pertinent to note here that eminent leader Dadabhai Naoroji, a Parsi, had strongly pitched for equal treatment to all Indians in 1886 when the Aligarh School was trying to prevent Indian Muslims from joining the Congress.[6]

---

[4]Sheshrao More, *Congress Ni Ani Gandhiji Ni Akhand Bharat Kaa Nakarla*, p. 425.
[5]'Sardar Patel speech from Calcutta Maidan, 3rd January, 1948.' https://www.youtube.com/watch?v=40aannaRcUI&t=6s. Accessed on 23 August 2021.
[6]R.P. Masani, *The Grand Old Man of India*, Mysore: Kavyalay Publishers, 1968, p. 93.

Therefore, Savarkar was voicing the same demand as Naoroji in 1937—based on appeasement of none and equal rights for all—from the Hindu Mahasabha platform. It also shows the fall of the Congress from a party voicing equal rights for all in 1886 to a party favouring Muslim appeasement at any cost in 1937. So, this book will help the society at large in understating the true factors that led to India's partition and its consequences.

This book also seeks to explore the entire gamut of actions on Savarkar's part to prevent the formation of Pakistan and also answer as to whether Partition could have been prevented had the nation and the Congress heeded Savarkar's advice. It also provides a reply to those who say that Partition was a good, long-term augury for India as it divided the Muslim power. This is a fallacious argument, to say the least. It is full of incongruities in the light of the fact that since 1947, the Hindu population in today's Pakistan has declined by 92 per cent[7] and by almost 70 per cent in Bangladesh[8], while the Muslim population in India has grown over 500–600 per cent during the same period, as per our analysis. This also reveals the baselessness of the allegations of Muslim victimhood being repeatedly levelled by many senior Muslims leaders, communists and pseudo-secularists. If the charges were true, then Indian Muslims would have fled to Pakistan and Bangladesh—just like Hindus and non-Muslims fled the two countries to India because of the persecution they faced from a section of fanatical Muslims in those two countries after Partition.

Yet another facet that this book examines is the contribution of the revolutionary movement when India finally attained freedom in 1947. The impression we get from history books is that the passive fight of the Congress was the main reason behind Britain granting us Independence. However, when Clement Attlee, British prime minister at the time of India's independence, came to stay with

---

[7] Anand Ranganathan, 'The Vanishing Hindus of Pakistan: A Demographic Study,' *Newslaundry*, 9 January 2015, https://www.newslaundry.com/2015/01/09/the-vanishing-hindus-of-pakistan-a-demographic-study-2. Accessed on 15 July 2021.

[8] *Banglapedia: National Encyclopedia of Bangladesh*, https://en.banglapedia.org/index.php/Population. Accessed on 2 September 2021.

the acting governor of West Bengal, Justice P.B. Chakraborty, as his guest at Calcutta in 1956, he told Chakraborty in a discussion that Gandhi's influence over the British was 'minimal' in the British decision to grant Independence to India and that there were other factors responsible that impacted the British's move.[9] These factors, according to Attlee, were the spectre of fear created by Bose's Azad Hind Fauj (Indian National Army [INA]) episode[10] and also the threat of lakhs of Indian soldiers returning from Europe after the end of World War II, who wanted the British to leave India against the services they had rendered to the British empire in the war. The British feared that the returning Indian soldiers might revolt against the British's act of persecuting those Indian soldiers who had joined the Azad Hind Fauj after being made prisoners of war by Germany and Japan in World War II and who were later caught by the British Indian forces following the fall of Bose's army. Attlee also mentioned the 1946 mutiny of navy soldiers at Bombay dock as one of the final reasons for the British's departure.

It would be pertinent to recall Savarkar's militarization call to Hindus to join British Indian forces in 1939 at the outbreak of World War II. This informs of the important role that Savarkar played in the evolution of the Indian nation as we see it today. In 1937, Savarkar had suspected that separatist Muslims would demand India's partition in the future. (The word 'Pakistan' was in public domain since 1932 when the name was coined by Choudhary Rahmat Ali while studying in Cambridge and when Mohammed Ali Jinnah too was living in London.) Therefore, the following year, Savarkar called upon the Hindu youth to join the army as British Indian soldiers and get arms training in view of the future threat to the unity and integrity of India. With the start of World War II, he intensified his drive for the militarization of Hindus. Savarkar was the only leader to perceive this threat at that time. He repeated his

---

[9]Maj. Gen. (Dr) G.D. Bakshi, S.M., *Bose or Gandhi: Who Got India Her* Freedom, K.W. Publishers Pvt. Ltd; First edition, 2019, p. 61.
[10]This is well described by historian R.C. Majumdar in his book *History of Bengal* (B.R. Publishing Corporation, 2011). P.B. Chakraborty himself shared this with Majumdar in a letter that he wrote to him.

clarion call with greater vigour after the Muslim League adopted the resolution demanding the formation of Pakistan in 1940.

Savarkar prophetically observed that Muslim leaders, as part of their future, separatist strategy, were facilitating the recruitment of Muslim soldiers in the British Indian army, taking advantage of the war in which Britain needed more troops to fight the Axis forces. But he noticed that the number of Hindu soldiers in the army was less than Muslims as per the Hindu–Muslim population ratio in the country.[11] Savarkar was finally proved correct when lakhs of Hindus joined the defence forces as soldiers following Savarkar's campaign and that of his party, the Hindu Mahasabha, leaving Muslim League leaders extremely alarmed. The Muslim League leaders officially objected to increased recruitment of Hindu soldiers several times between 1941 and 1944. The shrewd League leaders perhaps knew that due to the Congress's weak-kneed strategy, India would concede Pakistan and, on the day of Partition, the army strength of Pakistan vis-à-vis India's would play a big role in determining the final size of the two nations. Over 90 per cent of the Muslim soldiers of the undivided British Indian army chose to go with the Pakistan army and very few joined the Indian army, thus proving Savarkar correct.[12] Interestingly, Savarkar's words proved prophetic when in 1948, within months of Partition, the newly created Pakistan tried to swallow Kashmir through masked military intervention. It was a development in which India finally lost almost one-third of Kashmir to Pakistan.

Had Savarkar not given the call of militarization to Hindus and had the military strength of India been inferior as compared with Pakistan at the time of Partition, the new Islamic nation might have tried to swallow more areas of partitioned India, apart from Kashmir. Savarkar's ideology and actions had a major impact even when the last nail was being driven into the coffin of British rule in India. Sadly, the nation is unaware of this.

---

[11]B.R. Ambedkar, *Thoughts on Pakistan*, Prabhat Prakashan, 2020, p. 85.
[12]'Muslims in Indian Army,' *Dawn*, 15 March 2010. https://www.dawn.com/news/842925/muslims-in-indian-army. Accessed on 27 July 2021.

The last chapter of this book deals with how the absence of Savarkarian vision has affected our national psyche and prevents us from realizing our true potential. It illustrates with examples how the lack of Savarkarian vision has led to distortions in history which, in turn, have affected our national vision and left our mind fractured in many other areas. It further analyses what today's India would have been like had the Savarkarian vision been implemented soon after Independence.

But a more important issue that the book tries to analyse is the Savarkarian belief vis-à-vis the Congress's that complete non-violence against an enemy is a perversion of virtue because aggression from an unprincipled enemy has to be met with aggression which, he strongly believed, is necessary for maintenance of permanent peace. This Savarkarian belief was, in turn, rooted in the beliefs of the Hindu deity Lord Parshuram, who had said that the principle of non-violence against a cruel aggressor is cowardly, and a sin and that for establishing peace, even a pious Brahmin should take up weapons. India's answer to Pakistan after the 2019 Pulwama attack was perhaps based on this belief.

The book analyses Savarkar's unalloyed nationalism with new instruments and proves that it doesn't discriminate between people on the basis of religion and that it could be an answer to all the present ills of the country including the challenge of obscenity in films and OTT (over-the-top) platforms. It even proves that if propagated properly, Savarkar's brand of nationalism has the power to assimilate even those Muslims and Christians who want to remain in the national mainstream but are misguided.

NOT A HAGIOGRAPHY

No one can deny that patriotism evokes emotions. Rather, demonstration of patriotism without emotions isn't possible. However, when one is writing on a person like Savarkar, whose every warning about the threats to India's national security is coming true today and who has been loathed by divisive forces to prevent him from emerging as an icon of India's new generation, one has to keep emotions away to bring the true Savarkar before the nation. Therefore, we have looked at his shortcomings too. We believe a seminal work that could perhaps change the thinking of a vast section of people about an important aspect of the nation is incomplete without a mention of the shortfalls of a man of Savarkar's stature.

Otherwise, it could add to the culture of sheer hypocrisy in this country, partly based on emotions and partly due to the designs of the divisive forces wherein only a positive side of a great personality is presented and his shortcomings are sought to be buried. That amounts to writing unfair history. And distorted history is harmful for a nation's future and against Savarkar's own principle of true Nation First. In India, this has put spokes in the path of the nation's goal of becoming a Vishwaguru.

The year 2022 will be the Diamond Jubilee year of India's independence and the nation looks forward to celebrating it with the required fervour despite the ugly shadow of the COVID-19 crisis that the country faces. But the nation can't forget that it is also the 75th year of the tragic story of India's partition which saw 1.5 million deaths and plunder and rape of thousands of women in what was nothing less than medieval vandalism. It was the greatest catastrophe to hit humanity in the twentieth century, perhaps even greater than the Nazi holocaust. But the pressures of vote-bank politics have worked overtime in this country to ensure that the nation forgets this tragedy and doesn't draw a lesson from it. This book is also an attempt to ensure that the country draws the right lessons from that gory episode to prevent its recurrence. In that sense, this book is a guide to preventing another Partition in the future.

Completing this book gives both me and Pandit a deep sense of fulfilment. Both have been long-time admirers of Savarkar's contribution as a great thinker. But we believe that we have maintained enough distance from the subject of the book to appear as dispassionate. In this work, we have drawn extensively from the original sources on Savarkar, many of which are written by Savarkar himself. It has been of immense value to us because Savarkar, a great literary figure, wrote almost 6,000 pages in his lifetime.

We thank authors Akshay Jog and late Balarao Savarkar, Yuvraj Krishan and B.N. Jog, whose works we have referred to draw our own new conclusions. Balarao Savarkar, secretary to Veer Savarkar, was what personal secretary Mahadev Desai was to Mahatma Gandhi. The admirable job of record keeping that Desai did for Gandhi, Balarao performed for Veer Savarkar. The greatness of both Gandhi and Savarkar won't have shown so much in the public domain but for the passionate work of these two men.

We also place our gratitude here for late writer, Padma Vibhushan Dhananjay Keer, whose seminal work on Savarkar was of immense value to us, no less than Babasaheb Ambedkar, whose writings have helped us greatly in understanding the strategy of pan-Islamists. We have also drawn from the work of late general secretary of the Rashtriya Swayamsevak Sangh (RSS), H.V. Sheshadri, who was the keenest observer of the tragic story of India's partition and therefore express our gratitude to him. We would also like to thank the other authors whose work we have cited in this book. We thank Mumbai-based senior journalist Ashok Shinde for his help in making available the source material. We also thank Ranjit Savarkar, chairman, Swatantryaveer Savarkar Rashtriya Smarak, for providing rare photographs of Savarkar. Finally, we thank our publisher, Rupa Publications, for giving us the opportunity to write this book.

Uday Mahurkar

INTRODUCTION: DAWN OF THE SAVARKAR ERA

In the past seven decades, quite a few books and thought-provoking articles have appeared in the English language on Savarkar—deemed a political pariah when the Marxists, pan-Islamists and, in the later scenario, their extended brothers (the pseudo-Gandhians) held sway over the system. Some of the literature written by die-hard Savarkar admirers was largely limited to Savarkar the revolutionary. Of course, they devoted significant space to the social revolution that he brought about during his internment (nazarqaid/nazarbandi) in Ratnagiri from 1924 to 1937.

During this period, he led the most potent movement against untouchability in Indian history and called this the Hindu Sangathan (consolidation). Its high point was the opening of the first-ever Hindu temple in Ratnagiri in recent history that allowed the entry of untouchables—namely the Patit Pavan Mandir. Top leaders, from Gandhi to Ambedkar, lauded the movement.

Another set of writers of the far Left, pan-Islamist and of exclusive Muslim mindset condemned Savarkar either in their books or in their newspaper columns for his 'divisive thinking' and 'his harsh treatment of Muslims'; some going as far as accusing Savarkar—not Mohammed Ali Jinnah—of being responsible for the nation's partition! The same lot has gone to great lengths to defame Savarkar and make him unacceptable to the new generation by focusing on his clemency petitions to the British seeking his release from rigorous imprisonment—first from the Cellular Jail in Andaman and Nicobar and then from the Ratnagiri jail, where he passed the last three years of his rigorous imprisonment before being set free by the British in 1924 and allowed to do non-political work within the precincts of Ratnagiri district.

Most of his petitions to the British rulers sought clemency for all the prisoners who were with him in the jails and not only for himself.[1] Interestingly, even Savarkar himself didn't try to hide these clemency petitions, which he saw as quite normal in revolutionary thinking in which the best way out in such a situation was to get out of the the enemy's clutches and continue the fight. He has described his motive behind these petitions in detail in his Marathi book *Andamanchya Andheritun (From the Darkness of Andaman)*[2] and also threw light on this in his famous work, *My Transportation for Life*[3]. He says he tried to impress his fellow prisoners by giving the example of Chhatrapati Shivaji, the national hero who tried the same ruse to come out of Aurangzeb's captivity at Agra in 1666. Savarkar also gave them the example of Shivaji's treaty with Aurangzeb's general Mirza Raja Jai Singh—the Treaty of Purandar—when he was cornered by the Rajput general in 1665. The rationale behind Savarkar's thinking was that emerging victorious in a national battle was more important than anything else.[4] In a situation where you are in captivity, the only way to achieve your objective is to free yourself from the shackles at any cost. A die-hard follower of Shivaji Maharaj, Savarkar had even tried to flee British custody after his arrest in London in 1910, when he jumped into the sea near the French coast from the ship in which he was being brought to India. Unfortunately, he was caught again in a few hours. So to weigh Savarkar's action against Gandhian tools is travesty of truth.

Savarkar stayed true to his objective of promoting revolutionary methods while he lived in Ratnagiri from 1924 onwards. Here, a number of revolutionaries came to meet him in secrecy, which included Vasudeo Balwant Gogate, who shot at the acting governor of Bombay, Sir John Ernest Buttery Hotson, at Fergusson College,

---

[1]Vinayak Damodar Savarkar, *Mazi Janmathep, Vol. II*, Lakhey Prakashan, 2018, p. 148.
[2]Veer Savarkar, *Andamanchya Andheritun (From the Darkness of Andaman)*.
[3]Veer Savarkar, *My Transportation for Life*, Prabhat Prakashan; First edition, 2020.
[4]Acharya Balarao Savarkar, *Swatantryaveer Savarkar: Ratnagiri Parva*, Swatantryaveer Savarkar Rashtriya Smarak, 2020, p. 295.

Pune, on 22 July 1931.[5] According to Vamanrao Chavan, Bhagat Singh and Rajguru (who, like Savarkar, was a Brahmin from Pune) had paid a secret visit to Ratnagiri to seek Savarkar's guidance for their revolutionary activity.[6] When Chavan shot at a British sergeant at Dhobi Talav in Bombay on 26 April 1934, Savarkar was suspected to be a part of the conspiracy. His house in Ratnagiri was searched and he was put in jail for 15 days on this occasion. In fact, Savarkar started his behind-the-scenes activity of supporting revolutionaries as soon as he was released from jail and put in nazarqaid.

In the same year, when plague broke out in Ratnagiri, Savarkar was moved to Nashik with some conditions. There too he started meeting revolutionaries. One of them was Dhundiraj Thengadi, who was later arrested along with 30 other revolutionaries on the charge of overthrowing British rule.[7] Savarkar's activities in Nashik became so suspicious that the British collector there called him to his office and warned him against not following the conditions on which he was released from jail.

ONE BRAVE HEART INSPIRES ANOTHER

Interestingly, the Left and pan-Islamist writers have not just deliberately ignored Savarkar's writings about the justification behind his clemency petitions but have gone further and found a cunning way of contrasting Savarkar's patriotism and his mercy petitions with Bhagat Singh's sacrifice in embracing the gallows with a smiling face after conviction in the Saunders murder case. They appropriated Bhagat Singh and projected him as a face of Left ideology, thus contrasting the patriotism of Hindutva revolutionary forces with that of communists. This is contradictory in itself as communism and patriotism are most contrasting terms today, when Indian communists refuse to condemn communist China despite its aggression on India.

---

[5]Ibid.
[6]Ibid.
[7]Akshay Jog, *Veer Savarkar: Allegations and Facts*, Pune, 2019, p. 61.

These writers also deliberately ignore the fact that Bhagat Singh was highly inspired by Savarkar's famous book *1857: India's First War of Independence*, something that is well-recorded.[8] They also sidestepped something that was revealed by Savarkar himself in 1952—that he had played a role in Subhas Chandra Bose's decision to flee to Japan and float the Azad Hind Fauj to fight British occupation of India. Savarkar said he gave the advice to Bose, during his June 1940 meeting with him at Bose's Bombay residence, based on his belief that on the world stage an enemy's enemy has to be regarded as a friend and used for our national objective and that no country is a permanent enemy or a permanent friend in the comity of nations because national interest is the only thing that is permanent. Within six months of this meeting, Netaji fled India.[9]

The complete appropriation of Bhagat Singh by communists requires a close look in the light of a plethora of evidence that is available. Questions were raised about his autobiographical essay titled 'Why I am an Atheist', which was published by a Left historian. Incidentally, all the original letters and his works in the form of articles and poems he wrote while in jail and before that are available in national archives but not the manuscript of this essay. Another reason given by Left strategists for declaring him as an atheist is a book on Lenin that he had in his jail cell. But the fact that he had four other books with him when he went to the gallows, including one on Maharana Pratap and another on Guru Gobind Singh and yet another on Punjab's romantic legends, Heer-Ranjha, is overlooked by the Left propagandists.

Further, the last line of Bhagat Singh's last letter to his younger brother Kultar Singh from jail said, *'Jo rab nu manzoor* (Whatever God ordains)'. Would a man who wrote an essay titled 'Why I am an Atheist' take the name of God in his last letter?[10]

The justifiable explanation given by non-communists for the

---

[8]Dhananjay Keer, *Veer Savarkar*, Popular Prakashan Pvt. Ltd; Second edition, 2019, p. 60.
[9]Balarao Savarkar, *Abhinav Bharat Sangata Bhashane* (SS Vol. 8), p. 48.
[10]Anilesh Mahajan and Subhash Sharma, *Rashtrawadi Bhagat Singh*, p. 2, 3, 8, 9, 20 and 21.

book on Lenin which Bhagat Singh read is that in those days Lenin was a symbol of the fight against imperialism. Bhagat was fighting British imperialism and found it convenient to read the book. In fact, while in Ratnagiri, Savarkar himself imparted lessons on Lenin to budding revolutionaries who saw him as a bulwark against modern imperialism.

Bhagat Singh, along with Chandra Shekhar Azad, was, in fact, the founder of the Hindustan Socialist Republican Association (HSRA), a nomenclature that was selected only because it symbolized the fight against British imperialism and was apparently inspired by Lenin's revolution against Russian imperialism, which then was not very old. To say that they had embraced communism of the variety we have seen across the globe in the later years and see even now and which runs counter to the idea of nationalism would be too farfetched. Moreover, Bhagat Singh's uncle, revolutionary Ajit Singh, was helping Savarkar in spreading unrest in the army.[11] Despite such evidence, Bhagat Singh has been hijacked by communists.

But the most unimpeachable evidence of the fact that Bhagat Singh drew inspiration from Savarkar and understood his spirit of *Vasudhaiva Kutumbakam* (the world is a large family) is found in Bhagat's own writings. In his article titled 'Vishwa Prem', which appeared in a magazine called *Matwala* on 22 November 1924, Bhagat Singh says, 'We describe Savarkar as an arch anarchist and vitriolic revolutionary but ultimately he was a brave believer in world brotherhood.'[12] This matches with what Savarkar has written on the last page of his epic work *Hindutva*, where he says, 'A day will come when the world will have to face the force of Hindutva. Equally certain is that whenever Hindus come to hold such a position and dictate terms to the whole world, those terms cannot be different from the terms which Gita dictates or the Buddha lays down.'[13]

There is further evidence of Bhagat Singh not being a classical

---

[11] Balarao Savarkar, *Abhinav Bharat Sangata Bhashane* (SS Vol. 8), p. 34.

[12] Datta Desai and Prof. Chamanlal, *Shahid Bhagatsinh Samagra Vangmaya*, Manovikas Prakashan; First edition, 2016, p. 401.

[13] V.D. Savarkar, *Hindutva* (SS Vol. 10), Hindi Sahitya Sadan, 2003, p. 104.

communist in his famous jail diaries in which he has quoted six times from Savarkar's work, *Hindu Pad-Padashahi*. And the quotes nowhere indicate that he had communist leanings. For example, one quote says, 'It is easy to break the shackles of political bondage but very difficult to break the shackles of cultural bondage.' Another quote says, 'It is good to die rather than accept conversion (to other religious faith) but it is even better to fight and defeat the violent forces ranged against Dharma and die in doing so.'

POLITICS OF AN ASSASSINATION AND BEYOND

There are even more glaring cases of how, contrary to available evidence, a systematic campaign of calumny has been led against Savarkar on the issue of Gandhi's assassination. This evidence proves that he was not just innocent, but had even opposed the anarchist ways of Nathuram Godse and Narayan Apte, Gandhi's killers, and their followers in the Hindu Mahasabha. Stories have repeatedly surfaced in the media quoting Left and Muslim leaders accusing Savarkar of Gandhi's assassination, along with Godse and Apte, despite the fact that Savarkar was acquitted in the case by court. They say Savarkar was let off only because of lack of evidence, which gave him the benefit of the doubt.

This accusation is patently false, and is proved by the fact that just before India's partition, Godse, as a member of the Hindu Mahasabha, repeatedly accused Savarkar and other senior leaders of the party such as Dr S.P. Mukherjee, B.S. Munje and L.B. Bhopatkar of being passive in opposing the Congress and Gandhi. Once, Godse and his colleague Apte violently opposed Savarkar at the party convention held at Barshi in Maharashtra on 15 December 1946. This was the time when Partition looked certain and the situation was becoming dire in respect of Hindu–Muslim riots. The meet decided that in such a delicate situation, the Hindu Mahasabha should support the interim government led by Pandit Nehru, which had been in power for three months at that point. Godse and Apte opposed the proposal. But when Bhopatkar expressed his opinion that the Hindu Mahasabha could be dissolved as a party when the time comes, Godse, in a fit of rage, chased him with a knife! Bhopatkar would have been stabbed had the other members not intervened.

Savarkar even chided Godse for interrupting and bullying Gandhi in a public meeting in June 1947, two months before Partition. This was the period when Godse and Apte were opposing Gandhi's alleged Muslim-appeasement policies.[14] It was, therefore, not surprising that as the editor of two newspapers *Agrani* and *Hindu Rashtra*, Godse repeatedly criticized the Hindu Mahasabha leadership including Savarkar for being unable to protect Hindu interests and called upon the youth to act independently sidestepping the senior Hindu Mahasabha leadership. Almost the entire Hindu Mahasabha leadership was in disagreement with the anarchist ways of Godse and Apte. In fact, both before and after Independence, Savarkar had himself preached in the form of speeches and articles that anarchist ways are justified when one is fighting for independence from a foreign power but totally untenable when used against your own country's leadership because this can lead to anarchy, which no independent nation can afford.[15]

On being accused in Gandhi's assassination, and then being acquitted, Savarkar was for some time a broken man. He just couldn't believe that he who had sacrificed the most for the nation in terms of suffering physical torture would have to go to jail in independent India. In fact, when Savarkar was made an accused by the Nehru government, most of the Cabinet members including the then law minister Ambedkar had opposed it. But they all had to bow to the wishes of Nehru, who was bent upon prosecuting Savarkar in the case.[16]

Yet, according to new evidence, Ambedkar secretly met Savarkar's lawyer and Hindu Mahasabha leader Bhopatkar in Delhi and inspired him to fight the case vigorously telling him that he

---

[14]Akshay Jog, *Swantantrya Veer Savarkar: Akshep Ani Vastav*, Mrutanjay Prakashan, 2019, p. 110.
[15]Balarao Savarkar, *Savarkaranchi Abhinav Bharat Sangata Bhashane* (SS Vol. 8), p. 63.
[16]Akshay Jog, *Veer Savarkar: Allegations and Facts*, Pune, 2019.

(Ambedkar) felt that the case against Savarkar was very weak and that he would be ultimately acquitted.[17] In fact, Ambedkar had such sympathy for Savarkar that he came to the Delhi court at least twice, once with his wife and another Congress leader, Kakasaheb Gadgil. On 22 June 1949, when the hearing began in the court of Justice Atma Charan, Ambedkar sat in the front row with his wife and Gadgil to ensure that the judge noticed his presence. It is pertinent to note here that Savarkar and Ambedkar shared something special. They were the only two leaders in the last hundred years, apart from Munje, who could comprehend the strategy of pan-Islamists to develop a Muslim-dominated polity in India based on Muslim appeasement which, in turn, was based on false Muslim victimhood theory.

Savarkar opposed Gandhi on the ideological plane but invariably showed him respect at a personal level. He didn't allow his ideological differences to turn into personal prejudice. When talking about Gandhi, Savarkar would always address him as 'Mahatmaji'. In one of his articles dated 3 August 1928, Savarkar clarified his view on Gandhi in clear terms. He said:

> ... We want to do and say only those words that will be useful to support and assist Mahatma ji as it is appropriate to fight in unison. Whenever we find national interest is compromised, we will definitely try to stop him. That too for the sake of the nation. Otherwise, our motto is: Vayam Panchadhikam Shatam (from Mahabharat, it means we are all together and hence 105–100 Kauravas and 5 Pandavas).[18]

In 1943, when Gandhi went on a 21-day fast, Savarkar sent a telegram to Sir Tej Bahadur Sapru saying, 'Mahatma Gandhi's life is not so much his own as it is a national asset.' When Gandhi was released from detention in Aga Khan palace, Pune, in May 1944, Savarkar released a statement saying: 'Given the old age of Gandhiji, his deteriorating health and his recent severe illness, the

---

[17]Ibid.
[18]*Shraddhanand*, 3 August 1928.

government's decision has brought a sigh of relief to the nation.'[19]

Interestingly, Savarkar and Gandhi came face to face only twice in their careers and on both the occasions, they showed mutual respect for each other. The first occasion was the 1909 Dussehra celebration of Indian students in London while Gandhi was on tour to the United Kingdom (UK) from South Africa. Gandhi, the chief guest, expressed hope that India would reap the fruits of Savarkar's sacrifice and patriotism.[20] The second occasion came when Gandhi visited Ratnagiri in 1927 and praised Savarkar's work to remove untouchability with his own unique model. Interestingly, a resolution passed by the Congress at its 1923 Kakinada (Andhra Pradesh) session sought Savarkar's release from rigorous imprisonment at a time when Savarkar had been shifted from the Cellular Jail in Andaman to Ratnagiri jail.

The Savarkar vilification campaign, of which besides the Congress most of the so-called secular parties have been part, began in full earnest when recently a senior Congress leader dubbed Savarkar as an enemy of Hindu–Muslim unity and an architect of Pakistan in what was complete falsification of history.[21] Around the same time, the mercy petition charge was added to it in what was a 'put-down-Savarkar-at-any-cost campaign'. What was surprising about the campaign was that even Pandit Nehru, Savarkar's biggest political rival, and his daughter, Mrs Indira Gandhi, never made these charges against him. On the contrary, Mrs Gandhi praised Savarkar more than once as prime minister and even released a stamp to commemorate him.

Significantly, in a surprising gesture before he died, Pandit Nehru, a broken man then, knocked down by India's humiliating

---

[19] Akshay Jog, *Swantantrya Veer Savarkar: Akshep Ani Vastav*, Mrutunjay Prakashan, 2019, p. 104.

[20] Dhananjay Keer, *Veer Savarkar*, Popular Prakashan Pvt. Ltd; Second edition, 2019, p. 64.

[21] Indo Asian News Service (Lahore), 'Mani Shankar Aiyar says Savarkar was first proponent of two-nation theory', *Hindustan Times*, 7 May 2018, https://www.hindustantimes.com/india-news/mani-shankar-aiyar-says-savarkar-was-first-proponent-of-two-nation-theory/story-5YUjO7R36lIkUAw3bsG1oL.html, accessed on 31 August 2021.

defeat against China in the 1962 war, invited the RSS to take part in the 1963 Republic Day parade in Delhi.[22] In response to his invitation, a contingent of RSS volunteers dressed in khakis took part in the parade. Nehru never explained as to how he became an admirer of an organization that he had virtually accused of Gandhi's assasination in 1948. But inferences can be precisely drawn from the prevailing circumstances and the history of the Independence struggle. He had closely seen how Gandhi's policy of complete non-violence and 'Hindu–Muslim unity at any cost' had failed to prevent horrendous communal violence at the time of Partition.

Nehru had also experienced how his own neglect of India's defence requirements due to his pacifist beliefs had proved costly to India in the Indo-China war of 1962, in which India's lack of defence preparedness was the main reason behind its humiliating defeat. The RSS had always preached strong self-defence against aggressors and scores of RSS volunteers have contributed in various ways towards maintaining internal security.[23]

These two things perhaps compelled Nehru to self-introspect and see the Congress's and his own blunders of the past in new light. It is not out of place to surmise in retrospect that this resulted in his belated appreciation of the RSS. Had Nehru lived longer, he would have perhaps changed his opinion on Savarkar too.

SAVARKAR'S HINDUTVA

In contrast to how Savarkar has been presented by a group of politicians and Left-Liberals, this book explores Savarkar's political and national security vision with its multifaceted aspects. The book is, in fact, a new interpretation of Savarkar's Hindutva ideology of unalloyed nationalism in the spirit of true Nation First, five decades after he left this world. We have also analysed the two

---

[22]M.G. Chitkara, *Rashtriya Swayamsevak Sangh: National Upsurge*, APH Publishing Corporation, 2004, p. 275.

[23]M.S. Golwalkar, *Bunch of Thoughts*, p. 224.

stepping stones to understanding Savarkar's thinking: the history of the Congress's Muslim appeasement as well as the history of pan-Islamism in the country.

Contrary to what the anti-Savarkar lobby alleges, Hindutva puts the nation before everything else including religion, caste and regional pride. We have tried to bring out the true Savarkar, who, in fighting for Hindu rights amid Muslim appeasement, was actually fighting for equal rights. Put differently, Savarkar was not demanding special rights for Hindus but was opposing Muslim appeasement at the cost of Hindu rights. His Hindutva was, in fact, a Hindu-protective view and not a Hindu-supremacist view.

As the Hindu Mahasabha president, Savarkar himself made this crystal clear in 1938 in his reply to a press interview question at Lahore. He said, 'Myself and Jinnah are not birds of the same feather. While I am for equal treatment for all and no concessions, Jinnah is for more and more concessions for Muslims.'[24] Savarkar's manifesto for an independent India, which he made in the 1930s, further specified his Hindutva vision in unequivocal terms. The manifesto clearly said, 'In independent India, all religions and castes will have equal rights. Should any one hinder the *puja-archana* (prayers) of religious minorities (read Muslims and Christians), the State will step in and ensure that they are able to offer prayers in the way they do.' However, after saying this he holds out a warning, 'However, the nation will not allow creation of a State within a State in the name of (religious) "Minoritism".'[25]

A further evidence of the contours of his nationalism can be seen in his statement issued in 1945 which was a public appeal to the constituents of the non-Mohamedan constituency of Bombay (there were separate electorates then). In this statement, Savarkar said the Hindu Mahasabha recognized all citizens of India as one and didn't believe in majority and minority. He said a meritorious Parsi would have the first chance in an appointment if he is found

---

[24] Dhananjay Keer, *Veer Savarkar*, Popular Prakashan Pvt. Ltd; Second edition, 2019.
[25] Ibid. 236, 281, 282.

to be more meritorious than Hindu and Muslim candidates. It was on such perfectly democratic and just national principles that the approved constitution of the Hindu Mahasabha took its stand.[26]

The most prominent trait of Savarkar's ideology is that it is able to identify closet Islamists or communists, people who are inwardly anti-Hindus but masquerade as moderates or patriots and whose number in today's India is fairly large. In that sense, Savarkar's unalloyed nationalism is a prism through which the nation can identify pseudo-patriots from the true patriots.

A good example was of Sir Mirza Ismail, generally described as a great statesman, a visionary of good governance and a friend of some of the greatest men of pre-Independence India such as industrialist G.D. Birla and Nobel Laureate Sir C.V. Raman. Ismail was the prime minister of princely states such as Mysore, Hyderabad and Jaipur. Despite his pioneering efforts in good governance and modernizing the princely states for which he worked as Diwan, Ismail was a closet Islamist. When he was the prime minister of Jaipur, he made the knowledge of Urdu compulsory for passing and promotion in Jaipur state civil service, thus clearly attempting to make a pathway for Muslim domination in Jaipur, where 90 per cent citizens were Hindus. The Hindu Mahasabha, with public support, started an agitation against his pro-Muslim policies. In a statement issued against Ismail on 6 November 1944, a good four years after the Muslim League's Pakistan Resolution, Savarkar said, 'Even Sir Mirza is hand in glove with many a leader of the Muslim League. Was not Sir Mirza actually congratulated to his great relish by Yunus (a Muslim League leader) on his making Urdu compulsory in Jaipur and did he not want him to go [the] whole hog in a letter dated 20-6-1944?' The letter to Ismail was the biggest evidence of the charges against him.[27]

Though today's secularists would have seen this as a misplaced agitation, the incident also helps us understand the kind of pro-Muslim, pseudo-secularism that was practised in independent

---

[26]S.S. Savarkar and G.M. Joshi, *Historic Statements of V.D. Savarkar*, p. 187.
[27]Ibid.

India. In a nutshell, appeasement of Muslims at the cost of Hindu rights in the name of minority protection is India's true story over the past century. Savarkar had seen it happening, and repeatedly predicted its consequences from 1937 onwards.

In 1937, when Savarkar was released from internment at Ratnagiri, Subhas Chandra Bose and some other Congressmen wanted him to join the Congress.[28] Savarkar made the greatest sacrifice of his career when he refused to join the most popular party of the day on the ground that it was indulging in unabashed appeasement of Muslims at the cost of Hindu rights and that this would prove very costly to the nation in the near future. This was one of Savarkar's many prophecies that came true and that too within just 10 years of his warning when India was partitioned.

Thereafter, between 1937 and 1945, he put his entire might to prevent the formation of Pakistan. For Savarkar, the indivisibility of India—from Sindh to the North-east and from Kashmir to Kanyakumari—was an article of faith. His reply to Jinnah's Pakistan scheme was 'Pakistans may come and Pakistans may go, but Hindustan goes for ever.' He tried a series of measures to thwart the Pakistan scheme even as the Congress was caving in before Jinnah's make-believe Muslim victimhood theories and after the violence he triggered following his Direct Action call. For example, he played a major role in non-Congress and non-Muslim League efforts to prevent Partition, going to great lengths to adjust with third-party leaders for a common goal. He found the Congress's decision to keep away from the census suicidal in the face of the British efforts to divide Hindus and Muslims and achieve their goals with the help of the Muslim League. The Congress had been keeping away from enumeration of population by the British on the grounds that such census along religious lines was detrimental to Hindu–Muslim unity. This resulted in various Hindus and groups of the Hindu pantheon not taking part in the census, thus resulting in a decrease in the Hindu population over a period of time. This deeply affected

---

[28]Dhananjay Keer, *Veer Savarkar*, Popular Prakashan Pvt. Ltd; Second edition, 2019, p. 225.

Hindu interests vis-à-vis Muslims. Therefore, he implored the followers of the religions of the Hindu pantheon such as Sikhs, Jains and Buddhists and even the tribals to join the census and record their names as Sikh Hindus, Buddhist Hindus, Jain Hindus and tribal Hindus. The accuracy of Savarkar's prediction can be gauged from the fact that in Bengal, where due to tribals not recording themselves as Hindus, Muslims became a majority, which, in turn, impacted the division of Bengal at the time of Partition.[29]

EVOLUTION AS A NATIONALIST THINKER

Interestingly, when it comes to Savarkar's take on Muslim appeasement and his emphasis on Hindu consolidation, there is wide gap between the pre-1910 Savarkar (the year he was sentenced to 50 years rigorous imprisonment in the Jackson murder case and other sedition charges) and the post-1923 Savarkar (the year his book *Hindutva* was first published under the pseudo name 'Maratha'). The pre-1910 Savarkar had a different take on Muslims. This was the period when he gave his famous 1909 Dussehra speech at London in Gandhi's presence in which he described the various communities of India including Muslims as a rainbow that enriched India's cultural traditions. The revolutionary Asaf Ali, who was present on the spot, described Savarkar's speech as the best he had ever heard.

This was also the period when the revolutionary movement started by Savarkar from Nashik—known as Abhinav Bharat (it was known as Mitra Mela from 1899 to 1904)—used to celebrate Ganesh festival and on one occasion even invited Sayed Haider Raza, promoter of Swadeshi movement from Delhi, as a chief guest. While talking about Hindus' fight with radical Muslims during the medieval period, Savarkar writes in *Hindutva*, 'The moral victory was won by the Hindus when Akbar came to the throne and when Dara Shukov was born.' In doing so, Savarkar perhaps drew from the celebrated letter written by Shivaji to Aurangzeb in 1679

---

[29] *Modern Review*, June–November 1941.

protesting against re-imposition of the anti-Hindu jizya tax, which was withdrawn by Akbar. In this letter, Shivaji asked Aurangzeb to emulate his great grandfather Akbar, whom he described as 'Jagadguru'.

During the same period, Ibrahim Khan, a friend of the known gymnast and wrestler of Vadodara Rajratan Manikrao, used to go to Nashik to teach horse riding to the members of Abhinav Bharat, whose aim was to produce revolutionaries in the national fight against the British.[30] Manikrao had established the Manikrao Akhada in Vadodara with the help of the then legendry reformist Vadodara ruler, Maharaja Sayajirao Gaekwad III. Sayajirao also kept in touch with the revolutionaries led by Savarkar from the backdoor. So, what transpired between 1910 and 1923 that made Savarkar come out with a book that defined the foundation of Hindu nation and preached Hindu consolidation against growing Muslim aggression?

The answer lies in the experience of Muslim behaviour he had in the Cellular Jail at Andaman and Nicobar. Here, Muslim convicts as well as Muslim employees of the prison used to try and convert depressed Hindu convicts to Islam using various ruses.[31] When Savarkar saw this, he stood as a bulwark against their activity by providing guidance and inspiration to the Hindu convicts and standing up to these Islamic missionaries in jail.

In 1921, Savarkar was moved from the Cellular Jail in Andaman to the Ratnagiri jail in the Konkan region of Maharashtra. Here, too, Savarkar witnessed the conversion activity of the Muslims, thus giving him a close insight into Muslim thinking. It was in Ratnagiri jail i.e., around 1922, that Savarkar wrote his epic work *Hindutva*. While in jail, he had kept himself abreast of the Congress's dealings

---

[30] V.M. Bhat, *Abhinav Bharat athava Savarkaranchi Krantikari Gupta Sanstha*, G.P. Parchure Prakashan Mandir, 1950, p. 27.

[31] News 18, 'Veer Savarkar Believed Some Muslims, and Christians Possess "All Essential Qualifications of Hindutva", Claims Biography,' 19 August 2019, https://www.news18.com/news/books/veer-savarkar-believed-some-muslims-and-christians-possess-all-essential-qualifications-of-hindutva-claims-biography-2275599.html. Accessed on 24 August 2021.

with pan-Islamic Muslims on various issues including the Khilafat movement.[32] He learnt about key political developments from Muslim and Congress prisoners in Ratnagiri jail. His book, which calls for Hindu consolidation to protect Hindu religion and culture from the activities (read conversion) of pan-Islamists and pan-Christians, was also influenced by these negative reports that he got in jail. The answer to this, he obviously thought, was defining the foundations of nationalism in precise terms by reminding the Hindus and the followers of the religions of the Hindu pantheon—Buddhists, Sikhs and Jains—about their common strengths.

There is another important issue that needs to be mentioned here. The entire separatist movement called Pakistan was based on the Muslim thinking that Muslims were the rulers of India in 1820 when the British gained full control over India after fighting many battles. When the Congress was formed in the closing year of the nineteenth century, the separatist Muslims propounded the theory that after ruling India for 800 years, Muslims won't get justice from Hindus in a post-British era. Many amongst the Muslims went further and expected that as former rulers of India before the British came, they should get special treatment or a separate country.

But here the moot question is: did the British take charge of India from the Muslims in 1820? The answer is negative. It was a wrong interpretation of history and a fallacious belief of divisive Muslims calculated to suit their separatist strategy. This is because the British had won India from the Marathas and not Muslims. One of the few leaders who exposed this fallacy at the time of the Independence movement was Savarkar. It was he who said that the reins of India passed on to the British from Maratha hands[33] and not Mughals and therefore the Muslim belief was based on a false premise.

Savarkar believed that Hindu–Muslim unity would be achieved when we (the system and politicians) stop appeasing religious

---

[32]V.D. Savarkar, *Mazi Janmathep* (*Samagra Savarkar, Vol. 2*), Continental Prakashan, 2018, p. 493.
[33]V.D. Savarkar, *Historic Statements by Savarkar*, G.P. Parchure, 1967.

minorities and, at the same time, justly deal with every section of the society.³⁴ Another criterion is to discard the false Muslim heroes from our history books in schools such as Tipu Sultan, who persecuted Hindus on an unimaginable scale, but under pressure from Marathas and the British showed kindness to selected Hindus to curry favour with the Hindu population, whose support he needed to save his kingdom.³⁵ India has to replace these false heroes with true Muslim heroes such as the Telugu Muslim general of the Marathas, Ibrahim Khan Gardi, the great medieval Muslim ruler of Kashmir, Sultan Zain-ul-Abidin, Emperor Akbar, his great grandson and the great Muslim symbol of syncretic culture, Dara Shukoh, Bahadur Shah Zafar and Emperor Shah Alam II. In the same history books, we can highlight the recent Muslim heroes such as the great revolutionary Ashfaqullah Khan, Brigadier Mohammed Usman, Havaldar Abdul Hamid and Indian army soldier, Aurangzeb.

Knowledge of true history is essential for national character building. There is little mention of true Maratha history except the period involving Shivaji and Peshwa Bajirao I. The knowledge of the dominance that local Hindus, in the form of Marathas, achieved over the Mughal Sultanate after Bajirao, despite the challenge from the Islamic fundamentalists, is simply missing in common people today. The true history is that the Mughal emperors were completely dependent on the Marathas for their survival from 1750 onwards after Peshwa Balaji Bajirao struck a treaty with the Mughals guaranteeing protection to the emperor on certain conditions. From this point to 1803, except for a brief period in between, it was the Marathas who ran the Mughal empire as its protectors. Even after the Mughal–Maratha connection got dissolved in 1803, before the might and skill of General Arthur Wellesley (afterwards rechristened Lord Wellington, the hero of the

---

³⁴Veer Savarkar, *Hindu Rashtra Darshan* (SS Vol. 10), Prabhat Prakashan, 2020, p. 19.
³⁵V.D. Savarkar, *Six Glorious Epochs of Indian History*, Mumbai: Bal Savarkar, 1971, p. 223.

Battle of Waterloo that brought an end to Napoleon Bonaparte's career and twice the prime minister of Great Britain), it was the Marathas that the British continued to fight in the form of the princely states of the Maratha confederacy—the states of Peshwa, Gwalior, Indore and Nagpur. The only significant Muslim ruler that the British surmounted during this period was the Nizam of Hyderabad.

And it was not that in this period between 1745 and 1803, the Muslims didn't try to break free from Maratha tutelage. They did but failed. In 1759, the eighteenth-century Delhi-based Islamic preacher and revivalist and the precursor of the Wahhabi movement in India, Shah Waliullah Muhaddis Dehlvi, wrote a letter to the Afghan invader Ahmad Shah Abdali to defeat the Marathas and 'free Islam from the clutches of Hindu Kafirs'.[36] This letter led to the third battle of Panipat in 1761 and the terrible defeat of the Marathas at the hands of the Afghan invaders and their Indian Muslim supporters such as Najib Khan, the Rohilla Yousafzai Pashtun. But within a few years, the Marathas recovered from the shock and re-established their supremacy over the Mughal emperor in Delhi.[37]

The turning point was the 1763 Battle of Rakshasbhuvan in present-day Maharashtra in which the Marathas, led by Peshwa Madhavrao and his uncle Raghunathrao, inflicted a crushing defeat on the Nizam of Hyderabad, a former noble of the Mughal court who had broken free but was seen as part of the Mughal pantheon because of being a Turani Mughal in origin. The Maratha victory at Rakshasbhuvan sent a clear signal to the Mughal empire that even after the defeat at Panipat, Marathas were a force to reckon with in Hindustan. After Mahadji Scindia became the head of the Scindia family from 1767 onwards, the Maratha affairs were back to the former level except for some years following Peshwa Madhavrao's death in 1772. But before that, Scindia captured Delhi

---

[36] Y. Krishnan, *Understanding Partition: Separation Not Liquidation*, Bharatiya Vidya Bhavan, 2002, p. 293.
[37] Sita Ram Goel, *Muslim Separatism: Causes and Consequences*, p. 52, 54.

and reinstated the emperor on the throne of Delhi. The emperor was under British protection for a brief period. Later from 1784 to 1794, Mahadji Scindia straddled across India like a colossus in his capacity as a protector of the Mughal emperor and extracted from the emperor an edict banning cow slaughter throughout the Mughal empire and got the emperor to bestow the holy districts of Mathura, Gokul, Vrindavan and Harsud as Jagir to the Peshwa.

ONE ICON, MANY LENSES

As a nationalist, Savarkar was unique in several senses and perhaps has no parallel. Savarkar the great Bhavishya Vakta (prognosticator) remains largely unexplored. He had predicted in *Hindutva*, seven to eight decades ago, a series of problems that India is facing today on the national security front, from Assam to Kashmir, including the insurmountable Muslim problem which is preventing India from exploring its full potential and as a result its rise as Vishwaguru—as has been foretold by many great men including Sri Aurobindo, Swami Vivekananda and Savarkar himself.

Equally great was Savarkar the cultural icon and the purifier of Marathi and Hindi languages. After Shivaji, Savarkar was the first person who undertook the work of purification of Marathi by replacing Persian words with Sanskrit ones. Very few people know that Hindi words such as 'Doordarshan' for 'television', 'Mahapour' for 'mayor' and 'Paarshad' for 'municipal councillor' were coined by Savarkar. It is a pity and a measure of the intellectual bankruptcy in the country that so little is known about the true contribution of such a multifaceted personality and patriot as Savarkar.

Ironically, all these years, Veer Savarkar was virtually on the sidelines except during phases when his name was heaped with calumny by his political and ideological detractors. He was quoted selectively; some of his strong statements against Muslim appeasement or pan-Islamist Muslims were wrongly used in order to drive home the charge that Savarkar was divisive. Today, Savarkar's ideology based on national security and Nation First is clearly coming into currency. This was clearly visible when India sent fighter aircrafts to bomb radical Wahhabi seminaries located at Balakot in Pakistan in February 2019 as a riposte for the killing of 42 Indian security jawans at the hands of Pakistan-sponsored terrorists.

It was more evident later when the duo of Prime Minister Narendra Modi and Home Minister Amit Shah showed uncommon fortitude to free Jammu and Kashmir from the clutches of Articles 370 and 35A of the Indian Constitution, which hit at the core of principles of democracy.

We have attempted to uncover the real Savarkar through many lenses, very different from those used by most in the past. The chapters of the book will also throw light on why Savarkar didn't succeed in the final run at that time, despite being ideologically and politically correct. We hope to place the true Savarkar before the nation so that our countrymen can learn from his mistakes, if any, and comprehend his true value for the unity and integrity of our nation.

1

DEADLOCK AT ALIGARH

A flag with the Crescent and a star, hoisted on the midnight of 14 August 1947, over 336.4 thousand sq. miles, marked the creation of one of the world's largest Islamic countries.[1] On that day, Muslims of the Indian subcontinent achieved 'Pakistan' under the leadership of Mohammed Ali Jinnah. It was the result of a long political strategy primarily shaped by the Aligarh Movement, and marked by separatism. No wonder then that Jinnah had said that 'Aligarh is the arsenal of Pakistan.'[2]

The moorings of the Aligarh Movement can be traced to Sir Syed Ahmed Khan (1817–98), recognized as a Mohammedan social reformist, educationist and founder of the Indian Patriotic Association and the Muhammadan Anglo-Oriental College (M.A.O. College in 1875), later known as the Aligarh Muslim University (AMU).

The majority Hindu community, in fact, actively helped Syed Ahmed's venture of the M.A.O. College as a token of unity. The maharajas of Patiala and Vizianagaram as well as middle-class Hindus contributed towards the establishment of the college.[3] However despite this, he and a section of Muslims in pre-Independent as well as post-Independent India have taken advantage of the liberal nature of Hindus. Syed Ahmed's political vision for Muslims and the conceptualization of his separatist two-

---

[1] *After Partition*, Publications Division, 2016, p. 21.
[2] Yuvraj Krishan, *Understanding Partition: India Sundered, Muslims Fragmented*, Mumbai: Bharatiya Vidya Bhavan, 2002, p. 127.
[3] Lal Bahadur, *The Muslim League: Its History, Activities and Achievements*, Agra Book Store, 1954, p. 115.

nation theory are generally ignored by an Indian society that has typically distorted notions about history. The contribution of his separatist thinking to the creation of Pakistan is best illustrated by his respectable status in today's Pakistan, where there are institutions named after him such as the Sir Saiyad University of Engineering and Technology and Sir Saiyad College of Medical Sciences for Girls, among others.[4] In the official history of Pakistan, historian S. Moinul Haque has described Syed Ahmed Khan as the 'founder of the Muslim nation'.[5]

INSIDE THE MIND OF A SEPARATIST

Two lectures delivered by Syed Ahmed before a large and very influential audience of Mohammedans—on 18 December 1887 in Lucknow and on 14 March 1888 in Meerut—are historical milestones and provide a deep insight into his mind and ultimate goal.[6] A critical understanding of the points raised by Syed Ahmed is the key to understanding Muslim politics in British India.

These speeches were delivered just three years after the formation of the INC, and in context of the Congress's demands and protection of Muslim interests. Congress leaders argued that if India was part of the British empire, Indians should get all the rights that were enjoyed by citizens of Britain. The Congress demanded that Indians be made part of legislative assemblies and civil services. Syed Ahmed believed that if these demands were accepted, Hindus would have an upper hand over Muslims because of the several natural and social advantages they enjoyed vis-à-vis Muslims.

Syed Ahmed warned Muslims against the parliamentary system of governance. He said,

---

[4]http://aligarhmovement.com/Sir_Saiyad_Institutions. Accessed on 29 July 2021.
[5]Sheshrao More, *Congress Aani Gandhijinee Akhand Bharat ka Nakarala*? Rajhans Prakashan; First edition, 2012, p. 38.
[6]Speech of Sir Syed Ahmed at Meerut [1888]. http://www.columbia.edu/itc/mealac/pritchett/00islamlinks/txt_sir_sayyid_meerut_1888.html. Accessed on 20 May 2021.

They want to copy the English House of Lords and the House of Commons. The elected members are to be like members of the House of Commons; the appointed members like the House of Lords. Now, let us suppose the Viceroy's Council is [to be] made in this manner. And let us suppose first of all that we have universal suffrage, as in America, and that everybody, chamars and all, have votes. And first suppose that all the Mahomedan electors vote for a Mahomedan member and all Hindu electors for a Hindu member; and now count how many votes the Mahomedan members have and how many the Hindu. It is certain the Hindu members will have four times as many, because their population is four times as numerous. Therefore, we can prove by mathematics that there will be four votes for the Hindu to every one vote for the Mahomedan. And now how can the Mahomedan guard his interests? It would be like a game of dice in which one man had four dice, and the other only one.

He continued,

In the second place, suppose that the electorate be limited. Some method of qualification must be made; for example, that people with a certain income shall be electors. Now, I ask you, O Mahomedans! Weep at your condition! Have you such wealth that you can compete with the Hindus? Most certainly not. Suppose, for example, that an income of Rs. 5,000 a year be fixed, how many Mahomedans will there be? Which party will have the larger number of votes... Leaving aside the question as to the suitability of members with regard to population, let us suppose that a rule is laid down that half the members are to be Mahomedan and half Hindus, and that the Mahomedans and Hindus are each to elect their own men. Now, I ask you to pardon me for saying something which I say with a sore heart. In the whole nation, there is no person who is equal to the Hindus in fitness for the work. I have worked in the (Viceroy's) Legislative Council for four years, and I have always known well that there can be no man more incompetent or worse fitted for the post than myself.[7]

These arguments were used against Hindus and their natural numerical superiority was depicted by Syed Ahmed as Hindu majoritarianism. But the irony was that at the same time, the Muslim leaders suitably forgot the situation of majority Hindus during the medieval era of Muslim rule when Hindus were treated like serfs. During the pre-Independence era, even in Muslim states such as Hyderabad, Hindus were discriminated against. They particularly overlooked the acts of medieval Muslim invaders and rulers to convert Hindus to Islam at the point of the sword and the trauma it caused to the Hindu society as a result. For example, the eighteenth-century South Indian Muslim ruler Tipu Sultan committed untold atrocities on the Hindus of Kerala and Coorg, breaking temples, converting lakhs of Hindus to Islam and abducting their women.[8] This was almost three centuries after the death of liberal Mughal emperor Akbar, who tried to liberalize Islam and bring relief to Hindus.

Interestingly, Syed Ahmed was so committed to his strategy that he went as far as opposing the selection of administrators through competitive exams by a giving an argument that was used widely by separatists to depict that India was not one nation. Playing on India's caste system and ethnic and geographical diversity, they projected castes as different nations. Syed Ahmed also depicted Hindus and Muslims as different nationalities—a major part of the strategy of pan-Islamist and separatist Muslims in India till this day.

He said,

> I am going to speak of the evils likely to follow the introduction into India of the competitive principle. I do not wish to speak in the interest of my own co-religionists,

---

[7]Speech of Sir Syed Ahmed at Lucknow [1887]. http://www.columbia.edu/itc/mealac/pritchett/00islamlinks/txt_sir_sayyid_lucknow_1887.html. Accessed on 20 May 2021.

[8]V.D. Savarkar, *Six Glorious Epochs of Indian History*, Mumbai: Bal Savarkar, 1971, p. 223.

but to express faithfully whether I think the country is prepared for competitive examination or not. What is the result of competitive examination in England? You know that men of all social positions, sons of Dukes or Earls, of darzies and people of low rank, are equally allowed to pass this examination. Men of both high and low family come to India in the Civil Service. But as regards Indians, the case is different. Men of good family would never like to trust their lives and property to people of low rank with whose humble origin they are well acquainted (a pointer towards the Hindu caste system).

Everyone can understand that the first condition for the introduction of competitive examination into a country is that all people in that country, from the highest to the lowest, should belong to one nation... But this is not the case with our country, which has people with different nations. Consider the Hindus alone. The Hindus of our Province—the Bengalis of the East and the Mahrattas of the Deccan—do not form one nation. If in your opinion the peoples of India do form one nation, then no doubt competitive examination may be introduced; but if this be not so, then competitive examination is not suited to the country.

The third case is that of a country in which there are different nationalities which are on an equal footing as regards the competition, whether they take advantage of it or not. Now, I ask you, have Mahomedans attained such a position as regards higher English education, which is necessary for higher appointments, as to put them on a level with Hindus or not? Most certainly not.[9]

Significantly, while accepting the incompetence of Muslims, Syed Ahmed denied the historical cultural unity of the Indian subcontinent. According to him, not only do Hindus and

---

[9]Speech of Sir Syed Ahmed at Lucknow [1887]. http://www.columbia.edu/itc/mealac/pritchett/00islamlinks/txt_sir_sayyid_lucknow_1887.html. Accessed on 20 May 2021.

Muslims belong to different 'nations', but even Hindus of different provinces do not belong to the same nation. He also projected castes as part of different nationalities. While the fact is since the time of Ptolemy, 300 years before Christ, 'India' is known as one geographical unit to the world. In fact, Kautilya, better known as Chanakya, claimed in his *Arthashashtra* that this geographical unit is the region of one empire.[10]

Syed Ahmed tried multiple ruses to promote Muslim interests. He knew full well that though it was difficult for Muslims to get political power through the legislature or civil services, they could achieve military power very easily by increasing their strength in the army. So he stressed on militarization of Muslims. He said:

> A second error of Government of the greatest magnitude is that it does not give appointments in the army to those brave people whose ancestors did not use the pen to write with; no, but a different kind of pen nor did they use black ink, but the ink they dipped their pens in was red, red ink which flows from the bodies of men. O brothers! I have fought the Government in the harshest language about these points. The time is, however, coming when my brothers—Pathans, Syeds, Hashimi, and Koreishi; whose blood smells of the blood of Abraham—will appear in glittering uniform as Colonels and Majors in the army. But we must wait for that time. Government will most certainly attend to it; provided you do not give rise to suspicions of disloyalty (to the British rulers).[11]

As part of his strategy, Syed Ahmed emphasized that Muslims joining the Congress were not true representatives of the community, thus the Congress was not representing Muslims. A few who joined the Congress were dismissed in the following words:

---

[10] Chanakya, *Kautilya's Arthashastra*, Epoch 9, Sloka 1.
[11] Speech of Sir Syed Ahmed at Lucknow [1887]. http://www.columbia.edu/itc/mealac/pritchett/00islamlinks/txt_sir_sayyid_lucknow_1887.html. Accessed on 20 May 2021.

> It is said that Prince Humayun Jah (of Nizam family) joined it (Congress). Let us suppose that Humayun Jah, whom I do not know, took part in it; yet our position as a nation will not suffer simply because two men stand aside. No one can say that because these two Raïses took part in it, that therefore the whole nation has joined it. To say that the Mahomedans have joined it is quite wrong, and is a false accusation against our nation... It was necessary and incumbent on me to show the falsity of the impression which, by taking a few Mahomedans with them by pressure or by temptation, they wished to spread, that the whole Mahomedan nation had joined them.[12]

Syed Ahmed and his successors regarded the Congress as a Hindu organization. They portrayed Congress rule as Hindu Raj, a ploy that was later effectively used by the flagbearer of Syed Ahmed's two-nation theory, the Muslim League.

He also used threatening language against Hindus when he said,

> Some Hindus think that by joining the Congress and by increasing the power of the Hindus, they will perhaps be able to suppress those Mahomedan religious rites which are opposed to their own, and, by uniting, annihilate them. But I frankly advise my Hindu friends that if they wish to cherish their religious rites, they can never be successful in this way. If they are to be successful, it can only be by friendship and agreement. The business cannot be done by force; and the greater the enmity and animosity, the greater will be their loss. I will take Aligarh as an example. There Mahomedans and Hindus are in agreement. The Dasehra and Moharrum fell together for three years, and no one knows what took place [that is, things remained quiet]. It is worth noticing how,

---

[12]Speech of Sir Syed Ahmed at Meerut [1888]. http://www.columbia.edu/itc/mealac/pritchett/00islamlinks/txt_sir_sayyid_meerut_1888.html. Accessed on 29 July 2021.

when an agitation was started against cow-killing, the sacrifice of cows increased enormously, and religious animosity grew on both sides, as all who live in India well know.[13]

Syed Ahmed threatened Bengali Hindus that if they tried to make the Congress movement successful, Muslims would make their lives miserable. In fact, it was the genesis of the partition of Bengal that happened many years later. It also showed how Muslims would treat their opponents where they were in the majority, thus revealing to the world the dangers of Muslim majoritarianism in the name of minoritism, a phenomenon India is witnessing even now.

He said,

In Bengal, the Mahomedan population is so great that if the aspirations of those Bengalis who are making so loud an agitation be fulfilled, it will be extremely difficult for the Bengalis to remain in peace even in Bengal. These proposals of the Congress are extremely inexpedient for the country, which is inhabited by two different nations who drink from the same well, breathe the air of the same city, and depend on each other for its life. To create animosity between them is good neither for peace, nor for the country, nor for the town.[14]

Syed Ahmed laid the foundation of not only the M.A.O. College but also the long-term Anglo–Muslim alliance that was detrimental to the goals of national unity. He preferred to be a subject of the British rather than Hindus. He took reference from the Koran to justify the Anglo (read Christian)-Mohammadan alliance as an

---

[13] Speech of Sir Syed Ahmed at Meerut [1888]. http://www.columbia.edu/itc/mealac/pritchett/00islamlinks/txt_sir_sayyid_meerut_1888.html. Accessed on 29 July 2021. Cow protection is an essential part of Hindu texts and history. According to Dr Ambedkar: 'Islamic law does not insist upon the slaughter of the cow for sacrificial purposes and no Musalman, when he goes to Haj, sacrifices the cow in Mecca or Medina'. (*Thoughts on Pakistan*, Prabhat Prakashan, p. 267) Later, in 1938, Jinnah put a condition to compromise with the Congress that Muslims should have the freedom to perform cow slaughter.

[14] Speech of Sir Syed Ahmed at Meerut [1888]. http://www.columbia.edu/itc/mealac/pritchett/00islamlinks/txt_sir_sayyid_meerut_1888.html. Accessed on 29 July 2021.

alliance of the people of the book (read Abrahamic faiths) against the majority community (Hindus)

> No Mahomedan can say that the English are not 'People of the Book'. No Mahomedan can deny this: that God has said that no people of other religions can be friends of Mahomedans except the Christians. He who had read the Koran and believes it, he can know that our nation (read Muslim nation) cannot expect friendship and affection from any other people. At this time, our nation is in a bad state as regards education and wealth, but God has given us the light of religion, and the Koran is present for our guidance, which has ordained them and us to be friends.
>
> Now God has made them rulers over us. Therefore, we should cultivate friendship with them, and should adopt that method by which their rule may remain permanent and firm in India, and may not pass into the hands of the Bengalis (read Hindus). This is our true friendship with our Christian rulers, and we should not join those people who wish to see us thrown into a ditch. If we join the political movement of the Bengalis, our nation will reap loss, for we do not want to become subjects of the Hindus instead of the subjects of the 'People of the Book'. And as far as we can we should remain faithful to the English Government.
>
> By this, my meaning is not that I am inclined towards their religion. Perhaps no one has written such severe books as I have against their religion, of which I am an enemy. But whatever their religion, God has called men of that religion our friends. We ought—not on account of their religion, but because of the order of God—to be friendly and faithful to them.
>
> We can mix with the English in a social way. We can eat with them, they can eat with us. Whatever hope we have of progress is from them. The Bengalis (read Bengali Hindus) can in no way assist our progress. And when the Koran itself directs us to be friends with them (the British), then there is no reason why we should not be their friends. But it is necessary

for us to act as God has said. Besides this, God has made them rulers over us. Our Prophet has said that if God place over you a black Negro slave as ruler, you must obey him. See, there is here in the meeting a European, Mr. Beck. He is not black. He is very white. Then why should we not be obedient and faithful to those white-faced men whom God has put over us, and why should we disobey the order of God?[15]

The so-called association of 'People of the Book' did not remain bookish but eventually translated into reality through the Aligarh College.

Syed Ahmed encouraged Muslims to adopt separatist goals by telling them about legends from the past:

Think for a moment who you are. What is this nation (read Muslim nation) of ours? We are those who ruled India for six or seven hundred years. From our hands, the country was taken by Government into its own. Is it not natural then for Government to entertain such thoughts? Is Government so foolish as to suppose that in seventy years we have forgotten all our grandeur and our empire? Although should Government entertain such notions, she is certainly wrong; yet, we must remember she has ample excuse. We do not live on fish, nor are we afraid of using a knife and fork lest we should cut our fingers. Our nation is of the blood of those who made not only Arabia, but Asia and Europe, to tremble. It is our nation which conquered with its sword the whole of India, although its peoples were all of one religion. I say again that if Government entertains suspicions of us, it is wrong. But do her the justice and admit that there is a reasonable ground for such suspicions. Can a wise ruler forget what the state of things was so short a time ago?[16]

---

[15]Speech of Sir Syed Ahmed at Meerut [1888]. http://www.columbia.edu/itc/mealac/pritchett/00islamlinks/txt_sir_sayyid_meerut_1888.html. Accessed on 29 July 2021.

[16]Speech of Sir Syed Ahmed at Meerut [1887]. http://www.columbia.edu/itc/mealac/pritchett/00islamlinks/txt_sir_sayyid_lucknow_1887.html. Accessed on 29 July 2021.

That the British conquered India from Muslims and therefore they should hand over the nation to Muslims before leaving India was an extremely fallacious argument. The great social reformer, Justice Mahadev Govind Ranade very clearly denied this argument:

> In the first place, it should be noted that the immediate predecessors of the British rulers of India were not the Mahomedans, as is too often taken for granted, but they were the Native rulers of the country, who had successfully thrown off the Mahomedan yoke. Grant Duff (noted British historian) indeed describes the Marathas as 'our predecessors in conquest in India, whose power was gradually gaining strength, before it found a head in the far-famed adventurer, Shivaji Bhonsle'. Except in Bengal and on the Coromandel Coast, the powers displaced by the English conquest were not Mahomedan but native Hindu rulers who had successfully asserted their independence. Among these Native Powers, the first place must be assigned to the members of the Maratha Confederacy. The Maratha power took its rise in Western Maharashtra, and the sphere of its influence soon extended to the Central Deccan, Karnatak, and Southern India as far south as Tanjore, including Mysore. On the north, it embraced Gujarat including Kathiawad, Berars, Central Provinces up to Cuttack, Malwa in Central India, Bundelkhand, Rajputana, and Northern India including Delhi, Agra, the Doab and Rohilkhand. Bengal and Oudh were invaded, but were protected from conquest solely by the interposition of the British armies. For fifty years, the Emperors at Delhi were made or unmade by the agents of this Power. In these limits, the power was in the hands of native chiefs, who were either members of the Confederacy or old rulers in subordinate alliances with the Confederacy. The two buffer Mahomedan States at Hyderabad and Mysore were completely under the same influence. The secret of a combination which extended its sway over such a vast territory, and held it together for over a century, cannot but

be a matter of absorbing interest to the British Rulers of India.

...The recognized head of the Confederacy was the Peshwa who was not only the chief military leader in his own country, but was also the deputy to the Delhi Emperors kept virtually as puppets in the Moghul Palace. For all practical purposes, therefore, it may be safely stated that, except in Bengal and on the Madras Coast, the chief power in the country was in the hands of the Native Hindu Rulers controlled by the Maratha Confederacy. The Mahomedan influence had spent itself, and the Hindus had asserted their position and become independent rulers of the country with whom alone the British Power had to contend for supremacy.[17]

This proves how false Syed Ahmed's claims were in his pursuit of what later turned out to be the two-nation theory, which eventually led to India's partition. In fact, he even anticipated partition of India in very clear words, when he said:

I wish to explain what method my nation—nay, rather the whole people of this country—ought to pursue in political matters. I will treat in regular sequence of the political questions of India, in order that you may have full opportunity of giving your attention to them. The first of all is this—in whose hands shall the administration and the Empire of India rest? Now, suppose that all English, and the whole English army, were to leave India, taking with them all their cannon and their splendid weapons and everything, then who would be rulers of India? Is it possible that under these circumstances two nations—the Mahomedans and the Hindus—could sit on the same throne and remain equal in power? Most certainly not. It is necessary that one of them should conquer the other and thrust it down. To hope that both could remain equal is to desire the impossible and the

---

[17]Justice Mahadev Govind Ranade, *Rise of the Maratha Power*, Diamond Publications, 2018, p. 4.

Map 1

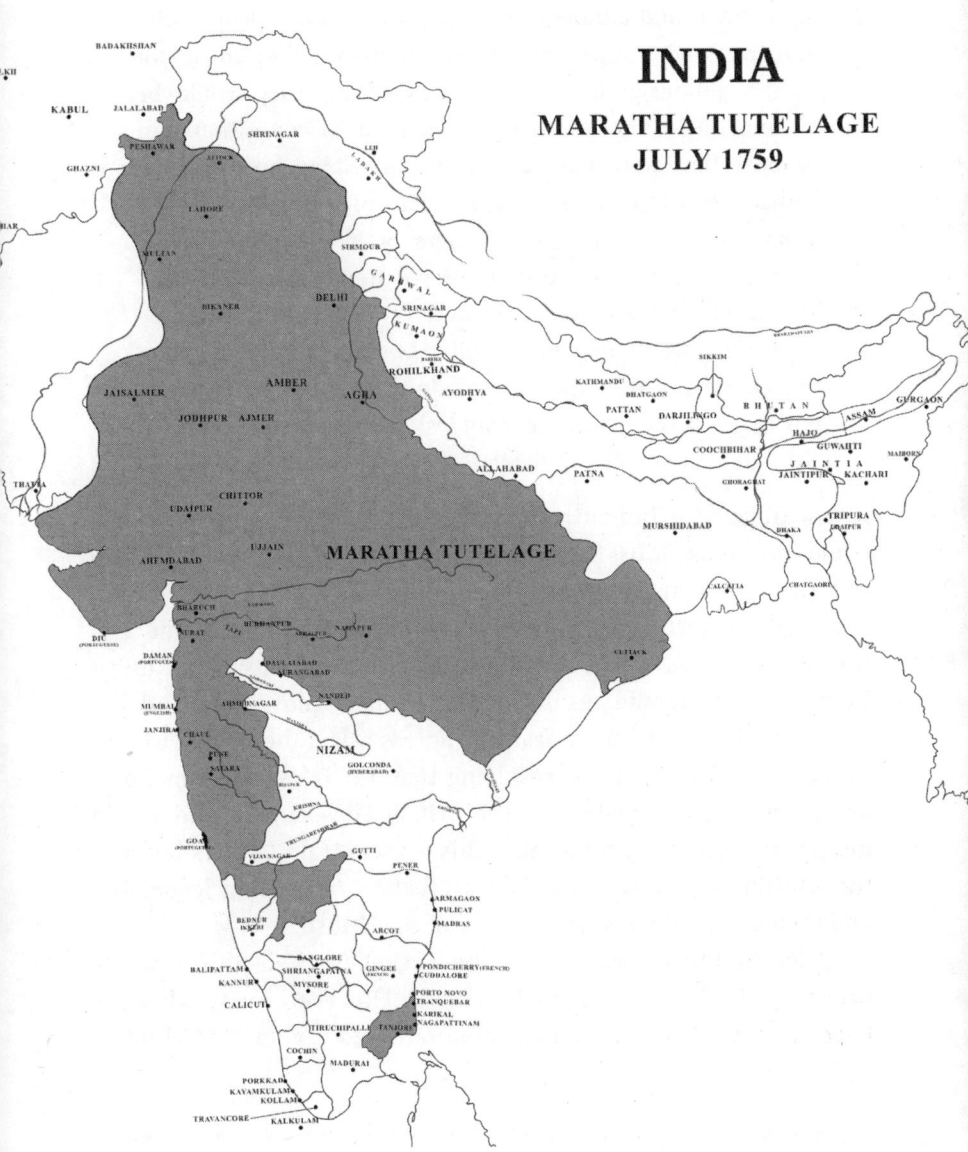

Note: Map showing the Maratha empire including the tributary states in 1759. This includes Peshawar, Multan and Attock.
Map courtesy: Rahul Bhole and Vinit Kanojia

inconceivable. At the same time, you must remember that although the number of Mahomedans is less than that of the Hindus, and although they contain far fewer people who have received a high English education, yet they must not be thought insignificant or weak. Probably they would be by themselves enough to maintain their own position. But suppose they were not. Then our Mussalman brothers, the Pathans, would come out as a swarm of locusts from their mountain valleys, and make rivers of blood to flow from their frontier in the north to the extreme end of Bengal. This thing who, after the departure of the English, would be conquerors would rest on the will of God. But until one nation had conquered the other and made it obedient, peace could not reign in the land. This conclusion is based on proofs so absolute that no one can deny it.[18]

It is a tragedy of Indian history that a majority of Indian leaders could not sense this threat and lived in their utopia trying to win over Muslims or preventing them from joining the Muslim League by resorting to minority appeasement which in the end turned out to be a loaded gun against the majority community. Even after facing the results of the Khilafat movement and the Pakistan resolution, an ignorant Congress asked the British to quit India on 27 April 1942 by resolving that 'the question of majority and minority is a creation of the British Government and would disappear on their withdrawal.'[19] This was contrary to facts because the Muslim separatism was first a creation of Muslim leadership and then the divide-and-rule theory of the British.

Clearly, the extracts from the speeches cited above amply prove Syed Ahmed's separatist streak. However, many Muslims have tried to depict him as a moderate and a votary of Hindu–

---

[18]Speech of Sir Syed Ahmed at Meerut [1888]. http://www.columbia.edu/itc/mealac/pritchett/00islamlinks/txt_sir_sayyid_meerut_1888.html. Accessed on 29 July 2021.
[19]B.K. Ahluwalia and Shashi Ahluwalia, *Rajaji and Gandhi*, New Delhi: Allora, 1978, p. 121.

Muslim unity. They cite the works of Tara Chand, a Left-oriented historian who selectively quoted Syed Ahmed as an official historian of the Indian government to sell him as a moderate. Samples of some of Syed Ahmed's moderate speeches were given for tactical purposes.

In the speech delivered at Patna on 27 January 1883, Syed Ahmed said:

> Now both of us live on the air of India, drink the holy waters of the Ganges and Jamuna. We both consume the products of the Indian soil. We are together in life and death; living in India...in consideration of the fact that we both belong to the same country, we are a nation, and the progress and welfare of the country, and of both of us, depend on our unity, mutual sympathy, and love, while our mutual disagreement, obstinacy and opposition and ill-feeling are sure to destroy us.[20]

Addressing the Hindus of the Punjab around the same time, he crossed all limits of flattering Hindus. He complained that he was not regarded as a Hindu, and said, 'You have used the term Hindu for yourselves. This is not correct. For, in my opinion, the word Hindu does not denote a particular religion, but, on the contrary, everyone who lives in India has the right to call himself a Hindu. I am, therefore, sorry that although I live in India, you do not consider me a Hindu.'[21]

The truth of the matter is that Syed Ahmed spoke in two voices—the moderate one meant only for the consumption of moderate Hindus, who too had donated huge amounts of money for the Aligarh College, and the hardline, separatist voice to inspire his Muslim brethren in Aligarh and beyond.

That the Aligarh Movement was deeply rooted in Muslims worldwide during the first decade of the twentieth century is further reinforced by Sir Ziauddin Ahmad, an Aligarh Muslim

---

[20] Tara Chand, *History of the Freedom Movement in India*; Volume II, Publications Division, M/O Information and Broadcasting, Govt of India, 1 January 2016, p. 357.
[21] Ibid. 359.

leader (then in Germany), who warned another leader Abdullah Suhrawardy, in these clear words:

> You know that we have a definite political policy at Aligarh, i.e. the policy of Sir Syed. ... I understand that Shyamji Krishna Varma has founded a society called the 'Indian Home Rule Society' and you are also one of its vice presidents. Do you really believe that the Mohammedans will be profited if Home Rule be granted to India? ... There is no doubt that this Home Rule is decidedly against the Aligarh policy... What I call the Aligarh policy is really the policy of all the Mohammedans generally—of the Mohammedans of Upper India particularly.[22]

In fact, noted revolutionary and lawyer Asaf Ali wrote to Pandit Shyamji Krishna Varma in September 1909: 'I am staying with some Muslim friends who do not like me to associate with nationalists; and, to save many unpleasant consequences, I do not want to irritate them unnecessarily.'[23]

Such was the sense of mistrust that Muslims even opposed the Congress president Dadabhai Naoroji's developmental proposal in 1886 that demanded the examination for the Indian Civil Service (ICS) be held not just in England but also in India. Some British Members of Parliament (MPs) also promised to propose a suitable Bill in the British Parliament to the effect.

Dadabhai faced united opposition from Muslims. The Patriotic (Muslim) Association and the likes of Islamia Anjuman complained against Dadabhai's proposal. Even the Nizam supported the Muslim agitation. They sent petitions and leaflets to the MPs of the British Parliament.

At heart, Dadabhai was furious at this agitation. A Parsi and a true nationalist, he felt especially grieved to know that Shabuddin, a senior Muslim leader, whom he had always described as a nationalist, had also joined the cries of opposition to his proposal.

---

[22]Dhananjay Keer, *Veer Savarkar*, Popular Prakashan Pvt. Ltd; Second edition, 2019, p. 33.
[23]Ibid.

In a letter to Kazi Shabuddin, dated 15 July 1887, Dadabhai wrote, 'How your action has paralyzed not only our own efforts, but the hands of the English friends and how keenly I feel this, more so, because you have based your action on selfish interests that because the Moslems are backward, you would not allow the Hindus and all India to go forward. How you have retarded our progress for a long time!'[24]

A NEW CULT

The city of Aligarh has been well-known for its lock industry, but the deadlock created by the Aligarh Movement hindered the process of unity and the progress of the Indian nation, long after Syed Ahmed's death in 1898.

Thanks to the seeds sown by him, the Aligarh policy continued unabated even after his departure. The Secretary of M.A.O. College, Nawab Mohsin-ul-Mulk, Munir Nawaz Jang, also known as Syed Mehdi Ali, took forward Syed Ahmed's legacy. On the basis of a letter written by Dunlop Smith, private secretary to the Viceroy and Governor General of India, Lord Minto[25], William Archbold (Principal of M.A.O. College) guided Mehdi Ali to dispatch a representation to the British Indian government signed by some Muslims saying that a deputation should go to the Viceroy, even though its members were not elected representatives. Archbold suggested that the loyalty to the Crown should be expressed in clear terms in the address to be presented to the Viceroy.[26]

This Muslim delegation came to know that the next step of reforms in the legislative councils was already being contemplated by the British. In fact, the first attempt to introduce reforms was made in 1892 when Viceroy Lord Dufferin pushed the Indian

---

[24]R.P. Masani, *The Grand Old Man of India*, Mysore: Kavyalay Publishers, 1968, p. 93; Vinayak Savarkar, *Inside the Enemy Camp*, Independently Published, 2019, p. 21.
[25]Gilbert Elliot-Murray-Kynynmound, First earl of Minto, was Viceroy of India (1905–10).
[26]Lal Bahadur, *The Muslim League: Its History, Activities and Achievements*, Agra Book Store, 1954, p. 35.

Councils Act 1892, which allowed separate representation to Muslims in legislative councils through nomination in the name of justice. Muslims welcomed it with both hands. What propelled the Dufferin administration to give this separate representation to Muslims is not exactly known. In fact, such an objective is not even mentioned in the actual Act but was later introduced as a guiding principle while implementing it.[27]

This was the period when the Indian revolutionary movement was lifting its head again after the suppression of the 1857 struggle. The great revolutionary Vasudev Balwant Phadke, who wanted to reignite the fire of the 1857 Revolution, had been caught by the British and left to die in Aden Jail in Yemen under inhuman conditions. Between 1860 and 1890, many Bhil rebellions had to be quelled by the British. And so perhaps it is not illogical to infer that the British move to grant separate representation to Muslims was aimed at thwarting any common Hindu–Muslim attempt to challenge the British rule.

The Muslim delegation met the Viceroy on 1 October 1906 and demanded 'adequate, real, and genuine Mahomedan representation'[28] in the Senates and Syndicates of Indian universities, municipal and district boards, provincial councils, Viceroy's council and executive council. They also made sweeping demands such as seeking Muslim nomination on the Bench of different courts and employment in government service without qualifying in competitive exams.

To justify their demands, the delegation argued:

> The Mahomedans of India number, according to the census taken in the year 1901, over sixty-two millions or between one-fifth and one-fourth of the total population of His Majesty's Indian dominions, and if a reduction be made for the uncivilized portions of the community enumerated under the heads of animist and other minor religions, as well as

---

[27] B.R. Ambedkar, *Thoughts on Pakistan*, Nabu Press, 2011, p. 239.
[28] B.N. Jog, *Threat of Islam: Indian Dimensions*, Mumbai (Bombay): Unnati Prakashan, 1994.

for those classes who are ordinarily classified as Hindus but properly speaking are not Hindus at all, the proportion of Mahomedans to the Hindu majority becomes much larger. We therefore desire to submit that under any system of representation extended or limited a community in itself more numerous than the entire population of any first class European power except Russia may justly lay claim to adequate recognition as an important factor in the State.

We venture, indeed, with your Excellency's permission to go a step further, and urge that the position accorded to the Mahomedan community in any kind of representation, direct or indirect, and in all other ways affecting their status and influence should be commensurate, not merely with their numerical strength, but also with their political importance and the value of the contribution which they make to the defence of the empire, and we also hope that your Excellency will in this connection be pleased to give due consideration to the position which they occupied in India a little more than hundred years ago and of which the traditions have naturally not faded from their minds.[29]

Clearly, history has been falsified in this context by overlooking the fact that when the British established their sway over India in 1820, they took power from the hands of the members of the Maratha confederacy and not Muslims.

The main driver of these demands was Aga Khan, a known liberal at that time and only a half-Muslim, being from the Khoja sect.[30] He made intelligent use of the Hindus' thirst for freedom and held these demands as a loaded gun against the Hindus, telling them that if they accepted the Muslim demands, they (Hindus)

---

[29] Address presented to H.E. Lord Minto, Viceroy and Governor General of India, by a deputation of the Muslim community of India on 1st October 1906 at Simla; and reply thereto, http://www.columbia.edu/itc/mealac/pritchett/00ambedkar/ambedkar_partition/appendices/12app.html. Accessed on 17 July 2021.

[30] The Bombay High Court in its judgement of 1866 declared Ismaili Khojas to be half-Muslim and half-Hindu.

would strengthen nationalism as that would bring Muslims and Hindus on the same page on national issues. And if they didn't, nationalism would be weakened to that extent.

The demands that the Muslims made were not as a minority. Dividing Hindu sects, they claimed that 'the proportion of Mahomedans to the Hindu majority becomes much larger'.[31] It was a new kind of 'divide and rule'. They did not make special demands on the British as a backward community but as former rulers of India. Most importantly, their claims were based on 'not merely with their numerical strength, but also with their political importance'[32] which continued in independent India as 'vote bank politics'.

Syed Ahmed's successors felt the need for a political party to safeguard Muslim rights and to inculcate loyalty to the British in the hearts of Muslims.[33] Immediately after the All India Muhammadan Educational Conference at Dacca (Bangladesh) on 30 December 1906, a political session of the conference was held under the presidentship of Mushtaq Hussain Zuberi, alias Nawab Viqar-ul-Mulk, honorary secretary of the M.A.O. College. It was resolved that a political association to protect the interests of the Muslims be established. The All India Muslim League, better known as the Muslim League, was thus born in December 1906.[34]

Thereafter, the Muslim League president Sir Syed Ali Imam placed a 12-point demand before the British, whose tone was similar to that of Aga Khan.

- Communal representation in accordance with their numerical strength, social position and local influence on district and municipal boards.
- An assurance of Muhammadan representation in the

---

[31] Address presented to H.E. Lord Minto, Viceroy and Governor General of India, by a deputation of the Muslim community of India on 1st October 1906 at Simla; and reply thereto, http://www.columbia.edu/itc/mealac/pritchett/00ambedkar/ambedkar_partition/appendices/12app.html. Accessed on 17 July 2021.
[32] Ibid.
[33] Lal Bahadur, *The Muslim League: Its History, Activities and Achievements*, Agra Book Store, 1954, p. 43.
[34] Ibid.

- governing bodies of universities.
- Communal representation in provincial councils; representatives to be elected by special electoral colleges composed of Muhammadan landlords, lawyers, merchants and representatives of other important interests, university graduates of a certain standing and members of district and municipal boards.
- The number of Muhammadan representatives in the Imperial Legislative Council should not depend on their numerical strength, and Muhammadans should never be in an ineffective minority. They should be elected as far as possible (as opposed to being nominated) to assert their political authority, election being by special Muhammadan colleges composed of landowners, lawyers, merchants, members of provincial councils, fellows of universities, etc.

Efforts of these separatist Muslims bore fruit a few years later when a series of reform measures—known more commonly as the Morley-Minto Reforms—were enacted in 1909 by the British Parliament. On 23 February 1909, during the second reading of the Indian Council Bill, Morley said,

> The Mahomedans demand three things. I had the pleasure of receiving a deputation from them, and I know very well what is in their minds. They demand the election of their own representatives to these councils in all the stages, just as in Cyprus, where I think, the Mahomedans vote by themselves… Secondly, they want a number of seats somewhat in excess of their numerical strength. Those two demands we are quite ready and intend to meet in full. There is a third demand that, if there is a Hindu on the Viceroy's Executive Council—a subject on which I will venture to say something to your Lordships before I sit down—there should be two Indian members on the Viceroy's Council and one should be a Mahomedan.[35]

---

[35] John Morley, *Indian Speeches (1907–09)*, Rarebooksclub.com, 2012, p. 126.

Thus, the Indian Councils Act of 1909 (also known as the Morley-Minto Reforms) created two types of members on legislative councils: (i) Nominated or official member, (ii) Non-official members or those elected from different franchises or electorates. Broadly, these franchises were Muslims, landlords, chamber of commerce, members of municipal committee and university senate.[36] Only the Muslim franchise was based on religion and no other religion was included in the franchises. Only Muslims could vote for Muslim candidates in separate Muslim electorates. Safeguarding Muslim interests became the utmost important condition for getting an electoral position. Muslims got 'plural' voting rights through this Act. A Muslim could vote in Muslim franchise as well as a trader, landlord or graduate. A Muslim could also be eligible to contest and vote in all these categories (landlords, chamber of commerce, members of municipal committee and university senate). Again, British official and Muslim non-official members could easily form majority in the councils. It became a big hurdle for unity and national interest. It divided Hindus and Muslims into two watertight compartments.

Like the Muslims, the Congress too could have approached Lord Minto in advance with the plea that it wouldn't support reforms at the cost of division of India. But the party, in its Lahore session (1909), only recorded 'its strong sense of disapproval of the creation of separate electorates on the basis of religion'[37] and objected to 'the excessive and unfairly preponderant share of representation given to the followers of one particular religion; the unjust, invidious, and humiliating distinctions made between Moslem and non-Moslem subjects of His Majesty in the matter of the electorates, the franchise and the qualifications of candidate.'[38]

---

[36]Anil Chandra Banerjee, *Indian Constitutional Documents: 1757–1939; Vol. II*, Read Books, 2006, p. 228.

[37]Anil Chandra Banerjee, *Indian Constitutional Documents: 1757–1939; Vol. II*, A. Mukherjee & Co., 1948, p. 270.

[38]A. Tripathi, *The Extremist Challenge: India between 1890 and 1910*, Calcutta: Orient Longmans, 1967, p. 205.

Congress leader Sir Tej Bahadur Sapru (who later formed the Liberal Party of India) came out openly against these special demands made by the Muslims. In a long letter published in *The Tribune* on 6 June 1909, soon after the Morley-Minto Reforms were passed, Sapru, a moderate leader but proud of his Hindu heritage, upbraided the Congress leadership for its feeble opposition to the special demands of the Muslims and warned that the future of the Hindus would be in danger if the same trend continued. He said:

> ... Will the Hindus even now awaken to their sense of duty towards themselves, their past and future? How long are we going to cry hoarse over the prospect of separation (from Muslims)? It seems to me that the Hindus shouldn't trouble themselves about separation. It is (separate electorates and representation according to political importance as demanded by Muslims) the most mischievous doctrine that is being preached that has not got the hallmark of recognition. Its real mischief lies not so much in its immediate effect as in the possibilities which it suggests.

Gopal Krishna Gokhale, better known as Gandhi's political mentor, himself expressed to William Wedderburn (one of the Congress founders), the disquiet he felt over 'the not only unjust but monstrously unjust' representation granted to the Moslems.[39] In his statement, Gokhale made three strong, historical points about the reforms in spite of his moderate thoughts:

1. The Muslims of this land have descended from the Hindu stock. Their attitude has undergone a change due to forced conversion. Hindus are far ahead of Muslims in matters of numerical strength, wealth, education and social conscience. The present national awakening has been achieved mainly by Hindus. They are moderate and submissive and also weakened by caste differences.

---

[39] Amales Tripathi, *The Extremist Challenge: India between 1890 and 1910*, Orient Longmans, 1967, p. 205.

2. Muslims claim they ruled over India for 500 years. It must however be remembered that Hindus ruled for several thousand years prior to it and even before the arrival of the British. Hindus had established their rule by defeating the Muslims.
3. It is strange that those who do not owe their allegiance to India are getting better representation than those with patriotic fervour.[40]

A moderate leader with full faith in constitutional politics, Gokhale's thoughts therefore deserve special consideration. His statement that the national awakening was mainly due to the efforts of Hindus deserves special emphasis. His observation about the moderate and submissive nature of Hindus is full of insight.

However, contrary to Gokhale's strong stand against the Morley-Minto Reforms, his disciple Gandhi supported the reforms by giving his own logic, thus overlooking the divisive agenda of a section of Muslims, who were pan-Islamists.

Writing about the reforms on 21 June 1909, Gandhi said,

> I think it is reasonable that Muslims should be appointed to the Viceroy's council. If Lord Minto has ordered such an appointment, I think he is justified. I make no distinction between Hindus and Muslims. To me, both are sons of Mother India. My personal view is that since numerically Hindus are in a great majority, and are, as they themselves believe, better placed educationally, they should cheerfully concede to their Muslim brethren the utmost they can. As a satyagrahi, I am emphatically of the view that the Hindus should give to the Muslims whatever they ask for, and willingly accept whatever sacrifice this may involve. Unity will be brought about only through such mutual generosity.[41]

---

[40]B.N. Jog, *Threat of Islam: Indian Dimensions*, Mumbai (Bombay): Unnati Prakashan, 1994, p. 103; N.R. Phatak, *Adarsh Bharat Sevak*, Mauj Prakashan Griha, p. 80.

[41]Dhananjay Keer, *Mahatma Gandhi: Political Saint & Unarmed Prophet*, Popular Prakashan; Revised second edition 2020 (1973), p. 150.

This is the key to understanding Gandhi's future policy of Hindu–Muslim unity. As a satyagrahi, Gandhi never felt any need to tender advice to the Muslims as the word 'mutual' always remained one-sided and had no meaning except that it involved sacrifices on the part of Hindus alone in the national struggle. What Gandhi wrote on that fateful day in June 1909, he kept repeating for decades. In fact, he later added a rider to the effect that without Hindu–Muslim unity there would not be swaraj (self-governance/independence) for India. The appropriate interpretation of what Gandhi said would be 'Hindu–Muslim unity at Hindu cost', as there was hardly anything that the Muslims sacrificed for Hindu–Muslim unity during that phase, as the sequence later showed.

Significantly, the Congress of that time, which was not led by Gandhi, had strongly opposed the special concessions given to the Muslims in the reform. So, it is logical to believe that 'Hindu–Muslim unity at Hindu cost or Muslim appeasement at any cost' became the cornerstone of the Congress only after Gandhi came to lead the party after 1916.

The politics of Hindus and Muslims converted into the politics of Muslims and non-Muslims with the implementation of the Morley-Minto Reforms. Even though Hindus were in the majority and were waging a moderate as well as a revolutionary struggle against the British, they were nowhere in the political scenario as a community. Separate electorates made Muslims a separate power centre of Indian politics.

In the final analysis, the historical chronology shows that it was not just the British who resorted to 'divide-and-rule' policy, as is generally believed by historians and even impartial scholars, but it is the Muslims who united with the British with a clinical strategy to get more share in power, keeping national interest aside.

2
CONGRESS SURRENDERS TO MUSLIM GRAVAMIN POLITICS

In its eagerness to present a united front against the British policy of dividing Hindus and Muslims by enticing the latter, the Congress signed the Lucknow Pact in 1916. This is often seen as the foundation of Muslim appeasement in the country. Under this pact, the Congress, headed by Bal Gangadhar Tilak, conceded to Muslims, led by Jinnah, 200–300 per cent more representation than Hindus in the councils of the Hindu-majority provinces/states. At the same time, it failed to ensure the same degree of privilege to Hindus in the Muslim-majority states. Of course, there was a clause in the pact stating that Muslims will get more representation: 'Provided that Mahomedans shall not participate in any of the other elections (from other electorates) to the Legislative Councils.'[1] It was a settlement that at least other electorates or constituencies would be 'safeguarded' for 'non-Muslims'.

By giving disproportionate representation to Muslims in the form of separate state electorates, the pact made them hungry for more and more concessions. And so when the author of the pact, Lokmanya Tilak, went to Varanasi, he faced stiff opposition from Hindu Mahasabha leaders, including Madan Mohan Malaviya and B.S. Munje, who had earlier fought against the British policy of giving special concessions to Muslims. They questioned Tilak on

---

[1] *Indian Documents*, Vol. II, p. 290. This means that Muslims made some promise in exchange for the huge favour shown to them in the councils under the pact. However, it was highly disproportionate and totally against a level-playing field.

selling Hindu interests to Muslims. Tilak's reply was in parts logical but was that of a leader tired of the British's divide-and-rule policy: 'Nothing more was possible under the circumstances. This pact is for a period of 10 years only. If we want, we can get it changed (in future). If we were to give up negotiations (with Muslims), nothing could have been gained. It would have provided full opportunity to the British to yield nothing (in the matter of representation to locals in States legislatures).'[2]

Later in conversation with D.G. Dalvi, a Bombay Congress delegate, Tilak clarified: 'The Hindus had overthrown Muslim rule twice and would do so again if such a situation arose. But in existing circumstances, there was no go but to avoid a triangular fight and win over the Muslims to the national struggle to drive away Britishers.'[3] On another occasion, while speaking on the same subject, Tilak called the Lucknow Pact a necessary settlement (and not surrender) to present a united front against the British attempts to drive a wedge between Hindus and Muslims in India. In fact, he also prevailed upon the Muslims to agree to some conditions in lieu of the benefits they were getting from the pact. However, despite Tilak's efforts and assertions, it was clear that the Lucknow Pact had opened the doors for a Muslim-appeasement policy, which was to ultimately lead to India's partition and continues to bedevil the nation till this day and impede its progress.

However, it is incorrect to assume that the saga of Muslim appeasement started only in 1916. A study of the Congress's history reveals that the party had pro-Muslim leanings from the time of its formation in 1885. There existed an undying urge in the party to draw Muslims into the Congress movement at any cost against the diversionary tactics of the Aligarh School of Syed Ahmed Khan, which remained steadfastly loyal to the British and opposed the Muslims wanting to join the Congress as part of its overall strategy to oppose Hindus' progress.

---

[2]B.N. Jog, *Threat of Islam: Indian Dimensions*, Mumbai (Bombay): Unnati Prakashan, 1994, p. 133, 134.

[3]Dhananjay Keer, *Lokmanya Tilak: Father of the Indian Freedom Struggle*, Popular Prakashan; Third edition, 2016 (1959), p. 364.

This slowly took the form of some kind of Muslim veto in the party when Congress founder A.O. Hume, in keeping with the party's quest to win Muslim support, circulated a draft resolution in 1887. It said:

> No subject shall be passed by the Subject committee or allowed to be discussed by the President, to the introduction of which the Hindu or Muslim delegates as a body, object unanimously or nearly unanimously. And if after the discussion on any subject, which has been admitted for discussion, it shall appear that all the Hindus or all the Mohamedan delegates, as a body, are unanimously or nearly unanimously opposed to the resolution which it proposed to pass on thereon, such resolution shall be dropped without reference to whether those who oppose constitute the majority or the minority.[4]

Taking advantage of this veto in the later years, Muslims opposed the ban on cow slaughter and also truncated 'Vande Mataram' saying that it constituted idol worship.

In fact, there is unimpeachable evidence to prove that even Muslim leaders who initially joined the Congress such as Badruddin Tyabji, the third president of the Congress, were under the influence of the Aligarh School and looked to protecting Muslim interests from within the party as their foremost duty. Tyabji was initially a progressive, national leader and genuinely believed in Hindu–Muslim unity. He initially opposed the Aligarh School argument that Muslims should distance themselves from the Congress as the party's progressive ways would benefit educated and advanced Hindus more than Muslims. He argued, 'The way to do it is by raising ourselves (Muslims) in the scale of progress rather than preventing other people from enjoying the right which they are qualified.'[5]

---

[4]Source material for a *History of the Freedom Movement in India*, Vol. 2, p. 67.
[5]B.N. Jog, *Threat of Islam: Indian Dimensions*, Mumbai (Bombay): Unnati Prakashan, 1994, p. 46.

However, due to constant pressure from the Aligarh School, particularly from top leaders such as Syed Ahmed and Nawab Amir Ali, a confused Tyabji gave in to the their demands on one hand, and on the other hand, admitted before the Congress founder Hume that attaining Hindu–Muslim unity was proving to be impossible. He even suggested that the mandatory annual Congress meetings be prorogued for five years or till Hindu–Muslim unity was achieved and even drop the idea with dignity, if it was impossible.

However, before giving this advice to Hume, Tyabji had walked right into the Aligarh School's lap when he wrote a letter to Syed Ahmed, who was opposing the Congress's move for a unified India:

> ...We can no more stop the Congress then we can stop the progress of education. But it is in our power by firm and resolute action to divert the course the Congress shall take. My strong conviction is that the Mussalmans by united action can confine the Congress to such topics only as they may think desirable or safe for discussion... My policy therefore would be to act from within than from without.[6]

In the same letter to Syed Ahmed, who always maintained that India is not one nation, Tyabji wrote: 'I am not aware of any one regarding India as one nation and if you read my inaugural address, you will find it distinctly states that there are numerous communities of nations in India.'[7]

Thus, the Congress's first-ever Muslim president committed himself to protecting and furthering Muslim interests when he was to act in a non-partisan manner as the party head, when he should have focussed on the common good of all Indians. And many subsequent Muslim leaders of the Congress followed the Tyabji model.

After the Lucknow Pact, Hindu–Muslim relationship underwent a complete change in a span of few years with Mahatma Gandhi slowly taking over the Congress leadership. From one of settlement,

---

[6]Source Material for a *History of the Freedom Movement in India*, Vol. 2, p. 70.
[7]Ibid. 71.

the relationship started assuming the tone of Hindu surrender to Muslim demands in the name of Hindu–Muslim unity and in the garb of jargons such as *Ganga-Jamuni tehzeeb* or the shared culture of Muslims and Hindus in north India as described by some. The main reason behind this change was Gandhi's belief that without Hindu–Muslim unity swaraj was not possible. Therefore, winning Muslim support became a priority, in addition to his total lack of knowledge about the Islam-centric strategic mind of Muslim leaders and history.

One has to delve into Gandhi's past to decipher the roots of this Gandhian thinking. Back in South Africa, during the anti-apartheid movement that he led, there were a large number of Gujarati Muslims who had settled there for business purposes. They mainly belonged to a few districts of south Gujarat such as Bharuch and Surat and a few of the Saurashtra region such as Porbandar, Gandhi's birthplace. Some of them were top business magnates who funded his movement in South Africa and so Gandhi was dependent on them for help.

However, a more significant cause of Muslim appeasement that marked his entire career is an episode in South Africa which is generally ignored and doesn't find a mention in any of his own writings, including his autobiography. In March 1905, Gandhi delivered four lectures under the aegis of the Theosophical Society in Johannesburg on 'Hinduism and Comparative Religions'. In one of them, he said, 'The zeal or passion of Islam was a mighty force. It had been the cause of many good deeds but some times of bad ones too. In India, a majority of converts came from lower classes'.[8] He also said that it was Hinduism which gave Mohammedanism its Akbar and that Sikhism was a direct result of Islam. He, however, concluded that all religions teach us to live in harmony and mutual kindness.

However, he soon found that despite their truthfulness, his views on Islam had greatly offended the local Muslim community.

---

[8]*Collected Works of Mahatma Gandhi* (CWMG), Vol. 4, 23 May 1904–4 November 1905, p. 272.

Muslims vehemently protested, writing a series of letters to Gandhi who, in his defence, quoted from the *Encyclopaedia Britannica* to prove the veracity of his statements, adding that it was a historical fact that Islam had spread by force. The Muslim protests, however, continued despite Gandhi reiterating that he had spoken in good faith and with a view to understand each other and that he didn't mean any offence to Muslims. The protests were so strong that he had to apologize to the Muslims in June 1905 to bury the controversy. Yet, a section of young Muslims remained unconvinced and continued to run a campaign against Gandhi. Finally, in April 1906, Gandhi sorrowfully apologized once again to the entire Muslim community saying that Muslims should forgive him if he had committed an error in what he had said.[9] Thereafter, he was careful never to wound Muslims sensibilities which later graduated to unabashed Muslim appeasement.

KHILAFAT: GANDHIAN FOLLY AND ITS FALLOUT

Fired with fanciful ideas of Hindu–Muslim unity, Gandhi saw a great opportunity to forge it using the pan-Islamic Khilafat agitation that started in 1919 to reinstate the Sultan of Turkey, seen as their Khalifa by a section of Indian Muslims. The Sultan had been unseated by western powers, including Britain, with the cooperation of Turkey's own liberal Muslim subjects as a result of World War I in which the central powers, including Turkey, eventually lost. The Muslim agitation was led by pan-Islamist brothers Maulana Mohammad Ali and Maulana Shaukat Ali and had the support of a large section of the Indian ulema (the Muslim clerics) particularly the radical Deobandi ulema, and leaders such as Maulana Abul Kalam Azad and Maulana Hasrat Mohani. Gandhi declared Hindu (or the Congress) support to the pan-Islamic movement of the Muslims and used it to launch the non-cooperation movement against the draconian Rowlatt Act 1919

---

[9]Dhananjay Keer, *Mahatma Gandhi: Political Saint & Unarmed Prophet*, Popular Prakashan; Revised second edition, 2020 (1973), p. 87.

and the Jallianwala Bagh killing of innocent Hindus and Sikhs by General Dyer.

This impractical alliance was fraught with disastrous consequences as Muslims cared little for the Congress agenda and were concerned with only the success of the Khilafat agitation. The Hindus, at large, were not attracted by the Congress–Muslim alliance; in fact, they felt some kind of disconnect with it. What added to this was Gandhi's refusal to a suggestion that some conditions should be imposed on the Muslims against such unequivocal Congress support to a purely Muslim religious cause and that too a pan-Islamic one that gave fillip to extraterritorial loyalties at the cost of national integration. One of the suggestions made was that the Congress should seek a ban on cow slaughter by Muslims in lieu of the support to the Khilafat movement. Even Khilafat leaders such as Maulana Bari spoke up against cow slaughter but their voices were drowned as other Khilafat leaders were not in unison.[10] Gandhi too rejected the suggestion point blank saying there couldn't be any preconditions when it came to a genuine friendship between two friends. He begged Hindus not to insist on the prohibition of cow slaughter by Mahomedans.[11]

Not just that, Gandhi also looked the other way, despite his steadfastness to the ideal of non-violence, when the Maulanas involved in the movement recited violent verses from the Koran centred around the concept of jehad and killing of Kafirs while taking potshots at the British government on the Khilafat issue. When Swami Shraddhanand cautioned Gandhi that such verses could also be used against Hindus in future, Gandhi brushed it aside saying, 'They (the Maulanas) are alluding to the British.'[12]

He also justified the call of some Muslim leaders of the Khilafat movement to invite the Amir of Afghanistan to invade India to

---

[10] P.C. Bamford, *Histories of the Non-cooperation and Khilafat Movement*, Government of India Press, 1925.

[11] Chettur Sankaran Nair, *Gandhi and Anarchy*, BiblioLife, 2009, p 44.

[12] B.R. Ambedkar, *Thoughts on Pakistan*, Nabu Press, 2011, p. 152; *The Liberator*, 26 July 1926, p. 149.

free it from British rule.[13] He said, 'I would, in a sense, certainly assist the Amir of Afghanistan if he waged war against the British Government. That is to say, I would openly tell my countrymen that it would be a crime to help a Government which had lost the confidence of the nation to remain in power.'[14]

The Congress support to the Khilafat might not have been well received, but due to Gandhi's persuasion, almost the entire Congress leadership came out in support of the movement, including orthodox Arya Samaj leaders such as Lala Lajpat Rai and Swami Shraddhanand, apart from the then Shankaracharya of Puri. They were all oblivious to the fact that that the unconditional Congress support to pan-Islamism was laying a disastrous foundation of future Muslim appeasement. Only one political leader, Munje, of the Hindu Mahasabha, opposed the Congress–Khilafat alliance; perhaps he was the only one who foresaw the consequences of such a compromise by the Congress with pan-Islamists and the far-reaching effect it would have on the nation.[15]

Other than that, what Shraddhanand had told Gandhi came true within months of the Congress support to the Khilafat movement. The Moplah Muslims of Kerala, who have mostly followed the radical Ahl-e Hadith brand of Wahhabism for decades, broke free from the British and declared their own Sultanate (Khilafat) in 1921 under the leadership of one Ali Musaliar, who posed as Khalifa. The hostilities first began between the British security forces and the Moplahs, but as they grew, the Moplah ire fell on Hindus. They started untold atrocities against the local Hindus, making no distinction between Hindu and British kafirs. Thousands of Hindus were killed, hundreds of Hindu women were raped and converted and innumerable temples demolished by the jihadi Moplahs over

---

[13] B.N. Jog, *Threat of Islam: Indian Perspective*, Mumbai (Bombay): Unnati Prakashan, 1994, p. 141,142,144,151.
[14] *Collected Works of Mahatma Gandhi* (CWMG), Vol. 23, 6 April–21 July 1921. http://www.gandhiashramsevagram.org/gandhi-literature/mahatma-gandhi-collected-works-volume-23.pdf. Accessed on 30 July 2021.
[15] B.N. Jog, *Threat of Islam: Indian Perspective*, Mumbai (Bombay): Unnati Prakashan, 1994, p. 160, 161, 165.

a period of three months.

The petition by the Rani of Nilambur, signed by 2,000 affected Hindu women, to Lady Reading, the wife of the then viceroy, Lord Reading, describing the Moplah atrocities on Hindus, is a saga of blood-curdling stories.[16] However, the Congress party and Gandhi tried to play down the entire episode so that it didn't derail their Hindu–Muslim unity project.

However, several leaders including Mrs Annie Besant and Congress leader Sir Chettur Sankaran Nair, who presided over the 1897 Amravati session of the Congress, were shaken by the scale of atrocities and wrote about it bluntly. Besant's description was heart rending as she blamed Gandhi for looking the other way. She described how two Hindu Dalits refused to convert at the point of sword and were killed by the Moplah jihadis.[17] Ambedkar's description of the atrocities in his book is chilling to say the least:

> The Hindus were visited by dire fate at the hands of the Moplas. Massacres, forcible conversions, desecration of temples, foul outrages upon women, such as ripping open pregnant women, pillage, arson and destruction—in short, all the accompaniments of brutal and unrestrained barbarism, were perpetrated freely by the Moplas on the Hindus until such time as troops could be hurried to the task of restoring order through a difficult and extensive tract of the country. This was not a Hindu–Muslim riot. This was just a Bartholomew.[18]

It is significant to note that after the Khilafat–Congress cooperation yielded disastrous results, several political leaders saw the error in judgement and denounced it. The most brutal admonition of the Congress and Gandhi came from Ambedkar in his book *Thoughts on Pakistan*. He wrote,

---

[16] Veena Hardas and B.S. Munje, *Dharmaveer Dr Balkrushna shivram munje yanche charitra*, Part-II, Nagpur: Lakhe Prakashan; Second edition, 2013, , p. 55, 56, 57.

[17] Chettur Sankaran Nair, *Gandhi and Anarchy*, BiblioLife, 2009, p. 135.

[18] B.R. Ambedkar, *Pakistan or the Partition of India*, Samayak Prakashan; First edition, 2013, p. 178.

> The blood-curdling atrocities committed by the Moplas in Malabar against the Hindus, were indescribable. All over Southern India a wave of horrified feeling had spread amongst the Hindus of every shade of opinion, which was intensified when certain Khilafat leaders were so misguided as to pass resolutions of congratulations to the Moplas on the brave fight they were conducting for the sake of religion. Any person could have said that this was too heavy a price for Hindu–Muslim unity. But Mr Gandhi was so much obsessed by the necessity of establishing Hindu–Muslim unity that he was prepared to make light of the doings of the Moplas and the Khailafatis who were congratulating them. He (Gandhi) spoke of the Moplas as the 'brave God-fearing Moplas who were fighting what they considered as religion and in a manner they considered as religious.'[19]

Ambedkar was referring to the toning down or even changing of the resolution in the Congress session at Ahmedabad, in December 1921 following the Moplah episode. The draft of the original resolution was stern against the Moplahs, but was changed under pressure from Muslim leaders including Mohani, who brazenly said that Moplahs had acted according to the dictates of their religion. The final resolution was evasive. It mildly blamed Moplahs for their action against Hindus, but put the blame for the bloodshed mainly on the law-enforcing authorities and the British.[20]

Gandhi's reaction was hard to decipher. He admitted that the Khilafat was a blunder, yet he was advising Hindus to be killed instead of defending them, saying:

> My error! Why, I may be charged with having committed a breach of faith with the Hindus. I asked them to befriend Muslims. I asked them to lay their lives and their property

---

[19] https://archive.org/stream/thoughtsonpakist035271mbp/thoughtsonpakist035271mbp_djvu.txt. Accessed on 30 July 2021.
[20] Dhananjay Keer, *Mahatma Gandhi: Political Saint & Unarmed Prophet*, Popular Prakashan; Revised Second Edition, 2020 (1973), p. 414; *The Liberator*, 26 August 1926.

at the disposal of the Mussalmans for the protection of their holy places. Even today, I am asking them to practice ahimsa, to settle quarrels by dying but not by killing. And what do I find to be the result? How many temples have been desecrated? How many sisters come to me with complaints? As I was saying to Hakimji yesterday, Hindu women are in mortal terror of Mussalman goondas. In many places, they fear to go out alone. How can I bear the way in which his little children were molested? How can I now ask the Hindus to put up with everything patiently? I gave them the assurance that the friendship of Mussalmans was bound to bear good fruit. I asked them to befriend them, regardless of the result. Who listens to me? And yet I must ask the Hindus even today to die and not to kill.[21]

Gandhi's response and the Congress's Khilafat compromise, which had clearly shown the dangers from the Congress's appeasement, and as a result, increasing Muslim fanaticism, had a ripple effect in terms of Hindu reaction. On one hand, it led to Veer Savarkar writing *Hindutva* in Ratnagiri jail in 1923, an epic work that defines the fundamentals of Hindu nationalism, better defined as unalloyed nationalism.

On the other hand, it resulted in Dr K.B. Hedgewar, originally a Congress worker of Nagpur who went to jail during the Khilafat movement and before that a revolutionary of the Anushilan Samiti, starting the Rashtriya Swayamsevak Sangh (RSS) in 1925 as a Hindu bulwark against the rising Muslim appeasement and Islamic fanaticism. Hedgewar's transformation from a simple Congress worker to a defender of Hindu faith and culture is interesting. Once Hedgewar and a Muslim leader named Samiulla Khan were travelling for a conference during the Khilafat days. Hedgewar casually asked Khan that the 'Gandhian cap is accepted by everyone nowadays. Why don't you wear that instead of [the]

---

[21]*Collected Works of Mahatma Gandhi* (CWMG), Vol. 29, 16 August–26 December 1924, p. 185. https://www.gandhiashramsevagram.org/gandhi-literature/mahatma-gandhi-collected-works-volume-29.pdf. Accessed on 19 July 2021.

Turkish skull cap?' Samiulla answered: 'I am a Muslim first. This cap is my religious symbol. So, there is no question of doffing it.'[22] Hedgewar understood that when Hindus removed their turbans for the Gandhian cap, Muslims kept their skull caps intact. Therefore, their closeness to the Congress was for an Islamic cause and not for a common cause.

Yet another fallout was Arya Samaj leader Swami Shraddhanand moving away from Gandhi and the Congress. Swamiji had, on Gandhi's insistence, suspended the customary Shuddhi movement (reconversion to Hinduism from Islam and Christianity) in deference to Gandhi's call for Hindu–Muslim unity and had even addressed a massive Muslim gathering atop Delhi's Jama Masjid during the height of the Khilafat/non-cooperation movement. However, after the Moplah carnage, he found himself completely disillusioned with Gandhi's obsession with Hindu–Muslim unity at any cost.

After failing to persuade Gandhi to leave the wrong course, Swami Shraddhanand left him and the Congress as well and restarted the reconversion movement with renewed vigour under the banner of the Hindu Mahasabha. The huge success of his reconversion drive ignited the ire of the Muslims. To them, the final trigger was the conversion of the Malkana (Muslim) Rajputs to the Hindu fold under his inspiration, resulting in a plot to murder Swamiji.

According to political activist, writer and historian Sita Ram Goel, in 1926, the Tablighi Jamaat, which had then recently emerged out of the radical Deoband School to tackle the threat of reconversion by the Arya Samaj, hired Abdul Rashid to kill Swamiji on 3 December 1926.[23] Rashid went to meet Swamiji, asked his attendant to fetch him a glass of water and then pumped four bullets into Swamiji when he was bedridden. On being caught, Rashid said he had planned to kill Madan Mohan Malaviya too.

---

[22]N.H. Palkar, *Dr. Hedgewar Charit*, Lokhit Prakashan, 2014, p.108.
[23]Sita Ram Goel, *Time for Stock Taking Whither Sangh Parivar?* Voice of India, 1997, p. 422.

The students of the Deoband School, whose ulema were working in close unison with the Congress against the British, offered special namaz (prayers) to Allah to give Rashid a place in heaven. The ulema of the Deoband School were, in fact, the main supporters of the Congress during the freedom movement because of the party's strategy to protect Muslim interests from within the Congress.

However, it was Gandhi's response to Rashid's act that shocked everyone. Instead of condemning him, Gandhi defended him and held the media and both Hindu and Muslim communities responsible for the condemnable act. He said:

> I wish to plead for Abdul Rashid. I do not know who he is. It does not matter to me what prompted the deed. The fault is ours. The newspaper man has become a walking plague. He spreads the contagion of lies and calumnies. He exhausts the foul vocabulary of his dialect, and injects his virus into the unsuspecting, and often receptive minds of his readers. Leaders 'intoxicated with the exuberance of their own language' have not known to put a curb upon their tongues or pens. Secret and insidious propaganda has done its dark and horrible work, unchecked and unabashed. It is, therefore, we the educated and the semi-educated class that are responsible for the hot fever which possessed Abdul Rashid. It is unnecessary to discriminate and apportion the blame between the rival parties. Where both are to blame, who can arbitrate with golden scales and fix the exact ratio of blame? It is no part of self-defense to tell lies or exaggerate.[24]

He further added:

> If we cleanse our hearts, we shall be able to see that Swamiji has served us in his death as much as he served us when living. Let us purify our hearts with his blood, and fight, if need be, for our rights in a peaceful and satyagrahi way. Let every

---

[24]*Collected Works of Mahatma Gandhi* (CWMG), Vol. 37, 11 November 1926–1 January 1927, p. 457. https://www.gandhiashramsevagram.org/gandhi-literature/mahatma-gandhi-collected-works-volume-37.pdf. Accessed on 19 July 2021.

Mussalman also understand that Swami Shraddhanand ji was no enemy of Islam, that his was a pure and unsullied life, and that he has left for us all the lessons of peace written in his blood. Now you will, perhaps, understand why I have called Abdul Rashid a brother, and I repeat it, I do not even regard him as guilty of Swami's murder. Guilty, indeed, are all those who excited feelings of hatred against one another.[25]

Gandhi's pro-Muslim bias—evident from his observation that 'the Mussalman as a rule is a bully, and the Hindu as a rule is a coward',[26] and his reference to Rana Pratap, Chhatrapati Shivaji and Guru Gobind Singh, who successfully fought against Muslim rule, as 'misguided patriots'[27]—was reinforced when he didn't give the same privilege, as enjoyed by Rashid, to the armed revolutionaries such as Bhagat Singh and Udham Singh, who were fighting against the Britishers. After Bhagat Singh's act of killing British officer John Saunders, who was responsible for Lala Lajpat Rai's death, Gandhi warned:

> The Bhagat Singh worship has done and is doing incalculable harm to the country... The deed itself is being worshipped as if it was worthy of emulation. The result is goondaism and degradation wherever this mad worship is being performed. The Congress is a power in the land, but I warn Congressmen that it will soon lose all its charm if they betray their trust and encourage the Bhagat Singh cult whether in thought, word or deed.[28]

---

[25] *Collected Works of Mahatma Gandhi* (CWMG), Vol. 37, 11 November 1926–1 January 1927, p. 445. https://www.gandhiashramsevagram.org/gandhi-literature/mahatma-gandhi-collected-works-volume-37.pdf. Accessed on 19 July 2021.

[26] '(17) Psychology of Fear', https://www.mkgandhi.org/g_communal/chap17.htm. Accessed on 25 May 2021.

[27] *Collected Works of Mahatma Gandhi* (CWMG), Vol. 31, 22 March–15 June 1925, p. 137. https://www.gandhiashramsevagram.org/gandhi-literature/mahatma-gandhi-collected-works-volume-31.pdf. Accessed on 30 July 2021.

[28] *Collected Works of Mahatma Gandhi* (CWMG), Vol. 53, 2 July–12 October 1931 p. 152. https://www.gandhiashramsevagram.org/gandhi-literature/mahatma-gandhi-collected-works-volume-53.pdf. Accessed on 19 July 2021.

After Udham Singh shot dead Michael O'Dwyer in March 1940 and took heroic revenge of the Jallianwala Bagh massacre, Gandhi called it an 'insane act'[29]. The Congress even passed a resolution sympathizing with O'Dwyer. It stated:

> The Working Committee has learnt with deep regret of the assassination of Sir Michael O'Dwyer and the wounding of Marquess of Zetland and others by a person said to be an Indian. The Committee does not attach any political significance to this unfortunate act of violence. Nevertheless it wishes to reiterate its conviction that all such acts are injurious to the national cause.[30]

The Congress didn't learn any lesson from the Khilafat chapter and its aftermath, but went a step further when Deshbandhu Chittaranjan Das, a member of the Swarajya party within the Congress, struck the Bengal Pact in 1923 with the Muslims in Bengal on the eve of an important election. The pact allowed Muslims:

1. The authority to indulge in cow slaughter without opposition from Hindus.
2. Sixty per cent reservation in jobs to Muslims in Bengal and 80 per cent reservation in jobs in the Calcutta Municipal Corporation.
3. Ban on the Hindu community taking out religious processions from near the mosques.

The pact however faced stiff opposition from a section of Congress leaders including Niranjan Pal and was rejected by a majority vote in the Kakinada Congress session in 1924, which followed the pact.[31]

Maulana Abul Kalam Azad, the Congress president during the most crucial period before Partition, and widely regarded as a

---

[29]*Collected Works of Mahatma Gandhi* (CWMG), Vol. 78, 23 February–15 July 1940, p. 55. https://www.gandhiashramsevagram.org/gandhi-literature/mahatma-gandhi-collected-works-volume-78.pdf. Accessed on 30 July 2021.

[30]Ibid. 56..

[31]B.N. Jog; *Threat of Islam: Indian Perspective*, Mumbai (Bombay): Unnati Prakashan, 1994, p. 188.

towering symbol of Hindu–Muslim unity, shocked everyone by his views on the Bengal Pact, which were published in his autobiography *India Wins Freedom*. He called the rejection of the Bengal Pact as the first seed of Partition and eulogized Chittaranjan Das for creating a great nationalist atmosphere amongst the Bengal Hindus by signing the Bengal Pact.[32] By Azad's call for Hindu–Muslim unity, Hindus should have allowed cow slaughter by Muslims and changed the course of their processions in case a mosque came in the way. Hindu processions being taken from near mosques and cow slaughter, in addition to the reconversion movement of the Arya Samaj led to a spate of riots in the country—from Malabar to Multan and Kohat, and from Saharanpur to Gulbarga. The pattern of these riots indicated that Muslim's conduct during the non-cooperation/Khilafat movement was dictated by the policy of deriving advantages by cooperating with Hindus against the British. However, when that strategy did not provide the desired advantages for the community, owing to the failure of Khilafat and non-cooperation movements, the Muslims reverted to their old game of deriving advantages by supporting the British against the Hindus.[33]

Clearly, the Congress used one yardstick when it came to Hindus and another, a softer one, when it came to the Muslims in its eagerness to woo the Muslim community. Not surprisingly, the repeated pro-Muslim biases shown by the Congress and its leaders gave credence to a veered logic that put the entire Hindu community on the defensive when it came to Muslim-related issues. In turn, Muslims became more aggressive in making unjust demands on the Hindu community. Even though the Congress commanded maximum support of the Hindus, which was more than the Hindu following of the Hindu Mahasabha, the party's pro-Muslim attitude shook the confidence of Hindus, who started showing signs of helplessness.

---

[32] Abul Kalam Azad, *India Wins Freedom*, Orient BlackSwan, 1988, p. 21.
[33] R.C. Majumdar, *History of the Freedom Movement in India*, South Asia Books, 1988, p. 223, 224.

Did the Congress's move in the direction of Hindu–Muslim unity at any cost, or clearly at Hindu cost, and open association with radical maulvis instead of progressive Muslims, lead to a change in the progressive, liberal Muslim leader, Mohammed Ali Jinnah? Was this change driven by the ambition to grab Muslim leadership and in doing so, having no qualms about taking the radical route when the Congress itself was openly wooing radical Islamic preachers? The most glaring example was that of Maulana Mohammad Ali, the Khilafat leader who had also been the Congress president for three years. In his speech at the Khilafat conference in 1926, he said, 'Conversion of every non-Muslim is the duty of every Muslim. The day I would succeed in converting Gandhiji would be the golden day of my life.'[34]

Sheshrao B. More, a scholar of Muslim politics, insists that Jinnah, like most Muslim leaders of his time, had a separatist streak from the beginning, but differed from others because of his sophistication.[35] Jinnah might have been driving towards a Muslim-centric polity even in his early years, may be under pressure from the Muslim community, just like in the case of Tyabji. He is known to have been protecting Muslim interests from within the Congress, even while maintaining a liberal face on the surface.

The course of history shows that Jinnah, described as the 'ambassador of unity' by Sarojini Naidu,[36] used Congress leaders, from Tilak to Gandhi, to increase the bargaining power of the Muslim League which he used to encash during negotiations with the British. Though he did not join the Khilafat movement led by Gandhi, he never opposed Khilafat demand. On the contrary, he

---

[34]Veena Hardas and B.S. Munje, *Dharmaveer Dr Balkrushna shivram munje yanche charitra*, Part-II, Nagpur: Lakhe Prakashan; Second edition, 2013, p. 199.

[35]B.N. Jog; *Threat of Islam: Indian Perspective*, Mumbai (Bombay): Unnati Prakashan, 1994, p. 188.

[36]Saquib Salim, 'When Sarojini Naidu called Mohammad Ali Jinnah "An Ambassador of Unity"', *Heritage Times*, 28 October 2019. https://heritagetimes.in/sarojini-naidu-mohammad-ali-jinnah-ambassador-of-unity/. Accessed 19 July 2021.

was the leader of the Khilafat delegation of the Muslim League which met the British prime minister in London in 1919.[37]

If one looks at his conduct as a Muslim League member and simultaneously as a Congressman in his early years, Jinnah was never as great a liberal as he was believed to be. He depicted himself as playing a balanced mediator between the League and the Congress, but the advantage of his mediation mostly went to the Muslims. Another way to look at it is that he was always weighed down by Muslim pressure and like other Muslims leaders, always claimed that he was suggesting concessions for the Muslim community for the greater good of Hindu–Muslim relations and to bring Muslims into the national mainstream. True, he opposed the Congress alliance with the Khilafatists, but one cannot forget the fact that he played a key role as Tilak's follower in drafting the 1916 Lucknow Pact. Plus, if one sees in retrospect, even his stand against the Khilafatists might have been driven by political needs, as he didn't command a big following then and needed to oppose those Muslims leaders who did.

His stand as a Muslim League leader in 1924 gives a clear indication of his penchant to snatch special concessions for Muslims. The meeting of the Muslim League on 24 May 1924 in Lahore, presided over by Jinnah as president, put conditions for any Constitution of India acceptable to Muslims. In this, the first condition was aimed at keeping the Centre weak 'with full autonomy to the provinces with central government functions being confined to matter of general and common concern'. This condition was also in contradiction of the Government of India Act of 1935 aimed at a strong Centre, which could have prevented Partition had it not been abandoned in the wake of World War II. One of the other conditions was that the mode of representation in elected bodies shall guarantee adequate and effective protection to minorities in every province and would be through separate electorates but with the provision that no majority shall be reduced

---

[37]Sheshrav More, *Congress Ani Gandhijini Akhand Bharat Ka Nakarla?* Rajhans Prakashan; Fourth edition, 2020, p. 89.

to a minority and even to equality.[38]

The moment for Jinnah to turn openly communal arrived after the Simon Commission[39] came to India in 1928 and was boycotted by all except the Muslim League led by Mian Muhammad Shafi[40] and the Justice Party of Madras. The Congress boycotted the commission for having no Indian member on it and for its one-sided nature. Later, the Congress called an all-party conference to demonstrate to the British rulers that Indians were capable of setting the national agenda on their own without a Simon Commission.

Both the Hindu Mahasabha and the Muslim League, led by Jinnah, participated in the conference. However, the views of the Muslim League differed on representation of various communities in state legislatures and on separating Sindh from the then Bombay province. Jinnah also wanted other concessions from the Congress, including separate electorates for Muslims, more in proportion to their numbers.

In the meantime, Motilal Nehru's Nehru Report, seeking dominion status for India and recommending joint electorates based on fair play and rejecting the special demands of the Muslims, started creating waves to the detriment of the Muslim League and Jinnah. Jinnah called an all-party conference at Calcutta to discuss this report.

Opposing Jinnah's pro-Muslim demands at this conference, well-known educationist and politician Dr Mukund Ramrao (M.R.) Jayakar, who had been associated with both the Hindu Mahasabha and the Congress and had also been the director, along with Jinnah, on the board of *The Bombay Chronicle*, said: 'The word

---

[38] R.C. Majumdar, *History of the Freedom Movement in India*, South Asia Books, 1988, p.223, 224.

[39] The Simon Commission was a group of seven MPs from Britain who were sent to India in 1928 to study constitutional reforms and make recommendations to the government. Originally named the Indian Statutory Commission, it came to be known as the Simon Commission after its chairman Sir John Simon.

[40] The League had by then split into two parts, one led by Shafi and the other by Jinnah.

communalism has acquired a most extraordinary significance these days. If I venture to speak for Hindu rights, I am a communalist, but if a Muslim with nationalist tendencies fights for Muslim rights, he still remains a nationalist. There is no use hiding the fact that all the amendments put forward by Mr Jinnah had their origin in communal spirit.'[41] Jayakar clearly and rightly analysed Jinnah one last time before he finally emerged in all his true colours.

After the denial of his demands at the all-party meeting, Jinnah convened an All Parties Muslim Conference at Delhi in 1929 and took a giant step towards realizing his ambition. He openly donned Muslim colours by presenting a charter of 14 demands on behalf of the Muslim community:

1. The form of the future constitution should be federal with residuary powers vested in the provinces. The central government to have control only of such matters of common interest as may be guaranteed by the Constitution.
2. Uniform measure of autonomy shall be granted to all provinces.
3. All legislatures in the country and other elected bodies should be reconstituted on the definite principle of adequate and effective representation of minorities in every province without reducing the majority of any province to a minority or even equality.
4. In the central legislature, Muslim representation should not be less than one-third.
5. The representation of communal groups should continue to be by means of separate electorates as at present, provided that it should be open to any community at any time to abandon its separate electorate in favour of joint electorates.
6. Any territorial redistribution that might at any time be necessary should not in any way affect the Muslim majority in the Punjab, Bengal and North-West Frontier Province.
7. Full religious liberty, that is, liberty of belief, worship,

---

[41]B.N. Jog, *Threat of Islam: Indian Perspective*, Mumbai (Bombay): Unnati Prakashan, 1994, p. 197, 198, 230, 231.

observances, propaganda, association and education should be guaranteed to all communities.
8. No bill or resolution, or any part thereof should be passed, in any legislature or any other elected body, if three-fourths of the members of any community in that particular body oppose such a bill or resolution or part thereof, on the ground that it would be injurious to the interests, of that community.
9. Sind should be separated from the Bombay Presidency.
10. Reform should be introduced in the North-West Frontier Province and Balochistan on the same footing as in other provinces.
11. Provision should be made in the Constitution giving Muslims an adequate share along with the other Indians, in all the services of the State and in local self-governing bodies having due regard to the requirements of efficiency.
12. The Constitution should embody adequate safeguards for the protection of Muslim culture and for the protection and promotion of Muslim education, language, religion, personal laws and Muslim charitable institutions and for their due share in the grants-in-aid given by the State and by local self-governing bodies.
13. No cabinet, either central or provincial, should be formed without there being a proportion of at least one-third Muslim ministers.
14. No change shall be made in the Constitution by the central legislature except with the concurrence of the States constituting the Indian federation.[42]

On a closer look, one can trace the foundations of Pakistan to these demands, the major features of which include a weak Centre, provincial autonomy, promoting Muslim religious and political interests at the cost of Hindu rights, separation of Sindh from Bombay province, and on the other hand, no territorial

---

[42] D.R. Mankekar, *The House that Jinnah Built*, Padma Publications, 1944, p. 32.

redistribution affecting the Muslim majority in Punjab, Bengal and the North-West Frontier Province.

Now it was clear that Jinnah had decided the political course of his life promoting pro-Muslim agenda at Hindu cost and used it to become the undisputed leader of the Muslims. However, he managed to achieve his goal sooner than later as one sees. His stand also indicated that he was coming under the influence of the first visionary of Pakistan, Sir Muhammad Iqbal.

A descendent of a Kashmiri Pandit family, Iqbal was considered to be one of the greatest poets of Urdu and Persian in the Indian subcontinent, but, at the same time, was the main figure behind the partition of India and the creation of Pakistan. His life can be broadly divided into two parts: the first part (before 1906) during which he penned the patriotic song 'Sare Jahan se Accha', or 'Tarana-e-Hindi', which is virtually sung as India's second national anthem, and referred to Lord Ram as Imam-e-Hind; and the second and the more important part being responsible for the birth of Pakistan and lakhs of deaths due to Partition.

With the formation of the Muslim League in Dhaka in 1906, Iqbal started turning towards puritanical Islam. In 1907, he became an office bearer of the Muslim League and thus lunged further towards separatist thoughts. Eventually, he emerged as a great preacher, expounding his own philosophy woven around Islam and its principles. In the second part of his career, his core dream was of having a separate nation for Indian Muslims by partitioning India. In 1910, within just six years of penning 'Tarana-e-Hindi', Iqbal, a complete pan-Islamist now, penned 'Tarana-e-Milli', endorsing pan-Islamism. It ran thus:

> *Chin-o-Arab hamaaraa, Hindoositan hamaaraa*
> *Muslim hai ham, vatan hai saaraa jahaan hamaaraa*

> (Central Asia and Arabia are ours, Hindustan is ours,
> We are Muslims, the whole world is our homeland)

He wrote another poem titled 'Wataniyat', in which he called for the destruction of the concept (which is referred to as an 'Idol' in his poem) of nationalism, which is in contradiction to pan-Islamist thinking that aims at converting the entire world to Islam. It ran thus: 'You should show the old panorama to the world, O Mustafaa's follower! You should destroy this idol.'

Iqbal's dream of a separate country for Indian Muslims was partly implored by Syed Ahmed Khan's vision that as former rulers of India, Indian Muslims can't allow themselves to be ruled by Hindus, their former subjects, in case the British left this country. While Syed Ahmed persevered for continuation of British rule in India and slighted those few Muslims who joined the Congress, Iqbal went a step further and said the community's full aspirations would be fulfilled only when it carves out a separate Islamic nation out of India.

In 1930, at the Allahabad Muslim League session, Iqbal outlined his vision for a separate nation for Indian Muslims comprising Punjab, Sindh, North-West Frontier Province and Balochistan, which precisely forms today's Pakistan. Speaking at the session, he said: 'I would like to see the Punjab, North-West Frontier Province, Sind and Balochistan amalgamated into a single state. To me, self-government within the British Empire, or without the British Empire, the formation of a consolidated North-west Indian Muslim state appears to be the destiny of the Muslims, at least of North-west India.'[43] Thus, Iqbal became the first politician to articulate what would be known as the two-nation theory in clearer terms than Syed Ahmed—that Muslims are a distinct nation and hence deserve political independence from other regions and communities of India.

Two years later in 1932, Choudhary Rahmat Ali, a Muslim student of Gujjar origin from India's Hoshiarpur district studying in Cambridge University, coined the word 'Pakistan' for this proposed nation in a pamphlet titled *Now or Never: Are We to Live or Perish*.[44] In this pamphlet, he implored the Muslims to

---

[43]Sir Muhammad Iqbal's 1930 Presidential Address to the 25th Session of the All-India Muslim League, Allahabad, 29 December 1930, http://www.columbia.edu/itc/mealac/pritchett/00islamlinks/txt_iqbal_1930.html. Accessed on 30 July 2021.

[44]Full text of the pamphlet *Now or Never*, published by Choudhary Rahmat Ali as

break away from India to form a separate Islamic State, the time for which he thought was most opportune at that moment.

The time was also opportune for Jinnah's rise as the undisputed leader of the Muslims in India. It coincided with Gandhi becoming the supreme leader of the Hindus after he refused to attend the first Round Table Conference in London in 1930 following Viceroy Lord Irwin's refusal to give him any assurance on his demand for a new Constitution and dominion status for India. Leaders of other parties attended the conference. Muslim leaders were unaffected by Gandhi's absence, as they were busy playing their own game of seeking more and more concessions in connivance with the British. However, as Gandhi launched the Salt Satyagraha in India that year, the Hindu leaders attending the conference in London such as Munje and Tej Bahadur Sapru lost face as they were seen as traitors by the Hindu populace, which had started seeing Gandhi and the Congress as patriots. This was in spite of the fact that Munje demanded complete independence from British rule at the conference and also opposed special demands of the Muslims, thus protecting Hindu rights. The British prime minster Ramsay MacDonald dropped a hint of what was to come when he harped on the need for special powers to be vested in the Viceroy to protect the interest of the minorities, which, he said, was the British government's responsibility.

Significantly, in a few years of Jinnah's 14 demands came the British Communal Award after the second Round Table conference of 1931, which in many ways addressed many of Jinnah's demands. Interestingly, the second Round Table Conference was attended by Gandhi following a compromise with the British in the form of the Gandhi–Irwin Pact, but he could make no impact on the Muslim League and Muslim demands. He also failed to prevent the Muslim League and other Muslim representatives from allowing him to be the sole representative of all Indians at the conference.

'Founder of Pakistan National Movement', in which the word 'Pakistan' appears to have been used for the first time in a document (1933). http://www.columbia.edu/itc/mealac/pritchett/00islamlinks/txt_rahmatali_1933.html. Accessed on 19 July 2021.

Apart from giving representation to Muslims far in proportion to their numbers in the Communal Award (which came soon after the conference), the British cunningly tried to divide the entire society coming under the Hindu pantheon by planning separate representation in legislatures for Sikhs, Buddhists, Jains and Depressed Classes (now known as Dalits). But here one saw a combative Gandhi, who vehemently opposed the provision to divide the Hindu society by going on fast unto death while being imprisoned in Yerwada jail. He opened negotiations with Depressed Classes led by Ambedkar and M.P. Raja and other leaders and conceded seats to them from the Upper Caste quota in what was later known as the Poona Pact. Munje played a key role in drafting the pact as he was close to Ambedkar. The pact prevented the British from interfering in the internal affairs of the Hindu community.

However, when it came to the separate electorates given to Muslims in the Communal Award, Gandhi first rejected the award as 'anti-national'[45]. Nehru described it as 'utter negation of nationalism and meant to divide Hindustan into communal compartments.'[46] This instilled a sense of hope that the Congress had finally come around and would resolutely oppose it. However, the Congress's official stand on the award a few days later virtually meant that it had accepted it.

H.V. Seshadri explains the Congress's volte-face in his landmark book *The Tragic Story of Partition*. He writes that when the Muslim League came to know that the Congress would oppose the award tooth and nail, it got in touch with a key Muslim leader and former Congress president, Dr Mukhtar Ahmed Ansari, and urged him to persuade the Congress to accept the award in the greater interest of Hindu–Muslim unity. The appeal was made in the form of a telegram to Ansari by League leaders Aga Khan and Jinnah on the advice of the British Secretary of State, Samuel Hoare. It showed how the Muslim leaders, including the ones in the Congress,

---

[45]B.N. Jog, *Threat of Islam: Indian Dimensions*, Mumbai (Bombay): Unnati Prakashan, 1994, p.210.
[46]Ibid.

and the British were hand in glove when it came to furthering Muslim interests. Ansari, who had initially called the award 'a cup of poison' at the time of its announcement, softened his stand after the telegram from Aga Khan and Jinnah.

Soon after this came the Congress's final stand that 'it would neither accept nor oppose the award'. The episode also showed how the Congress's nationalist Muslims were playing the Muslim League game of protecting common Muslim interests and also gave an idea about the real reasons behind Partition in the next decade.[47]

Ambedkar describes the unfairness of the Congress to the Hindus vis-à-vis the Muslims thus:

> The Communal Award is iniquitous inasmuch as it accords unequal treatment to the Hindu and Muslim minorities in the matter of electorates. It grants the Muslim minorities in the Hindu Provinces the right of self-determination in the matter of electorates, but it does not grant the same right to the Hindu minorities in the Muslim Provinces. In the Hindu Provinces, the Muslim minority is allowed to choose the kind of electorates it wants and the Hindu majority is not permitted to have any say in the matter. But in the Muslim Provinces, it is the Muslim majority which is allowed to choose the kind of electorates it prefers and the Hindu minority is not permitted to have any say in the matter. Thus, the Muslims in the Muslim Provinces having been given both statutory majority and separate electorates, the Communal Award must be said to impose upon the Hindu minorities Muslim rule, which they can neither alter nor influence.[48]

The Communal Award also highlighted the attitude of the Congress as well as that of the Muslims vis-à-vis the patriotic attitude of Indian Christians, led by educationist Dr S.K. Dutta. The

---

[47] H.V. Seshadri, *The Tragic Story of Partition*, Sahitya Sindhu Prakashan, 2015, p. 98, 99.
[48] B.R. Ambedkar, *Pakistan or the Partition of India*, Samayak Prakashan; First edition, 2013, Chapter VI.

community (Indian Christians) refused to be drawn into the British net and instead took a nationalist stand on the Communal Award, saying that raising special demands at the cost of majority rights would split the nation. The Christian's stand, expressed by Dr Dutta before the Minority Committee of the Conference—which also included Muslim representation—was very strong and unequivocal against any special concessions to religious minorities. He said,

> According to the League of Nation's Charter, the minorities can merely demand the right to follow their religion and freedom from coercion by followers of the other faiths. However, the charters preferred by the parasites growing on the body of the Indian nation in the name of community and religion contain such aggressive claims that if they were conceded, the very name of democracy will cease to exist in the Constitution.[49]

The Christian stand in a way reminded how the Congress, despite claiming to be an organization of all Indians, had totally left the path of true nationalism in its quest for elusive Muslim support.

This support eluded the Congress in the provincial elections held in the winter of 1936–37, the results of which proved that even after years and years of Muslim appeasement, the party remained the lowest political priority for Muslims. The Muslim voters voted mainly for the Muslim-led parties, except in the North-West Frontier Province, where the Congress did well because of the hold of Khan Abdul Ghaffar Khan and his brother, Dr Khan Abdul Jabbar Khan. The party could win only 26 of the total 492 Muslim-reserved seats nationwide. In fact, the Congress could get only 58 candidates to fight on the total 492 Muslim-reserved seats. The Muslim representation in the All India Congress Committee (AICC) in 1936 also showed the party's poor hold over Muslims. Out of 143 AICC members only six were Muslims. However, the polls established the Congress as the most popular party amongst

---

[49]B.N. Jog, *Threat of Islam: Indian Dimensions*, Mumbai (Bombay): Unnati Prakashan, 1994, p. 220, 221.

Hindus. The party won an overwhelming 715 seats out of the 836 non-reserved constituencies. However, even the Muslim League didn't do too well in these polls. The party won only 108 seats of the total 496 Muslim seats, as Muslim voters voted for regional Muslim-dominated parties.

From this point onwards, Jinnah was hell-bent on making the Muslim League the sole representative of Muslims and himself the supreme Muslim leader. His problem was Muslim-majority areas such as Bengal, Punjab and Sindh, where he couldn't so much play on Muslim fears and where other Muslim leaders, such as Sir Sikandar Hayat Khan of the Unionist Party in Punjab and Abul Kasem Fazlul Huq of the Krishak Praja Party in Bengal, didn't want to pursue a totally anti-Hindu line and were keen to take the local Hindus along.

Jinnah then resorted to a three-pronged strategy to achieve his objectives:

1. Taking recourse to extreme fanaticism in the Muslim-minority states by playing on Muslim fears to bring pressure on both the Congress and the Muslim leaders of the Muslim-majority states.
2. Playing strategically in the Muslim-majority states to bring the Muslim leaders of the states under his sway, directly or indirectly.
3. Taking the lead in political negotiations with the British to project that he was the main and the sole representative of Muslims in India in dealing with the British.

Interestingly, while deciding upon this strategy, Jinnah was also keen on sharing power with the Congress in provinces such as Uttar Pradesh, where the League had done better than in other provinces in the 1937 elections. One of the reasons behind this was perhaps his attempt to draw Muslims leaders from other parties into his fold by raising his stature as a leader and holding out loaves of power. He officially declared his party's willingness to cooperate with the Congress in running the Uttar Pradesh ministry. However, the Congress virtually turned down his offer by putting such stiff conditions for accepting Jinnah's proposal that these would have finished the Muslim League on the political horizon. Soon after this, the Congress launched a mass contact programme amongst Muslims under Nehru's leadership to win Muslim support by explaining the Congress's objectives.

These two moves incensed Jinnah so much that he immediately embarked upon his three-pronged strategy, in which he used the trump card of 'Islam in danger' to win Muslim support.

Around the same time, the Congress tried to sow seeds of discontent in the Muslim League even as a by-election was being held in the Jhansi-Hamirpur constituency in June 1937 following the death of the elected League candidate. The move was particularly foolish and misdirected because the provincial elections had proved the Congress's lack of Muslim support on ground. Thanks to this communal pitch, the League won the elections against the Muslim candidate of the Congress with a handsome margin.

It convinced Jinnah that one of the best ways to become the leaders of all Muslims and thwart the Congress was to raise the 'Islam in danger' bogey, which he achieved following his election as the president of the Muslim League at Lucknow in October 1937. Depicting the Congress as a Hindu party aiming to put down Muslims, he opposed 'Vande Mataram' as being against Muslim tenets, being an idol-worshipping poem, and denounced Hindi as state language that was thwarting Urdu, the Wardha scheme of education promoting Hindi and also the tricolour. Jinnah played on the Congress's act of putting stiff conditions before the Muslim League for sharing power with Muslims in Uttar Pradesh. He told the Muslim world that even in a limited type of self-rule in the form of provincial autonomy, the Congress was preventing the Muslim League from sharing power with it and thus the Congress's was a Hindu rule.

As a next step, he set up two committees to probe the manufactured allegations of atrocities of the 'Hindu Congress' against Muslims. One of them was set up under the Nawab of Pirpur, Muhammad Mehdi. The Pirpur Committee report depicted the Congress rule as anti-Muslim and opposed the tricolour, 'Vande

Mataram', and went a step further by opposing the Congress's and Hindu's objection to cow slaughter. The demand for allowing cow slaughter by the Muslim League constituted the last straw on the camel's back when it came to the Hindu–Muslim unity scheme of the Congress.

A committee was also set up by the Bihar Provincial Muslim League under the leadership of Mohammed Sharif to look into the condition of Muslims under the Congress rule in Bihar. Like the Pirpur Committee report, it turned out to be a bundle of lies to project the Congress as anti-Muslim and the Muslim community reeling under the onslaught of Congress's Hindu tyranny.[50]

The worst thing these reports did was to change the complexion of Indian politics. They incited less communal and moderate Muslim leaders to turn overtly communal and anti-Congress in order to find favour amongst Muslim voters. Otherwise, they feared, Jinnah's agenda would swallow their leadership. Even Fazlul Huq, who had opposed Jinnah earlier but had later sought the Muslim League's help to save his ministry in Bengal, joined the League. He was so overwhelmed by Jinnah's communal propaganda that he tried to match Jinnah by publishing a booklet titled *Muslim Sufferings under Congress Rule*, in which he virtually incited the Muslims by levelling unsubstantiated charges against the Congress. The Muslims played Gravamin politics against provincial Congress governments, which as Ambedkar describes in his book *Pakistan or Partition of India*, 'means politics in which the main strategy is to gain power by manufacturing grievances'.[51]

THE CONGRESS: CHASING A MIRAGE

In terms of strategy to meet his objective of emerging as the supreme leader of Indian Muslims, Jinnah was far ahead of the Congress. He tried various ways to force the established Muslim

---

[50]B.N. Jog, *Threat of Islam: Indian Perspective*, Mumbai (Bombay): Unnati Prakashan, 1994, p. 233, 235, 324.
[51]Dr B.R. Ambedkar, *Pakistan or Partition of India*, Samayak Prakashan; First edition, 2013, p. 220.

leadership in the country to join him. On the other hand, the Congress was virtually strategy-less; its objective of gaining Independence solely with Hindu–Muslim unity was like chasing a mirage. For example, Jinnah skillfully used the Shahidganj mosque controversy in Lahore which became a point of confrontation between Muslims and Sikhs in 1935 to force the Punjab chief minister, Sikandar Hayat Khan, to join hands with the League.

Shahidganj was originally a mosque that went over to the Sikhs during the time of Maharaja Ranjit Singh and even the court had upheld the Sikh ownership of the property. The controversy however started when a rumour went around that the Sikhs wanted to demolish the structure. This gave Jinnah an opportunity to further his communal agenda as Muslims cutting across party lines started an agitation to take control of the mosque. The leadership of the agitation naturally shifted to the Muslim League elements. Muslims from across north India started pouring into Lahore.

The control of the affair went out of the hands of Hayat Khan, who had to knock at Jinnah's doors to douse the raging fire. Reportedly, Jinnah made a conditional offer that if Khan would join hands with the Muslim League, he would help withdraw the agitation. Khan was forced to join the League, after which Jinnah withdrew the agitation. The controversy soon cooled down and the property remained in the possession of the Sikhs. It was a great example of Jinnah displaying strategic thinking and letting off one mosque in exchange of an entire province. Had this happened in a Congress-ruled state, Jinnah wouldn't have called off the agitation but instead would have allowed it to boil.[52]

Confident of growing Muslim support, Jinnah declared that the Congress should recognize his party as the authoritative representative organization of Indian Muslims and Gandhi as the leader of the Congress and Hindus. It was only on this basis, he said, he would hold any further negotiations.[53]

---

[52]Ram Gopal, *Indian Muslims: A Political History 1858–1947*, Asia Pub. House, 1964, p. 280.
[53]Anita Inder Singh, *Origins of Partition of India*, OUP India; New edition, 1991, p. 29.

The Congress's surrender before the Muslim League came in a series of events that shook the foundation of the fundamentals of nationalism. What was glaring was that the Muslim leaders of the Congress were playing a role from inside to make the Congress cave in before the League's agenda in what allegedly appeared to be a spirit of common Muslim brotherhood aimed at promoting the Muslim agenda.

When the Muslim League launched an attack on the Wardha scheme of education, some of the Congress leaders started promoting Hindustani. Gandhi himself said that there was little difference between Hindi and Hindustani, and maintained that 'there is no difference between Hindustani and Urdu. Written in the Devanagari script, it is called Hindi, and written in the Arabic script, it is called Urdu'.[54] The leader of the Opposition and other Muslim members in the Central Provinces and the Berar Legislative Assembly also insisted that the name 'Vidya Mandir' (under the Wardha scheme of education) was unacceptable to them as it constituted an attack on Islamic culture. They announced that they would have to appeal to the governor if the government persisted on 'foisting' the scheme on Muslims.[55]

The surrender on Vande Mataram was total. A local education board in Congress-ruled Central Provinces and Berar issued a circular to all the headmasters of Marathi and Urdu schools to the effect that 'in future, the Vande Mataram song should be recited daily at the time of prayer'.[56] But with Muslims taking strong exception, the Central Provinces government stated in a memorandum to all commissioners in April 1939 that local boards can permit the singing of this song in schools under their management; they should however 'not compel the Muslim pupils either to sing it or to remain present when it is sung against their

---

[54] *Collected Works of Mahatma Gandhi* (CWMG), Vol. 33, p. 453.
[55] Muslim Response to the Educational Policy of the Central Provinces and Berar Government (1937–39); 11 November 2006. http://www.suedasien.info/analysen/1460.html. Accessed on 26 May 2021.
[56] Ibid.

will.'[57] In 1939, education minister of Bihar, Dr Syed Mahmud, a hard-core Congress leader, ordered the education and other departments not to make Vande Mataram compulsory.[58] In the Budget session of the Central Provinces Legislative Assembly in March 1938, the leader of the Opposition and other Muslim members stated that singing Vande Mataram was impracticable. C. Rajagopalachari, popularly known as Rajaji, who was the chief minister of Madras province, said that Vande Mataram should be done away with as it created bitterness amongst the Muslims.

Eventually, a committee set up by the Congress on the issue, which included Pandit Nehru and Netaji Subhas Chandra Bose, suggested that only the first two stanzas of the song be sung in Congress functions. This was accepted by the Congress Working Committee (CWC) in October 1937. The Muslim League put a complete ban on singing of Vande Mataram. It was, in a way, a psychological war waged by Jinnah and Muslim leaders to blackmail the Congress and project it as anti-Muslim in spite of the Congress's numerous attempts to woo the community.

There was no immediate response from the Congress to the Muslim League on its demand for legalizing cow slaughter until much later when Gandhi virtually expressed his helplessness at some Muslims insisting on cow slaughter. This was when outwardly the Congress remained wedded to cow protection.

In *Thoughts on Pakistan*, Ambedkar described the unending Congress appeasement of Muslims as 'the dark age of Indian politics of modern times,'[59] and believed that it had made Hindus feeble. The Congress greatly reduced the Hindu society's will to fight against Muslim fanaticism and put it virtually in a 'lame duck' mode.

The Hindus had now lost all vigour to fight divisive forces, unlike during the Partition of Bengal by Lord Curzon in 1905 under the ostensible plea of achieving administrative efficiency but which

---

[57] MPSA, GCPB/Education Department, File No. 3-70/1939.
[58] Milind P. Sabnis, *Samagra Vande Mataram*, Vol. II, Saptahik Vivek, p.160.
[59] Dr B.R. Ambedkar, *Thoughts on Pakistan*, Prabhat Prakashan, 2020. Also, Dhananjay Keer, *Veer Savarkar*, Popular Prakashan Pvt. Ltd, Second edition, 2019, p. 232.

was meant to weaken the nationalism movement in Bengal. The subsequent reunification of the state under Viceroy Lord Hardinge in 1911 following massive protests by Bengalis over a period of six years—using boycott to bombs as weapons—is an epoch-making event in India's freedom struggle. It gives great hope to nationalists even today when it comes to overcoming divisive forces.

The British's decision to partition Bengal was to break the back of nationalists in Bengal in the form of a Congress movement. This movement also aimed to bring Muslims under its fold in the face of the machinations of the Aligarh School, which supported British rulers as part of its pan-Islamic agenda. The partition was welcomed by Muslims because the new East Bengal province, which also included Assam, made it a Muslim-majority province, with Dacca as its capital.

The Muslims' celebration of the partition, however, created hatred for them in the mind of the local Bengali Hindus, who launched a massive movement against the division with all their combined might—the kind of which modern Indian history has rarely seen. The hardliners and the moderates in the Congress used the boycott of British goods as their weapon and the revolutionaries used their bombs—all combined to create such pressure on the British that they had to reverse their decision to please the Bengali Hindu sentiment. One of the reasons for the reversal of the decision was also the terrible economic losses that the British suffered due to the six-year struggle.

Sadly, more than three decades later, the hard-line nationalist Hindu element, which had played a major role in forcing the British to reunite Bengal after partitioning it, was dead. The nation couldn't show the same resolve of 1905–11 to prevent its Partition.

The commencement of World War II in 1939 became the test for both the Congress and Jinnah on how best to play their cards to gain their objectives. The British establishment in India came under severe pressure of the war. Jinnah took full advantage of the situation to take forward his avowedly communal politics, while the Congress being wedded to non-violence simply refused to support the war.

With Gandhi's intervention, the Congress modified its stance identifying the Axis Powers (Germany, Italy and Japan) as the aggressors and threat to world peace but continued with its earlier stance that Britain should decide the time frame to leave India once the war was over. The Congress demanded assurance from the British that India would be freed from British rule after the war. The demand was made by Nehru and Rajendra Prasad before Viceroy Lord Linlithgow on behalf of the Congress. But the demand was summarily rejected by the Viceroy, who saw it as arm-twisting and refused to yield. As a result, in a totally thoughtless move, the CWC directed all the provincial governments of the Congress in the seven Hindu-majority provinces to resign in protest, forcing governor's rule in these states.

This shifted, in one stroke, the balance of power in favour of Muslims and Jinnah. First, all the Muslim chief ministers of Punjab, Sindh, Bengal and Assam extended full support to the British in its war efforts. Next, Jinnah forwarded four demands in return of help in war efforts:

1. After the war, a new Constitution should be made for India.
2. The British should make constitutional reforms with the consent of two communities only.
3. The legitimate aspirations of the Arabs in Palestine should be fulfilled by the British.
4. The Indian Army should not be sent against any Muslim nation outside India.

With his back to the wall, owing to the Congress's non-cooperation, the Viceroy had to accept all of Jinnah's four demands, thus giving him a lead over the Congress and almost declaring him a British ally in war efforts. From this point onwards, the decline in the Congress's position before the British was fast as Jinnah used the war card to press his communal agenda with the help of his undeclared ally, the British. Adding to his list of communal demands, he sought that Urdu be declared as the national language of India. He became more aggressive and demanded that the Congress shouldn't be allowed to assume power in the seven provinces where it had resigned in protest. If it (the Congress) wished to do so, Jinnah threatened a civil war.

In his analysis of the Congress's change in stance from one of settlement with the Muslims to appeasement of the community, Ambedkar said,

> Appeasement means buying off the aggressor by conniving at his acts of murder, rape, arson and loot against innocent persons who happen for the moment to be the victims of his displeasure. On the other hand, settlement means laying down the bounds which neither party can transgress. Appeasement sets no limits to the demands and aspirations of the aggressor. Settlement does. The Congress has failed to realize that the policy of concession has increased Muslim aggressiveness, and what is worse, Muslims interpret these concessions as a sign of defeatism on the part of the Hindus and the absence of the will to resist. This policy of appeasement will involve the Hindus in the same fearful situation in which the Allies found themselves as a result of the policy of appeasement which they adopted towards Hitler.[60]

A NATIONALIST EMERGES

It was at this stage, when the dark clouds of pro-Muslim nationalism were hovering over the Indian horizon, that Savarkar stepped on to the national political scene after his release from internment in Ratnagiri, which was preceded by 14 years of rigorous imprisonment.

During this period, in addition to being a great revolutionary, he had also acquired the image of a great social reformer due to the movement against untouchability that he ran in Konkan from 1924 to 1937. In fact, his work on Dalit emancipation was pioneering. As a Brahmin, he himself performed the thread ceremony of Dalits to give them respectability and also organized massive anti-caste

---

[60] B.R. Ambedkar, *Thoughts on Pakistan*, Nabu Press, 2011, p. 286.

dinners. This put Savarkar on collision course with orthodox Brahmins. But he remained undeterred as he was firmly wedded to Hindu unity and reform by rooting out social perversions from the Hindu society. Such was his passion that Maharashtrian social reformer V.R. Shinde had once remarked that had Savarkar not joined politics in 1937 and continued with his work of social reform for a few more years, he would have banished untouchability from large parts of India.

Significantly, by the time he was released, Savarkar had also emerged as a great nationalist thinker because of his book *Hindutva*, which when seen along with Savarkar's Hindu Rashtra manifesto, gave the country a new definition of nationalism called 'unalloyed nationalism'. Though Savarkar got the book first published in 1923 under the pen-name Maratha, he could give his name to the book only in 1928, four years after being released from rigorous imprisonment in Ratnagiri jail. Incidentally, when the book landed in the hands of Swami Shraddhanand before his murder in 1926, he was simply mesmerized by the definition of 'Hindutva' as given by Savarkar and described it 'as the dawn of a new age'[61]. Even as Swamiji heaped praises on the author of the book, he remained unaware of his real identity.

Following his release, when Savarkar decided to join politics, he had a choice. He could have joined the Congress because some of the leaders of the party, including Subhas Chandra Bose, invited him to join them. In fact, amongst those very keen on Savarkar joining the Congress Socialist Party were party leaders S.M. Joshi and Achyut Patwardhan, but Savarkar turned down the offer. A great nationalist and visionary, Savarkar knew that the Congress had gone so far ahead on the path of Muslim appeasement that it was impossible for it to retrace its steps. Above all, he well knew that the Congress's acceptance of Muslims' anti-national demands would tear Hindu–Muslim relations apart rather than bringing them together, thus eventually breaking the nation.

---

[61]Dhananjay Keer, *Veer Savarkar*, Popular Prakashan Pvt Ltd; Second edition, 2019, p. 262.

Savarkar considered it his national duty to free the nation from the web of the Congress's politics of giving special rights to Muslims at Hindu cost. He was firm in his conviction that his was a fight for equal treatment and not special treatment for Hindus, unlike Jinnah. So, when the Hindu Mahasabha leader and the great nationalist B.S. Munje decided to step down and offer the party's presidentship to Savarkar, the great revolutionary-cum-thinker proudly and graciously accepted it. Savarkar firmly believed that till the Muslims continued to demand special concessions at the cost of Hindu rights, Hindus needed a special party to protect their interests against Muslim aggression. That was in fact his justification for joining the Hindu Mahasabha.

Interestingly, before Savarkar came to the political scene efforts were made by top political leaders such as Pandit Madan Mohan Malaviya and Munje to counter the Congress's approach. However, these efforts didn't succeed beyond a point in terms of mass support because of Gandhi's and the Congress's phenomenal public hold, which could be attributed to Gandhi's saintly demeanour and the party's extraordinary mass-mobilizing abilities.

Munje was a leader of great standing. He had been able to convince the British to recruit Hindus from all castes in the army instead of just martial castes. The present homogeneous character of the Indian army was actually initiated by Munje. He also convinced the British to recruit Indians higher up in the army hierarchy up to the rank of junior commissioned officers.

Munje's high sense of patriotism is demonstrated by the simple fact that he vacated his chair as Hindu Mahasabha president in 1937 and offered it to Savarkar in the hope that Savarkar, with an unparalleled track record of sacrifice behind him and being a Hindutva ideologue, would be able to counter the Congress. He hoped that Savarkar would mobilize the masses and get them away from the Congress on to the path of unalloyed nationalism. Savarkar too put his career on the sacrificial alter by joining the Hindu Mahasabha because had he joined the Congress with a little compromise in his ideological beliefs, he could have risen to any level in that party.

However, for Savarkar, the nation was bigger than position, as always. He once again prepared himself to make sacrifices for his country. In doing so, Savarkar, in a sense, chose the path of Maharana Pratap and eschewed the one followed by his adversary and Emperor Akbar's favourite, Raja Man Singh.[62]

---

[62]Dhananjay Keer, *Veer Savarkar*, Popular Prakashan Pvt. Ltd; Second edition, 2019, p. 230, 321.

3

UNDERSTANDING SAVARKAR'S HINDUTVA

The end of the second decade of the twentieth century was a turbulent time for Indian politics. It was marked by rising pan-Islamism among the Muslim masses even as the Hindus were surrendering their rights and identity by following the Congress's pacifist ideology. It was at this critical juncture that Veer Savarkar proposed his doctrine of Hindu nationalism through his book *Hindutva*.

Nationalism was the cornerstone of Savarkar's ideology, and everything else—caste, regional and religious considerations—were secondary. He encouraged Hindus to be unapologetic, and believed that when Hindus were non-discriminating towards other religions, they should take measures to protect themselves when attacked. This, he believed, was necessary to create a level-playing field. Savarkar was all for 'one man, one vote'—a just, democratic principle that the Congress destroyed with its theory of placating pan-Islamist Muslims by giving them special concessions. Further, his theory of Hindu nationalism was a counter to the narrative created by supporters of the two-nation theory (that Hindus and Muslims are two separate nations, coined by Syed Ahmed Khan) that 'India is neither a nation nor a single geographical unit.'[1]

---

[1] Sayyid Amir Ali in 1899 said, 'You are well aware that the land of Hindustan is inhabited by different nations following different religions. They have no sense of unity and nationality even in the name.' (Lal Bahadur, *The Muslim League: Its History, Activities and Achievements*, Agra Book Store, 1954, p. 27).

The word 'Hindutva' (Hindudom), Savarkar believed, has the ability to represent the whole history of India:

> The ideas and ideals, the systems and societies, the thoughts and sentiments which have centered around this name are so varied and rich, so powerful and so subtle, so elusive and yet so vivid that the term Hindutva defies all attempts at analysis. Forty centuries, if not more, it had been at work to mould it as it is. Prophets and poets, lawyers and law-givers, heroes and historians, have thought, lived, fought and died just to have it spelled thus. For indeed, is it not a result of countless actions—now conflicting, now commingling, now cooperating—of our whole race? Hindutva is not a word but a history. Not only the spiritual or religious history of our people as at times it is mistaken to be by being confounded with the other cognate term Hinduism, but a history in full. Hinduism is only a derivative, a fraction, a part of Hindutva.[2]

THE MAKING OF A HINDU NATION

Savarkar maintains that the words 'Hindu', 'Hindi', 'Hindustani' and 'Indian' have the same etymological origin in the river 'Indus', and refer to the human settlements in the Indian subcontinent on the banks of the Indus River since the ancient Indus valley civilization. Describing the Hindu nation as an ancient and continuous tradition that is stupendous and solid as the Himalayas that border our north, he says,

> Ever since the Vedic ages in the past, our forefathers had been shaping the formation of our people into a religious, racial, cultural and political unit. As a consequence of it all, growing organically the Sindhus of the Vedic time have grown today into Hindu Nation, extending over India and holding India in common as their Fatherland and their Holy Land. No other

---

[2]V.D. Savarkar, *Hindutva*, Hindi Sahitya Sadan, 2003, p. 3.

nation in the world, excepting perhaps the Chinese, can claim a continuity of life and growth so unbroken as our Hindu Nation does. The Hindu Nation is not a mushroom growth. It is not a treaty nation. It is not a paper made toy. It was not cut to order. It is not an outlandish makeshift. It has grown out of this soil and has its roots struck deep and wide in it. It is not a fiction invented to spite the Muslims or anybody in the world.[3]

Savarkar endeavoured to prove that the Hindu nation was an organic being, unlike several cut-and-paste entities that were considered 'nations' in the West. It made him analyse the deeper connection Hindus had with the seven rivers led by the Indus that emanate from the Himalayas. His description of the rise of the Sapta Sindhu (seven rivers) nation was poetic to say the least when one looks at the thread he used to describe it. He said that out of their gratitude to the perennial network of waterways that run through the land like a system of nerve-threads and that wove them into a being, Hindus very naturally took to themselves the name Sapta Sindhus. Sapta Sindhu was an epithet, according to him, which was applied to the whole of Vedic India in the world's oldest record, the *Rig Veda* itself. He explained the divine love and the homage the Aryans or the cultivators as they essentially were, bore to these seven rivers presided over by the Sindhu, which to them were but a visible symbol of the common nationality and culture.[4]

So, how did the Sindhu nation become a Hindu nation? Savarkar explains that even at the very dawn of history, these people were known to themselves as Sindhus, but as per definite records, they were also known to their surrounding nations as Sapta Sindhus. The letter 's' in Sanskrit is at times changed to 'h' in some of the Prakrit languages, both Indian and non-Indian. For example, he observes that the word 'Sapta' has become 'Hapta' not only in Indian Prakrits but also in European languages. So, we have 'Hapta', i.e., week, in India and 'Heptarchy', i.e., a state or region consisting of seven autonomous regions/government by

---

[3]Veer Savarkar, *Hindu Rashtra Darshan*, Prabhat Prakashan, 2020, p. 34.

[4]V.D. Savarkar, *Hindutva*, Hindi Sahitya Sadan, 2003, p. 5.

seven rulers, in Europe. 'Kesari' meaning 'lion' in Sanskrit becomes 'Kehari' in old Hindi. 'Saraswati' becomes 'Harhvati' in Persian and 'Asur' becomes 'Ahur'[5]. He says there is evidence to prove that the Vedic name of our nation, 'Sapta Sindhu', finds a mention as Hapta Hindu in the *Avesta* (religious text of the Zoroastrian faith). Thus, Savarkar insists that we belong to the nation of the Sindhus or Hindus, a fact that was well known to our learned men even in the Puranic period.[6]

Expounding his theory on the evolution of the Hindu nation further, Savarkar says our frontier provinces through which the Indus flowed still clung to their ancient name Sindhu Rashtra and throughout Sanskrit literature, we find Sindhu Sauveers (brave people of Sindh) recognized as an integral and an important part of our body politic. In the great Mahabharata war, the king of Sindhu Sauveers, Jayadratha, figures prominently and is said to have been closely related to the Bharatas, descendants of Bharat. Savarkar observes and adds that although the limits of the Sindhu Rashtra shifted from time to time, the language that the people spoke then, as they do now, marks them out as a people by themselves, from Multan to the sea. He says the name 'Sindhi', which it bears, is an emphatic reminder that all those who speak it are Sindhus and are entitled to be recognized as a geographical and political unit in the commonwealth of our Indian people.

Expounding on the term 'Bharat Khand' (the Indian subcontinent), which too came to be used to identify India in ancient times, he says the epithet 'Bharat Khand' almost succeeded in overshadowing the cradle name of our nation, Hapta Hindu, but foreign nations seem to have cared little for it. As our frontier provinces continued to be known by their ancient name, our immediate neighbours—the Avestic Persians, the Jews, the Greeks and others—clung to our ancient name Sindhus or Hindus.

---

[5]Ahura is a designation of a type of deity inherited by Zoroastrianism from the prehistoric Indo-Iranian religion. In the *Rig Veda*, 'asura' denotes the 'older gods', such as the 'Father Asura' (10.124.3). https://iranicaonline.org/articles/ahura-1-type-of-deity. Accessed on 31 July 2021.

[6]V.D. Savarkar, *Hindutva*, Hindi Sahitya Sadan, 2003, p. 5.

In his efforts to evolve his theory and back it up with credible and strong evidence, Savarkar also drew from foreign analogy to underline how Avestic Persians knew us as Hindus and how through the Greeks almost all of Europe and later on America came to know us as Hindus or Indians. He says even the Buddhist monk and Chinese pilgrim to India Hiuen Tsang insisted on calling us Shintus or Hintus. He goes on to add that barring a few examples, such as Afghanistan being called Shweta Bharat (White India) by the Parthians, very rarely had foreigners forgotten our cradle name.

In his definition of 'Hindu', Savarkar beautifully used different meanings of the word 'Sindhu' to describe territorial boundaries. He says:

> The word Sindhu in Sanskrit does not only mean the Indus but also the Sea—which girdles the southern peninsula—so that this one word Sindhu points out almost all frontiers of the land at a single stroke. Even if we do not accept the tradition that the river Brahmaputra is only a branch of the Sindhu which falls into flowing streams on the eastern and western slopes of the Himalayas and thus constitutes both our eastern as well as western frontiers, still it is indisputably true that it circumscribes our northern and western extremities in its sweep and so the epithet Sindhusthan calls up the image of our whole Motherland: the land that lies between Sindhu and Sindhu—from the Indus to the Seas.[7]

Mountstuart Elphinstone, one of the founders of British Raj in India, defined 'Boundaries of India' in his book *The History of India* as: 'India is bounded by the Hemalaya Mountains, the river Indus, and the sea. Its length from Cashmir to Cape Comorin is about 1,900 British miles; and its breadth from the mouth of the Indus to the mountains east of the Bharamputra considerably upwards of 1,500 British miles.'[8]

---

[7]Ibid. 24.
[8]Mountstuart Elphinstone, *The History of India*, 1841, p. 1.

He was not the first foreigner to define Indus as the western boundary of India. The Greek writers Arrian, Strabo and Eratosthenes, though they spoke of Indians beyond the Indus, strictly limited India to the eastern side of that river. Arrian says 'this river (Indus) Alexander crossed at daybreak with his army into the land of the Indians.' In the course of this description, he again explicitly declares that the Indus is the western boundary of India from the mountains to the sea.[9]

Chhatrapati Shivaji's goal was to extend his Hindavi Swarajya up to India's natural boundaries. Barthelemy Carre, a cleric of the French East India Company, noted the interesting conversation he had with Shivaji's Governor of Chaul port in Konkan during his India visit in 1668: 'I then asked him about Sevagy, his master, and he told me that he is intended to push his conquests from the river Indus, which forms the boundary of the kingdom of Cambaye, to the Gange, far beyond the rich provinces of Bengal.'[10] When the Maratha confederacy was at its peak, Govindrao Kale, the Maratha ambassador to the Nizam, expressed his joyous feelings to Nana Fadnavis, an influential minister and statesman of the Maratha empire, through a letter in 1793. He wrote:

> From the river Attock to the Indian Ocean extends the land of Hindus, Hindusthan (land of Hindus), not Turkasthan (land of Muslims). These have been our frontiers from the times of Pandavas to Vikramaditya. They preserved them and enjoyed the empires. After them came effete rulers and the Muslims conquered our Kingdom but now everything has been restored to us and re-won under the Peshwas and by the valorous sword of Mahadji Shinde! The Hindu Empire is established, the fame of our victory goes sounding around.[11]

Savarkar defined Hindu as everyone who regarded and claimed this Bharatbhoomi—from the Indus to the Seas—as his 'Fatherland'

---

[9]Ibid. 441.
[10]Surendra Nath Sen, *Foreign Biographies of Shivaji*, Saptarshee Prakashan; First edition, 2020, p. 244.
[11]Veer Savarkar, *Hindu Rashtra Darshan*, Prabhat Prakashan, 2020, p. 33.

and 'Holy Land'.[12] Fatherland, according to him, means the race that evolved in India, whose ancestors as emperors, lawmakers, reformers and leaders of the society were born here and contributed to the land. Holy Land means the land of one's prophets and seers, of one's god-men and gurus, the land of piety and pilgrimage.

It was this unique combination of Fatherland and Holy Land that defined a Hindu. Christians, Muslims, Parsis or Jews who have been living in India for generations cannot be considered Hindus, because although their Fatherland is India, their Holy Land is outside India. Similarly, Japanese or Chinese Buddhists consider India as a Holy Land, but they have their Fatherland outside Indian boundaries.

By his definition of Hindu, Savarkar placed a greater emphasis on the Hindu civilization as represented by a common history, common heroes, a common literature and art, a common law and jurisprudence and common fairs and festivals, rites and rituals, ceremonies and sacraments rather than just a religion.[13]

A LEAGUE OF INDIC FAITHS

Savarkar maintains that Hinduism in general is used to indicate Vedic faiths. However, non-Vedic faiths such as Jainism, Buddhism, Sikhism and even faiths such as animism have originated in the Hindu Holy Land. Therefore, 'Hinduism' means the 'ism' of the Hindu—like of Indic faiths or league of all 'isms' of Indian origin— meaning primarily all the people who reside in the land that extends Sindhu (Indus) to Sindhu (Ocean).

Savarkar believed that Indian Muslims, even if they profess a different religion, can be considered Hindus, since they are citizens of Hindusthan and the words 'Hindu' and 'Indian' have the same origin. Savarkar was ready to call Muslims Hindu with some prerequisites, which he had evolved. He said:

---

[12]Ibid. 3.
[13]V.D. Savarkar, *Hindutva*, Hindi Sahitya Sadan, 2003, p. 68.

> It may be that at some future time the word Hindu may come to indicate a citizen of Hindusthan and nothing else; that day can only rise when all cultural and religious bigotry has disbanded its forces pledged to aggressive egoism, and religions cease to be 'isms' and become merely the common fund of eternal principles that lie at the root of all that are a common foundation on which the Human State majestically and firmly rests.[14]

What he meant was till such a world evolves, the distinctions based on religion and culture would remain. Significantly, in a letter to the Shias of Lucknow, Savarkar once wrote, ' ... Whoever thinks that this Hindustan is not only their birth land but also their religious land, Holy Land and Fatherland, are all Hindus for us.'[15] He also had very positive things to say about the Muslim Bohras' and Muslim Khojas' love for the nation.[16]

He further contends that Hinduism must necessarily mean the religion(s) that are peculiar and native to this land and its people. If we are unable to reduce the dissimilar tenets and beliefs to a single system of religion, we will cease to maintain that Hinduism is a system and to consider it a set of systems consistent with, or contradictory or even conflicting with, each other.[17]

Savarkar averred that no nation has ever been free from sects and sections, dissimilarities and differences within its fold. He says:

> A nation is not marked out as a separate unit because its people have no subdivisions and diversities amongst themselves but because they, as a whole, present a more homogeneous unity amongst themselves than they have in common with all other alien national units; because they differ definitely and immensely more from all other peoples in the world than they differ amongst themselves from each other.[18]

---

[14]Ibid. 56.
[15]*Kesari*, 1 August 1939.
[16]V.D. Savarkar, *Hindutva*, Hindi Sahitya Sadan, 2003, p. 68.
[17]Ibid. 73.
[18]Veer Savarkar, *Hindu Rashtra Darshan*, Prabhat Prakashan, 2020, p. 34.

Using examples from around the globe, Savarkar proves that Hindus are a nation by themselves.

> No people on the earth are so homogenous as to present perfect uniformity in language, culture, race and religion. Even those who deny the fact that the Hindus could be called a nation by themselves, do recognize Great Britain, the United States, Russia, Germany and other peoples as nations. What is the test by which those peoples are called nations by themselves? Take Great Britain as an example. There are at any rate three different languages there; they have fought amongst themselves dreadfully in the past, there are to be found the traces of different seeds and bloods and race.[19]

Savarkar argued that if on the basis of just a common language, a common culture and a common Holy Land the western nations claimed nationhood, then Hindus had a greater claim to be called a nation since they too possess a common country so well marked out as Hindusthan and a common language, Sanskrit, from which all their current languages are derived/nourished and which forms even today the common language of their scriptures and literature. After all, Sanskrit is a language that is held in high esteem as the sacred reservoir of ancient scriptures and the tongue of their forefathers. Justifying his stand further that the Hindus were a nation by themselves, Savarkar said their social festivals and cultural forms are not less common than those we find in England and they (Hindus) also possess a common Holy Land.

Dwelling further on the features that constitute a nation, he said the Vedic rishis are the Hindus' common pride; their grammarians Panini and Patanjali, their poets Bhavabhuti and Kalidas, their heroes Shri Ram and Shri Krishna, Shivaji and Maharana Pratap, Guru Gobind Singh and Banda Singh Bahadur are a source of common inspiration. Savarkar saw the Hindu caste system as quite flexible and explained that through the practice of Anuloma and

---

[19] Veer Savarkar, *Hindu Rashtra Darshan*, Prabhat Prakashan, 2020, Karnavati session.

Pratiloma (inter-caste marriages), their seed and blood continued to get commingled since the days of Manu.

Explaining further, Savarkar said the Hindus' prophets, Buddha and Tirthankara Mahavira, Kanada and Adi Shankaracharya, are held in common esteem and like their ancient and sacred language, Sanskrit, their scripts too are fashioned on the same basis and that the Nagari script has been the common vehicle of their sacred writings since centuries. Lending an emotional touch but steeped in realism, he further said the Hindus' ancient and modern history are common and similarly their friends and enemies are in common and that they have faced common dangers and won common victories. Taking his line poetically forward, he said that the Hindus are one in national glory, one in national disasters, one in national despairs and one in national hope and they are welded together during eons of a common life and a common habitat.

However, above all, he said that Hindus are bound together by the dearest, most sacred and most enduring bonds of a common Fatherland and a common Holy Land, and these two being identified with one and the same country, our Bharatbhoomi, our India, the National Oneness and homogeneity of Hindus have been reasserted. If the United States, with its warring crowds of African-Americans, Germans and Anglo-Saxons, having a common past not exceeding four or five centuries, put together can be called a nation, then Hindus must be entitled to be recognized as a nation par excellence, Savarkar emphasized.

Truly, Hindus as a people differ most markedly from any other people in the world than they do amongst themselves, Savarkar remarked and asserted that 'all tests whatsoever of a common country, race, religion and language that go to entitle a people to form a nation, entitle Hindus with greater emphasis to that claim'. And finally he observed with hope that whatever differences divide Hindus amongst themselves are rapidly disappearing owing to their awakening of the national consciousness and the Sangathan and social reform movements of today.[20]

---

[20]Veer Savarkar, *Hindu Rashtra Darshan*, Prabhat Prakashan, 2020, p. 7.

Savarkar maintained that our country was endeared to us because it had been the abode of our race, people, and our dearest and nearest relations. India's independence meant the independence of our people, our race and our nation. Therefore, he emphasized that as far as the Hindu nation was concerned to Hindus, Indian Swarajya or Indian Swatantra meant the political independence of the Hindus, or the freedom that would enable them to grow to their full potential.

Interestingly, he points out that it was only geographically speaking that India as a land and a state was absolutely independent of any other non-Indian powers when an Alauddin Khilji or an Aurangzeb ruled over it. However, that kind of independence proved a veritable death warrant to the Hindu nation, and impelled Rana Sanga, Maharana Pratap, Guru Gobind Singh, Bir Banda, Shivaji and Bajirao to fight and ultimately win and establish a Hindu empire under the Marathas, the Rajputs, the Sikhs and the Gurkhas throughout our motherland. Their actions saved our Hindudom or Hindutva from the clutches of non-Hindu aggression, he said. This, he emphasized, proves that mere geographical independence does not mean the independence of the Hindu nation.

Explaining the real meaning of Swarajya, Savarkar opines that for Hindus, Hindusthan's independence is worthwhile only if it ensures their Hindutva—i.e., their religious, racial and cultural identity. Swarajya is thus more than the mere geographical independence of a stretch of earth called India. There was no point in fighting and sacrificing one's life for a Swarajya (mere territorial independence) at the cost of our Svatva (self-existence) or Hindutva itself![21]

INDIAN NATIONALISM AND HINDUTVA

Indian nationalism, a creation of the colonial Hindu mind, is not synonymous with Hindu nationalism because the former denies or at least doesn't appreciate India's glorious past. In his 1904 article

---

[21] Ibid. 13, 14.

titled 'Bias of English Educated People', Lokmanya Bal Gangadhar Tilak precisely depicted the mentality of neo-colonials. Countering their view, he said:

> It would be wrong to say that three or four religions are prevalent in India and therefore Hinduism is not nationalism. On the basis of population, the community of Hindus is large and Hindutva is the bond that binds such a large group. Breaking this bond, or failing to hold it strong by neglecting it, entails scattering two-thirds of India's population like sand particles. If someone believes that breaking Hinduism in this way would produce positive results from a national perspective, they are delusory.

He said he was prepared to concede that apart from Hindutva, there might be other means to unite the 300 million people of India, but it is also equally important to keep in mind that 200 million out of that 300 million people are united due to Hindutva. He argued that to sustain their (Hindus) bond is more convenient and necessary from the national point of view.[22]

To clarify the differences between Savarkar's Hindu nationalism and Indian nationalism, which was coined by the INC,[23] Savarkar explained the origin and history of Indian nationalism in detail during his presidential address at the Nagpur session of the Hindu Mahasabha in 1938.

> The immediate effect of Western education was that the two first generations of Hindus who were influenced by it were totally carried off their feet and they fell in love with everything Western. They looked upon the British rule as a Godsend. They prayed for its permanence. Fed on the

---

[22] A.J. Karandikar, *Krantikarak Tilak ani Tyancha Kaal*, Kaal Prakashan, p. 61.

[23] Congress objective (b) : 'The eradication, by direct friendly personal intercourse, of all possible race, creed, or provincial prejudices amongst all lovers of our country, and the fuller development and consolidation of those sentiments of national unity that had their origin in their beloved Lord Ripon's ever memorable reign.' (Anil Chandra Banerjee, *Indian Constitutional Documents 1757–1939, Volume II*, A. Mukherjee & Co., 1948, p. 83).

Western literature and history and cut off from any contact with Hindu thoughts and Hindu policy, they naturally came to the easy conclusion that if but they imitated the West and especially England in every detail of individual and collective life, they and their country would be benefited and saved... Like all other ideas and sentiments, their notion of patriotism also was borrowed, readymade from England. So they thought or rather believed, without thinking at all, that the only bond of a territorial unity, the only fact of residing in a common geographical unit was by itself the most efficient, nay, the only efficient factor to mark out a people into a nation...[24]

According to western thinking on nationalism, since Hindus, Muslims, Christians, Parsis and others had been inhabiting the territorial unit called India for centuries together, they must be a nation by themselves, irrespective of the fact that they differed so much in religion, language, culture, race and historical development. Savarkar contended this view on nationalism and said these features had nothing to do with a common nationality because a territorial unit must also be a national one. According to the western concept of nationalism, if India was a territorial unit and called a country, then it must also be a national unit, he said. He asked if it was at all so, then all of us must also be Indians only and cease to be Hindus or Muslims, Christians or Parsis. He said the leaders of those first generations of English-educated people, being mostly Hindus, erroneously tried their best to erase their identity as Hindus and thought it below their dignity to take any cognizance of the Hindu–Muslim division and transformed into 'Indian patriots' overnight.

Savarkar further stated it was very easy for them to cease being Hindus because western education had taught them that Hindutva meant nothing else but Hinduism, which to them meant a veritable bundle of superstitions. They had no occasion, Savarkar observed, to stop and think of the other and the most fundamental concepts

---

[24] V.D. Savarkar, *Hindu Rashtra Darshan (Samagra Savarkar, Vol. 10)*, Veer Savarkar Prakashan, 1994, p. 36.

of Hindutva, of Hinduness, in all its racial, cultural and historical bearing. Since they found it easy to renounce their Hindu-ness and merge themselves into an Indian identity and see themselves as Indians alone, they expected it to be equally easy for Muslims to forget their identity and merge themselves entirely and totally into the Indian people, the Indian nation, which to those 'Indian patriots' already seemed a fact as tangible as the territorial unit India.

Savarkar said, the Hindus, with their synthetic thinking always prone to philosophies with a universal urge, found nothing objectionable in the ideal of uniting the whole of India into a consolidated political unit. Savarkar conceded that the ideal of politics itself ought to be a human state—all mankind for its citizen, the earth for its motherland. And, according to him, if all of India, with one-fifth of the human race, could be united irrespective of religious, racial and cultural diversities, merging them all into a homogeneous whole, it would be but a gigantic stride taken by mankind towards the realization of that human political ideal.

Drawing more analogies, Savarkar said that the new concept of an Indian nationality was founded on the common bond of a territorial unity of India, as the Hindus for one found nothing revolting even in that assumption. This was, he explained, due to the fact that their national being had already been identified with that territorial unit, India, which to them was not only a land of sojourn but a home, their Fatherland, their motherland, their Holy Land all rolled into one. To them, Indian patriotism was but a synonym of Hindu patriotism as well as the territorial unit. Therefore, in their opinion, an Indian nation was but a territorial appellation of the Hindu nation.

Commenting on the British attitude, he said that they dreaded and hated any genuine and fruitful rise of Indian nationalism. Therefore, on one hand, they encouraged and surreptitiously fuelled the fanatical hatred, enmity and distrust which the Muslims bore to the Hindu nation, thus rendering any efficient national unity as delusive as a mirage and, on the other hand, encouraged the Hindus, at least in the beginning, to pursue that mirage with avidity so that the rise of a homogeneous Hindu nation might be ruled out of practical politics.

He further explained that the consolidation of our Hindu nation was not in virtue of the new cult of Indian nationality or the proclaimed intentions of the INC, but in spite of its efforts, direct or implied, to suppress our racial and religious consciousness as Hindus. The territorial patriots, according to Savarkar, wanted us to cease to be Hindus, at least as a national and political unit and some of them actually took pride in disowning themselves as Hindus and expected the same of Muslims.

However, the Muslims remained Muslims first, Muslims last and Indians never, Savarkar analysed,[25] till at last, things came to such a pass that the proposal to divide India itself into two parts—the Muslim India and the Hindu India—was blatantly put forward and their readiness to ally themselves with a non-Indian Muslim nation against the Hindus was avowed by no less a representative Muslim body than the Muslim League.[26] This was the sorry fate, which Savarkar said, resulted from the vain hopes of these Hindu patriots of the Congress, who from the best of motives but with a thoughtless belief and the blindest of policies, persisted in their efforts of consolidating all Indians into one undivided and indivisible Indian nation, irrespective of religions, races and cultures and based only on the common bond of a territorial unity!

Here, Savarkar, though harsh on Muslims, was not wrong if one takes into consideration the results of the 1945–46 Central Assembly polls, the last central and provincial elections in pre-Partition British India. In this election, almost 87 per cent of the total Muslim votes cast went to the Muslim League, around 10 per cent to other Muslim candidates and only 3 per cent to the Congress's Muslim candidates (there were separate electorates then).

Savarkar believed that the Congress, at the time of its formation, committed the serious mistake of overlooking this

---

[25]V.D. Savarkar, *Hindu Rashtra Darshan (Samagra Savarkar, Vol. 10)*, Veer Savarkar Prakashan, 1994, p. 43.
[26]Veer Savarkar, *Hindu Rashtra Darshan*, Prabhat Prakashan, 2020.

fundamental social and political principle that in the formation of nations, religious, racial, cultural and historical affinities count immensely, in fact, more than their territorial unity or the fact of having a common habitat. On the part of the followers of territorial nationalism, the historical tragedy was that they became a party to territorial division of the nation.

NATIONALIST AND RATIONALIST; PREACHER AND PRACTITIONER

Savarkar was not only a Hindu nationalist but a Hindu rationalist too. He stood for the progress of culture (Sanskriti Samvardhan) rather than just protection of culture (Sanskriti Sanrakshan). According to him, the discriminations prevailing among Hindus had not originated by birth but by books (*janmajaat nahi pothijaat*). He vehemently opposed untouchability and fought tooth and nail to uproot it from society. Though he opposed cow worship purely on religious grounds and wanted a scientific temper to support the practice, he nevertheless was a votary of cow protection.[27]

Savarkar observed that progress of the western countries had been possible only when they disowned superstitions and religious orthodoxy and accepted science. Similarly, he urged Hindus to follow contemporary ideas in all matters of life rather than *'Shruti-Smriti-Puranoktaas'* (as per ancient holy books and codes).[28] He encouraged them to test the knowledge in ancient scriptures, their laws and learnings on the touchstone of science and to follow fearlessly the path that contributes to the good of the nation.

Few leaders in Indian history can claim Savarkar's commitment to social unity. He was not just a preacher but a practitioner too. He was one of the first Hindu leaders in the country who cut across party lines to will that he be cremated in an electric crematorium and that his mortal remains be taken to the crematorium by people of all four Varnas, including a Dalit.

---

[27] V.D. Savarkar, *Vigyan Nishtha Nibandh*, Swatantryaveer Savarkar Rashtriya Smarak Trust, p. 49.
[28] Ibid. 79.

Savarkar pointed out to some self-imposed sanctions by Hindus in their extreme anxiety to protect their religion which ultimately stood as hurdles in their progress. As explained below, these seven shackles that originated in the Medieval Era were sturdy even in the twentieth century.[29]

Prohibition of touch (Sparshabandi)

Savarkar insisted that untouchability must be condemned and abolished not only as the need of the hour but also as the command of true religion; not only as a policy or as an act of expediency but also as a matter of justice; and not only as a matter of obligation but also as a service to humanity. The orthodox Hindus touched animals such as bullocks and buffaloes, they could endure the presence of a dog or a cat in their houses, but not the presence of their co-religionist Hindu Mahars or Bhangis though they were human beings, he bewailed. These Hindus feared that their sacred God would be polluted by the mere sight of a Hindu Bhangi. 'He is not God who can be desecrated'[30] was the epigrammatic Savarkarian reply to the orthodox.

The removal of untouchability, he added, implied purification and salvation of such misguided orthodox touchables also.[31]

During his stay at Ratnagiri, Savarkar and his reformist team regularly visited hills, villages and towns where the untouchables lived. This team studied their ways of living, taught them cleanliness, guided them and worshipped with them. They took the Chambhars into the quarters and temples of the Mahars and the Bhangis into the quarters and temples of the Dhors.[32] Savarkar supported Dr Ambedkar's movement of temple entry for untouchables by appealing to the Hindus of Nasik through an open letter.

---

[29]V.D. Savarkar, *Jatyuchhedak Nibandh*, Swatantryaveer Savarkar Rashtriya Smarak Trust, p. 64.
[30]Dhananjay Keer, *Veer Savarkar*, Popular Prakashan, Pvt. Ltd; Second edition, 2019, p. 182.
[31]Ibid.
[32]Ibid. 196.

Prohibition of rites sanctioned by the Vedas (Vedoktabandi)

Savarkar believed that the Vedas were not the monopoly of Brahmins alone but the glorious heritage of the whole mankind. He was invited by the 'untouchables' (whom he addressed as ex-untouchables) to preside over the 19 May 1929 conference at Malvan in Ratnagiri district. The conference sang Vedic hymns in a body. Savarkar distributed sacred threads among the so-called untouchable Hindus and declared amid a thunderous applause:

> A battle royal has been raging for the last seven generations over the right of studying the Vedas. Here are the Vedas. Here is the sacred thread. Take these two. Is that all? Even non-Hindus read the Vedas. Why should not the Hindu Mahars read them? The feud over this problem was a useless task. Let us expiate the sins we committed. We are all responsible for our political subjugation. That is the past. Now let us declare on oath that we shall rectify our past blunders and win back our weal, wealth and glory.[33]

During the Ganpati festivals initiated by Savarkar in Ratnagiri, a Bhangi (so-called untouchable) Hindu sang Vedic hymns and the Gayatri Mantra, the sacred privilege enjoyed till then by Brahmins alone.

Inter-dining (Rotibandi)

Even the inter-dining of all Hindu castes was a difficult task till the 1930s. Savarkar arranged several 'Sah Bhojans' or inter-dining programmes to break this shackle. He incessantly preached: 'Eat with anybody. Eat anything that is medically fit and clean. That does not deprive you of your religion. Remember, the root of religion is not the dish or the stomach, but the heart, soul and the blood!'[34]

Many Hindus had converted to Islam or Christianity by swallowing a slice of bread chewed by non-Hindus rather than by

---

[33] Ibid. 182.
[34] Ibid. 239.

a sword stroke. Savarkar believed that if a Muslim or a Christian did not become a Hindu by eating food cooked by a Hindu, then why should the Hindu religion be flushed out by partaking of food cooked by a Muslim? He wondered if the digestive power of the Hindu religion had become so weak. He maintained that his Hindu brothers would continue to remain Hindu even after eating and digesting food cooked by anyone in the world, irrespective of their faith.[35]

Inter-caste marriages (Betibandi)

Several examples of inter-caste marriages—Anulom and Pratilom Vivah—are well recorded in Hindu scriptures. Savarkar explained what he meant by breaking of 'betibandi':

> If a Hindu with desirable qualities such as love, character, and capacity to beget healthy offspring chooses a spouse from another caste, then such an alliance should not be condemned simply because their castes are different. Such a couple should not be considered as unworthy of cohabitation. Breaking the prohibition of intermarriage does not imply forcibly marrying off girls of one caste into another caste.[36]

Savarkar blessed and supported many inter-caste couples. He believed that permission for such mixed marriages was extremely desirable not only for the removal of birth-based caste distinction, but also for the success of the re-conversion movement. However, he was opposed to the marriage of a Hindu with a non-Hindu, if it took place without bringing the partner into the Hindu fold. In his opinion, such a precaution was necessary for the collective good of the Hindu nation. On the flipside, this is exactly the principle followed by most Muslims and Christians while marrying Hindu women. So, this principle of Savarkar too was in the realm of equal treatment.[37]

---

[35] Vinayak Damodar Savarkar, *Mazi Janmathep*, Vol. II, Lakhey Prakashan, 2018, p. 281.
[36] Veer Savarkar, *Hindutva che Pancha Pran*, Veer Savarkar Prakashan, 1994, p. 85.
[37] Ibid.

Prohibition on pursuing certain occupations (Vyavasayabandi)

Savarkar believed that monopoly over certain professions had kept the caste system alive. Everyone should be free to choose and perform an occupation according to one's skill and liking and not according to one's caste. He sarcastically suggested that for driving a car, one should check the licence of the driver and not of his grandfather.[38]

Prohibition of seafaring (Sindhubandi)

Savarkar explained the historical reasons for a ban on seafaring. He said these had come into force because the natives had been made to suffer all sorts of humiliations by the foreign invaders (read Muslim as well as Portuguese invaders) who had come from distant lands and across the seas and forced them to accept Islam and Christianity. These invaders committed all sorts of atrocities on the natives including dishonour of their women and they, in turn, realized that chivalry alone won't work against these aggressors. Therefore, Savarkar said the community (Hindus) went into a shell and for the purpose of self-preservation imposed the restriction on seafaring. As a result, Hindus lost not only commercial, but also cultural and strategic ties with the rest of the world.

Prohibition of reconversion (Shuddhibandi)

Savarkar maintained that any non-Hindu who was keen to adopt the Hindu religion or a person whose ancestors were Hindus and wanted to come back should be welcomed by Hindus. Of course, this conversion should be done by their will and not by force. Savarkar suggested that each person who came forward for Shuddhi (reconversion) should only be asked if he was becoming a Hindu out of conviction or if someone was trying to force the dharma on him.[39]

Savarkar's belief in reconversion of Hindus without any coercion had historical support. The invading Shakas and Huns ultimately

---

[38] V.D. Savarkar, *Jatyuchhedak Nbandh,* Swatantryaveer Savarkar Rashtriya Smarak Trust, p. 66.

[39] *Shraddhanand,* 26 January 1928.

adopted faiths of Indian origin, but foreign rulers with Abrahamic faiths came to India with the aim of religious domination. There was no Muslim in India before the Islamic invasion. Savarkar estimated that of 70 million Muslims, 5 million may have direct foreign ancestors but the remaining 65 million have Hindu ancestors that were part of Hindu society once upon a time.[40] The visionaries of the Pakistan movement, such as Jinnah (Hindu Gujarati from Raghuvanshi caste) and Iqbal (a Hindu Kashmiri Pandit) had Hindu forefathers. In fact, making a historical observation about conversion by Muslim invaders, Savarkar said that Muslims seized far more Hindu land throughout India by conversion than by conquest.[41]

Initially, Hindus started reconversion by making changes in the rituals and codes (smruti), but the momentum was lost with time. During the reign of Ranbir Singh, the Maharaja of Jammu and Kashmir, from 1856–85, Muslims from Poonch and Rajouri and some from the Kashmir valley assembled and appealed to the Maharaja that they be accepted in their basic Hindu religion. When the Maharaja asked the Pandits about the reconversion of their relations, the Pandits refused to accept them back into the Hindu religion because of their own dogmas.

Other than these shackles, Savarkar further pointed out the suicidal tendency of Hindus in the application of liberal individual virtues on the war front with the enemy. He said:

> Suicidal morbidity had completely possessed the Hindu mind for a long time. This morbidity paralysed their own might of offensive and counter-offensive. Far greater than the Muslims could ever attempt were the defeats inflicted on themselves by these morbidity virtuous Hindus! If a comparatively mild term is to be used for this infatuation—this mental imbalance of the Hindus, which caused disastrous losses for themselves— we have to call it a perverted sense of Hindu virtues.[42]

---

[40] V.D. Savarkar, *Sphut Lekh*, p.4. www.savarkarsmarak.com. Accessed on 20 July 2021.
[41] Veer Savarkar, *Six Glorious Epochs of Indian History*, Prabhat Prakashan; First edition, 2020, p. 240.
[42] Ibid. 176.

Virtue, he felt, was not the absolute term, and considered virtues and vices as only relative terms. No virtue could be unqualified and absolute under every circumstance or at every place, and in practice or in ethical code. A virtue should be called a virtue only to the extent to which it was useful to the best interests of human society. It should be considered a vice and discarded forthwith the moment it begins to cause harm to mankind. No doubt, ahimsa (non-violence), kindness, chivalry even towards the enemy women, protection of an abjectly capitulating enemy, forgiveness (often regarded a glorious emblem for the brave) and religious tolerance were all very noble virtues. However, the blind, slovenly and sometimes even impotent adoption of all these virtues, irrespective of any consideration of propriety of time, place or persons, he felt, had horribly vanquished them in the millennial Hindu–Muslim war on the religious front. He invoked the society, and said, 'O thou Hindu society! Of all the sins and weakness, which have brought about thy fall, the greatest and most potent are thy virtues themselves.'[43] He was also a strong votary of retaliation against the aggressor with matching fury and believed that a super diabolic counter offence was the only answer to a diabolic invasion.[44]

Savarkar's mantra for the growth of the Hindu society was practical Hindutva, with elements that focussed on the removal of untouchability, Shuddhi or reconversion, Akhada movement for physical strength and Swadeshi to strengthen the Hindu nation.

THE GREAT HINDU DREAM

Savarkar preached and followed Hindutva as unalloyed nationalism. '*Varam janahitam dhyeyam kevalaa na janastutihi* (Not praise of people, public welfare alone!)' was the mantra of Savarkar's life, even as a teenager. He started the Abhinav Bharat Society to overthrow British rule at a time when British Raj was considered a boon. He established the Patit Pavan Mandir, a temple

---

[43]Ibid. 196.
[44]Ibid. 188.

open to all, when orthodox Hindus opposed temple entry of the so-called lower castes. In the times of appeasement under the name of Hindu–Muslim unity, he stood for equal rights for all. Though dubbed as communalist, he did not stop fighting for Akhand Bharat. In the era of Panchsheel and non-violence as foreign and security policy of India, he advocated militarization of the youth and upgradation of the armed forces.

Not just Savarkar, but both his brothers were involved in the armed struggle for freedom. Ganesh and Vinayak were sentenced to life imprisonment in Andaman. The family's property that was confiscated by the British was not handed over to them even in the 1960s. However, despite all these, Savarkar remained unfazed. 'I got back three-fourth of Hindusthan freed from Britishers, is my property not included in Hindusthan? That's all. I am very satisfied', was his response.[45]

Once in a private conversation, when his biographer Dhananjay Keer mentioned Savarkar as a defeated leader on the front of Akhand Hindusthan, Savarkar replied, 'What people consider as a defeat, I don't. ... I am successful if you see victory and defeat on the basis of principles. Some people believe that I could be a President. Yes, if I compromised with my principles, I would be. But for principles I am sitting on the ruins of my life.'[46]

Savarkar insisted that every nationalist who was keen to truly serve the nation could follow his advice and champion issues that were in the interests of the people, irrespective of their popularity. A sincere servant of the people would not embrace or reject a principle or policy that was in national interest solely with an eye on whether he would be applauded or humiliated.[47] His unrelenting commitment to the Hindu nation and his mission to propagate it amongst the people is well demonstrated by a message he sent to Vishwanath Agrawal, a Hindu Mahasabha leader of Uttar Pradesh,

---

[45]V.D. Savarkar, *Sphut Lekh (Samagra Savarkar Vol. 8)*, Mumbai: Veer Savarkar Prakashan, 1994, p. 55.
[46]Dhananjay Keer, *Krutadnya Mi Krutarth Mi*, Popular Publication, 1995, p. 263.
[47]V.D. Savarkar, *Samajik Bhashane (Samagra Savarkar Vol. 8)*, Mumbai: Veer Savarkar Prakashan, 1994.

in 1955 when he was contesting the provincial assembly election as a candidate. While wishing him success for the election, Savarkar told Agrawal that even if he lost the election, it wouldn't constitute a failure because betrayal of the Hindu nation was a failure.[48]

Savarkar was in a different class as an unalloyed nationalist as is evident from his clinical statement in 1942 regarding what constitutes nationalism: 'If nationalism means that the Hindus should cease to be Hindus, even culturally, racially or religiously, while all other non-Hindu Indians despise to adopt that attitude in their own cases, then such a nationalism is the most criminal and dastardly betrayal of our true national soul and ancestral heritage.'[49]

Savarkar sowed a seed, and saw a dream for the coming Hindu generations.

> The seed of the banyan tree is so trivial as to be smaller than the mustard seed. But it holds within itself the rich promise of a luxuriant expanse. If you wish, O Hindus, to prosper as a great and glorious Hindu Nation under the sun, and you well have a claim on it, that State must be established under the Hindu Flag. This dream would be realized during this or coming generation. If it is not realized, I may be styled a day-dreamer, but if it comes true, I would stand forth as its prophet. I am bequeathing this legacy to you.[50]

He was certain that a day would dawn when mankind would have to face the force of 30 crore people, with India—their Fatherland and their Holy Land—as their basis of operation. Backed by history and bound together by ties of a common blood and culture, he said, they would dictate their terms to the whole world. But he was equally certain that whenever Hindus would come to occupy such a position and dictate terms to the whole world, those terms would not be very different from those dictated by the Gita or the

---

[48] V.D. Savarkar, *Historic Statements by Savarkar*, Parchure Prakashan, 1967, p. 238.
[49] Ibid. 66.
[50] Dhananjay Keer, *Veer Savarkar*, Popular Prakashan Pvt Ltd; Second edition, 2019, p. 556.

Buddha. The last lines of his epic work *Hindutva* say: 'A Hindu is most intensely so, when he ceases to be Hindu; and with a Shankar claims the whole earth for a Benares "Waranasi Medini!" or with a Tukaram exclaims my country! Oh brothers, "the limits of the Universe—there the frontiers of my country lie".'[51] So, Savarkar uses the analogy of Sant Tukaram to emphasize the Hindu principle of Vasudhaiva Kutumbakam, which means 'the world is one family'.

Savarkar's definition of pristine nationalism can foster true national unity and help India realize its goal of becoming a Vishwaguru. His idea of Hindutva was rooted in secular Hindu culture, which is catholic or all-encompassing and sees all religions as equal. While many saw him as divisive because of his opposition to Muslims for their tendency to make special demands on the Hindus, whenever a set of Muslims acted in favour of true national unity, casting aside their false Muslim victimhood theories, Savarkar was quick to acknowledge them. He was willing to welcome Muslims when they stood for true national unity, as highlighted by Shia Muslims of Lucknow, who passed a resolution in 1939 that declared that any Muslim who slaughtered cow would be seen as an enemy of Hindu–Muslim unity. They also refused to object to playing of music by Hindu processions that passed by mosques. In his letter to the leader of the Shia Muslims, Savarkar welcomed this resolution and maintained that such genuine gestures from the Muslim community could pave the way for real Hindu–Muslim unity. He also underlined his principles for forging Hindu–Muslim unity thus:

> Hindu Mahasabha, without any hatred, reciprocates by showing respect to the religious sentiments of our fellow Shia Muslims. While playing musical instruments is the fundamental right of every citizen, Mahasabha will sincerely try that no Hindu does this purposely in front of a mosque to deliberately hurt the sentiments of Muslims. The Hindu Mahasabha is fully ready to cooperate with the national

---

[51] V.D. Savarkar, *Hindutva*, Hindi Sahitya Sadan, 2003, p. 104.

attitude pursued by these Shias. Not only this, we have a strong desire to continue friendship with such nationalist and just brothers. When the rest of the non-Hindus are also ready to show same zeal for true unity, the dream of national unity of Hindus and non-Hindus will not be difficult to realize.[52]

On one particular Dussehra, Savarkar along with other Hindu Mahasabha leaders went to Ratnagiri and visited the main Muslim leaders of the town to express their brotherhood. While Savarkar explained the aims of the Hindu Mahasabha, which were based on equal treatment and no concessions, to the Ratnagiri Muslim leaders, the Muslims too welcomed him with great warmth. He also visited the local Christian Mission and explained the Hindu Mahasabha's objectives. He told the Christians, 'Hindu Dharma's aim is not against any one. Hindus never hate other religions but they want same rights as their Christians, Muslims and other brothers.'[53]

Savarkar's Hindutva is culturally Hindu but its effect is secular. Therefore, the Hindutva of Savarkar and the RSS doesn't discriminate between Hindus and others. Savarkar's Hindu Rashtra constitution, in which he guarantees equal rights to all religions, clearly underlines this fact. However, the ideological enemies of Savarkar and the RSS have cunningly projected their Hindutva as sectarian by suppressing the secular element in it.

---

[52] V.D. Savarkar, *Aitihasik Rajkiya Nivedane* (*Samagra Savarkar, Vol. 8*), Mumbai: Veer Savarkar Prakashan, 1993, p. 14.

[53] Akshay Jog, *Veer Savarkar: Allegations and Reality*, 2019, p. 100, 102.

4

INDIA HAILS THE PROPHET OF REVOLUTION

Before Savarkar took over the Hindu Mahasabha's leadership, the party's following was in thousands. However, after Savarkar's elevation, in a matter of no time, it reached lakhs due to his magnetic appeal. He put all his might to enhance the stature of the party. Several veteran revolutionaries such as Bhai Parmanand, Ashutosh Lahiri and Baba Madan Singh Gaga too joined the Mahasabha. An intellectual like S.P. Mukherjee told Savarkar several times that he was a man of academics and not politics, but due to Savarkar's great appeal, he finally joined the party.[1]

Savarkar's rise as the president of the Hindu Mahasabha was followed by his maiden speech in that capacity at Ahmedabad in 1937. Till this day, selected portions of this speech are targeted by the anti-Savarkar and anti-RSS lobby to depict the ideologue of Hindutva as divisive and Savarkar as the father of Pakistan. However, a closer look at the original contents of the speech reveals a diametrically opposite picture. It gives the impression that during the freedom movement, the battle on the sidelines was between Savarkar's true secularism on one hand, and Muslim communalism and the Congress's pseudo-secularism, on the other hand, the last two based on granting special rights to Muslims at the expense of Hindu rights. In fact, in this particular speech, Savarkar emphasized that the Hindu Mahasabha firmly believed in the just, democratic

---

[1]Balarao Savarkar, *Swatantryaveer Savarkar, Akhand Hindusthan Ladha Parv*, 2020, p. 381.

and nationalist principle of one man one vote—irrespective of caste, creed or religion and that the Hindu Mahasabha was more national than even the Congress. While guaranteeing protection to the religion, culture and language of the religious minorities, he warned that 'Hindus shall no longer tolerate any aggression on the part of the Muslims on their (Hindus') right to equal liberty to guard their religion, culture and language.'[2] He made it clear: 'If the non-Hindu minority is to be protected, then surely the Hindu majority must also be protected from any aggressive minority in India.'[3]

In this historic speech, which laid out the contours of Savarkar's compromise-less nationalism, he gave a warning to India and the Hindus to be on guard against the designs of the Muslims when the British left India. He said, 'Let us (Hindus) not be blind to the fact that Muslims continue to cherish fanatical designs to establish Muslim rule in India.' At the end, he warned, 'Let us work for harmony; let us hope for the best but let us be on guard.'[4]

Significantly, what had heightened Savarkar's anxiety about the Muslims' designs was the separation of Sindh from the Bombay Province which was exactly in keeping with the prediction of the first architect of Pakistan, Sir Muhammad Iqbal. In his 1930 speech at the Allahabad session of the All India Muslim League, he had predicted Sindh as part of the future Muslim State in the north-west of India. The demand had also figured in Jinnah's charter of 14 demands earlier in 1929. The name 'Pakistan' for the proposed Muslim homeland, coined by Choudhary Rahmat Ali at the time of the second Round Table Conference in London in 1932, had already been in public domain for almost five years, though less known. Significantly, Sindh was finally separated from Bombay Province in 1936, nearly a year before Savarkar became the Hindu Mahasabha president. The suggestion made by Rahmat Ali, the separation of Sindh and Iqbal's speech had convinced Savarkar that Muslim politics in India would henceforth go in the direction of

---

[2]Veer Savarkar, *Hindu Rashtra Darshan*, Prabhat Prakashan, 2020, p. 23.
[3]Ibid.
[4]Ibid., 1937 speech.

demanding a separate nation in the name of Islam and a feeble Congress would cave in before the Muslim League's strategy. These were perhaps the key reasons why he had used harsh language for Muslims in his Ahmedabad speech. He was perhaps the first Hindu political leader of note, apart from B.S. Munje, to see through the Muslim game plan.

Savarkar also spoke of Hindus and Muslims as being 'two nations living within India'[5]. His utterances on the issue need to be seen in totality in order to understand the deceptiveness of the allegations of the anti-Hindutva lobby against him.

He said:

> It is safer to diagnose and treat a deep-seated disease than to ignore it. Let us face unpleasant facts as they are. India cannot be assumed today to be a Unitarian and homogenous state, but on the contrary, there are two nations in the main—the Hindus and [the] Muslims in India. And as it has happened in many countries in similar situation in the world, the utmost we can do under the circumstances is to form an Indian State in which none is allowed to have special weightage of representation and none is paid an extra price to buy his loyalty to the State. Mercenaries are paid and bought off, not the sons of the motherland to fight in its defence.[6]

He also reiterated that when the time was ripe, such centuries-old cultural, religious and national antagonism between Hindus and Muslims could be solved. Clearly, he treated the two-nation theory as a disease that had to be cured and not ignored.

His emphasis on unalloyed nationalism is clear when he says,

> Let the Indian State be purely Indian. Let it not recognize any invidious distinctions whatsoever as regards the franchise, public services, offices, taxation on the grounds of religion and race. Let no cognizance be taken whatsoever of being Hindu, Mohammedan, Christian or Jew. Let all citizens of that

---

[5] Veer Savarkar, *Hindu Rashtra Darshan*, Prabhat Prakashan, 2020, p. 23.
[6] Ibid.

Indian State be treated according to their individual worth irrespective of their religious or racial percentage in the general population.[7]

Savarkar made the most pertinent point in his very first speech as president—that nationalism or loyalty to the motherland can't have a price. This is particularly relevant even today when a section of Indian Muslims continue to demand and enjoy special concessions.

Savarkar was convinced that the Hindu Mahasabha had a historic role to play in protecting the interests of the Hindus in their only land on earth, when these were being attacked by the Muslim League and compromised by the Congress in their pursuit of Hindu–Muslim unity, which was but a mirage. 'It is better to stand in the last row of patriots than in the first row of betrayers,' he said, asserting his firm belief that the Congress's policy of giving special rights to Muslims at the cost of Hindu rights was a betrayal to the nation.[8]

Around the same time, Savarkar made two additional historic statements that showed his commitment to Hindu ideals and his understanding of the Muslim psyche and strategy. In the first, he said, 'I would reject even Indrapad (seat of Lord Indra) if that is the reward I am offered for becoming a non-Hindu and instead would prefer to die as the last Hindu.'[9] Addressing Muslims who were demanding special concessions at the cost of Hindu rights as a precondition for joining the freedom struggle, and were becoming increasingly aggressive in making these demands, he said, 'If you come, with you, if you don't, without you. If you oppose, in spite of you, Hindus would continue to wage the freedom struggle.'[10]

India wouldn't have been partitioned had the Congress followed this golden principle while dealing with Muslims and not be misled by the belief that India's independence wasn't possible without Hindu–Muslim unity.

---

[7] Veer Savarkar, *Hindu Rashtra Darshan*, Prabhat Prakashan, 2020, 1937 speech.
[8] *Collected Works of Veer Savarkar*, Prabhat Prakashan.
[9] Balarao Savarkar, *Swatantraveer Savarkar, Hindu Mahasabha Parva*, 2020, p. 68.
[10] Veer Savarkar, *Hindu Rashtra Darshan*, Prabhat Prakashan, 2020, p. 20.

SAVARKAR STEALS THE CONGRESS'S THUNDER

Even though Savarkar's mass-mobilizing capacities were inferior to Gandhi's as he chose to eschew the path of populist politics, and suffered severe health problems in between, he didn't turn into an arm-chair ideologue, as many would perhaps be tempted to believe, after he came out of the internment in Ratnagiri. Rather, he made an electrifying tour of the nation explaining his unalloyed nationalism to the people in spite of his health problems.

Savarkar had his task cut out for him. Apart from protecting the political interests of the Hindus, he also had to protect their cultural interests. And for doing so, he didn't wield any special power. The only means left open to him was launching a campaign for national awakening amongst the Hindus through extensive touring. Each and every stop of his tour had a meaning for the nation; his underlying theme being unity of India in the face of numerous challenges.

During his presidential years (1937–43), he traversed through almost every major city of British India and princely states, from Sindh to Assam and from Kashmir to Travancore. The places where the annual sessions of the Hindu Mahasabha were organized under his leadership pointed towards a pan-India presence of the organization: Karnavati (Ahmedabad), Nagpur, Calcutta, Madurai, Bhagalpur and Kanpur. Some interesting accounts of his travel throw light on his influence on the Hindu masses.

His first stop was at Kolhapur, where he bowed before the seat of Chhatrapati Shivaji and exposed the anti-princes policy of the Congress. He declared that princely states were the power centres that were ahead of even the British in ushering in reforms in several cases and had helped sustain the Hindu culture as well as the revolutionaries in the face of British tyranny. His way of looking at the princely states was radically different from the Congress, which saw them, in most cases, as British supporters only. He viewed the princely states as the centres where the population was free from British persecution and, therefore, these states were very valuable as part of Savarkar's nation-building plan.

The best example is provided by the case of Vadodara state, which was led by the legendry, reformist ruler Sayajirao Gaekwad III. The first Indian ruler to make girl's education compulsory in 1907, even before the British could do it in the areas under their direct rule, he also established a network of libraries covering almost every village of his state, apart from introducing a series of other reform measures.

In the 1930s, the Congress opposed even Sayajirao. In reply, the commander-in-chief of his armed forces, General Nanasaheb Shinde, protested to Gandhi in a strongly worded letter saying that the Maharaja was one of the most progressive rulers in India and the Congress's attack on him was most unwarranted. Gandhi saw force in Shinde's argument. Savarkar, in fact, condemned Congress leaders who launched a campaign against Hindu states without evaluating their importance. 'Some of the princely states are as large as independent countries in Europe...what party of our chatterbox politicians and slogan-ridden ideologues had succeeded in effecting actually social or industrial or military progress on such an extent as, say for example, the Hindu States of Baroda, Mysore, Travancore or Gwalior have recorded?'[11]

Significantly, Sayajirao supported the revolutionaries in a big way including the Abhinav Bharat Society, Savarkar's revolutionary group which he had formed to overthrow the British in 1903. The Maharaja's own barber Shankar Wagh was a member of this society.[12] Since Savarkar could foresee that the Muslim League, Muslim princes, the Congress and Britishers would agree for the partition of India, he insisted that not only British India, but Portuguese India, French India, the princely states and even Nepal was a part of United India (Akhand Bharat). Hence, the movement for freedom and unity should be strengthened in these parts as well.[13]

In fact, so firm was his belief, that in his 1940 presidential speech, Savarkar described the Hindu princely states as power

---

[11] Veer Savarkar, *Hindu Rashtra Darshan*, Prabhat Prakashan, 2020, 1940 speech.

[12] Dhananjay Keer, *Veer Savarkar*, Popular Prakashan Pvt. Ltd; Second edition, 2019, p. 62.

[13] Veer Savarkar, *Hindu Rashtra Darshan*, Prabhat Prakashan, 2020, p. 91.

centres of the Hindu nation. He said:

> It is not want of resources, Oh Hindus, which forces you to be so helpless and hopeless, but it is the want of practical insight in political realities to know your resources; and the tact to use them. The Hindu Sanghatanists possess an insight into political realities [and] they would soon find that the Hindu States are, in fact, nearly the only centres of the organized, military, administrative and political Hindu strength and are bound to play a more active and more decisive part in the near future in moulding the destiny of the Hindu Nation than any other factor within our present reach.[14]

This was a masterly reading of the situation and equally masterly prediction on the part of a political, security and social visionary. The princely states indeed played a most pivotal role in the formation of the Indian Republic.

He also warned the states thus: 'If Hindudom is uprooted, the Hindu States also must fall down and wither as inevitably as the limbs of a body that ceases to live.'[15] In fact, his prediction about Hindu princely states was very detailed. While expressing his conviction that the Hindu princely states would surely stand for United India, he also mentioned that taking these states along would reduce the threat of internal anarchy and external aggression. He expressed hope thus: 'The pan-Hindu ideology was sure to stir up, sooner or later, the latent fire in the blood of our historic forefathers which flows in the veins of our Hindu Princes and make them realize that their duty required them not only to sympathize with but to lead the Hindu movement.'[16]

These words came true when Maharana Bhupal Singh of Mewar refused the Nawab of Bhopal's lucrative offer to join Pakistan. He also prevented Jodhpur and Jaisalmer—the two other major Hindu states on the western frontier that were being enticed

---

[14]Ibid. 212.
[15]Ibid. 1940 session.
[16]Ibid. 119, 120, 121.

by Jinnah, through the Nawab of Bhopal—from joining Pakistan.[17] The Maharana refused the offer in the following words: 'My choice was made by my ancestors (read Maharana Pratap). If they had faltered, they would have left us a kingdom as large as Hyderabad. They did not. Neither shall I. I am with India.'[18]

On 1 June 1947, while sending a message on the coronation ceremony of Chhatrapati Shahaji Maharaj, Savarkar could foresee the threat from the neighbouring Muslim state of Hyderabad. So, he advised the Maharaja: 'Let the heritage of Shivaji the great inspire him and enable him not only to meet but to forestall any anti-Hindu aggression on Maharashtra.' He said the military and air forces of all Hindu states should immediately be raised to such a standard as to render them a bulwark of Hindudom. 'The future is big with great possibilities; if but Hindudom recovers its self-consciousness, we may yet regain all that is lost.'[19]

However, one should not misconclude that Savarkar wanted 'Princistan' within India. During his Baroda visit in January 1938, he said: 'I believe that the Maharaja of Nepal will lay his crown and the Maharaja of Kolhapur will shed his turban on the altar of independence.'[20] In fact, the Hindu Mahasabha meeting in New Delhi on 9 and 10 August 1947 called for the merger of all the princely states within India for a strong and united nation. This was one of the points discussed in the 12-point agenda at the meeting.[21]

Savarkar kept a close watch on the political and religious activities in the princely states. In July 1942, he requested the Maharao of Sirohi to abolish the tax taken from Jains for pilgrimage of Jain temples at Abu. He told the Maharao that the State of Sirohi would gain more than what it would lose in money by the removal

---

[17] This has been well-described by V.P. Menon in his famous book titled *Integration of the Indian States* (Orient BlackSwan; First Edition, 2014).
[18] Balraj Krishna, *Sardar Vallabhabhai Patel: India's Iron Man*, Rupa Publications, 2013, p. 286.
[19] V.D. Savarkar, *Historic Statements by Savarkar*, G.P. Parchure, 1967, p. 121.
[20] Balarao Savarkar, *Swatantryaveer Savarkar: Hindu Mahasabha Parv*, p. 100.
[21] Balarao Savarkar, *Swatantryaveer Savarkar: Akhand Hindusthan Ladha Parv*, p. 485.

of the taxes. It would earn thereby, the sympathy of the Hindu Mahasabha in particular and Hindudom in general, which, he said, constitutes a bedrock on which alone the security and prosperity of Hindu states all over India can be broadly based.

Savarkar launched a campaign against Mirza Ismail, Dewan of the Hindu state of Jaipur, who made Urdu compulsory for state public services jobs and had pursued pro-Muslim policies. In October 1945, he advised the Dewan of Travancore to bring all primary schools under government control as they became the illegitimate hub of conversion of Hindu children. He gave befitting replies to separatist Muslims of Kashmir and Baroda states. He also thanked the Maharaja of Tripura, who gave shelter to migrant Bengali Hindus.[22]

The Hindu Mahasabha and its affiliated organizations were active in these princely states. These included the Travancore State Hindusabha and the Shuddhisabha; the Kolhapur State Hindusabha and the Shuddhisabha; the Bhopal State Hindusabha; the Nizam State Hindu Mandal; the Gwalior State Hindusabha; and the Kutch-Kathiawar State Hindusabha. As against this, the Congress totally failed in reading the importance of the princely states in the evolution of new India till India became independent and Sardar Vallabhbhai Patel took up the task of integrating the princely states.

Savarkar's grip over issues of national security was unmatched, and this was revealed during his trip to Nagpur, where he called upon the Hindus to prepare themselves to defeat the Pakistan scheme and warned that the existence of Kashmir would be in danger if the pan-Islamist designs of a section of Muslims were not curbed. Just like his prophetic words about Pakistan, Savarkar issued this warning on Kashmir at a time when nobody was able to foresee that the Valley's existence would be under threat.

Savarkar openly attacked the Congress's call to the Maharaja of Jammu and Kashmir to abdicate his throne and transfer power to the Muslims as they were in majority in the state. Savarkar exposed

---

[22]Balarao Savarkar, *Swatantryaveer Savarkar, Akhand Hindusthan Ladha Parv*, p. 48, 401.

the Congress's pro-Muslim attitude by arguing that the party didn't give the same advice to the Nizam of Hyderabad or the Nawab of Bhopal, two Muslim-ruled princely states in which Hindus were in majority.[23] In August 1945, while supporting Sheikh Abdullah's 'Quit Kashmir' movement against the Maharaja of Kashmir, Pandit Nehru even threatened the Kashmiri Hindus by saying: 'If non-Muslims want to live in Kashmir, they should join the National Conference or bid goodbye to the country. If Pandits do not join it, no safeguards and weightages will protect them.'[24]

Revolutionary Savarkar was overwhelmingly received by Hindus on a pan-India canvas. In February 1938, a sea of people welcomed him in Delhi on his first-ever visit. Although Savarkar was unwell and needed assistance, he couldn't ignore the thundering response of the people. He took medical help and then he was put in a chariot and taken in a procession that continued for five miles. Leaders of eminence such as Dr Munje, M.S. Aney, Bhai Parmanand, Dr M.R. Jayakar and Lala Narayan Dutt accompanied the procession. Here, Savarkar reiterated his commitment to cultural nationalism by changing the Urdu slogan 'Zindabad' to 'Amar Rahe' in chaste Hindi.[25]

'ME AND JINNAH: NOT BIRDS OF THE SAME FEATHER'

In May 1938, Savarkar landed in Lahore. This was less than two years before the Muslim League's Lahore resolution demanding a separate nation for Indian Muslims which eventually changed the course of India. Savarkar's speech at Lahore showed the difference between the equal-treatment-emphasizing Hindu Mahasabha on one side and the pro-Muslim Muslim League and the Congress on the other.

His statements presenting the principles of unalloyed nationalism

---

[23]Dhananjay Keer, *Veer Savarkar*, Popular Prakashan Pvt. Ltd; Second edition, 2019, p. 229, 230.
[24]Balraj Krishna, *Sardar Vallabhbhai Patel: India's Iron Man*, Rupa Publications, 2014, p. 345.
[25]Dhananjay Keer, *Veer Savarkar*, Popular Prakashan Pvt. Ltd; Second edition, 2019, p. 233.

in no uncertain terms resonated throughout the country. They found great appreciation from leading newspapers too. In response to a question, Savarkar told the media that he and Jinnah were not birds of the same feather because he stood for equality and no concessions while Jinnah asked for more and more concessions for Muslims. He said that the need of the hour for the Congress was to assume the role of a Parliament in which all parties could participate, but unfortunately it was performing the role of a partisan party.

He also laid down the principles of just nationalism based on equal treatment for all: 'Either there should be joint electorates without reservation of seats for any community in legislatures and local bodies, or there must be separate electorates with reservation of seats for minorities either on population basis or according to a system of weightages equally applicable to all minorities.'[26]

These words show that the greatest visionary of all time could foresee that the violations of these just principles by the Muslim League, no less than the Congress, would irrevocably lead to the formation of Pakistan. *The Tribune*, the most popular newspaper of Punjab then as now, was impressed—as evident in its editorial:

> As a matter of fact, Mr Savarkar's anchor as a sincere and true nationalist holds. The several speeches made by him during the last three days (in Lahore) unmistakably show both the general soundness of his political views and the fervor and intensity of his love of country and freedom. His conception of an ideal modern State is one in which no difference is made between people on the score of community, religion and caste. Holding this view, and this is undoubtedly the only correct view, it is only right that he should want the Congress, which is India's supreme national organization, not to recognize religion, class and community and to stand for equal rights for all citizens.[27]

---

[26]Dhananjay Keer, *Veer Savarkar*, Popular Prakashan Pvt. Ltd; Second edition, 2019, p. 236.
[27]*The Mahratta*, 20 May 1938.

Savarkar's next stop was Amritsar, where as many as 60,000 people participated in a procession in which he was enthusiastically received. Akali Dal leader Master Tara Singh, who held Savarkar in high esteem for the importance that Savarkar gave to Sikhs in his Hindutva scheme, cancelled his tour to rush to Amritsar to receive Savarkar. In his reply to the address given by the Sikhs, Savarkar advised the community not to get entangled in the web of non-violence (Gandhi's ahimsa) and asked them to follow the ideals of Guru Gobind Singh. When a kirpan was presented to him, Savarkar said that a kirpan to a Maratha was of no use when those people for whom the kirpan was sacred had lost its meaning and spirit under the influence of the doctrine of complete non-violence. This revealed the aim of his great national mission—reliving the spirit of Maharana Pratap, Chhatrapati Shivaji and Guru Gobind Singh to reintroduce virility in a nation that was fast losing it under the spell of slogans of complete non-violence. Later, at a speech in Amritsar, Savarkar held out a warning to the Congress thus: 'The more you run after Hindu–Muslim unity, the further it runs away from you.'[28] He virtually said that the Hindu–Muslim problem was a creation of the Congress as actually there didn't exist such a problem. He added that the Parsis, the Jews and the Christians inhabiting this land had never claimed special rights and they have declared that they don't want separate electorates.[29]

His next important stop was Sindh, a region that (along with the Sindhu River) was a special place for Savarkar. In *Hindutva*, he has passionately described as to how these were intrinsically linked with the rise of the Hindu nation and that it was from the banks of the Sindhu river that the Hindu civilization sprang. The receptions accorded to Savarkar in the Sindh Province during his 10-day visit starting from 1 September 1938, were exceptional, gauging by the people's enthusiasm and sheer numbers. It took five hours for his procession to reach its destination in Karachi! The role of the main organizer in Karachi was played by his Andaman jail mate Baba

---

[28]Ibid.
[29]Ibid.

Madan Singh Gaga, a Gadar party Sikh leader.

In this conference, Savarkar stressed on military training of the youth in Karachi. Sukkur's enthusiasm came only next to Karachi in welcoming Savarkar. Here, addressing the Sindh Hindu conference, Savarkar sounded a timely warning to the local Hindus. He asked them to boycott the Congress if they wanted to save themselves in the future from the party's partisan pro-Muslim policies that could greatly affect Sindh. The warning was very apt as the Congress leaders had failed to prevent the partition of Sindh from Bombay Province, and its eventual separation from India.

Then, in October 1938, Savarkar, leading the Hindu Mahasabha and the Arya Samaj in an agitation against the atrocities of the Nizam of Hyderabad on his state's Hindu population, showed himself as man of action and not merely words. The Hindus and Sikhs of Hyderabad suffered under the medieval tyranny of the Nizam and his prime minister Syed Qasim Razvi as the Hindus were disallowed to take out processions, have their schools impart education to their children in their mother tongue and renovate their temples.[30] Savarkar rightly saw this as an opportunity to project the situation as a forerunner of the things to come for Hindus if the Muslim League politics was allowed to flourish and the Congress continued to cave in before the Muslim demands.

Significantly, he rightly foresaw the situation as the Congress, which was allegedly supporting and even instigating the Kashmiri Muslims against their Hindu ruler as they were in a majority, refused to follow the same logic in the case of Hyderabad. In fact, Gandhi even called and implored Munje to convince Savarkar and the Arya Samaj to end the agitation. Munje told the Mahatma that Savarkar and the Hindu Mahasabha knew well where to stop, even as the Arya Samaj was on the verge of withdrawing the agitation under Congress pressure.

Savarkar gave a send-off to several batches of volunteers that entered Hyderabad to offer civil resistance. Eventually, over 15,000 volunteers, led by eminent leaders such as Senapati Bapat, L.B.

---

[30]Dhananjay Keer, *Veer Savarkar*, Popular Prakashan, 1966, p. 240.

Bhopatkar, D.K. Sathe, Dr Laxman Vasudev Paranjape and Bapurao Joshi from Maharashtra, Baba Madan Singh Gaga, Pandit Narayan Swami and Chandrakiran Sarada from other provinces, and the Hyderabad Hindu Mahasabha leader, Yashwantrao Joshi, landed in jail. The first batch of volunteers from Maharashtra that entered Hyderabad was incidentally led by Nathuram Godse.

In keeping with his principle of restoring old, original Hindu names of places which had been renamed by Muslim invaders, Savarkar, and for that matter every Hindu Mahasabhaite, always called Hyderabad by its old name, Bhagyanagar. This name has been mentioned by Hindu historians since the time of Shivaji and in Shivaji's own correspondence and his State papers.

Interestingly, much later in December 1941, while leading the agitation against the government ban on the Hindu Mahasabha's Bhagalpur session, Savarkar showed the same fire as in the Hyderabad struggle. The government insisted that the session would threaten communal harmony keeping in mind the Hindu Mahasabha's strong stance against Muslim appeasement and the upcoming Eid festival. The ban was obviously under pressure from the Muslim leadership as the Muslim community had a strong presence in Bihar and many of its leaders were pan-Islamists.

However, under Savarkar's leadership, the Hindu Mahasabha led a landmark agitation for liberty, holding huge demonstrations. All classes of Hindus and even Sikhs and Jains participated in the stir. Though Savarkar was arrested while he was proceeding to Bhagalpur, the session was held under the leadership of Tilak's grandson, Dr G.V. Ketkar, who read out Savarkar's presidential address even as the lion was in jail. Like the Hyderabad struggle, the Bhagalpur agitation proved that Hindus as a community, otherwise so emasculated due to the Congress's pacifist politics on Muslim-related issues, could lead a struggle on their own and that too cutting across caste lines. It once again established the cultural and religious unity of Hindus and the Hindu pantheon.

Guru Golwalkar, the second Sarsanghchalak of the RSS, wholeheartedly supported the Bhagalpur movement. Guruji visited Hindu Mahasabha leaders Dr Munje and Bhai Parmanand when they were imprisoned. During his speech, Guruji said, 'The strength of the Hindu society is tested by such a movement. It is the duty of the Swayam Sevaks to participate in such a battle.'[31]

Hyderabad now figured in Savarkar's speeches wherever he went. In December 1938, Savarkar attended the Aryan conference at Sholapur on the request of the Arya Samaj, which wanted Savarkar's valuable direction for its Hyderabad struggle. Around the same time, Savarkar attended the annual Hindu Mahasabha session at Nagpur, Munje's hometown. Not surprisingly, the atmosphere in the city was electrifying. Savarkar's procession here took five hours to reach its destination. Flowers were showered on him from an aeroplane, even as Buddhist representatives from Japan attended the conference in keeping with Savarkar's definition that those religions which were born in India were part of the Hindu pantheon. Savarkar delivered an epic speech at the session, in which he defined the principles of nationalism once again, but this time along with the rights and duties of the religious minorities. He also laid down principles of a sound foreign policy and national and international politics. The Hyderabad struggle against the Nizam's tyranny was the prime focus at the Nagpur session.

Savarkar's visit to Bengal, two months later, was equally or perhaps more electrifying in terms of the public response it received. Such was the effect of his logical oratory and magnetism that it captivated eminent personalities such as N.C. Chatterjee and Dr S.P. Mukherjee, the latter being the great discovery of Savarkar on this tour of the Hindu Mahasabha. The success of Savarkar's Bengal tour was best reflected in the pro-Congress newspaper, *Amrita Bazar Patrika*, which in an editorial warned the Congress against surrendering before the unholy demands of the Muslim League.

Next, in March 1939, Savarkar received a rousing reception in Monghyr (Munger) in Bihar, where he presided over a provincial Hindu Mahasabha conference. The local newspaper

---

[31] Balarao Savarkar, *Swatantryaveer Savarkar: Hindu Mahasabha Parv 1937–1940*, Swatantryaveer Savarkar Rashtriya Smarak, 2020.

Prabhakar averred that the recognition he received as a leader was unparalleled in the annals of the town.[32] Here, Savarkar explained the difference between Hindutva and Hinduism. He said that Hindutva constituted all those aspects and aspirations which the word 'nationalism' comprised.

The local press in Bihar, impressed by the logic of his ideological line, felt that Savarkar had created an atmosphere of great enthusiasm amongst the Hindus. *Amrita Bazar Patrika*, one of India's oldest newspapers, published an enthusiastic report on this visit:

> A thrill passed through the audience when Sj. Savarkar was found putting his hands on the head of five Santhal boys, who in Santhali, claimed that they belonged to Hinduism and sought Sj. Savarkar's lead to guide their destiny. When one of them garlanded him with a wreath of Sylvan blossoms, Sj. Savarkar embraced them with joy.[33]

In June 1939, Savarkar received an overwhelming response at the Mahakoshal Provincial Hindu Conference in Jabalpur, where his arguments against the unjust treatment of the majority and the resultant danger to Hindustan were much appreciated. In the same month, 'Hyderabad Day' was observed by the Hindu Mahasabha all over the country. The arrests of party volunteers and Savarkar's exposition on the Hyderabad struggle and its true purport for India had great impact in the Central Provinces, Berar and Maharashtra. In the end, the struggle against the Nizam's despotism, in which the Hindu Mahasabha and the Arya Samaj took a leading part, bore fruit when the Nizam, overwhelmed by public pressure, announced reforms and offered 50 per cent reserved seats to Hindus in the elected legislature for the first time.

The successful termination of the Hyderabad struggle established Savarkar as a great organizer for the Hindutva cause, who could bring the fight on the issue of Muslim appeasement

---

[32] Dhananjay Keer, *Veer Savarkar*, Popular Prakshan Pvt. Ltd, 2019, p. 242.
[33] Joya Chatterji, *Bengal Divided: Hindu Communalism and Partition, 1932–1947*, Cambridge University Press, 2002, p. 195.

to a successful end by an effective mix of strategy and force, in spite of the Congress. Most of all, it reignited hope in that set of Hindus who felt emasculated by the Congress's compromises with Muslims.

It was not surprising that more than two lakh Hindus attended the Calcutta session of the Hindu Mahasabha in December 1939.[34] The Viceroy, who happened to be in Calcutta on the day, told his seniors in London that,

> [The] Hindu Mahasabha was gradually emerging, and with considerable vigour. [They] have just held a monster-meeting here [in Calcutta] from which there has emerged a series of resolutions highly communal in character and condemnatory of the Congress ... I will not be surprised, things being as they are, if the Mahasabha were to succeed in stealing a certain amount of Congress thunder.[35]

The Viceroy's report also showed the marked bias of the British in describing the Hindu Mahasabha's fight for just rights against Muslim aggression as 'communal'.

During his Assam visit in November 1941, Savarkar was virtually welcomed as the king of Hindus. He delivered lectures in more than 100 gatherings and addressed around seven lakh Hindus.[36] In Kashmir, the far end of Hindustan, thousands of Hindus virtually saw Savarkar as an incarnation of God and invoked his blessings. Thousands touched his feet in devotion and kissed his hands in spite of his fervent disapproval of such display of emotion. Such thrilling scenes of devotion and deification were common features of Savarkar's tours, and not just in Kashmir.[37]

These tours were characterized by two key features. Savarkar

---

[34]Dhananjay Keer, *Veer Savarkar*, Popular Prakashan Pvt. Ltd; Second edition, 2019, p. 253.
[35]Joya Chatterji, *Bengal Divided: Hindu Communalism and Partition, 1932–1947*, Cambridge University Press, 2002, p. 135.
[36]Balarao Savarkar, *Swatantryaveer Savarkar, Hindu Mahasabha Parva*, p. 117.
[37]Dhananjay Keer, *Veer Savarkar*, Popular Prakashan Pvt. Ltd; Second edition, 2019, p. 317.

attended anti-caste dinners, organized at his behest by the Hindu Mahasabha alongside his political programmes, to remove untouchability. He also made it a point to attend RSS gatherings and parades, as he sincerely believed that the RSS would turn into a massive mass movement that would change the course of Indian history once it had attained a certain stature. Savarkar had inspired RSS founder Dr Keshav Baliram Hedgewar and, in fact, much of the RSS's ideological content came from Savarkar's book, *Hindutva*. It was natural that Savarkar conducted himself as a father figure to the RSS but also advised the Sangh whenever he disagreed with it ideologically.

Some analysts have tried to create an impression that Savarkar and the RSS disagreed on several points. This is, in fact, a misnomer. Except disagreements on a couple of occasions, Savarkar and the RSS remained on the same page. One major disagreement happened when Savarkar's statements based on his belief in science questioned the religious sanctity of the cow.[38] Savarkar had his own scientific reasons to say that the cow should be seen from the point of view of science only and not from the religious angle. The RSS naturally opposed this approach and in a way rightly so. However, some writers have picked up this episode to depict major differences between the RSS and Savarkar.

Savarkar had predicted the future greatness of the RSS with commanding confidence and by drawing interesting analogy. On 30 July 1939, while addressing a meeting, Savarkar said:

> Many waves of victory and defeat arose over the unfathomable ocean of Hindutva, but the ocean remained the same. Dr Hedgewar established the Sangh keeping this in mind. I thank him for this. Just like the tiny fish in the palms of Manu grew larger and saved Manu's boat during the cataclysm, similarly I believe that this organization of Dr Hedgewar will become giant and save the country today.[39]

---

[38]V.D. Savarkar, *Vigyannisht Nibandh*, Uttkarsha Prakashan, 2008, p. 49.
[39]Balarao Savarkar, *Swatantryaveer Savarkar, Hindu Mahasabha Parva*, p. 299.

With the start of World War II, Savarkar began propagating the militarization of Hindus. He exhorted the Hindu society to take advantage of the military training imparted by the RSS under Dr Hedgewar's great mission of Hindu organization—the mission to unite and organize Hindus. Savarkar maintained that Dr Hedgewar had wrung his heart to bathe the Hindu society in the nectar of vitality, and with fearlessness had given the message of pride to the Hindu society. He said when Congress leaders were trying to drag the Hindu society down in the name of nationalism, it was the duty of the youth to wholeheartedly participate in Dr Hedgewar's mission of Hindu organization for the security of the Hindu nation.

Savarkar also advised on how to settle disagreements amongst Hindu factions. Addressing 2,300 office-bearers of the RSS, on 17 June 1943, he said: 'For many years, I have been following the activity of the Sangh. Many more Hindu volunteer organizations, like [the] Sangh, are now flourishing. All of these institutions should decide on their own key areas and contribute for the advancement of Hindutva without competing with one another.'[40]

It should also be recalled that during Savarakar's funeral procession in 1966, 2,000 RSS volunteers lined up the route and sounded the final post at Bombay Central.[41]

The Congress leadership was stung by this growing public response to Savarkar and the Hindu Mahasabha. In an astounding move which had no justification, it declared a boycott of the party, dubbing it as communal. Yet, it was crystal clear that a significant but silent section of the Congress, particularly at the lower level, continued to appreciate Savarkar for his courage in upholding the Hindu cause on the touchstone of true principles of democracy and justice under extremely trying circumstances.[42] This section

---

[40]A.B. Savarkar, *Swatantryaveer Savarkar: Akhand Hindusthan Ladha Parv 1941–1947*, Swatantryaveer Savarkar Rashtriya Smarak, 2020, p. 247.
[41]Dhananjay Keer, *Veer Savarkar*, Popular Prakashan Pvt. Ltd; Second edition, 2019, p. 546.
[42]It was this Congress section, called the right-wing section of the party led by Sardar Patel, which through the medium of D.P. Mishra, chief minister of the

in the Congress, though powerless against the writ of Gandhi, was unhappy with the Congress's Muslim-appeasement policy and admired Savarkar in the heart of hearts for his forthright stand on the issue. This is reflected in the intermittent visits that Congress leaders paid to him publicly and secretly when he was waging a battle against the Muslim League and the Congress for protecting Hindu rights. This was the same faction—known as the Sardar Patel faction—which after the death of Gandhi and Patel waged an internal battle against the ultra-liberals within the Congress, identified with Pandit Nehru, for the protection of Hindu rights. Till this faction was strong within the Congress, the Bharatiya Jana Sangh, a forerunner of the Bharatiya Janata Party (BJP), couldn't rise beyond a point in Indian politics as Hindu issues were addressed from within the Congress, at least partially.

Hurt by the Congress's attitude based on political untouchability, seven key political and public leaders including Savarkar, Dr Ambedkar of the Independent Labour Party, Jamnadas Mehta and N.C. Kelkar of the Democratic Swarajya Party, and Sir Chimanlal Setalvad, Sir V.N. Chandavarkar and Sir Cowasji Jehangir on behalf of the Indian Liberals denounced the Congress as a party that believed in annihilating all parties, as in the case of Fascist and Nazi regimes. This, they said, would be a deathblow to democracy.[43] Savarkar had emerged as the biggest critic of the Congress and with a considerable degree of public support. So, it was not surprising that media publications supporting the Congress attacked Savarkar for leaving his original stand and joining hands with the liberals. But in reality, Savarkar, by aligning with non-Congress leaders, had in this episode demonstrated political flexibility and Chanakya Niti so necessary in politics.

Central Provinces, and Barrister Ramrao Deshmukh, tried to win Savarkar's support after Partition had been announced, and Punjab and Bengal were engulfed by communal conflagration, in which Hindus were at the receiving end. Sardar Patel's silent support was obvious in this move. This group was obviously reacting owing to the realization that Savarkar's prophecy that Muslim appeasement would eventually lead to Partition had come true.

[43]P.R. Lele, *War and India's Freedom*, Popular Book Depot, 1940, p. 89.

Little did he know than that these traits would be put to the ultimate test very soon.

THE 1940 RESOLUTION: WATERSHED IN EVERY WAY

Savarkar was about to enter the most important phase of his political career. On 23 March 1940, Prophet Savarkar's prophecies about Muslim appeasement leading to the formation of Pakistan came true when the Muslim League, under the direct guidance of Jinnah, passed a resolution at the League session in Lahore. They demanded a separate nation for the Muslims of the Indian subcontinent comprising areas where Muslims were in a majority. This came to be known as the Pakistan Resolution.

The operative part of the resolution read: 'In the regions where Muslims are in a majority (e.g. North West and eastern regions like Bengal), separate states would be carved with due regard to geographical contiguity. The provinces amongst such Muslim-majority States should be independent and sovereign.'[44] The resolution also dictated how Muslims should be treated in the rest of India where they are in the minority: 'Adequate, effective and mandatory safeguards shall be specially provided in the Constitution for them and other minorities for the protection of their religious, cultural, economic, political, administrative and other rights and interests in consultation with them.'[45]

From 30 per cent reservation in 1927 and plea for minority rights, the Muslim League, led by Jinnah, had now proceeded to claim that Muslims were a separate nation and therefore eligible for equal rights with Hindus in terms of representation, and offered to safeguard the interests of the minorities. Obviously, he saw his fight for Pakistan as a war and he believed that everything was fair in love and war.

Jinnah had been preparing ground for this historic resolution

---

[44] Y. Krishnan, *Understanding Partition: Separation Not Liquidation*, Bharatiya Vidya Bhavan, 2002, p. 388.
[45] Ibid.

from 1937 onwards by raising the false bogey of Muslim victimhood under Hindu oppression led by the Congress. He had threatened a civil war in case the Congress assumed power at the Centre. The impulsive and foolish resignation of the Congress provincial ministries on the issues related to World War II was celebrated by Jinnah as a 'Deliverance Day'. Savarkar was the only leader of note who had seen through Jinnah's game and had been repeatedly warning the Congress and the Hindus of the nation about the Muslim League's strategy. And now his prophecies had come true to the last dot.

Some Muslim and communist historians promote the Muslim League's victim card narrative that the atrocities against Muslims during the Congress regime led to Pakistan. However, even Jinnah didn't believe it! In his speech at Aligarh in 1944, he dwelt on how the seed of Pakistan had emerged. He said:

> Pakistan was not the product of the conduct or misconduct of Hindus... Pakistan started the moment the first non-Muslim was converted to Islam in India long before the Muslims established their rule. As soon as a Hindu embraced Islam, he was outcast not only religiously but also socially, culturally and economically. As for the Muslim, it was a duty imposed on him by Islam not to merge his identity and individuality in any alien society. Throughout the ages, Hindus have remained Hindus and Muslims have remained Muslims, and they had not merged their entities—this was the basis of Pakistan.[46]

Interestingly, Pakistan was not the final agenda of the dreamers of 'Pakistan'. Rahmat Ali, who had developed this idea, had a bigger dream. According to him, in the beginning, Pakistan would consist of Punjab, the North-West Frontier Province, Kashmir, Sindh and Balochistan only. Later, encouraged by the reception from the subcontinent to the Muslim League's 1940 resolution, an emboldened Rahmat Ali unravelled the second part of his

---

[46]Yuvraj Krishan, *Understanding Partition: India Sundered, Muslims Fragmented*, Mumbai: Bharatiya Vidya Bhavan 2002, p. 288.

programme embracing Bangistan, which was to include Bengal and Assam, and afterwards in 1942, he added Osmanistan, comprising Hyderabad (Deccan), Siddiqistan in Bundelkhand and Malwa, Faruqistan in Bihar and Orissa (now Odisha), Haidaristan in United Provinces of Agra and Oudh, Muinistan in Rajasthan, Maplistan in the Madras Presidency, Safiistan in Western Ceylon (Sri Lanka) and Nasaristan in Eastern Ceylon.[47] In the maps he had visualized, he renamed the Indian subcontinent as 'Dinia' (an anagram of India with the position of 'd' changed) with the ultimate aim of *'Pakasia*: The Historic Orbit of the Pak Culture'.[48] However, small or big, the dreamers of Pakistan could visualize and achieve it only because of Hindu weaknesses as had happened in medieval history too.

The Pakistan Resolution came as a shock to the Congress, which had been talking about no independence without Hindu–Muslim unity. But instead of opposing the Muslim League, the Congress conceded Partition within just one month of the Lahore resolution. How it happened is both interesting and painful.

The initial reactions of the Congress leaders were very apt. They opposed the resolution tooth and nail stating various reasons. Rajaji called the two-nation theory a mischievous idea which will bring destruction.[49] Nehru, who always blissfully but wrongly believed that Muslims' communal aggression would subside against the common economic needs of Hindus and Muslims, said: 'We will have nothing to do with this mad scheme. The whole problem has taken a new complexion and there is no question of settlement of negotiations'.[50] After these statements made by Congress leaders, it appeared to be a foregone conclusion that the party would oppose the Partition demand with all its might.

---

[47] Choudhary Rahmat Ali, *Pakistan: The Fatherland of the Pak Nation*, Cambridge Pakistan National Liberation Movement, 1947, p.116.
[48] Ibid.
[49] B.N. Jog, *Threat of Islam: Indian Dimensions*, Mumbai (Bombay): Unnati Prakashan, 1994.
[50] Ibid. 259.

Map 2

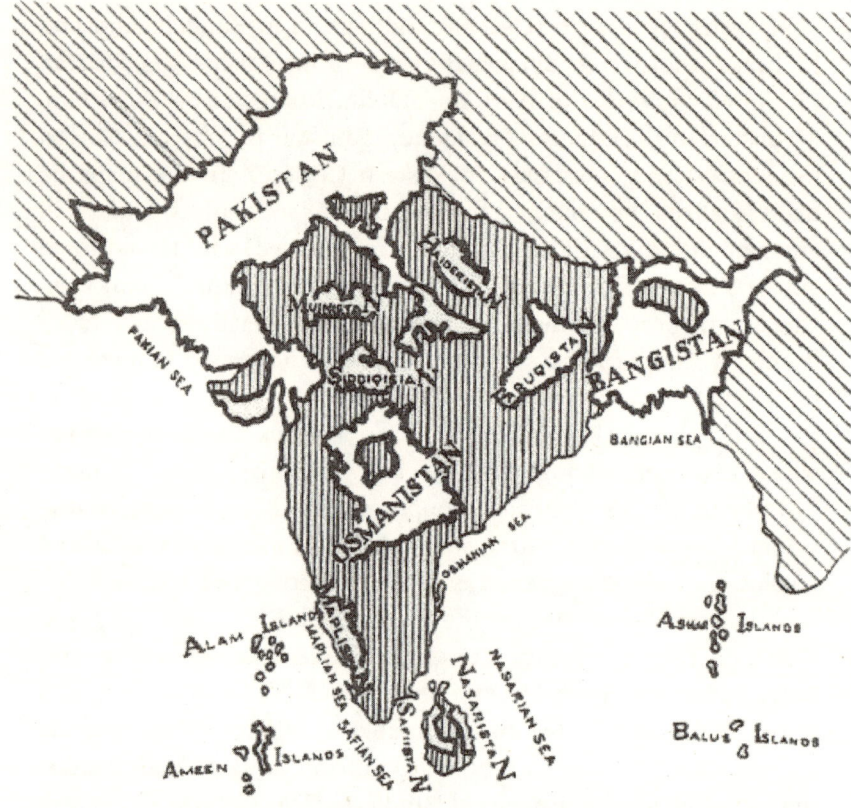

Note: Islamic Map of India as visualized in 1942 by Choudhary Rahmat Ali, who coined the term 'Pakistan' in 1932. Map reproduced from his book *Pakistan: The Fatherland of the Pak Nation* (page 116) published in 1946, in which Rahmat Ali visualized a fragmented India converted into seven mini Pakistans under different names, apart from today's Pakistan. This is, in fact, the dream of today's pan-Islamists in India.

Rahmat Ali's vision was:
1. Muinistan (Rajasthan)
2. Haideristan (Agra and Awadh area in United Provinces)
3. Bangistan (Bengal)
4. Faruqistan (Bihar and Odisha)
5. Siddiquistan (Bundelkhand and Malwa)
6. Osmanistan (Hyderabad)
7. Maplistan (Madras Presidency)

However, in a dreadful development, the Congress conceded Partition when Gandhi reacted in two voices, opposing the Partition demand on one hand, and on the other hand, expressing his helplessness in opposing it in the name of non-violence and the right of self-determination on the part of different peoples of India.

In fact, Gandhi had conceded Partition even before the 1940 Pakistan resolution. On 17 March 1940, a week before the resolution was passed, Gandhi cleared his stand on using force against vivisection of India, which was published in the 23rd March issue of *Harijan*. He said:

> ... the Congress cannot forcibly resist the express will of the Muslims of India. Needless to say, the Congress can never seek the assistance of British forces to resist the vivisection. It is the Muslims who will impose their will by force singly or with British assistance on an unresisting India. If I can carry the Congress with me, I would not put the Muslims to the trouble of using force. I would be ruled by them for it would still be Indian rule.[51]

However, Gandhi's initial reaction to the resolution in the 30th March edition of *Harijan* was against the Partition demand: 'I am proud that I am a Hindu. But I have never approached as a Hindu to ask for Hindu–Muslim unity. My Hindutva doesn't accept any pact mentality.' However, in his next article in *Harijan* on 6 April 1940, he again dubbed Partition as bad for the nation but conceded it in the following words:

> ... the Muslims will be entitled to dictate their own terms. Unless the rest of India wishes to engage in internal fratricide, the others will have to submit to Muslim dictation if the Muslims will resort to it. I know of no non-violent method of compelling obedience of eight crore Muslims to the will of the rest of India, howsoever powerful a majority the rest

---

[51] *The Collected Works of Mahatma Gandhi* (CWMG), Vol. 78, 23 February–15 July 1940. https://www.gandhiashramsevagram.org/gandhi-literature/mahatma-gandhi-collected-works-volume-78.pdf. Accessed on 31 July 2021.

may represent. The Muslims must have the same right of self-determination as the rest of India has. We are at present a joint family. Any member can claim a division. ...But I don't believe that Muslims when it comes to a matter of actual division will want vivisection. Their good sense would prevail. Their self-interest will deter them. Their religion will forbid the obvious suicide which Partition would mean.

However, in his next reaction in the same publication (*Harijan*) on 13 April 1940, he virtually condemned the demand but with the logic of his own religious beliefs, which many had contested. He said:

Partition will be a total travesty of truth. My soul recoils to the very idea which believes that Hindutva and Islam represent antagonistic cultures and faiths. To accept such a belief amounts to negation of God Almighty. It is my belief to the core of my heart that Allah of Quran and Parmeshwar of Bhagavad Gita are one and the same. I will have to rise in revolt against the very concept that purports to establish that those who were Hindus a few generations back have changed their nationhood along with their conversion to Islam.

It is clear that Gandhi's and consequently the Congress's belief in complete non-violence was at the root of Gandhi's stand in accepting the Muslim right to self-determination. For, Gandhi's *Harijan* article of 6 April made it clear that according to him, the only solution to the Partition imbroglio was good sense prevailing amongst the Muslims and dissuading them to reject Partition.

What actually happened was exactly the opposite. A series of Muslim leaders—Sikandar Hayat Khan of Punjab (who had been compelled by Jinnah to join the League but had severe differences with him) and separatists such as Fazlul Haque, who didn't want Jinnah to hijack their leadership and consequently bring down their standing amongst the Muslim masses and who believed that physical partition of India was either impossible or detrimental to Muslim interests—opposed the Partition demand. However, Jinnah, a shrewd observer of the Muslim community's religious beliefs and attitude, had rightly guessed that even if fellow Muslim leaders opposed his demand, the Muslim masses would accept it with both hands. And that is exactly how things played out.

The demand seemed to appeal to the Muslim masses, one reason probably being the typical mindset of demanding more and more concessions as a minority, as proved by history. Another was Jinnah's false propaganda of injustice meted out to Muslims by the Hindus and the 'Hindu Congress' and his constant refrain that majority oppression on minority was the worst kind of oppression. His propaganda was eventually lapped up by the Muslim masses, rejecting the stands of the Muslim leaders who didn't agree with Jinnah.

The Aligarh Muslim University was one of the first to fall into Jinnah's lap. Jinnah already had some footing in the institution, which was any way an old seed of the separatist thought in the Muslim community. With the Partition announcement, the university became the main centre for a separate Muslim homeland. The entire propaganda of the Muslim League was in a way planned and executed from the university.

Yet, an important factor that made the Lahore resolution a starter was the World War II situation. The British were looking for Indian support on the war effort. In its Ramgarh session, held just a week before the Muslim League's Lahore resolution, the Congress had refused to cooperate with the British in their war efforts. Therefore, Viceroy Lord Linlithgow was eager to placate the Muslim masses while aiming for their support, especially since the Muslim community at that time was also the biggest supplier of recruits to the Indo-British Army. (This is before Savarkar launched the militarization campaign and swelled the number of Hindu recruits.) In fact, Jinnah had met the Viceroy on 13 March 1940, and conveyed his message that if Britain recognized and supported Muslim aspirations, the Muslim masses and the Muslim League would cooperate in the war efforts.[52]

---

[52]B.N. Jog, *Threat of Islam: Indian Dimensions*, Mumbai (Bombay): Unnati Prakashan, 1994, p. 271.

Not surprisingly, Jinnah's aim of emerging as the sole leader of Muslims and his Pakistan scheme received immediate British support. Lord Zetland, Secretary of State for India, virtually endorsed the Pakistan scheme when on 18 April 1940, less than a month after the Pakistan Resolution, he announced in the House of Lords in London that Britain would not force a Constitution on India which was not acceptable to the Muslim community. Britain reiterated this stand in August by issuing a declaration assuring Indian Muslims that power and responsibility would not be transferred to any government whose authority was not acceptable to large and powerful elements in India's body politic. These immediately vested the Muslim League with veto power on any constitutional change and geared the Muslim League both against the Congress and amongst the Muslim masses by virtually positioning Jinnah and the League as the sole representatives of Indian Muslims.[53]

Sadly, the 1940 resolution showed how the indomitable spirit of Hindus that had compelled the British to annul the division of Bengal in 1911 had completely broken down in the next 30 years.

Congress leaders could have immediately launched a public campaign against the Partition demand, which could have in turn created public pressure from the Hindus as well as a section of Muslims, howsoever small, on the Muslim League. It could have also organized a front of Muslim leaders and organizations who had initially opposed the Lahore resolution. In fact, chief ministers of the Muslim-majority provinces had initially opposed Jinnah's Pakistan scheme and therefore, this was an opportune time for the Congress. However, in the name of self-determination, Gandhi handed over eight crore Muslims to Jinnah on a platter.

Meanwhile, Gandhi's queer stance continued. In the 13th October issue of *Harijan*, he said:

> If the British was overthrown as a result of WW-II and an internal anarchy set in the strongest power in the land would

---

[53]Yuvraj Krishan, *Understanding Partition: India Sundered, Muslims Fragmented*, Mumbai: Bharatiya Vidya Bhavan, 2002, p. 127, 182, 183.

Savarkar with a rifle in hand as a
young revolutionary in London

A saga of unparalleled family sacrifice: The Savarkar family (1931)
(Sitting from left) Dr Narayan Savarkar, Ganesh Savarkar (holding daughter
Prabhat Vinayak Savarkar) and Vinayak Savarkar
(Standing from left) Shantabai Narayan Savarkar with son Ashok,
Maina Kale (sister) and Yamuna Vinayak Savarkar with son Vishwas

Great social reformer: Savarkar with Dalits, whom he administrated the *janoi* (sacred thread) as a Brahmin. The untouchables were barred from wearing the *janoi*

Savarkar at an inter-caste dinner in Ratnagiri. Savarkar's main weapon against the caste system was organizing inter-caste dinners, where the upper caste including Brahmins, and Dalits, dined together

Soon after his release from *nazarqaid* (internment) at Ratnagiri, Savarkar was splendidly taken in a procession in Poona, the city of his alma mater, Fergusson College

Savarkar at the all-important 1937 Karnavati (Ahmedabad) Hindu Mahasabha session, where he took over as party president, discarding the invite of some Congressmen who wanted him to join their party. It was here that he laid the contours of unalloyed nationalism or Hindu nationalism, based on the equal treatment for all against the Congress's Muslim-appeasement policies

Top Hindu Mahasabha leaders Bhai Parmanand (seated, extreme left) and B.S. Munje (standing, extreme left) with Savarkar at the Karnavati session of the Hindu Mahasabha

Inspiration to Subhas Chandra Bose: Savarkar with Netaji (standing) at their famous 4 June 1938 meeting in Bombay. In their second meeting in the city in 1940, Savarkar suggested that Netaji flee India and organize an anti-British military coalition with the help of Japan and Germany, an advise that he heeded

Savarkar in a mammoth procession in Karachi, Sindh, on 27 September 1938. When Sindh was bifurcated from Bombay State in 1936, Savarkar said the Anglo-Muslim coalition had taken the first step towards Partition and Pakistan

With the crafty British negotiator Sir Stafford Cripps, on 28 March 1942. Cripps, who had enticed Russia against Germany in World War II with his diplomatic skills, was bowled over by Savarkar's arguments on how India constituted one nation and not different nationalities. Savarkar's sterling performance was hailed by the Congress mouthpiece, *National Herald*

(Left to right) Dr Syama Prasad Mukherjee, Savarkar and Dr Munje after meeting with Cripps

Savarkar addressing a public meeting. There was nothing soft about Savarkar's approach in his speech. He was truthful, non-populist and blunt to the point of being unpalatable and, therefore, people said it was difficult to digest Savarkar's philosophy

Savarkar with Rashtriya Swayamsevak Sangh (RSS) Sarsanghchalak M.S. Golwalkar (Guruji) (extreme right) at the Mrityunjay Divas celebration on 24 December 1960, when Savarkar would have been released had he not been freed in 1937 after being sentenced to 50 years in jail for waging a war against the British

(From left) At the root of Pakistan: Mohsin-ul-Mulk (key person of the Simla delegation of 1906, which demanded special privileges for Muslims), Syed Ahmed Khan (founder of the Aligarh Movement and father of the two-nation theory) and Justice Syed Mahmood (son of Syed Ahmed Khan and the first Muslim to serve as a High Court judge in the British Raj)

Muslims and Congressmen at a function of the pan-Islamist Khilafat movement which the Congress backed and which sowed the biggest seed of Muslim appeasement that ultimately led to Pakistan

Mahatma Gandhi and Mohammed Ali Jinnah after the conclusion of one of the Gandhi-Jinnah talks. Gandhi went to meet Jinnah at his place 17 times to discuss Partition, but Jinnah didn't pay a single return visit

Dead bodies in Calcutta after Jinnah's Direct Action Call in 1946, which was almost a call to Islamic jihad. Jinnah's violence secured him Pakistan because non-violent Congress had no answer to it

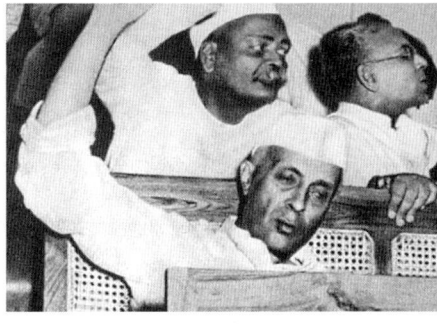

(Left) The Congress accepts Partition on 14 June 1947. For many Congressmen, Partition came as a relief, as they thought it would curb the horrendous communal riots, but what happened was exactly the reverse. Therefore, the Congress accepted both Partition and the price of complete non-violence
(Right) Nehru can be seen raising his hand in support of Partition

hold sway over India and this may be Hyderabad for ought I know. All the other bigger and Petty chiefs will ultimately succumb to the strongest power of the Nizam who will be the emperor of India.

He further added,

> If you ask me in advance, I would face anarchy to foreign rule, whether British or any other. I would unhesitatingly plump for anarchy, say, the rule of Nizam supported by the Chiefs becoming feudatory to him or supported by the border Muslim tribes. In my estimation, it will be cent per cent domestic. It will be Home rule, though, far from self-rule or Swaraj.

This astounding statement infuriated Savarkar to no end. He said Gandhi knew as little of Indian history as Hebrew.[54] He reminded Gandhi that the rule of an Alauddin Khilji or an Aurangzeb was also a cent per cent domestic rule, but the Hindus detested it as veritable hell. He then declared that any Muslim rule in future will be similarly hated and overthrown by a new Shivaji, a Bajirao or a Ranjit Singh.[55] Savarkar's words proved prophetic as evident from the fate suffered by Hindus in today's Pakistan, where they are oppressed, and Hindu girls are regularly abducted and converted to Islam. This hapless minority in Pakistan looks to a Ranjit Singh to rescue them. On the other hand, Gandhi was proved wrong when eight years later, his disciple Sardar Patel smashed the Pakistan inclinations of the Nizam, thus vindicating the Savarkar-led Hindu Mahasabha agitation against the Hyderabad State in 1939.

Significantly, the Hindu Mahasabha was perhaps the only party that truly understood the threat to India's unity and integrity in the Muslim League's Pakistan resolution and the Congress's meek surrender to Jinnah's aggression. It said that civil war would be inevitable if Partition was thrust on the nation, a prophecy

---

[54]Vinayak Damodar Savarkar, *Veer Savarkar's 'Whirl-wind Propaganda'*, S. Bhide, 1941, p. 239–58.
[55]Ibid.

which proved correct seven years later when lakhs of Hindus and Muslims were killed and scores of Hindu women raped in Partition riots.

Therefore, following the resolution, the party used to regularly hold programmes against the Pakistan scheme on 10 May, the opening day of 'India's first war of independence', which is how Savarkar had described the 1857 episode. Moreover, such anti-Pakistan programmes were also observed by the party on 23 March, the day the Pakistan resolution was passed, right till the day India was partitioned in 1947. This only showed the party's commitment to United India. Similarly, the Sikhs, who were the worst-affected community by Partition, and the Akali Dal threatened Direct Action against the Muslim League's move.

By 1941, there was a deadlock on the Indian political landscape. In a bid to resolve it, eminent jurist and liberal, Sir Tej Bahadur Sapru, convened a non-party conference in Bombay on 13 and 14 March 1941. Several top leaders stayed away from it, particularly from the Congress and the Muslim League, and the meet seemed doomed to fail in terms of its objective. Eventually, intellectual and legal luminaries attended the conference including Sir Nripendra Nath Sarkar, Sir Jagdish Prasad, Sir Chimanlal Setalvad, L.B. Aney, Pandit H.N. Kunzru and Dr S.P. Mukherjee besides Savarkar and Munje.

Savarkar played a crucial role in saving the conference when, on Sapru's request, he spoke eloquently on the representative character of the meet and gave evidence of his great intellect, flexibility on the political turf and grasp of issues facing the embattled nation. He asserted India's right for absolute Indian independence. He said there were leaders at the conference who disagreed with many of his views, but he didn't see why they shouldn't travel together so long as they had a common journey. Savarkar's virtual call to the leaders to agree on at least a common minimum programme for India's independence and related issues gave a boost to the conference in terms of its direction. Savarkar's acceptability amongst a vast section of the Indian leadership greatly increased after this meet, which showed him not only as a man wedded to administering bitter pills, but also as a man who was forward-looking, flexible and had a great grasp on issues grappling the nation.[56]

THEORETICAL HINDUTVA AT WORK

These qualities that Savarkar possessed were revealed once again when in 1941 he questioned the Congress's boycott of the 1941 census. In fact, the Congress, from 1920 onwards, had always opposed census work or population enumeration, which for any government—independent or foreign—is unavoidable purely for the sake of governance. In other words, the census has been an integral part of civil and electoral governance for various objectives such as delivery of public services and representation in legislatures. But the Congress had opposed it because it felt that the census figures would negatively affect its work of bringing Hindus and Muslims together and also lead to caste cleavages.

Questioning the party's hypocrisy, Savarkar asked, 'Why does the Congress not boycott elections? Electorals are also decided on communal basis.'[57] Having understood the mind of Muslim and Christian communal strategists, he always believed that not taking part in the census work would prove suicidal in many ways. For years, he had preached that numerical strength was also one type of strength and the demography recorded in this census would decide the destiny of Hindus, at least for the next decade. It proved true within five years when the Cabinet mission divided the regions on religious lines.

Muslim leaders had, since 1906, argued before the British that the proportion of Muslims to the Hindu majority becomes much larger if a reduction be made for the 'uncivilized portions' (the term was used by the 1906 delegation) of the community enumerated under the heads of animist (read tribals) and other minor religions (read Jainism, Buddhism and Sikhism), as well as for those classes

---

[56]Dhananjay Keer, *Veer Savarkar*, Popular Prakashan Pvt. Ltd.; Second edition, 2019, p. 290, 291.

[57]Balarao Savarkar, *Swatantryaveer Savarkar, Hindu Mahasabha Parva*, p. 29.

who are ordinarily classified as Hindus, but properly speaking are not Hindus at all. Therefore, by reducing Hindus to only caste Hindus, Muslims wanted to overtake the Hindus as a whole in power sharing.[58]

The Hindu Mahasabha was the only party that understood this diabolical plan and its long-term impact. So, it appealed to the government that the definition of Hindu as given by Savarkar should be adopted officially. This was Savarkar's counter to the Muslim League strategy which the Congress never understood.

The population to be recorded in the 1941 census was set to affect the political discussions relating to the Hindu–Muslim problem. So, a visionary Savarkar called upon the Hindus to actively cooperate in this exercise and record their numbers. He appealed to the extended Hindu pantheon including the animist tribals such as Santhsals and Bhils besides Sikhs, Jains, Buddhists, Arya Samajists and Lingayats to write 'Hindu' before or after the name of their sub-religion or group while registering in the census—i.e., Lingayat (Hindu), Sikh (Hindu), Buddhist (Hindu) or Hindu Santhals and Hindu Bhils. He made this appeal on the plea that India was their Holy Land and Fatherland. Savarkar issued instructions to regional and subregional Hindu Mahasabha units to cooperate with census officers. Mahasabha activists worked extensively even in tribal areas of Central India and convinced many tribes to record themselves as Hindus.[59]

He didn't stop at that. Fearing manipulation of numbers to inflate them for laying future claims by the Muslim League, especially in case of Muslim women in burkha, Savarkar asked the authorities to employ Christian and Anglo-Indian lady supervisors to verify Muslim women before registering their numbers. In fact,

---

[58]Address presented to H.E. Lord Minto, Viceroy and Governor General of India, by a deputation of the Muslim community of India on 1st October 1906 at Simla; and reply thereto, http://www.columbia.edu/itc/mealac/pritchett/00ambedkar/ambedkar_partition/appendices/12app.html. Accessed on 17 July 2021.

[59]Dhananjay Keer, *Veer Savarkar*, Popular Prakashan Pvt. Ltd, Second edition, 2019, p. 292, 293.

many rules related to census recording were modified after the Hindu Mahasabha's intervention.[60]

Significantly, Hindus and those like the Sikhs coming under the Hindu pantheon suffered terribly by the boycott of the census in 1921, 1931 and 1941 (in the last one the Hindu Mahasabha tried to limit the damage), under the thoughtless direction of the Congress as much as by attempts by a section of Muslims to increase their numbers. So, it was not surprising that between the 1931 and 1941 census, the Hindu population in Punjab (including Sikhs) turned into a minority from being in majority as compared to Muslims. It was 53 per cent in the 1881 census, 49 per cent in the 1921 census, 48 per cent in the 1931 census and 47 per cent in the 1941 census. The Muslim population, on the other hand, rose from 47 to 53 per cent in Punjab, thus gravely affecting the fate of Punjabi Hindus and Sikhs later when India was partitioned on the basis of religion and population.

In Bengal, the declining Hindu population due to, amongst others, the census policy of the Congress turned it into a Muslim-majority province by 1941. *The Modern Review,* one of India's most popular monthly magazines published from Bengal in those days, in its June and November 1941 issues squarely blamed the Bengal Muslim League for manipulation in the census. It also said that a large section of the local 14 per cent tribals didn't get covered by the census, thus clearly underlining the manipulation by the Muslim League. The boycott of the census by a section of Hindus, especially tribals, under the influence of the Congress policy was another important reason why Muslims became a majority in Bengal.[61]

The Congress policy of boycotting the census was one of the main reasons behind the partition of Punjab and Bengal. While it gave the suicidal direction to the people (read Hindus) to boycott the census saying it was communal to participate in the exercise, it

---

[60]Balarao Savarkar, *Swatantryaveer Savarkar, Hindu Mahasabha Parva,* p. 38.

[61]Dhananjay Keer, *Veer Savarkar,* Popular Prakashan Pvt. Ltd; Second edition, 2019, p. 293, 294.

relied on the same doubtful census figures while negotiating with the Muslim League and the British Cabinet Mission for determining the issue of Pakistan. What Congress did was virtually a double whammy for the Hindus.

In 1941, the two antagonists, Savarkar and Jinnah, one an upholder of the unity and integrity of India and another hell-bent upon breaking it, had a verbal duel which resonated in the nation's political circles. Speaking at the April 1941 session of the Muslim League in Madras, Jinnah condemned the Hindu Mahasabha as a hopeless and incorrigible body.[62] In the same address, he threatened the British saying that if the English failed to create an independent group of Pakistan states, others would come and do it, thus indicating that foreign Muslim powers would be forced to intervene if Britain didn't act on his demand.

Savarkar's response was Shivaji-like—strong as well as strategic. He warned the Congress to see the writing on the wall, come out of its illusions and stop misleading the masses on the issue of Pakistan.

Savarkar gave Jinnah back with logic and aggression. He said that the pan-Islamic alliance that Jinnah had threatened would be met by a Hindu–Buddhist alliance, from Jammu to Japan. He reminded him that in their history of 5,000 years, Hindus had defeated and absorbed many foreign invaders, from Shakas to Huns, and that the Marathas had swallowed the Mughal empire. He warned that the petty parasite states under the name of Pakistan would meet the same fate. He finally reiterated the ever-abiding truth—in India, 'Pakistans' may come and go but Hindustan goes on forever.[63]

Savarkar also used the occasion to unravel his formula for the creation of a united and powerful Indian State. According to him, in order to secure their safety, peace and security in India, Muslims should wholeheartedly and loyally incorporate themselves into the Indian nation on four fundamental principles, which are:

---

[62]V.D. Savarkar, *Historic Statements by Savarkar*, G.P. Parchure, 1967, p. 3.
[63]Vinayak Damodar Savarkar, *Veer Savarkar's 'Whirl-wind Propaganda'*, S. Bhide, 1941, pp. 359–75.

1. Independence and indivisibility of India as a nation.
2. Electoral representation in proportion to the population strength.
3. Public services on merit alone.
4. Guarantee of the fundamental rights of freedom of worship, language, script, etc., to all citizens alike.

Around the same time, Savarkar noticed that the seven new nominations made by Viceroy Lord Linlithgow didn't include a representative of Sikhs and the Depressed Classes. He urged the Viceroy to appoint a Sikh on the council besides nominating Dr Ambedkar, maintaining that 'there was no better candidate to fill the post than Ambedkar'.

INDIVISIBILITY OF INDIA: AN ARTICLE OF FAITH

On 26 July 1941, Savarkar attended the second round of the Sapru conference, where he got the United India resolution passed by the participants, thus indicating yet again that at a time when the atmosphere in the country was tilting towards Partition, he was the only person on the Indian turf for whom India's indivisibility was an article of faith. On 2 August 1941, explaining what Pakistan would entail in the future, Savarkar said:

> Hindus are the majority in India. The rule that comes through the democratic system would be Hindu rule, which is not acceptable to them. That is why they are opposing democracy all over India. They want to divide this country and create Pakistan here. The word 'Pakistan' itself is poisonous. 'Pak' means 'pure' in their language. So, in this country, Hindus are impure and by destroying their language, script, culture and religion, they want to establish Pakistan.[64]

Savarkar also exposed different shades of pro-Pakistan Muslim politics, saying: 'On one hand, they say that democracy is bad

---

[64]Balarao Savarkar, *Swatantryaveer Savarkar, Akhand Hindusthan Ladha Parva*, p. 92.

but on the other hand, they demand Punjab, Bengal and Sindh because there Muslims are in a majority. They want Hyderabad because its king is Muslim and they assert their right on Kashmir because majority of the people there are Muslim.'[65] When Congress president Acharya Kripalani, voicing his support for the demand for Pakistan, said, 'One state will be added with the formation of Pakistan, what else', Savarkar warned that it was beyond Kripalani's imagination the crisis Hindus would have to face if Pakistan came into existence.[66]

Interestingly, the Hindu supporters of Pakistan had argued that Pakistan should be given as a strategic move. It would be an economic failure and a poor Pakistan would then regret and surrender itself to India. Though their analysis was right, they concluded the problem wrongly. Savarkar, in his 1942 presidential address, countered that 'poor Pakistanis' would start plundering prosperous Hindu provinces. He said the pro-Pakistan Hindus, with their surrendering mindset towards religious fanaticism in their elusive search for so-called Hindu–Muslim unity, would end up offering more to Pakistan in terms of resources. It was a masterly prediction by Savarkar that came true later in Punjab.[67]

Some Hindus supported Partition to avoid violence and civil war. While predicting the future of Indo-Pak tensions, Savarkar asked where India would be when those who were now relatively weak and yet talking about civil war, once they get an independent footing as a State and sufficient time and money to organize themselves and that too when they are entrenched on the top of the powerful frontier ranges.[68]

Savarkar was so precise. As soon as it became independent, Pakistan attacked India in Kashmir in 1947 and snatched one-third area of the state. The subsequent wars forced by Pakistan on India in 1965, 1971 and 1999, besides the web of Pakistan-sponsored

---

[65] Ibid.
[66] Ibid.
[67] Veer Savarkar, *Hindu Rashtra Darshan*, Prabhat Prakashan, 2020, p. 197.
[68] Ibid. 196.

terrorism that continues to claim Indian blood, including that of patriotic Muslims, proves that Savarkar was the only person who could predict the price that India would have to pay in the future for allowing the formation of Pakistan.

Savarkar was once again prophetic when he predicted the future political situation in India and Pakistan.

> Mind well. Not a single person with Congressite mindset will remain in their Pakistan, but Muslims will remain as a minority in every province of your country, and will always put pressure on Congressite Hindus to bow before Pakistan. And every time for the hypocritical patriotism of Hindu–Muslim unity, you have to make this sacrifice! [69]

Aren't these two sterling predictions made by Savarkar, which have proved to be absolutely true, reason enough for India to officially see Savarkar as the father of India's national security?

---

[69] Ibid.

5
A NATIONALIST'S BATTLE FOR A UNITED INDIA

By the early 1940s, the Hindu Mahasabha, under Savarkar's able leadership, was making its presence felt not only in India's intellectual circles but at the international level as well. This was primarily due to its president's shrewd diplomacy and politics that was based on the protection of national interest. During his political leadership, Savarkar showed the uncanny ability to connect with the international media. He tried to make best use of the international situation during World War II to attain independence for United India by bringing pressure on the British rulers.

Therefore, international experts and media persons were naturally drawn to Savarkar's magnetic appeal and interviewed him on the World War II situation and his stand on various issues connected to Indian politics. These included Sir John Evelyn of *The Spectator*, London, Prof. Reginald Coupland of Oxford University, who came to study the political constitution of India, John Magruder of *The New York Times* and T.A. Raman, special correspondent of the North American Newspapers Alliance.[1] However, sadly, historians of the freedom struggle of almost all hues have, for various reasons, underplayed Savarkar's stellar role as the leader of a party unequivocally representing the majority and his skillful use of the international situation to bring pressure on the British.

---

[1]Dhananjay Keer, *Veer Savarkar*, Popular Prakashan Pvt. Ltd; Second edition, 2019, p. 301, 302.

It was during World War II that Savarkar demonstrated his strategic and diplomatic skills in pursuit of his nationalist goals. On 20 August 1941, he sent a cable to the US president, Franklin D. Roosevelt, asking him to come clear on whether the Atlantic Charter[2]—which was announced by Roosevelt and the British prime minister Winston Churchill—covered India or not and whether the US was willing to promise full political freedom to India within a year of the war's ending. He further told Roosevelt that if it was not so, then India can't but construe the declaration of the Atlantic Charter as another stunt like the war aims of the last Anglo-German war and that it was meant only to camouflage imperialistic aggressions. This challenge to the US president was broadcast throughout the world including the US, Germany, England and India. The statement was used by German propagandists to expose the hollowness of the Allied Power's war aims woven around peace, liberty and equality. In fact, the Germans used Savarkar's speeches on world politics as well as his retorts to leaders such as Roosevelt and Churchill in a big way in their broadcast network.

This created a situation in which Churchill was forced to clarify that the Charter applied only to those nations which were under the Nazi yoke. Using Churchill's statement, Savarkar now turned to Roosevelt once again by sending him a cable in which he questioned him on Churchill's statement. Roosevelt didn't respond. However, Savarkar succeeded in exposing the avowed objectives of the Allied Powers to prove his point that without getting carried away by war propaganda of the two sides, India (read the Congress leadership) should look for its own benefit first, as no nation involved in the war was actuated by moral or altruistic motives; they aimed to personally benefit from the war under the garb of high-sounding principles.

Interestingly, Savarkar had sent his first-ever cable to Roosevelt on 23 April 1939 after the US president had appealed to German

---

[2]The Atlantic Charter was a joint declaration released by the US president Franklin D. Roosevelt and the British prime minister Winston Churchill on 14 August 1941 following a meeting of the two heads of government in Newfoundland. The Charter provided a broad statement of US and British war aims.

Chancellor Adolf Hitler to refrain from putting human civilization in danger. Savarkar asked Roosevelt that if his appeal to Hitler was actually driven by his anxiety for safeguarding human freedom and democracy, then he should ask Britain to end the armed domination of India. 'A great nation like Hindustan can surely claim at least as much international justice as small nations do,' Savarkar told Roosevelt.[3]

Savarkar's idea of this great nation claiming its independence received a boost when a few years later, Japanese victories in the Eastern world, including its capture of Singapore and the destruction of two powerful British warships, created multiple problems for Britain. Savarkar's shrewd mind grasped the situation, and he started building pressure on Britain for nationalizing the government structure in India and for giving India a co-partnership in an Indo-British Commonwealth with other self-governing constituents, including Britain itself. In doing so, Savarkar warned the British that if Japanese forces, when they reach Indian borders, make a proclamation that their immediate objective is to free India from British clutches, such an announcement would capture the imagination of Indian people and would lead to incalculable political complications.[4] It was a master stroke in the form of a veiled threat.

CROSSING SWORDS WITH CRIPPS

The British empire faced an unprecedented crisis when Rangoon came under the Japanese army in March 1942. Savarkar sent Churchill a cable to the same effect seeking nationalization of the British Indian government (i.e., with more representation) and a co-partnership equal with Britain in an Indo-British Commonwealth. A similar pressure was also brought by the Congress. As a result, Churchill was virtually forced to announce

---

[3]Dhananjay Keer, *Veer Savarkar*, Popular Prakashan Pvt. Ltd; Second edition, 2019, p. 298.

[4]Savarkar's statement, 17 February 1942; Dhananjay Keer, *Veer Savarkar*, Popular Prakashan Pvt. Ltd; Second edition, 2019.

the British government's decision to send Sir Stafford Cripps, Lord Privy Seal and Leader of the House of Commons, to India to discuss the Indian situation in the political as well as the war context. One of the aims behind the decision was obviously to impress the American people about the British aims regarding India.

However, Cripps arrived in India on 22 March that year with a predetermined aim which became clear when he unravelled his scheme. It carried seeds of India's balkanization. It promised a new Indian Union with a dominion status association with Britain upon the end of the war, but granted Indian provinces the right to secede from the Union in the name of self-determination, if they so desired.

The Hindu Mahasabha accepted the first part but rejected the second. But shockingly, the Congress virtually accepted Partition while reacting to Cripps's proposal as exemplified in its April 1942 resolution. The resolution said that the Congress couldn't think in terms of compelling people of any territorial unit of India to join the Indian Union against their declared and established will. This it did after conceding in the same resolution that the Cripps scheme's second part could give fillip to fissiparous elements. However, the grounds on which the Cripps proposal was virtually rejected by the Congress were not the seeds of balkanization of India that it carried, but the fact that it didn't promise the defence portfolio to Indians in the Viceroy's executive council which Cripps had guaranteed to Indianize during war time.

The Congress's virtual support to the secession clause in the Cripps proposal gave further fillip to the Muslim League's Pakistan scheme. Earlier, Gandhi had indirectly endorsed the Pakistan scheme in the name of self-determination under the weight of his ultra-egalitarian ideology and now the Congress as a whole did the same thing. This virtually helped Jinnah in his efforts to emerge as the sole leader of Indian Muslims and brought down the stature of other established Muslim leaders. In fact, reacting to the Cripps mission's failure, Gandhi continued on the suicidal path. Writing in *Harijan*, he said there was no need for Indians to blame the British as Indian people themselves were responsible because attainment of Independence was impossible till India had solved the Hindu–Muslim communal tangle. In the same article, he wrote: 'If the vast majority of Muslims regard themselves as a separate nation having nothing in common with the Hindus and others, no power on earth can compel them to think otherwise.'[5]

The Congress's and Gandhi's stand before Cripps was astounding. In fact, senior Congress leader Dr Pattabhi Sitaramayya, while commenting on the 1942 Congress resolution a few years later, admitted: 'It is evident that the passage concedes the division of India into more than one State and gives a go-by to the unity and integrity of India.'[6]

Great conquerors such as Vikramaditya, Skandagupta and Chandragupta Maurya had fought both internal as well as external enemies to provide security to their countrymen and to weld India into one nation. More recently, the same vision, bravery and skill had been demonstrated by Maharana Pratap, Chhatrapati Shivaji and Guru Gobind Singh. However, now, with the Congress's abject surrender to the Muslim League's unjust demands, it appeared as if these great men had been born in some other country.

In this grim situation, in which India was fast sliding towards disintegration, Savarkar and the Hindu Mahasabha alone maintained the spirit of these great men as they waged a battle against both the pan-Islamism of the Muslim League and the Congress's surrender.

Reacting to the Congress resolution, Savarkar issued a historic statement. He said both the Hindus in the Congress and the section of non-Congress Hindus didn't believe him when he had been saying for almost three years, that the Congress would eventually surrender to the demand for Pakistan and even demonstrate that act as an acid test of Indian patriotism. He said: 'They wanted evidence to prove my assertions. Now here comes the evidence with vengeance. ...The Congress which calls itself as Indian National

---

[5]*Harijan*, 13 April 1942; B.N. Jog, *Threat of Islam: Indian Dimensions*, Mumbai (Bombay): Unnati Prakashan, 1994, pp. 276–77.
[6]B. Pattabhi Sitaramayya, *History of the Indian National Congress Volume II (1935–1947)*, Mumbai (Bombay): Padma Publications; First edition, 1947, p. 635.

Congress...has stabbed a stroke in the unity and integrity of the Indian nation in the back.'[7]

In his 1942 presidential address at the Kanpur session of the Hindu Mahasabha, Savarkar declared that 'self-determination is more dangerous than [the] Pakistan scheme'. He argued further that:

> The principle of self-determination cannot but form a veritable sword of Damocles kept hanging on the head of the Central State. It will be practically an invitation and instigation to any province to secede and blow up at a stroke the whole ground on which the Indian State has to stand. The majority of the Moslems, is the only ground behind the Pakistani demand for secession; but in admitting the principle of provincial secession, we shall have to face the demand on the part of any province at any time on any economical and any other conceivable ground to secede from the Central Government.[8]

The Congress's stand on the Cripps proposal revealed that independence of a divided India was the aim of the grand old party, while the Hindu Mahasabha wanted independence of United India. Therefore, not surprisingly, intellectuals of great standing reposed faith in Savarkar and the Hindu Mahasabha for guarding the unity and integrity of India. Liberal leaders such as Sir C.P. Ramaswami Iyer, Ramananda Chatterjee, V.S. Srinivasa Sastri and Sir V.N. Chandavarkar, who figured amongst the country's key intellectuals and were by no means communal, were concerned over the worsening situation marked by the Congress's meek surrender before the Muslim League's aggression. Appealing to Hindus to actively support the Hindu Mahasabha for the sake of the nation's unity and integrity, Sastri was blunt and even went to the extent of telling common Congress workers to support the Hindu Mahasabha to prevent the partition of their motherland. He said: 'We all cherish the unity of India and we will all resist any

---

[7] V.D. Savarkar, *Historic Statements by Savarkar*, G.P. Parchure, 1967.
[8] Veer Savarkar, *Hindu Rashtra Darshan*, Prabhat Prakashan, 2020.

attempt to break up what we take so much pride in.'⁹ Ramananda Chatterjee, editor of the *Modern Review* and regarded as the father of Indian journalism, while addressing a public meeting at Calcutta, said: 'I am sure if we are true sons and daughters of India it shall never be divided.'[10]

Interestingly, one of the highlights of Cripps's India visit was his interaction with Savarkar in Delhi in the presence of the luminaries of the Hindu Mahasabha, including Munje and S.P. Mukherjee. Cripps, whose skillful diplomacy had played a key role in setting Russia against Germany and had floored several Indian leaders, including Nehru, was virtually defeated by Savarkar's sheer knowledge of Indian history and his belief in the indivisibility of India that was based on unmatched logic.

Savarkar skillfully counteracted Cripps's argument that the right to self-determination, which Britain had proposed to the Indian people before giving them Independence, was not a new concept on the world stage. Cripps cited the examples of Canada and South Africa amongst other countries to support his argument. However, the diminutive Savarkar turned these arguments on Cripps's head, and said that the examples of India and Canada were not comparable because the Canadian States were already separate entities when they were asked if they would like to form themselves into an organic State or one unit. While India, he said, was already culturally and administratively a united entity.

Savarkar further reiterated that politically and administratively the British government admitted the oneness of India. Savarkar asked,

> Doesn't [the] British Government call the Government of India as Indian Government and its army and navy as Indian army and Indian navy and Bombay and Bengal as provinces of India. All these factors prove that India is already an undivided, centralized nation and State. So, the right to self-

---

[9]Dhananjay Keer, *Veer Savarkar*, Popular Prakashan Pvt. Ltd; Second edition, 2019, p. 306.
[10]Ibid.

determination is to be given to India as a whole and not to its administrative units.[11]

He also warned Cripps that any Congress–League pact that pointed towards the vivisection of India won't be binding on the Hindu Mahasabha.

As soon as the meeting between the Hindu Mahasabha and Cripps ended, Savarkar told his colleagues that his party will fight the Pakistan scheme to the last breath. When Savarkar returned to Bombay after the meeting, the governor of Bombay, Roger Lumley, 11th Earl of Scarbrough, met him and tried to explore his mind but was told that the Hindu Mahasabha could join a national government only if the Cripps scheme was freed from the secession clause. Cripps wanted to meet Savarkar for a second time, but he (Savarkar) believed it was futile to meet him again till the secession clause remained a part of the Cripps scheme.

Savarkar's logic not only silenced Cripps, but it also drew appreciation from the Congress mouthpiece, the *National Herald*. The newspaper said it disagreed with Savarkar on several points but must admit that 'he is one of the few men of our age who has made history and contributed to [the] reawakening of our people. He showed the old fire in him when he took up the thoughtless challenge thrown to the Hindu Mahasabha by the Government of Bihar and obtained a resounding victory at Bhagalpur. With Sir Stafford Cripps, he crossed swords which the former will never forget.'[12]

Savarkar displayed the same resolution when he was interviewed by well-known US journalist, Louis Fischer. Though his provocative questions to Savarkar virtually showed Fischer as a sympathizer of the Pakistan scheme, Savarkar replied to him with resolute calmness. To Fischer's question that the Pakistan demand had logic and why the Hindu Mahasabha doesn't concede, Savarkar replied with a blunt question: 'Why don't you (Americans) grant

---

[11]Dhananjay Keer, *Veer Savarkar*, Popular Prakashan Pvt. Ltd; Second edition, 2019, p. 304.

[12]*The Mahratta*, Pune, 28 August 1942.

"Negrosthan" to Negroes?'[13] In reaction, Fischer said that would be anti-national. In turn, Savarkar said just as the Negrosthan proposal was anti-national, the Pakistan demand too was anti-national in India. However, Fischer persisted with his argument and told Savarkar that if Pakistan was not granted, then Indian nationalists should be prepared for another Panipat. Savarkar retorted with his profound knowledge of world history: 'You should not forget the debacles in Dunkirk and Crete.'[14] After such retorts from Savarkar, Fischer was totally silenced and never crossed swords with him again. Perhaps the US journalist was unaware that he was taking on one of the intellectual giants of India.

Savarkar's penchant for keeping the international press informed about his political activities meant that his actions as the Hindu Mahasabha president were being observed on the global stage. He was already a known name in international forums, thanks to his international diplomacy and his earlier role as a great revolutionary whose case had been debated in the International Arbitration Court at The Hague as well as by ambassadors of leading western nations. Therefore, when Savarkar rejected Cripps's proposal, some elements from the outside world expressed surprise. To set the record straight, Savarkar sent a wire to *The New York Times* drawing an apt analogy. It explained why the Hindu Mahasabha appreciated the Cripps proposal to grant equal partnership with Britain but rejected the secession clause in it. He said Hindus are prepared to guarantee legitimate safeguards to the minorities but can never tolerate their efforts to create a State within a State, as the League of Nations put it. He said: 'Americans who went to war even with their kith and kin on the question of secession and saved the integrity of their union cannot fail to appreciate and uphold the Hindu opposition to vivisection of India.'[15]

It was clear that Savarkar was possibly the only leader on the

---

[13] Dhananjay Keer, *Veer Savarkar*, Popular Prakashan Pvt. Ltd; Second edition, 2019, p. 304.
[14] Ibid. 324.
[15] V.D. Savarkar, *Historic Statements by Savarkar*, G.P. Parchure, 1967.

Indian turf at that time who had such command over international issues along with the statecraft needed for the nation's benefit. This perhaps forced a rethink on the part of the Congress leadership. The party sensed that its surrendering response to Muslim separatism could prove politically fatal before the people, particularly in the backdrop of the public response that the Hindu Mahasabha received in the Hyderabad and Bhagalpur struggles for Hindu rights. Not only had the Congress acted in an uncharacteristic manner by declaring a boycott of the Hindu Mahasabha after the Hyderabad struggle, its feeble stance against Muslim aggression was being opposed by its own second-rung leadership and workers. So, in an astute move, the party's top leadership allowed Jagat Narain Lal, a former Hindu Mahasabhaite, to pass the Akhand Hindustan Resolution at the CWC meeting at Allahabad in May 1942, emphasizing the indivisibility of the nation and vowing to put down fissiparous tendencies in the country.[16]

This resolution was opposed by Rajaji (Chakravarti Rajagopalachari), who had been carrying on secret communication with the Muslim League to settle the Hindu–Muslim problem for quite some time, if necessary, by granting Pakistan through a plebiscite in Muslim-majority areas. In fact, five days before the Allahabad resolution, Rajaji had got a resolution passed by the Madras Congress Legislature supporting the Pakistan scheme if Muslims insisted on it.

Rajaji maintained that the Congress's Akhand Hindustan Resolution would impede settlement with the Muslim League. However, Rajaji's pro-Muslim League proposal at Allahabad was defeated by the CWC. He managed to get just 15 votes against 120 votes. But in the final tally, all this amounted to political chicanery only. On being questioned by party leader Abdul Latif of Hyderabad, the then Congress president Maulana Abul Kalam Azad replied that the Akhand Hindustan Resolution in no way affected the party's earlier resolution conceding the right to self-

---

[16]Dhananjay Keer, *Veer Savarkar*, Popular Prakashan Pvt. Ltd; Second edition, 2019, p. 304,305, 306, 307, 308, 314.

determination by provinces.[17] Significantly, all nationalist Muslims were prominent in opposing the Akhand Hindustan Resolution.[18]

Savarkar insisted that the Rajaji Plan had fundamental errors. Reacting to the plan during his visit to Rawalpindi in July that year, he said Rajaji's belief that the Hindu–Muslim problem would be solved by granting Pakistan to Muslims was totally erroneous because the formation of Pakistan would put Muslims in a more effective position to make further demands. It would be a folly to believe that Britain would grant India independence as soon as Hindu–Muslim unity is achieved.

'What force does Jinnah use to sway Britain which is at war with Germany and Japan? How many armies and lethal arms, such as tanks and aircraft, would he have? So, why should Hindus surrender their rights in the name of the improbable Swaraj?' Savarkar asked.[19]

Savarkar's unshakable faith in the indivisibility of India was questioned by a communication received from the Jammu & Kashmir National Conference, a pro-Pakistan Muslim body, after his visit to Jammu and Kashmir in July 1942. Here, he addressed a series of popular public meetings including three in Srinagar. The party that had earlier appreciated Savarkar's forthright and clear-cut stand on national issues tried to entrap Savarkar in the garb of democracy owing to his struggle for majority Hindu rights in Hyderabad. The party asked Savarkar to clarify whether he was prepared to apply his popular principle of majority rule to the Kashmir problem and support the claim of Muslim majority in Jammu and Kashmir.

Savarkar's reply was masterly and demonstrated his grasp on issues of national security. He skillfully and logically replied that his principle applied only to that majority that owed undivided loyalty

---

[17]Nazir Yar Jung (ed.), *The Pakistan Issue*, p. 119; H.V. Seshadri, *The Tragic Story of Partition*, Sahitya Sindhu Prakashan, 2015, p. 143.

[18]Dhananjay Keer, *Mahatma Gandhi: Popular Saint & Unarmed Prophet*, Popular Prakashan Pvt. Ltd, 1973, p. 700.

[19]Balarao Savarkar, *Swatantryaveer Savarkar: Akhand Hindusthan Ladha Parv*, p. 201.

and allegiance to the Indian nation and State, but didn't apply to that majority that affirmed to the Pakistani creed. He maintained that those who were not committed to the unity and integrity of India had no right to the democratic principle of representation in proportion to the population. The Kashmiri Muslims, he said, had never declared their consent to apply the principle they were demanding in Kashmir to majority Hindus in the Muslim States of Bhopal and Hyderabad and, therefore, had no right to ask him such a question. Savarkar further said that although Hindus were in a minority in Kashmir, they were part of a national majority and couldn't be seen as a separate entity.[20] Thus, Savarkar exposed the efforts of the party to use the principles of democracy for furthering pan-Islamist aims.

MEASURED RESPONSE TO QUIT INDIA

After the failure of the Cripps Mission, the Congress was under public pressure to do something spectacular against the British intransigence. As a result, the CWC met at Wardha in July 1942 and deliberated various options for 11 days. It finally agreed to Gandhi's suggestion that the Congress should call upon the British to leave India as the party believed that the Hindu–Muslim problem couldn't be solved till the British left the country.

However, the decision was not taken before major differences surfaced between top leaders on the issue. Gandhi and his lieutenants, including Sardar Patel and Dr Rajendra Prasad, believed that the time was opportune for such a call. But party president Maulana Azad and Nehru thought the time was inopportune as the Japanese army had already reached Burma and any such serious challenge to the British power at that juncture would be put down with an iron hand.

Gandhi, however, overrode them in the belief that the Japanese pressure would make the British more amenable if they were asked

---

[20]Dhananjay Keer, *Veer Savarkar*, Popular Prakashan Pvt Ltd; Second edition, 2019, p. 226, 227.

to quit India at that moment. Gandhi saw the impending agitation following such a call as a non-violent rebellion. The party gave the leadership of the movement to him.

It is widely believed that one of the reasons for the Quit India call was also the apparent fear in Gandhi's mind that the revolutionary fervour ignited by great revolutionaries such as Bhagat Singh and Savarkar was still alive amongst the common men and that some kind of safety valve was needed to give vent to the people's aspirations, albeit in a non-violent manner.

Gandhi gave the Quit India call on 8 August 1942. The very next day, all the major leaders including Gandhi were put behind bars. The British were adamant about not releasing Gandhi. So, a group of leaders gathered at Dr M.R. Jayakar's Bombay residence to force the British to release Gandhi. It included Congress leaders such as Bhulabhai Desai, K.M. Munshi, Allah Bux Soomro and Devdas Gandhi and, of course, Savarkar. Jayakar and Tej Bahadur Sapru implored Savarkar to speak on the subject of Gandhi's release. He responded positively but insisted that pressure should be applied for the release of other leaders too, including Netaji's elder brother, Sarat Chandra Bose. Savarkar was requested to take up the issue with the Viceroy, who had great respect for Savarkar's intellect and profound knowledge of issues. But due to ill health, Savarkar couldn't attend the second round of the conference the next day. He also missed his previously decided engagement with President Roosevelt's envoy, William Phillips, who was on a mission to India and was meeting prominent leaders separately to seek their views on the war as well as on the Indian political situation.

Meanwhile, owing to Savarkar's support on the issue of Gandhi's release, the assembled leaders issued a joint statement the next day seeking Gandhi's release, with Savarkar as one of the signatories to the appeal. However, when Savarkar discovered that his opinion that the release appeal should be for all the key leaders who were in jail was omitted, he issued a statement that his name was wrongly included as he was not present at the meeting where the decision to send this joint letter to the Viceroy was taken. This annoyed the other leaders present at the meeting. Clearly, Savarkar could have avoided embarrassing the leaders, but he was made of sterner stuff when it came to his beliefs.

Jinnah dubbed the Quit India call 'as an attempt by the Congress and Gandhiji to intimidate the British and establish a Hindu Raj'.[21] The virtual non-participation of the Muslims in the Quit India agitation was yet another proof of the divorce of the Muslim community from any public agitations against the British rulers, particularly after the failure of the Khilafat movement to protect their communal interest. The movement was almost entirely led by Hindus, with little support from Muslims in most parts of undivided India.[22]

The Hindu Mahasabha kept away from the call as it knew that the Congress had no solution to the Hindu–Muslim problem except surrendering to the demands of the Muslim League, including the demand for Pakistan in the name of self-determination. Savarkar's reaction to the Quit India call was measured, it being based on circumspection. He put three conditions before the Congress for joining hands with it in the larger interest of the nation:

1. The Congress should irreversibly stand for the unity and integrity of India.
2. It should promise that it won't accept any pact with the anti-national Muslim League.
3. It would accept Hindi with the Nagari (Devanagari) script as the Lingua Franca of India.[23]

In the same statement, Savarkar held out a warning saying that it was his considered opinion that Gandhi would agree to not one but many Pakistans.[24] Savarkar also didn't deviate from the

---

[21]R.C. Majumdar, *History of the Freedom Movement in India (Volume III)*, South Asia Books, 1988, p. 550, 562.
[22]Dhananjay Keer, *Veer Savarkar*, Popular Prakashan Pvt Ltd; Second edition, 2019, p. 543.
[23]Ibid. p. 322.
[24]Dhananjay Keer, *Veer Savarkar*, Popular Prakashan Pvt. Ltd; Second edition, 2019.

fundamentals of his thinking. When people were resigning their official positions in protest against the British's repressive measures during the Quit India movement, he strongly advised his supporters against resigning their posts in local bodies, legislatures, ministries, various governmental committees and the armed forces. The great visionary in him appealed to his supporters not to get carried away by emotions but conserve their energy for the real battle, the one for protecting India's unity and integrity. His advice would prove crucial just a few years later after the Muslim League's Direct Action call.

However, Savarkar's conditional offer for cooperation with the Congress had no effect on the party. On the contrary, the Congress's speed of Muslim appeasement acquired further momentum when it said that residual powers would be vested in the provincial governments along with the right to self-determination. Thereafter, things reached a point of no return when in a letter to Jinnah, Gandhi offered that the Congress would have no objection if the British transferred all power to the Muslim League on behalf of the Indian nation to avert Partition.[25] He said that the Congress could even join such a Muslim League government. According to Pyarelal Nayyar, Gandhi would have met Jinnah much earlier had he not been all of a sudden put into detention.[26]

The forceful momentum of the Quit India call continued for a few weeks and was marked by huge violence and bloodshed. It continued sporadically for a few months before receding. The violence following the administration's repressive measures was almost unprecedented on a public scale. According to an estimate, people killed in the violence, mostly at the hands of British forces, were in thousands. Besides, nearly 250 railway stations were burnt or damaged, 750 post offices were ransacked or damaged, 70 police stations were burnt and 3,500 telephone or telegram lines were cut.

---

[25]Pyarelal, *Mahatma Gandhi: The Last Phase, Vol. 1*, Ahmedabad: Navajivan Publishing House, 1956, p. 69.
[26]Ibid. 70.

The Quit India call is seen as a success by some as it worked up a strong current of nationalism amongst the people. But an honest assessment of the call shows that in terms of net result, it was a failure, as Gandhi and his supporters had not done any major planning to make the movement sustainable over a long period of time. They had also miscalculated as they didn't expect immediate arrest of all the top leaders and the utterly repressive measures by the British to put down the unrest. The British were, in fact, forced to act as the Japanese were closing in on them and as a result remaining passive on the issue would have affected the war efforts of the British and the Allied Powers.

Although the Hindu Mahasabha didn't join the movement, Savarkar was scathing in his condemnation of the repressive measures adopted by the British Indian government against the Congress leaders and the common people who joined the struggle and suffered on an unimaginable scale. He said the personal sympathies of the Hindu Mahasabhaites were with the Congressmen in their suffering for a patriotic cause.[27] He warned the British that nothing would solve the problem except the British parliament making an immediate proclamation granting India the status of a free and equal partner in the Indo-British Commonwealth. He also sent a cable to the British press warning the English people that British bayonets might suppress the violent outbursts of popular discontent but they can never appease the national discontent, thus telling Britain that its violent measures would only worsen the situation and fail to suppress the national aspirations.

Savarkar further revealed in a message to the people of Britain a five-point constitutional plan in the form of demands for securing cooperation of the Indian people in the war effort. These included:

1. Making India a free nation in the Indo-British Commonwealth, with equal status with Britain.
2. Indianization of the Central Executive Council, whose decisions would be binding on the Viceroy, who would

---

[27] Veer Savarkar, *Historic Statements by Savarkar*, G.P. Parchure, 1967.

however reserve the right to decide on matters of defence and internal security.
3. Indianization of the military forces.
4. Similar Indianized executive councils at the provincial level.
5. Framing of a national constitution on the constitutional demands after the end of the war.

Savarkar's clinical demands received much publicity in the British media including in such eminent publications like *The Times, Manchester Guardian, Yorkshire Post, Daily Herald* and *News Chronicle*.

However, these demands fell on deaf ears as Churchill insisted he had not become the British premier to preside over the liquidation of the British empire and informed the British parliament of the sufficient presence of British forces in India to tackle the situation.

Savarkar reacted to Churchill's blow to India's national aspirations with fury and logic. In his riposte, Savarkar reminded Churchill of the fate of Nebuchadnezzar II, the Babylonian king, who had to experience doom after a similar boastful tone.[28] He added that the future of India didn't lie in Churchill's lap, but in the lap of war gods.

Around this time, the Muslim League decided to send its delegations to foreign countries to win support for its Pakistan scheme on the basis of Muslim aspirations. Savarkar too decided to send a Hindu Mahasabha delegation abroad to explain the logic behind United India and expose at a global level the British propaganda that the Cripps mission had failed due to the internal conflicts of the Indian people and not due to the unwillingness of the British. However, both the Hindu Mahasabha and the Muslim League delegations could not leave India due to imposition of restrictions by the British citing the World War II situation.

By now, Jinnah and other Muslim leaders had become restive. They threatened Hindus with external pan-Islamic invasion.

---

[28]Veer Savarkar, *Historic Statements by Savarkar*, G.P. Parchure, 1967.

Savarkar questioned the military capacity and the contemporary global political position of Islamic countries such as Turkey, Persia and Afghanistan, and declared: 'I can only remind them that the Hindus have also some trump cards in their hand...the Hindus too have a united Hindu–Buddhist front from Jammu to Japan.'[29] Savarkar wasn't day dreaming. Several years ago, founder of the INA, Rash Behari Bose, who drew revolutionary inspiration from Savarkar in his young age, wrote him a letter in 1938 addressing him as 'My dear Savarkarji Maharaj'. He expressed thoughts on empowering Hindus thus:

> Instead of misusing our energy for the so-called Hindu Muslim entente, let us revive the Hindu spirit of old India... When the Hindus become strong, unified and powerful, I am sure our Muslim friends will gladly join us in the struggle for freedom. But what will happen to India I shudder to think, if the Hindus still cannot perceive the real situation and deceive themselves into the belief that all is well with the Hindus. Hindu Sangathan movement should be carried out to every corner of India. Hindu organisations should be strengthened in every conceivable way... The Hindu movement should not be confined to India alone. As I wrote in my last letter, the Buddhists are also Hindus, and every attempt should be made to create a Hindu block extending from the Indian Ocean up to the Pacific Ocean. For this purpose, the Hindu Sabha should take immediate steps for establishing branches of Mahasabha in Japan, China, Siam and other countries of the Pacific and sending their representatives for creating solidarity among the Eastern races.[30]

One can only imagine the fate of the separatists had the India National Army succeeded in its plan!

It was this interest—protecting Hindu rights—that was uppermost in Savarkar's mind when he directed the Hindu

---

[29] Veer Savarkar, *Historic Statements by Savarkar*, G.P. Parchure, 1967.
[30] T.R. Sareen, *Hindu Mahasabha Tryst with United India*, Eastern Book Linkers, 2019, p. 250.

Mahasabha to join hands with the Muslim League to form coalition governments in provinces such as Sindh and Bengal during 1941–42. Pseudo-secularists, leftists and pan-Islamists have used this episode to depict the Hindu Mahasabha and the Muslim League as two sides of the same coin. However, any judgement on Savarkar in this episode without considering his view and the related background is bound to be biased and lopsided.

According to the Census Report of 1941, non-Muslims constituted 45.7 per cent of the total population of Bengal; deducting Christians and 'others', Hindus must be taken to constitute 45.1 per cent of the population. However, even the official figures were not given due weight in the case of Hindus, as per the 1935 constitutional reforms. They were given only 80 seats (32 per cent) in the Bengal Legislative Assembly comprising 250 members. The Muslims got 119 seats (47.6 per cent) and found steady support from 30 Europeans. This arrangement totally excluded Hindus from the sphere of provincial administration. The Muslims became the rulers of Bengal as subordinate partners of the British Indian government. There was not a single Hindu minister in these Cabinets since 1937.[31] Savarkar had understood this well.

After the resignation of Congress ministries as part of the party's non-cooperation and boycott policy following differences with the British government over World War II, several provinces came under Governor's rule. In that situation, in order to protect Hindu interest, which would have otherwise got trampled (the British were already tilting towards the Muslim League following that party's cooperative attitude on World War II issues as compared to that of the Congress), the Hindu Mahasabha tried to form coalition ministries with the League and other Muslim-dominated parties such as the Krishak Praja Party in Bengal and Sindh. Apart from protecting Hindu minority, Savarkar also had the vision to sense the strategic importance of these two frontier provinces during the war.

---

[31] *Short Report of Hindu Mahasabha Relief Activities during Calcutta Killing and Noakhali Carnage*, Sagwan Press, 2018, p. 4.

His strategy was totally opposed to the Congress's boycott policy, as exemplified by his statement:

> In the Hindu-minority provinces, whenever a Muslim Ministry seemed inevitable whether it was sponsored by the Muslim League or otherwise and Hindu interests could be served better by joining it, the Hindusabhaites should try as a matter of right to capture as many seats as possible in the Ministry and do the best they can to safeguard the interest of the Hindu minority.[32]

Savarkar called his party's decision to join the Muslim League in coalition governments as 'responsive or aim-oriented cooperation'[33]. Explaining this further, Savarkar said:

> It means cooperating when the opponent is favouring our goal and opposing when the opponent goes against our aim. That means if the Muslim League is in a position to form the Government then join them to form a joint cabinet so as to get entry into the legislative assembly. That would make passing of anti-Hindu laws and anti-national resolutions difficult for the Muslim League. Also it would make easy for the Hindu Mahasabha to oppose such resolutions.[34]

Under this strategy, Savarkar asked S.P. Mukherjee to join the Muslim League's Fazlul Haq's Ministry in Bengal and get many pro-Hindu works done at the provincial level. In fact, Savarkar had congratulated the Sindh Hindu Mahasabha for joining the Muslim League ministry.

He, however, laid down certain broad principles to guide the representatives of the Hindu Mahasabha in the formation of such ministries. He said:

> They should oppose publicly every attempt on the part of the Muslims in the Ministry to support Pakistan or the

---

[32]Veer Savarkar, *Historic Statements by Savarkar*, G.P. Parchure, 1967.
[33]Akshay Jog, *Veer Savarkar: Allegations and Reality*, pp. 152–58.
[34]Ibid.

treacherous principle of self-determination to secede from India. The Provincial Hindusabhas should be left free in all other details, to agitate against any anti-Hindu step on the part of the Ministry in its collective capacity and if the Hindu Ministers are known to have recorded their protest against such steps, they should not be asked to resign from the Ministry. The leading principle which must be emphasized is that the boycott of a Ministry altogether is bound to be more often than not highly detrimental to Hindu interests. Under the present circumstances, the Hindu Mahasabha should try to capture as many positions of vantage as possible in order to assert the rights of the Hindu Party as an indispensable constituent factor, apart from the League or the Congress in any future constitution to be framed after the war.[35]

Thus, the basic difference between the Hindu Mahasabha and the Congress was that the former joined the government to resist Pakistan and protect Hindu interests amid Pakistani atmosphere, while Rajaji mooted the idea of a Congress–Muslim League coalition along with a plebiscite to concede Pakistan and therefore barter Hindu interests.

Revolutionary-turned-radical humanist M.N. Roy heaped high praise on Savarkar's willingness to join hands with Muslims and commended his sense of 'realism' and understanding in spite of his long incarceration and absence from politics.

It was on this issue of coalition governments that Savarkar and Jinnah came very close to meeting each other in 1942. Jinnah was keen to capture power in the Muslim-majority provinces, even with the help of the Hindu Mahasabha, because unlike the Muslim-minority provinces, he was unable to create a fear psychosis of Hindu domination in the minds of the Muslims in Muslim-majority provinces. His plan was to capture power here so that he could make an impression on the Muslims of these provinces which included Bengal, Sindh, Punjab and the North-West Frontier Province.

---

[35]Veer Savarkar, *Historic Statements by Savarkar*, G.P. Parchure, 1967.

Jinnah requested Dr Hemandas Wadhwani, a Hindu minister in the Sindh Cabinet whom he knew well, to arrange a meeting with Savarkar to discuss the possibility of a joint Hindu Mahasabha–Muslim League government in provinces. When Wadhwani extended Jinnah's invitation to Savarkar over tea, he put two conditions before Jinnah: first, Jinnah should suggest an alternative to the Pakistan (Partition) scheme and second, since he (Savarkar) was the leader of the majority, it is Jinnah who should come and see him. Jinnah responded by saying Savarkar must honour his invitation as he was elder to Savarkar in both age and politics and it was he who had invited Savarkar. But Savarkar again refused. So, Jinnah suggested that the two could meet and talk in a car. Savarkar turned down the offer, after which Wadhwani suggested that both should meet at his hotel room in Bombay, where he was staying. Both Savarkar and Jinnah agreed to this suggestion. Jinnah even expressed his high regard for Savarkar through Wadhwani.[36]

In the meantime, Jinnah even agreed to tone down his demands and agreed to population percentage-based representation in the proposed coalition ministries as Savarkar had demanded instead of 50 per cent seat for Muslims, which was his original proposal. But the Jinnah-Savarkar meeting was not destined to be. Due to some political developments, Jinnah conveyed to Wadhwani that he won't be able to meet Savarkar for two months and then the proposal died a natural death.

Though Savarkar was fully aware of the limitations of the Muslim-dominated coalition ministries, he wanted to use it as a stepping stone to secure Hindu interests in unfavourable circumstances. In a historic letter dated 14 January 1944 intercepted by the Intelligence Services at that time, Savarkar wrote to Sardar Ajit Singh, a prominent leader of the Sikh–League coalition government in Punjab:

> We cannot everyday stop every bill getting passed with the Muslim majority votes nor can we protect the Hindu-Sikh

---

[36]Dhananjay Keer, *Veer Savarkar*, Popular Prakashan Pvt. Ltd; Second edition, 2019, p. 340, 350.

interest as fully and completely in every case in the majority Muslim population. Under such circumstances, the minority has to either surrender absolutely to the majority and not enter the councils and the ministries or utilize whatever seats possible in the Legislatures, Ministries, Army and in fact all points of vantage to render our resistance power more and more effective. I believe that the latter course is the only policy which will strengthen the minority (in the Muslim-majority provinces) ...Look how the Muslims act even in the provinces where they are 10 or 4 % minority. They insist on entering the councils and having more seats, forming their independent blocks in the councils and acting always as a thorn in the sides of the Hindus to [the] best of their power. They never boycott the councils or ministries simply because they are in a minority of even one or two and they depend on the majority of other Muslims in other provinces to back them up.[37]

The power that the Hindu Mahasabha and the Akalis shared with the Muslim League in Bengal and Punjab and the resistance power and awareness they created amongst the local Hindus and Sikhs was one of the reasons why half of Punjab and Bengal remained with India when Partition became unavoidable. It finally destroyed Jinnah's dream of having the whole of Punjab and Bengal for Pakistan. The Hindu Mahasabha also had a role in the retention of Assam because the Muslim League and British designs were aimed at depriving India of Assam, besides the whole of Punjab and Bengal.

'SAVARKAR IS OUR CHURCHILL'

The year 1943 dawned with the political deadlock in India still in place. In an attempt to resolve the same, Gandhi undertook a fast in February that year. While appealing to Gandhi to end

---

[37] Abhilekh-patal.in Important Intercepts Supplied by Dib 1944 Identifier PR_000003015010 File No. HOME_POLITICAL_I_1944_NA_F-51-4.

his fast in national interest 'as his life was a national asset'[38], Savarkar once again warned the Congress and others not to exploit the fast to push constitutional changes without consulting the Hindu Mahasabha as the Mahasabha wouldn't tolerate any encroachment on Hindu rights or undermining of the nation's integrity.

However, during this very fast, Gandhi approved the C.R. Formula created by Rajaji, as suspected by Savarkar earlier. Gandhi had authorized Rajaji to negotiate with Jinnah on the basis of this formula. As Gandhi's personal secretary, Pyarelal says in his book that 'Gandhiji did not need a moment's consideration to give his approval to it (C.R. Plan).'[39] This again showed Savarkar's masterly grasp of the situation when it came to the unity of India.

The C.R. Formula or the Rajaji Formula, for settling the Hindu–Muslim problem, included the following points:

1. The Muslim League should first endorse the demand for Indian independence and form a transitional provisional government with the Congress after the British effect total transfer of power to Indians.
2. A plebiscite or referendum on the basis of adult franchise be held in the Muslim-majority areas of the North-west and the North-east to decide whether such areas desire secession.
3. If the provinces where the referendum is held demand separation from India, the outcome be upheld and separate treaties be signed with such ceded provinces on Defence, Commerce and Communication.[40]

Thus, the Rajaji plan offered almost all that the League had demanded in its Pakistan resolution in return of forming a

---

[38]Dhananjay Keer, *Veer Savarkar*, Popular Prakashan Pvt. Ltd; Second edition, p. 333.
[39]Pyarelal, *Mahatma Gandhi: The Last Phase*, Vol. 1, Ahmedabad: Navajivan Publishing House, 1956, p. 69.
[40]Ibid. 68, 69; B.N. Jog, *Threat of Islam: Indian Dimensions*, Mumbai (Bombay): Unnati Prakashan, 1994, p. 281, 282.

government with the Congress. His plan looked debilitating to say the least.

Reacting to the C.R. formula, Jinnah said: 'The scheme is only a shadow of Pakistan. It offers Pakistan which is handicapped and moth-eaten.'[41] He rejected the formula because he was against a plebiscite in Muslim-majority areas and wanted Partition before the British left India. He also did not want any conditions on his primary aim of claiming Bengal and Punjab for Pakistan without any division of those provinces. Therefore, in this context, the essential difference between the Muslim League and the Congress was that the former was demanding Partition before British departure, while the latter agreed to it through a plebiscite in the Muslim-majority areas after the British left the country.

However, what service Rajaji rendered to Jinnah by his C.R. Plan was revealed by Jinnah to well-known journalist Durga Das, in response to a question: 'I am in a happy position of being able to extract the best terms as they (Congressmen) want power and the British do not want to part with it.'[42] Jinnah's parting shot during this conversation was almost prophetic, writes Das. He said, 'You can depend on Rajagopalachari to use his sharp wits to define Pakistan for me.'[43]

However, notwithstanding these views, the plan was rejected by the Muslim League too. In its December 1943 Karachi session, the League demanded that the British rulers should quit India only after partitioning it. The party also made an action committee to oppose any move to form a constituent assembly for United India and achieve Pakistan. The League had now decided that it would achieve Pakistan, come what may. Although the League asked its cadres to remain aloof from the Quit India movement and not obstruct the Congress's programme, the massive violence and the massacres of Hindus that happened in 1946 as a result of the League's 'Direct Action' call were rooted in the deliberations of the Karachi session.

---

[41] Durga Das, *India: From Curzon to Nehru and After*, Rupa & Co., 2002.
[42] Ibid. 208.
[43] Ibid.

The Rajaji episode, which opened the floodgates to the Pakistan scheme with Gandhi's support, is a watershed in the pre-Independence movement. It needs to be looked at with deeper attention, especially in light of the statement issued by Pandit Nehru after Partition that had Gandhi stood firm against the Pakistan scheme, Congressmen would have followed him.[44]

It was, in fact, a travesty that this 'break-India' idea came from a person whose first name was 'Chakravarti', which in English means 'an ideal, universal ruler who protects the people from fissiparous forces'. This was reinforced by Savarkar when he expressed dismay at the fact that a true Raja (or king) protects his kingdom and not preside over its disintegration. Thereafter, he left no stone unturned in opposing the plan.

The Hindu Mahasabha tracked and opposed Rajaji relentlessly. When Rajaji undertook a tour to explain the contours and objectives of his plan, Mahasabha leaders and workers followed him to many places he visited, interacted with the people and tried to undo the poisonous effects of the scheme he was propagating. During this debate, Savarkar issued a hard-hitting statement:

> It is really unjust to look at Rajaji alone as the villain of this tragedy. His fault is that he allowed himself to become a willing tool into the hands of Gandhiji... Indian provinces are not private properties of Gandhiji and Rajaji so that they could make a gift of them to any one they liked.[45]

When American newspapers wanted to have Savarkar's views on the C.R. Formula, he issued a statement through the United Press International that as the main representative of Hindus in India, the Hindu Mahasabha stoutly opposed the proposal to break the Holy Land and Fatherland of Hindus and emphatically condemned the proposal to vivisect India by allowing Muslims to form separate, independent States. Savarkar sent the same statement in

---

[44]Leonard Mosley, *The Last Days of the British Raj*, Weidenfeld and Nicolson, 1961, p. 248.
[45]V.D. Savarkar, *Historic Statements by Savarkar*, G.P. Parchure, 1967.

the form of a cable to the then Secretary of State for India and Burma (Myanmar), L.S. Amery.

The Hindu Mahasabha's relentless public campaign against the C.R. Plan led to public ire against Gandhi and Rajaji. Rajaji's meetings were being disrupted by angry crowds opposed to any move to partitioning the nation. Savarkar's spirited opposition to the vivisection proposal also drew high praise from forces of United India. The Democratic Swarajya Party leader Jamnadas Mehta, who had compelled the British to release Savarkar from internment in Ratnagiri and enabled him to enter politics in 1937, drew an apt analogy while paying the following tribute to the Hindutva icon: 'Savarkar is our Churchill when it comes to protecting national interest while Rajaji is Chamberlain who appeased Hitler and made him a monster.'[46]

However, this overwhelming public response to Savarkar had no effect on the Congress leadership, which continued on the suicidal course of appeasing the Muslim League in its goal of convincing Jinnah to agree to the C.R. Plan.

However, Jinnah was a hard realist. He was unmoved even after correspondence from Gandhi in which he pleaded with Jinnah that even if Hindus and Muslims want to part ways, they should part as brothers and not as enemies and the Muslim League and the Congress should form a coalition government as a prelude to British departure. Several scholars cite the above Gandhi appeal (about Hindus and Muslims parting as friends) as a proof that Gandhi tried to prevent Partition. But they conveniently forget that Gandhi had conceded Partition by accepting the concept of self-determination in less than three weeks of the 23 March 1940 Muslim League resolution demanding a separate nation(s) comprising Muslim-majority provinces for Indian Muslims.

This correspondence was followed by Gandhi meeting Jinnah for 17 days at a stretch at his Bombay residence in September–October 1944 to make him accept his proposal for Partition. But Jinnah did not pay him a single return visit. During those

---

[46]Balarao Savarkar, *Swatantryaveer Savarkar: Akhand Hindusthan Ladha Parv*, p. 228.

17 days, Gandhi, while claiming that Hindu–Muslim unity was his life mission, made several attempts to placate Jinnah to make him accept his main proposal that Hindus, Muslims and others should first agree to come together to achieve Independence in a joint effort and then if Muslim-majority areas vote for Pakistan in a referendum, such areas would be separated from India and given to Muslims. On one particular Monday, Gandhi even broke his customary vow of silence for his parley with Jinnah.

Interestingly, at one point in the initial period of negotiations, Gandhi even said:

> It has never happened in history that converts and their descendants should regard themselves as a nation and say we are a very different nation than our ancestors... If India was one nation before the advent of Islam, then it must be one, indivisible land even though many a son of the land has adopted different faith.[47]

But this was a far cry for Jinnah, who wanted immediate Partition. In fact, he even had differences with Gandhi on the mode of plebiscite. While Gandhi wanted all the adults to participate in the Muslim-majority areas, which meant both Hindus and Muslims, Jinnah wanted only the Muslim adults to participate in it.[48]

Significantly, Gandhi conducted negotiations with Jinnah at the cost of his self-respect as well as of his party. Pyarelal later revealed that the behaviour of Jinnah's staff with Gandhi's men, who used to sit separately at Jinnah's residence, was disrespectful.[49]

V.P. Menon has aptly described how ill-timed Gandhi's negotiations with Jinnah were and how they served to strengthen him and the Muslim League. He says:

---

[47]Pyarelal, *Mahatma Gandhi: The Last Phase*, Vol. I, Ahmedabad: Navajivan Publishing House, 1956, p. 95.
[48]Yuvraj Krishan, *Understanding Partition: India Sundered, Muslims Fragmented*, Mumbai: Bharatiya Vidya Bhavan, 2002.
[49]Pyarelal, *Mahatma Gandhi: The Last Phase*, Vol. I, Ahmedabad: Navajivan Publishing House, 1956, p. 97.

The offer to discuss the partition of India with Jinnah was, to say the least, most inopportune. The League Ministries in Bengal, Sindh and North-West-Frontier-Province (NWFP) were in none too stable a position. Moreover, the refusal of Khizar Hayat Khan, the premier of Punjab, to change his Union Party's Ministry in Punjab into a Muslim League coalition Ministry had not enhanced Jinnah's prestige. In these circumstances, Gandhiji's move was calculated only to strength Jinnah's hands and further the cause of [the] Muslim League. This view was shared by some prominent Congressmen.[50]

When the Jinnah-Gandhi talks were adjourned, Savarkar issued a hard-hitting statement which appeared harsh at that time but was subsequently proved correct. He said:

It should be clearly noted that the proposal to vivisect our country has assumed a far more dangerous aspect today when the Gandhi-Jinnah talks are adjourned than it had on the day when the talks began. Mr Jinnah demands vivisection of India even more relentlessly than before. Gandhiji wants to placate that intolerable demand even more unrepentantly than before. The Moslems are openly claiming that they have nothing to do with the so-called Indian Nation, that they are a different Nation by themselves and that they want to cut off as many provinces of India as possible, utilize them as a territorial base to rear up an Anti-Hindu, Moslem State quite independent of any Central Indian Government. Gandhiji who claims confidently to get the Congress to support him is ready to hand over at any rate our four frontier provinces which form the natural and invulnerable frontier of our motherland, to the Moslems for the above treacherous objectives, for the mere asking of it—without firing a shot!! The tragedy of it all is that the Indian National Congress, which was ushered into existence to consolidate the Indian Nation has itself betrayed its sole mission, the very justification of its existence and

---

[50] V.P. Menon, *Transfer of Power in India*, Orient BlackSwan, 1957, p. 163.

falling a victim to the pseudo-nationalistic malady had dealt the unkindest cut of all at the 'Indian National Integrity'![51]

Nearly 5,000 meetings were held across the country and around 50,000 signatures were collected by the Hindu Mahasabha against the Gandhi-Jinnah talks.[52]

Large sections of the Congress leadership were opposed to such placation of Jinnah by Gandhi. In fact, he had proved his mentor Gopal Krishna Gokhale right, who had once remarked that Gandhi would be a great mass leader but when it came to political parleys, he will be a failure.[53] Even balanced intellectuals such as Srinivasa Sastri were compelled to say that it was impossible for a genuine nationalist to keep silent when the integrity of 'our motherland' was being bartered.

This was the stage when significant sections of Muslims were opposed to Partition for various reasons, including the leaders of the Khaksar movement, which had spoken severely against the Pakistan scheme. But by negotiating with Jinnah alone and that too in a style which depicted the highest kind of servility towards the League on the Congress's part, Gandhi brought down the standing of the other Muslim leaders amongst the Muslim masses. In fact, in many parts of India, the Muslim masses from now onwards began to see Muslims who were opposed to Partition as enemies of Islam, and Jinnah as their supreme leader.

But the supreme leader narrowly missed death on being attacked by a Khaksar movement fanatic. Savarkar condemned the attack for which Jinnah conveyed thanks through Savarkar's secretary. Savarkar had a very strong sense of propriety when it came to dealing with political rivals in their personal matters even while dealing with them sternly on the political turf.

But this was not always the case. There were occasions when Savarkar's utterances and actions stoked controversy and created

---

[51] V.D. Savarkar, *Historic Statements by Savarkar*, G.P. Parchure, 1967.
[52] Balarao Savarkar, *Swatantryaveer Savarkar: Akhand Hindusthan Ladha Parv*, p. 350.
[53] Satyagrahi, *Graha Ani Tare*, p. 60; Dhananjay Keer, *Veer Savarkar*, Popular Prakashan Pvt. Ltd; Second edition, 2019, p. 385.

further bitterness between the Congress and the Hindu Mahasabha. After the death of Kasturba Gandhi in 1944, which Savarkar mourned deeply[54], some Congressmen constituted the Kasturba Memorial Fund. Savarkar appealed to the people not to contribute to it as 'it was again going to be used for Muslim-appeasement purposes just as the Tilak Swaraj fund was used by the Congressites in [the] 1920s to further the pan-Islamic Khilafat movement against the ideals of Lokmanya Tilak'.[55] When it became known that Gandhi's followers were also planning to install a statue of Kasturba from the fund proceeds, Savarkar appreciated the act to honour 'a good patriotic women', but, at the same time, asked Congressmen whether they had ever cared to raise such statues for the widows of many martyred heroes who had also suffered and were a partner with their husbands in their nationalist pursuits including Satyabhama Tilak, Gopikabai Phadke, Madame Cama and many others. What he said was the bitter truth but Savarkar's stand on the Kasturba fund hurt Gandhi. Clearly, Savarkar could have avoided this controversy.

SENTINEL ON GUARD

However, there were other controversies that demanded Savarkar's attention. The Sindh Muslim League banned the Arya Samaj's sacred book *Satyarth Prakash*, which was penned by its founder, Dayananda Saraswati himself. Savarkar made a reasoned protest against the ban: '... Every scripture including [the] Bible has something or the other to say against other sects or religions. But no Hindu Ministry had ever contemplated any action against non-Hindu scriptures.'[56]

---

[54]Following Kasturba's death at the Aga Khan Palace, Savarkar sent a telegram to Gandhi to the effect: 'With a heavy heart, I mourn the death of Kasturba. A faithful wife and an affectionate mother, she died a noble death in the service of God and man. Your grief is shared by the whole nation.'
[55]'A Shabby Show: Congress Abandons Its Plan,' http://www.mea.gov.in/Images/attach/amb/Volume_09.pdf. Accessed on 31 July 2021.
[56]Dhananjay Keer, *Veer Savarkar*, Popular Prakashan Pvt. Ltd; Second edition, 2019, p. 342.

In a letter to the Viceroy, Savarkar warned that if the ban was not lifted, it could result in a similar demand to ban the Koran. Later, he met Viceroy Lord Wavell and repeated his stand. At the Bilaspur Hindu Mahasabha session that followed soon after, Savarkar said that had there been full-fledged Hindu Mahasabha ministries in the provinces, these would have banned the Koran until the ban on *Satyarth Prakash* was lifted.

The Congress refused to condemn the ban on *Satyarth Prakash* for the fear of antagonizing the Muslim community. This was yet another occasion when the Congress's pro-Muslim bias came to the fore. When Arya Samaj leader and a known former revolutionary, Bhai Parmanand, moved an adjournment motion in the Central Assembly over the *Satyarth Prakash* ban, the motion was defeated because the Congress kept mum over it. That Savarkar was the only political leader who condemned the ban proved once again that he was the true champion of Hindu interests.

In mid-1943, the British suppressed the Hur rebellion in Sindh following massive bloodshed by the Hurs, who had rebelled in support of some of their illegitimate demands and indulged in plunder and killing of Hindus. Their leader, the Pir of Pagaro, was charged and hanged by the British. Here again, the Hindu Mahasabha and the Muslim League clashed. The League demanded that the hanged leader's property should continue as a religious trust. Savarkar appealed to the government saying that the Hur gangs had looted Hindus during the rebellion and so the proceeds from the Pir's property should be used to compensate the losses incurred by the Hindus.[57]

However, there was more to the year than just plunder and bloodshed. Savarkar completed 60 glorious years in 1943 and this occasion was celebrated in Maharashtra with great fanfare and enthusiasm. Gandhi and Tilak were the only leaders who had been similarly honoured by people. People of great eminence were part of the reception committees that honoured Savarkar in places such

---

[57] Dhananjay Keer, *Veer Savarkar*, Popular Prakashan Pvt. Ltd; Second edition, 2019, p. 33.

as Poona (now Pune), Bombay, Amravati and Nagpur and offered funding to show support.

In Bombay, S.P. Paranjpe, a known intellectual and former principal of Fergusson College, Savarkar's alma mater, paid rich tributes to Savarkar. In the process, Paranjpe blamed Gandhi for mixing religion with politics. Savarkar's ardent admirer, Jamnadas Mehta, and known liberal leaders K.F. Nariman and Chandragupt Vedalankar were the other key speakers at this function.

In his reply, Savarkar reiterated that his fight was for 'one man, one vote', thereby indicating once again that he was not demanding special treatment for Hindus but only equal rights. He also stressed the point that the national majority can't be marginalized at the altar of Muslim-appeasement politics.

In the same year, Savarkar delivered a historic speech in Sangli on the occasion of the second millenary of Vikramaditya the Great. He defined the true contribution of the great ruler after whom a Hindu calendar—Vikram Samvat—is named. He said Vikramaditya had lived for 2,000 years in human memory because he fought invaders such as the Shakas and the Huns and demolished them to protect his people and liberate Bharatvarsh, and not because of his contribution to the promotion of arts, literature and learning which too was noteworthy. Savarkar believed the whole Hindustan felt inspired by Vikramaditya, the Hunari and Shakari, the conqueror of the Shakas and the Huns.

By the end of 1943, Savarkar was elected the president of the Hindu Mahasabha for the seventh time at its Amritsar session, despite his repeated requests to quit. Significantly, Savarkar wanted to leave the presidentship as he was weighed down by severe health problems, which had its roots in his painful incarceration at Andaman and Ratnagiri. But party leaders such as Munje repeatedly implored Savarkar to continue his tenure. His plea for exit on health grounds was not unjustified as he had to skip the Amritsar session itself due to an attack of bronchitis.

Notwithstanding his health issues, Savarkar took the lead in organizing the Akhand Hindustan Leaders' Conference at New Delhi on 7 and 8 October 1944. Over 300 leaders, including

Akali leader Master Tara Singh, His Holiness Sri Shankaracharya of Puri, Member of the Viceroy Executive Council (Department of Education) Sir Jogendra Singh, Commonwealth Relations Member to the then Government of India and one of the greatest champions of Hindu rights N.B. Khare, were present. Among the 300 sympathetic messages received, those from leading intellectuals such as Barrister Ramrao Deshmukh, Srinivasa Sastri and R.P. Paranjpe, asked Hindus to value the interests of the country more than those of a passing political party and wished the conference success. Shastri was very precise while echoing the nation-first principle of Savarkar, and said: 'Country is greater than [the] Congress. Keeping this in mind, the leaders inside the Congress should speak openly against the vivisection schemes.'[58]

Inaugurating the conference, Jamnadas Mehta condemned the idea of Pakistan with memorable resolution. He said: 'As a Hindu, I reject it; as an Indian, I repudiate it, and as an internationalist, I repel it.'[59] Mehta further called for a relentless war on the enemies of Hindustan which he said, were British imperialism, Muslim fanaticism, Congress's wobblings and our (people's) own apathy. Clearly, Mehta was at his scintillating best. His each and every word on this occasion carried weight in that delicate phase for the unity and integrity of the ancient nation.

Dr Radha Kumud Mukherjee, one of the greatest intellectuals of that time and a master of history and politics, presided over the conference. In his presidential address, he underlined the importance of the conference with a pun on the Congress leadership in memorable and historic words: 'A crisis of the first magnitude has been created in our national history by some great leaders who have convinced themselves that it is impossible for our mother country to attain her independence and the status which is her birth-right except on the basis of Hindu–Muslim unity.'[60] He

---

[58] Balarao Savarkar, *Swatantryaveer Savarkar: Akhand Hindusthan Ladha Parv*, p. 352.
[59] Dhananjay Keer, *Veer Savarkar*, Popular Prakashan Pvt. Ltd; Second edition, 2019, p. 358.
[60] Radhakumud Mookerji, Akhand Bharat, https://archive.org/details/akhandbharat035108mbp, p. 8. Accessed on 31 July 2021.

asserted that through millenniums of their history, the homeland of the Hindus had been nothing short of the whole of India and therefore, the leaders who thought otherwise and were giving a long rope to the Pakistan scheme were misreading history and politics. He laid down that Pakistan was unacceptable as a solution to the Hindu–Muslim problem as it was at the cost of the unity of the motherland.

Master Tara Singh declared at the conference that the Sikhs were the gatekeepers of India. He said that he had not come to lend support, but to seek support for the Sikh determination to guard the frontiers of United India, and sounded a warning that even if a majority of Hindus agreed to Pakistan, they had no right to force it upon the Sikhs.[61]

Savarkar delivered another illuminating speech on the occasion and explained the object of the conference while dwelling on its representative character. He hoped that there would be no difference of opinion on the main resolution.

The resolution unambiguously declared unflinching faith in the unity and integrity of India and said that Partition would be fatal to the best interests of the country as a whole and to every community. Leaders who came from all over the country including states such as Bengal, Punjab and Assam, which were on Jinnah's Partition radar, supported the resolution passed on the occasion.

The conference ended with great enthusiasm and determination of the nationalists to oppose Pakistan. This was the greatest demonstration of the nationalist opposition to the Pakistan scheme during this crucial phase. But even this steely determination ultimately failed against the evil designs of the Muslim League and the British and the timidity of the Congress, as proved by subsequent events leading to Partition.

The year ended with Savarkar stepping down as the president of the Hindu Mahasabha at the party's Bilaspur session, owing to health issues, and being replaced by S.P. Mukherjee.

---

[61]Dhananjay Keer, *Veer Savarkar*, Popular Prakashan Pvt. Ltd; Second edition, 2019, p. 358.

6

SAVARKAR'S LAST STAND: THE DARKEST HOUR

The New Year dawned with the Muslim League leader Liaquat Ali Khan extracting the principle of parity from Congress leader and noted lawyer, Bhulabhai Desai in the form of the informal Bhulabhai Desai–Liaquat Ali Pact (popularly known as the Desai–Liaquat Pact) finalized in January 1945. It meant that the Congress would treat 22 per cent Muslims in undivided India as 50 per cent in all political matters. In one stroke, the pact reduced Hindus to a minority in their motherland because they too were to be treated as 50 per cent despite their population being 75 per cent. With this, the Congress practically conceded that Hindus and Muslims are two seperate entities in India, which proved to be the first step for the realization of Jinnah's two-nation theory. It also resulted in the annihilation of another Congress claim—that it was the representative of all Indian peoples—because the party virtually allowed the League to project itself as the sole representative of Indian Muslims.

Commenting on the pact, well-known Pakistani author Prof. Sharif Al-Mujahid wrote:

> With Bhulabhai Desai, leader of the Congress Party in the Central Assembly in 1944, he (Liaquat Ali) proposed parity between [the] Congress and the League in any future set-up at the centre, and it became the core point in the Desai–Liaquat formula. This was the first time this cardinal principle which the League had long demanded in any coalition set-up, but was stoutly denied, had been conceded by the Congress

at any level. Once lifted beyond the pale of controversy, this key provision became the basis for the quota of seats for Hindus and Muslims/Congress and the League in the subsequent Wavell (1945) and interim government (1946) proposals. Thus, Liaquat's contribution assumes a milestone status in getting the principle of parity accepted. Jinnah was, reportedly, a little unhappy about Liaquat having contracted the Pact behind his back (since he lay ill at Matheran), but was fully alive to both its significance and its long-term implications. He, therefore, accepted Liaquat's explanation and exonerated him of any breach of trust, which Sir Yamin Khan alleges in his Nama-i-Aamaal. This was in sharp contrast to the treatment that Bhulabhai Desai had received at the hands of his Congress colleagues. Though blessed by Gandhi in his talks with Liaquat at the time, and despite his critical contribution in the INA trials (1945) and getting the prosecution charges of treason quashed, Desai was even denied a Congress ticket in the 1945–46 elections. Soon after, Desai, despite his great services to the Congress, died, broken-hearted—unwept, unsung, and unhonoured.[1]

This article reinforces the fact that the top Congress leadership was bungling on the Pakistan issue and that there was a substantial section in the party that felt otherwise but remained ignored. Further, Gandhi's role in the formation of the pact remains only partially explored. There is enough evidence to prove that Gandhi himself had initiated the pact through Desai to solve the political deadlock. He wanted the many leaders, who were still in jail following the British's repressive measures against the Quit India movement agitators, to be released. His other objective was to form the interim government at the Centre as a prelude to final Independence. The British also wanted an interim government as part of their World War II aims, the main British objective being

---

[1] Prof. Sharif Al-Mujahid, 'Liaquat Ali Khan: Hero and Legend,' *The Nation*, 17 October 2010. https://nation.com.pk/17-Oct-2010/liaquat-ali-khan-hero-and-legend. Accessed on 11 June 2021.

seeking cooperation of Indian leaders against advancing Japan in the war.

Dr N.B. Khare, then the member of the Viceroy's Executive Council, and the chief minister of the Central Province in 1937 and later a Congress-turned-Hindu Mahasabha leader, maintains that Desai revealed to him the true role of Gandhi in the pact:

> ... Bhulabhai Desai said, I will certainly tell you those reasons. Doctor, you know that after the unsuccessful Gandhi–Jinnah interview in September 1944, Dr Syed Mahmud, a member of the Congress Working Committee, was released from Ahmednagar jail. Naturally he went to Sewagram to see Gandhi after his release. Gandhi made him write to me a letter in which I was asked to contact Nawabzada Liaquat Ali Khan, the leader of the Muslim League Party in the Central Assembly and discuss with him the formation of a composite Government of India, consisting of the Congress and the Muslim League. I did not like to compromise with the Mussalmans in that fashion; I therefore ignored the letter by Dr Syed Mahmud at the behest of Gandhi and didn't even send a reply to it. But Gandhi ji, after waiting for about a fortnight for a reply, sent me a short letter in his own handwriting in Gujarati in which the last sentence was, 'This must be done.' I was therefore helpless on account of this Gandhi order and met Liaquat Ali and brought about the famous Bhulabhai–Liaquat Agreement which we both initialed. I took this draft to Wardha. Gandhi approved the draft and asked me to see Lord Wavell, the Viceroy, in this connection. Accordingly, I saw the Viceroy who was summoned to England for personal consultation to enable the British Government to consider the draft and take a decision about it. The British Government made slight changes in the draft and Wavell returned with that formula approved by the British Government under the name of Wavell Formula. The Simla Conference was held in July 1945 in pursuance of that formula. The main object of this conference was to establish

a Viceroy's Executive Council with the co-operation of the Congress and the Muslim League.[2]

Eminent jurist Sir M.C. Setalvad provides more evidence about Gandhi being the key author of the Desai–Liaquat formula. Setalvad says that Gandhi had himself made minor changes to the draft of the pact in his own handwriting when Desai went to Wardha between 3 and 5 January 1945 to show him the handwritten draft of the pact. In the appendix of his book, Setalvad has produced a photo copy of Desai's handwritten draft with minor changes made by Gandhi in the margins in his own handwriting.[3]

The scheme, when it became public through a press leak, was disowned by Gandhi, though he himself had pushed it through Desai. It was also denied by Liaquat Ali and Jinnah, whom Liaquat Ali had reportedly kept in the dark. Thus, the main architect of the Desai–Liaquat Pact was Gandhi, more than Desai, who unfortunately faced the music for the pact alone. However, to Gandhi and Desai's credit, the pact proposed joint electorates. However, bent upon dividing Hindus and Muslims as far as possible, the British did away with this clause too and pitched in for separate electorates.[4]

This was yet another occasion when Savarkar was the only national leader, and Hindu Mahasabha the only national party, who opposed the anti-national pact tooth and nail. Even Sapru, who had virtually sung Savarkar's tune some years ago on the issue of the unity of the nation and had supported joint electorates and adult franchise, accepted parity between Muslims and Hindus in electoral representation that the pact envisaged. Savarkar's reaction was resolute: 'Nothing could be more treacherous, anti-national and anti-Hindu. By such pacts and slavish surrender, they are not

---

[2]N.B. Khare, *My Political Memoirs, or, Autobiography*, J.R. Joshi; Second edition, 1971, p. 80.

[3]M.C. Setalvad, *Bhulabhai Desai*, Publications Division, M/O Information & Broadcasting, Govt of India, 2010.

[4]Dhananjay Keer, *Veer Savarkar*, Popular Prakashan Pvt. Ltd; Second edition, 2019, p. 363.

only strengthening the hands of the Muslims who would demand more as soon as you yield so far but the hands of Britain too.'[5]

SIMLA CONFERENCE: PICKING UP THE DIVISIVE THREAD

Though the British kept an outward show of trying to help a United India against machinations of the League, they picked up key elements of the pact to divide India. The pact gave a major fillip to the Pakistan scheme though the British claimed otherwise. In fact, the principle of parity between Hindus and Muslims was the main basis for the plan created by the Viceroy Lord Wavell to solve the political deadlock between the British, the Congress and the Muslim League. A major change made by the British was that the parity in the Wavell Plan was now to be between (upper) caste Hindus and Muslims, thus causing further division in the Hindu community, an issue on which Gandhi had fought tooth and nail in 1932 and brought about the Poona Pact to represent Hindus as one unit before the British. However, this principle was also given a pass by Gandhi this time, though he did express his unhappiness over it.

The Wavell Plan also came as a double whammy. It not only established the League as the sole representative of Muslims in India, but also deprived several powerful non-League Muslim leaders and parties from representing Muslims before the British, thus further puncturing the strategy of the forces of United India which were seeking to encourage these non-League Muslim leaders to oppose Jinnah's Pakistan scheme.

Wavell went to England in May 1945 with a draft of his plan, which aimed to end the political deadlock in India by forming an interim government of Indian leaders and securing their support in the British war efforts. With a few significant changes made, which were even more divisionary in nature, he got this plan ratified as the future road map for the Indian problem.

The theme of the plan was, thus, unmistakably based on the

---

[5] V.D. Savarkar, *Historic Statements by Savarkar*, G.P. Parchure, 1967.

main features of the Desai–Liaquat Pact, and in spite of being repudiated by both Gandhi and Jinnah and even Liaquat Ali, it set the tone for the Simla Conference in June 1945. The Wavell Plan for this conference was cast in a certain groove. Those who would oppose the plan had to be left out of the said government. Therefore, despite the pleading by Khare, then member of the Viceroy's Executive Council, the Hindu Mahasabha, which was the true representative of Hindu interests, was not called by Wavell, with reason: 'I will never extend the invitation of the Simla Conference to the leaders of the Hindoo Mahasabha because the Hindoo Mahasabha is more bitterly opposed to the British Empire than even the Congress.'[6] This firmly established the Congress as the representative of Indian Hindus and the Muslim League as the representative of Indian Muslims. Savarkar thundered that the Mahasabha had been left out because it was opposing Partition.[7]

However, beyond the Hindu Mahasabha's vehement opposition to the Muslim League's Partition plan, there were other reasons too for the party not being invited to the Simla Conference. It was an open secret that Rash Behari Bose, founder of the INA, was also the founder of the Japan branch of the Hindu Mahasabha. So, British officials were considering the Hindu Mahasabha as one of the probable parties to be negotiated with at the end of the war. Also, the party had launched the militarization programme for Hindus, which the British saw as beneficial to their wartime interests.

However, what happened thereafter changed the scenario for the Hindu Mahasabha and had a direct impact on the fate of India itself. On 3 May, the INA along with its Japanese allies surrendered Rangoon to the British and Allied forces, while Germany unconditionally surrendered to the Allies on 7 May. These events deeply affected the negotiation strength of the Hindu Mahasabha, which was now seen as a lightweight by Wavell and his team and therefore ignored.

---

[6]N.B. Khare, *My Political Memoirs, or, Autobiography*, J.R. Joshi; Second edition, 1971, p. 115.
[7]V.D. Savarkar, *Historic Statements by Savarkar*, G.P. Parchure, 1967.

The Wavell Plan envisaged an Indianized, 14-member Viceroy's Council to take over till the war ended, with five representatives to be nominated by the Congress and the Muslim League each. The rest four were to be representatives of other groups including the Depressed Classes, Sikhs, Christians and one Muslim nominee to be appointed by the Viceroy, supposedly from the Unionist Party (Punjab), which was opposed to the Muslim League's Partition plan.

On 24 June, Wavell met Congress President Maulana Abul Kalam Azad, Gandhi and then Jinnah. The conference began the following day. It hit a roadblock when Jinnah insisted that one Muslim member outside the Muslim League quota will also be nominated by his party, on which Wavell put his foot down. The Congress also proposed that its panel would consist of two Hindus, a Muslim, a Christian and a Parsi. Obviously, the Congress party could not allow its claim of being representative of all the Indian people to be rejected so easily.[8] On 29 June, Wavell asked the various groups to nominate their representatives, but Jinnah refused to send the Muslim League list until Wavell allowed nomination of all the Muslims on the council to be done by the League. The official and unofficial deliberations went on till 11 July, when Wavell again met Jinnah. On 14 July, he announced that the plan had failed due to Jinnah's intransigence.

The Congress's nomination plan, which was to include diverse religious groups, meant that Hindus would be in a hopeless minority in the council—75 per cent of the Hindu population would have got merely 28 per cent representation, with two representatives by the Congress and one representative of the Depressed Classes and Sikh each nominated by the Viceroy out of the 14, while 22 per cent of the Muslims would have got 50 per cent power share with a total of seven representatives.

This should have in fact made Jinnah happy. So, why did he reject the Wavell Plan? According to journalist Durga Das, before the final outcome of the conference was announced by Wavell,

---

[8] Durga Das, *India from Curzon to Nehru and After*, Rupa & Co., 2002, p. 215.

'... Jinnah had received a secret message from the "cell" of British Civil Servants in Simla which was in tune with the die-hards in London that if Jinnah stepped out of the talks, he would be rewarded with Pakistan.'[9] The journalist further writes that when he met Jinnah in the lift and asked him as to why he had spurned the Wavell Plan when he had won his point of parity for the Muslim League with the Congress, Jinnah's reply stunned him: 'Am I a fool to accept this when I am offered Pakistan on a platter?'[10] Das says, 'After painstaking inquiries, he learned from high officials and political sources that a sitting member of the Viceroy's Executive Council had sent a secret message to Jinnah through the League contacts he had formed.'[11]

The rejection of the Wavell Plan resulted in political dividends for Jinnah in the public domain. The Muslims, who were still divided amongst various parties, now started veering further towards Jinnah, as he was seen as one who could stand up to even the Viceroy with force. On the other hand, though the Hindu Mahasabha workers protested against the proposal of parity in the Wavell Plan, even demonstrating against it at Simla when the conference was in progress, the overall impact of its programme was limited. A protest week was observed against the plan by the Hindu Sanghatanists throughout India on a giant scale. Large meetings were held in Lahore, Amritsar, Delhi, Ajmer, Calcutta, Bombay, Poona, Nagpur, Mysore, Madras, Karachi, Patna and a thousand other cities, towns and villages. The audience at places such as Poona rising to about 50,000 condemned the Wavell Plan, the principle of parity and the supineness of the Congress as a national body. At places, the meetings were whimsically banned by the local authorities.[12] But on the whole, the party restricted itself to demonstrations and failed to give a direct action type of programme against the parity proposal. It was an average performance, not a

---

[9]Durga Das, *India from Curzon to Nehru and After*, Rupa & Co., 2002, p. 215–16.
[10]Ibid.
[11]Ibid. 216.
[12]V.D. Savarkar, *Historic Statements by Savarkar*, G.P. Parchure, 1967.

stellar one, which the situation demanded. Clearly, the fire that the party showed during the Hyderabad and Bhagalpur struggles was somehow missing now.[13]

If the Desai–Liaquat Pact, the INA's surrender of Rangoon and the Wavell Plan were political disappointments for Savarkar, he faced a major setback on the personal front too when in March 1945, he lost his elder brother and guide, the great revolutionary Ganesh, alias Babarao, Savarkar. His brother had spent several years with Savarkar in the Cellular Jail in Andaman, and had had a profound impact on Dr K.B. Hedgewar and his decision to found the RSS to protect Hindu interests against unwarranted Muslim aggression. Savarkar's youngest brother, revolutionary Dr Narayanrao Savarkar, was at Babarao's deathbed when he died at Sangli. Savarkar used to send him ₹100 a month for his upkeep. The trio's devotion to the nation is best exemplified by the fact that the last enquiry Babarao made at the time of his death was about the communist threat to Nepal.

Savarkar wrote moving letters to Babarao in his last years. One of them read:

> Our (of the trio) life work was one. In our generation, we have tried to repay our spiritual debt to our forefathers. No historian of modern Hindustan will fail to write in golden letters one separate chapter (on their contribution to the nation). Our political opponents have familiarized the title of that chapter as the Savarkar epoch. By giving to the countrymen two battle cries, 'Victory to the Goddess of Liberty' and 'Hindustan belongs to the Hindus' we have thus been instrumental twice in bringing about a fundamental revolution in the nation's ideology and active political life. The Lord of Death who is now standing by your side is meeting you, not like a foe, but like a friend. In sufferings as in happiness never did you drop down the banner of revolution.[14]

---

[13]Dhananjay Keer, *Veer Savarkar*, Popular Prakashan Pvt. Ltd; Second edition, 2019, p. 366.
[14]Balarao Savarkar, *Swatantryaveer Savarkar: Akhand Hindusthan Ladha Parv*, p. 373.

After the failure of the Wavell Plan, the Congress party president Abul Kalam Azad presented Gandhi a plan for winning Muslim support to keep the nation united against the divisive Muslim League agenda. The plan, which virtually meant creating a greater Pakistan or many Pakistans, albeit under the umbrella of United India, had the following points:

1. The number of Hindus and Muslims in Parliament and the Central Executive (Cabinet) should be equal.
2. Muslims alone should have a right to decide their role in the Constitution.
3. The states should have a right to secede from the Federation.
4. The head of the State should be a Hindu and Muslim alternately.

The plan said that when Muslims were convinced that Hindus were not using their numerical strength to bulldoze them, they would give up the idea of Pakistan. It also said that once India becomes independent, the economic, political and class interests will automatically prevail over religion-based considerations.[15]

Azad's suggestion list echoed in the Congress party resolution, passed only a few weeks later on 21 September 1945 at the party's national meet at Bombay, which was nothing but a reiteration of the 'self-determination' resolution of 1942. The resolution while talking about United India said:

> Nevertheless, the Committee also declares that it cannot think in terms of compelling the people in any territorial unit to remain in an Indian union against their declared and established will. While recognizing this principle, every effort should be made to create conditions which would help different units in developing a common and cooperative national life. ... Each territorial unit should have the fullest possible autonomy within the union consistently with a strong national State.[16]

---

[15]V.P. Menon, *The Transfer of Power in India*, Orient BlackSwan, 1957, p. 221.

[16]Indian Annual Register, Vol. I. p. 225, January–June 1942, https://dspace.gipe.

This secession clause however invited strong opposition from certain sections of the Congress and therefore it was decided to approach the Muslim population directly instead of the Muslim League.[17]

In the meantime, there were changes in the political matrix in Britain. In the general election held in mid-1945, the Churchill-led Conservative Party lost and the Labour Party won a landslide victory. Clement Attlee now replaced Churchill as the British prime minister. Almost immediately after this, Japan surrendered in World War II.

Under the changed circumstances, in which the British no longer faced war threat from Japan on India's eastern frontier, Wavell went back to London in the second half of August to ascertain the views of the new administration on the Indian problem. On his return, in mid-September, he immediately announced general elections to test the strength of various political parties, first at the central level and then at the provincial level. The Attlee administration was much more sympathetic to the cause of Indian freedom than the previous Churchill regime.

CHOOSING BETWEEN THE CONGRESS AND CONSCIENCE

Interestingly, as soon as elections were announced, known jurist and intellectual, M.R. Jayakar, tried to explore a United Hindu front in the elections against the Muslim League threat by approaching the then Hindu Mahasabha president S.P. Mukherjee. In response, Mukherjee, in his reply of 16 October, turned down the proposal and wrote:

> I am most anxious there should be no division among the Hindus at this crisis. In fact, ever since I became President of the Hindu Mahasabha, I have been pleading for a united front among as many nationalists parties as possible that may be agreed on the fundamental issues connected with the freedom

---

ac.in/xmlui/handle/10973/17984. Accessed on 31 July 2021.
[17] V.P. Menon, *The Transfer of Power in India*, Orient BlackSwan, 1957, p. 228.

of United India. Many now feel that there is no difference between the Congress and the Hindu Mahasabha in view of the Poona resolution and the open declaration against the league and the Pakistan issue by eminent Congress leaders. But this is not exactly the real case. ... The last few sentences (of the Poona resolution) are indeed ominous. The Congress there accepts self-determination of territorial units... Thus, we have before us three schemes for partitions of India: one of the Cripps type, the second of the League type and the third of the Congress type. The only body which will be uncompromising on the question of India's integrity will be the Hindu Mahasabha; others will differ on the areas that may be partitioned and on the method of determining such areas. The present Congress stand will not appease the League, but it will certainly create [extraordinary] complications on the main issues of division of India when the constitution-making body will start to function. I am told Sardar Patel and some others were opposed to any concession on the partition issue, but they had to yield in view of the threatened resignation of the President.[18]

Clearly, even after Savarkar's departure as the president, the Mahasabha continued to oppose the Partition proposals with all its might. Savarkar, suffering from fever and extreme weakness, was almost bed-ridden on the eve of the elections. His teeth were removed; so he was unable deliver a speech. Still, from his bed, he tried to wake up the Hindus when the crucial hour of the elections came. He issued clinical and impassioned statements, which implored the voters to save the country from ruin by their vote.

He said:

The real question before the voter in this election is not independence. Every Hindu Mahasabhaite and Congressite and all parties are united on that. Consequently, the real issue before the electorate is the Constituent Assembly which will

---

[18] National Archives, Roll No. 00155, File No. 833.

be called just after this election and which will necessarily be attended by the elected representatives who will have to deal with the very questions of Pakistan, Communal Award, Parity and such others. It will be here that strong and most trusted Hindu representatives will be required by the Hindus to represent their case and resist any aggression on our rights. And who else they can rely on but those who are elected independently on [the] Hindu Mahasabha ticket and are bound by their conscience as well as their prestige to stand by the Hindu Banner?[19]

Savarkar went a step further. By declaring 'Choose one: Congress or Conscience', he appealed to Hindu followers of the Congress to join hands with Hindu Sagathanists to realize the national goal. It was reminiscent of Chhatrapati Shivaji's appeal to Mughal commander Mirza Raja Jai Singh in 1665 to fight for the Hindu cause rather than fighting for the fanatic emperor, Aurangzeb.

Reminding Congressite Hindus of the sacrifices made by Hindu Sanghathanists for protecting Hindu temples and Hindu honour against Muslim aggression, Savarkar warned thus:

> Only last week a small boy of 9 was done to death in the dark simply because he was a staunch Hindu Sanghatanist member of the R.S.S. But remember if we few who are fighting for the Hindu cause are defeated, the blame of the defeat can never be attached to us who continued the good fight, but to those millions of Hindus who did not join the fight but kept on the fence and simply witnessed the Hindu banner sullied, the unity of India cut into pieces, the Hindusthan turned into Pakistan.[20]

As the Hindu Mahasabha headed into the elections, it had a fairly good all-India presence, as demonstrated by the response that Savarkar received throughout the country between 1938 and 1943. Having established the Hindu Mahasabha as a political party

---

[19] V.D. Savarkar, *Historic Statements by Savarkar*, G.P. Parchure, 1967.
[20] Ibid.112.

in the true sense, he had led the party in its defeat of Congress candidates in many important municipal, local and district board elections and by-elections to the legislatures. In 1941, the Congress suffered a significant defeat in Maharashtra when Jamnadas Mehta, supported by the Hindu Mahasabha, defeated the Congress candidate in the election to the Central Assembly. The former king of Ayodhya too won against the Congress in the United Province with the Hindu Mahasabha's support.[21]

In Bengal, where the Congress was by then a dwindling force, Ashutosh Lahiri, the general secretary of the Hindu Mahasabha, defeated the main opposition candidate of the Forward Block in the election to the Provincial Assembly. K.C. Neogy, supported by the Hindu Mahasabha, defeated the Forward Block candidate, Mujumdar, in Bengal in a by-election to the Central Assembly when a seat fell vacant due to the disappearance of Subhas Chandra Bose in January 1941. During the wartime, the party was part of the coalition government in Bengal and Sindh.

The party scored many electoral successes at Khamgaon, Patna, Munger, Katihar (Bihar), Suri (Bengal), Poona, Mahad, Bhagalpur and Sholapur, so much so that at some of these places, there was complete debacle for the Congress candidates. Some Congressmen withdrew their candidature or fought elections in a personal capacity in order to save the prestige of the grand old party in case of their defeats.

In Assam, the Congress could not even put up a candidate for a by-election to the Central Assembly and the Hindu Mahasabha candidate, Anang Mohan Dam, was returned unopposed to the Central Assembly.[22] In Kerala, a Hindu Mahasabha candidate was elected as the vice president of the Calicut District Council by defeating a Moplah Muslim in 1943.[23] Even in 1945, Hindu

---

[21] Balarao Savarkar, *Swatantryaveer Savarkar: Akhand Hindusthan Ladha Parv*, p. 37.
[22] Dhananjay Keer, *Veer Savarkar*, Popular Prakashan Pvt. Ltd; Second edition, 2019, p. 311.
[23] Balarao Savarkar, *Swatantryaveer Savarkar: Akhand Hindusthan Ladha Parv*, p. 279.

Mahasabha candidates won eight seats out of the 14 non-Muslim seats in Delhi municipal elections.[24] The party was emerging as a threat to the Congress in non-Muslim electorates in several areas.

Thus, the Hindu Mahasabha had gained much ground because of Savarkar's spirited stand on the issue of United India and for protecting Hindu interests. Faced with this imminent threat, the Congress created an elaborate plan to steal the Mahasabha's thunder. Flush with strength in terms of both funds and organization and backed by public support that it had acquired as a result of the Quit India movement, besides boasting an array of top and experienced leaders including Gandhi, the Congress decided to present itself as a bigger version of the Hindu Mahasabha when it came to the issue of keeping the country united.

The idea was not to gain Muslim votes but to prevent Hindu votes from going to the Hindu Mahasabha, the Congress's only possible rival for Hindu votes. The Congress campaign was combative and planned on multiple fronts. Sardar Patel was astutely employed against the Muslim League in a tone that was decidedly pro-Hindu and anti-Partition. In his anti-Pakistan and anti-Muslim League speeches that he delivered in public meetings after meetings, Patel thundered that the Congress won't allow the Partition of India, come what may. His speeches often had such lines as '*Talwar se talwar bhidegi* (Sword will face a sword)' while posturing against the Muslim League on the issue of Pakistan. On one occasion, he even said: 'There have been [a] series of mistakes by the Congress. Ever since the Congress abandoned unalloyed nationalism, the mischief has grown. From minority representation we have travelled to parity. Now it will never be repeated. [The] Congress will never go to the Muslim League.'[25]

Nehru too bellowed in a public meeting in Calcutta that there would be no compromise with the Muslim League. Then there were

---

[24]Ibid. 392.
[25]Dhananjay Keer, *Veer Savarkar*, Popular Prakashan Pvt. Ltd; Second edition, 2019, p. 368.

leaders such as the chief minister of the Central Provinces, Pandit R.S. Shukla, who threatened that if Pakistan was formed, Indian Muslims would be treated as foreigners.[26]

The most telling effect, however, was of the statement of Sarat Chandra Bose, Netaji's elder brother and leader of the Congress Parliamentary Party. Bose also thundered that the Congress could never allow Pakistan. Since he was the brother of Netaji, the true hero of the Indian people at that time, his statement carried a lot of heft.

On a second front, the Congress, many of whose leaders including Nehru were prepared to even act against the INA while concurring with British action against Japan, decided to defend the first three INA captives, Maj. Gen. Shahnawaz Khan, Col. Prem Sehgal and Col. Gurbax Singh Dhillon, who were captured by the British Indian army and brought to trial. Nehru and Bhulabhai Desai were fielded to defend the INA accused in the trial held in the Red Fort. Although the court verdict went against the accused, it did enough to help the Congress in the eyes of Hindus and the nationalists on the eve of the polls.

However, as soon as the elections ended, the Congress stopped showing sympathy for the INA accused. Further, as authors Chandrachur Ghose and Anuj Dhar quote, the then Congress general secretary Acharya Kripalani, in an intelligence report from the archives, dated 12 December 1945, said that the 'Congress sponsoring of the INA is intended for election purposes, and that after the elections, [the] Congress will drop the matter.'[27]

Incidentally, the Hindu Mahasabha too had given programmes in support of the INA but these failed to have an impact in the face of the Congress dramatics. This, and owing to multiple handicaps, the Hindu Mahasabha could never take its campaign to a crescendo. This was in spite of the fact that it had a powerful theme based on 'A vote for Congress was a vote for Pakistan', which

---

[26]Ibid. 367, 368, 369.

[27]Chandrachur Ghose and Anuj Dhar, *Conundrum*, Vitasta Publishing Pvt. Ltd; First edition, 2019, p. 798.

proved true 18 months later. Savarkar had already stepped down as party president because of serious health issues. Already missing the powerful presence of Savarkar, who was both the planner and executor for the Hindu Mahasabha, the party woefully lacked in resources and funds. This turned out to be a trickle against the river that the Congress commanded in terms of funds, overall resources and of course, public following. Plus, the Congress had on its side the sagely Mahatma, whose sheen the Hindu Mahasabha could not bedim in public eyes in spite of pointing out several of the blunders he made in decision-making.

The gullible voters voted for the Congress, forgetting all the warnings Savarkar and the Hindu Mahasabha leaders had given all these years in the face of the Congress's electric campaign. The Hindu Mahasabha's core constituency too gave away under the weight of the Congress campaign and shifted to the Congress. Perhaps somewhere, the Hindu Mahasabha's decision not to join Gandhi's Quit India call, although for justifiable reasons when seen in retrospect, also affected its public image. But on the whole, the party's wipe-out was shocking because it had done reasonably well in minor elections across the country between 1938 and 1942.

During 1945–46, the Hindu Mahasabha could not win a single seat in the Central Assembly of 102 seats. The smaller parties including the one led by Ambedkar were wiped out. However, a deeper analysis of the results shows that the Hindu Mahasabha was wiped out in terms of seats but not in terms of votes. It recorded 16 per cent of the total votes, which is an impressive figure by any yardstick. In fact, on his second visit to India in 1946 as part of the Cabinet Mission, when Cripps asked Hindu Mahasabha nominee Bhopatkar as to who his party was representing, Bhopatkar told him that the Hindu Mahasabha had secured 16 per cent votes in the Central Assembly polls. He also proposed that representation in the constitutional assembly should be given in proportion of percentage of votes gained by each party.[28]

---

[28]Balarao Savarkar, *Swatantryaveer Savarkar: Akhand Hindusthan Ladha Parv*, p. 418.

All the 30 Muslim-reserved seats went to the Muslim League, thanks to its most communal campaign in the name of Pakistan. The Congress won 57 seats besides two more seats through independent candidates, including Asaf Ali, who contested on behalf of the Congress as an independent from an open (non-Muslim) seat. Though the results were a big Congress victory, they were also a tragic rejection by Muslims of the Congress model of nationalism based on Hindu–Muslim unity, even after continuous appeasement of Muslims by the party for decades.

The results of the elections to the provincial assemblies that followed in January 1946 were no different. Of the 1,585 seats, the Congress won 923 and the Muslim League won 425. The League formed governments in Bengal and Sindh and afterwards managed to break the coalition government that the Congress, the Unionist Party and the Akali Dal had formed in Punjab almost at the point of sword. Though it was unable to capture power in the Muslim-majority North-West Frontier Province, where Congress leader Khan Abdul Ghafar Khan held sway, and also in Punjab, its victory on Muslim-reserved seats was most complete and virtually secured its demand for Pakistan. The League won on all the seats in Bombay, Madras and Orissa while winning between 80 and 90 per cent seats in all other provinces including United Provinces (present-day Uttar Pradesh), Bihar and Assam. The Congress's Muslim candidates were almost wiped out on Muslim-reserved seats as in the Central Assembly polls a month before. In these two polls (Central and Provincial), almost 87 per cent of the Muslim votes went to the Muslim League and only three per cent to the Congress's Muslim candidates.

A major feature of the polls was the Muslim League's highly communal campaign. The League leaders organized Muslim votes by roping in spiritual heads of major dargahs in the country and getting them to appeal to the Muslims to vote for the League in the name of Islam. These dargah heads, who commanded great community following, wiped out whatever little support the Congress had worked up amongst Muslims in rural areas. Significantly, the Muslim League purposely kept the definition of

Pakistan vague to befool the Muslim community. Many who voted for Pakistan thought that the new Muslim country that Jinnah had demanded for Muslims would include all the Muslim-majority areas spread across the country, like several mini-Pakistans.

In retrospect, when one analyses the results of the two elections, one feels that had the Congress as a whole changed its priorities and methods altogether and truly stuck to its pre-election, Hindu Mahasabha-like posture in defence of United India, it could have prevented Pakistan. Further, the party could have also brought enough pressure on Jinnah to yield to a strong Centre even in United India. For the Muslim League had failed to get absolute majorities in provincial elections in what comprises today's Pakistan and had, in fact, totally lost the elections in the North-West Frontier Province. However, unfortunately, the Congress had neither such resolve nor the skill or commitment to frustrate the British's divisive measures.

In fact, the Congress posturing as a nationalist party to the core during the campaigning in the two elections and then dropping it after the polls and coming back to its old pacifist ways was almost chameleon-like. Actually, as events subsequently proved, the Congress posturing at the time of elections constituted the biggest stab on Hindus' back and very similar to its recent ways when it has been indirectly supporting the most communal Muslim organizations, some of them bordering on anti-national activity.[29]

CABINET MISSION PLAN: MOVES AND COUNTERMOVES

With the declaration of the election results, it was now time for the constitution of the Constituent Assembly and the composition of the interim government. Only two parties remained on India's

---

[29]Uday Mahurkar, 'Rahul Gandhi's Wayanad Poll: Why a Closer Look at some Muslim Factions in the Area Is an Imperative,' *Daily O*, 8 April 2019, https://www.dailyo.in/politics/lok-sabha-elections-2019-rahul-gandhi-in-wayanad-muslim-appeasement-muslim-league-wahhabism-simi/story/1/30226.html. Accessed on 23 August 2019.

electoral spectrum: the Congress and the Muslim League, with whom the British would now deal. Meanwhile, the elected members of the provincial assemblies, under a formula, fixed party-wise members of the Constituent Assembly. The Congress got 292 members and the Muslim League 79 in the Constituent Assembly.

The atmosphere of insecurity in the country marked by communal tension was now rising as a result of the heat generated by the election campaigns. What added to the heat was the mutiny revolt in the Indian Navy's dockyards in early 1946 starting from Bombay dock. The revolt put real fear in the minds of the British and made them eager to leave India after handing over power. To further this objective, the British prime minister Attlee announced the Cabinet Mission's visit to India. He said:

> The Mission was going to India in a very positive mood. The temperature (in India) of 1946 was not the temperature of [the] 1920s, 1930s or even 1942. My colleagues were going to India with the intention of using their utmost endeavours to help her attain freedom as speedily and as fully as possible. We are mindful of the rights of the minorities and the minorities should be able to live free from fear. On the other hand, we cannot allow a minority to place their veto on the advance of the majority.[30]

The speech gave some hope to the protagonists of United India. But what they had not counted was the mood of the British bureaucracy or administration which, at the officer level, remained the same in spite of the change of political power in England.

The Cabinet Mission comprising Lord Pethick-Lawrence, A.V. Alexander and the old hand, Sir Stafford Cripps, landed in Delhi on 21 March 1946 to find a final solution to the Indian problem. The delegation stayed in India for three months and held a series of deliberations with political parties as well as a cross section of people. The delegation had to enlarge its scope of deliberation

---

[30]B.N. Jog, *Threat of Islam: Indian Dimensions*, Mumbai (Bombay): Unnati Prakashan, 1994, p. 298 .

when the Congress and the Muslim League failed to arrive at an agreement about the future shape of India. The Congress, through its president Maulana Azad, represented against the two-nation theory and in favour of a federal structure granting maximum freedom to provinces, which was basically the Azad view that was not in tune with many lower-rung Congress leaders.

Jinnah stuck to his Pakistan stand saying that the Muslims were already an independent nation. His scheme of Pakistan was to have Sindh, the North-West Frontier Province, Balochistan, Punjab, Bengal and Assam. Intellectuals such as Jayakar and Sapru agreed on separate electorates and parity between Hindus and Muslims at the electoral and administrative levels. Gandhi rejected the Pakistan scheme and said that a majority of Muslims in India were originally of Hindu origin and had adopted Islam as a result of forced conversions and so the Partition proposal was unjustified. However, what Gandhi and Azad told the delegation amounted only to semantics, as the Congress and Gandhi had already conceded Pakistan in the name of self-determination.

When the delegation enlarged its scope of deliberations following a deadlock between the Congress and the League, it also called the Hindu Mahasabha, which was represented by party leader Bhopatkar. The party stuck to its old, resolute stand against any attempt to divide India.

Though tilting more towards the Muslim League, the delegation wasn't prepared to grant everything to Jinnah because it had to maintain a semblance of balance, at least for the sake of public posture. So, to end the deadlock, the delegation proposed two alternatives, which were:

1. A sovereign state of Pakistan was offered to Jinnah as demanded by him but with only half of Bengal and Punjab. The other option was a group of the provinces as visualized and demanded by Jinnah in the name of Pakistan and another group/groups comprising the rest of the Indian provinces, with equal representation at the Centre to handle the portfolios of defence, foreign affairs and communication.

The states would have their own constitutions.
2. The second alternative was akin to forming independent states in a federation, with provinces having maximum powers and a federal government having minimum authority. The princely states were, of course, an undefined fourth group as part of the British's secret plan of allowing a 'Princesthan', which was also very palatable to Jinnah, who was always for India's division.

Jinnah reacted to the scheme as an intelligent strategist. Not wanting partitioned Bengal and Punjab, Jinnah opted for the second alternative. For the Congress too the second one was more agreeable. The subjects to be governed by a particular group's government would be decided by the groups themselves.

The Mission members also decided that the Constituent Assembly would be elected by the existing legislatures and would provide for appropriate representation of each community. The elected members would sit together for initial discussions and for that they should meet in three groups, namely:

1. Group A: Central Provinces, Bombay, United Provinces, Bihar and Orissa
2. Group B: Punjab, Sindh, the North-West Frontier Province and Balochistan
3. Group C: Bengal and Assam

As evident from the selection of states in the groups, the Mission proposal was loaded with a divisionary element. The grouping of Group B and Group C virtually meant yielding to Pakistan under a weak federal structure. It promised not just the whole of Bengal and Punjab to Jinnah, but also Assam. Clubbing Assam with the Muslim-majority Bengal, despite repeated warnings from the people of Assam and parties such as the Hindu Mahasabha, was the clearest indication of the delegation's intention and what it sought to achieve.

Significantly, out of the three groups, two groups would be controlled by the Muslim League on the strength of its majority. Jinnah reluctantly accepted the plan by getting a resolution passed by the Muslim League while expressing disappointment that his original Pakistan demand was rejected and even saying that the Muslim League's first priority was a clearly delineated, full Pakistan.

The Congress too expressed its unhappiness saying it didn't meet its aims and objectives but didn't reject the proposal either. It accepted the plan through a resolution and said 'the plan would play its part in drawing up the Constitution of an independent, united and democratic India'[31], while recording its dissatisfaction regarding the grouping scheme of provinces and a weak central authority. The Mission members said the 'Plan will retain the unity of India while giving minorities, particularly Muslims, an opportunity to safeguard their future.'[32]

After a long phase of uncertainty, things were finally falling into place and an interim government was in sight when Nehru took over as Congress President from Azad at its national session in July 1946. He immediately challenged several points of the plan in a press conference. In his opinion, it was none of the British's concern as to how Indians solve the minority problem and that no outside (read British) interference was acceptable. He also said that these were limiting factors to the sovereignty of the Constituent Assembly. Regarding the grouping scheme, he said in all probability there would be no grouping, as sections would decide against grouping. According to Nehru, there was a four to one chance of the North-West Frontier Province going against the grouping, so Group B would collapse. There was also every chance that Assam would refuse to go with Bengal. Finally, he said, 'Thus you see this grouping business approached from any point of view does not get on at all.'[33] He also expressed several reservations about the proposed federal structure.

---

[31]B.N. Jog, *Threat of Islam: Indian Dimensions*, Mumbai (Bombay): Unnati Prakashan, 1994, p. 301; V.P. Menon, *The Transfer of Power in India*, Orient BlackSwan, 1957, p. 277.

[32]B.N. Jog, *Threat of Islam: Indian Dimensions*, Mumbai (Bombay): Unnati Prakashan, 1994, p. 301.

[33]V.P. Menon, *The Transfer of Power in India*, Orient BlackSwan, 1957, p. 281.

His language virtually spelt out the Congress's refusal to join the proposed interim government. Clearly, Nehru was pleading for a strong central government and United India and in the process pouring cold water over Jinnah's scheme aimed at carving out a Pakistan through the back door under the umbrella of a weak federal structure with tacit support of the British. Nehru was perhaps trying to do justice to the aspirations of the Congress voters, who had in the recent election, voted overwhelmingly in favour of the party's promise of a United India. In fact, his bold stand was against the views of outgoing president Maulana Azad, who was in favour of a weak central authority. So, it was not surprising that Azad called this Nehru action 'a grave error on Nehru's part' in his autobiography.[34]

Expectedly, a livid Jinnah reacted furiously to Nehru's averments and condemned them at a press conference in which he accused the Congress of going back on its earlier word. He said: 'Pandit Nehru's interpretation of the Congress acceptance of Cabinet Mission's proposals is a complete repudiation of the basic form upon which the long-term scheme rests. This is simply because they (the Congress) have secured a brute majority of 292 members against 79 Muslims in the Constituent Assembly.'[35] Thus, he harked back to his theme of the late 1930s, when he accused the Congress of promoting majority domination and throttling the minority, thus raising a false bogey of Muslim victimhood. Jinnah now gave enough indications of not just countering Nehru's outburst but using it to full advantage for his Pakistan scheme.

Jinnah's response was expected to be doubly strong as the Congress and its supreme leader, Gandhi, had themselves, on more than one occasion, conceded the right of self-determination on the part of the provinces with a weak federal structure. These actions had whetted Jinnah's appetite for more and more concessions till he demanded a separate country itself.

---

[34]Maulana Abul Kalam Azad, *India Wins Freedom*, Orient BlackSwan, 1988, p. 143.
[35]Ibid. 138.

JINNAH'S JIHAD IN THREE PARTS

The Muslim League Council, called expressly by Jinnah, first denounced Nehru's stand and rejected the Cabinet Mission proposal and called upon the British to invite the League to form the government since the Congress had refused. The League gave its working committee the authority to pass a resolution calling for direct action by Muslims 'as all constitutional methods were exhausted for the Muslim league to achieve its objectives'.[36]

The Direct Action programme and its commencement were finalized for 16 August 1946. Jinnah's confident Liaquat Ali said, 'Direct Action means unconstitutional deeds. .... We don't want to omit any action from Direct Action. It means acting against the law'.[37] Sardar Abdur Rab Nishtar, a Muslim League leader of the North-West Frontier Province, said that 'now Pakistan could be achieved by bloodshed only. At the first opportunity we will have to take the blood of non-Muslims'[38]. Another League leader Firoz Khan Noon insisted that 'by our deeds even the hands of Genghis Khan and Halaku would hang in shame'.[39] Yet another leader and former chief minister of Bengal, Khwaja Nizamuddin, said, 'We can cause disaster by 101 ways. Bengali Muslims know what Direct Action means. They need not be given any direction.'[40] The mayor of Calcutta, Syed Muhammad Usman, was equally violent in his language: 'In the month of Ramzan, the first open war between Islam and Kafirs started and the Muslims got the permission to wage Jehad...the All India Muslim League has chosen this sacred month for launching jehad for achieving Pakistan... O Kafir! your doom is not far and the general massacre will come.'[41]

---

[36]V.P. Menon, *The Transfer of Power in India*, Orient BlackSwan, 1957, p. 284.
[37]Pyarelal, *Mahatma Gandhi: The Last Phase, Vol. I*, Ahmedabad: Navajivan Publishing House, 1956, p. 252.
[38]Ibid.
[39]Ibid.
[40]Ibid.
[41]Anita Inder Singh, *The Origins of the Partition of India, 1936–47*, OUP India; New edition, 1991, p. 182.

Jinnah's words after the resolution was passed clearly indicated that he was exhorting Muslims to resort to the old Islamic principle of jihad against non-Muslims. Describing the step as 'historic', he said, 'Never have we in the whole history of the League done anything except by constitutional methods. But now we are forced into this position. This day we say good-bye to constitutional methods.'[42] He alleged that the Congress and the Cabinet Mission were holding a pistol to the Muslim League, one of authority and other of mass struggle and non-cooperation. He said in the face of this pistol, the Muslim League too would pull out a pistol and use it for its objectives. When asked about the term 'pistol', he refused to elaborate as to what he meant. Jinnah's pistol was, in fact, the weapon of Islamic jihad—as proved by the subsequent bloodbath in Bengal marked by plunder, rape and conversion of Hindus.

Had the Congress, which had the full backing of the majority Hindu community, come with an equally strong and threatening statement on the League's open call for violence, it would have sent the right signal to Jinnah, who very well knew that Hindus were in a vast majority in the country while being a minority in Bengal. This is what Savarkar and the Hindu Mahasabha leaders had exhorted the Congress to do. Incidentally, the Congress and its top leaders had in the past differed with Gandhi on the issue of complete non-violence, but never tried to demonstrate it practically. This was the most opportune moment to counter Jinnah's violent threat with an equally threatening call. But the Congress not just missed the opportunity but tried to kowtow to Jinnah with a view to prevent him from carrying out his threat.

The morning of 16 August 1946 dawned with a Muslim League advertisement in newspapers with almost a direct exhortation to Muslims to indulge in violence. The Muslim government in Bengal, led by Huseyn Shaheed Suhrawardy, was ready to help in this civil jihad. It declared a public holiday on that day despite protests by opposition parties. Muslims equipped with elaborately distributed

---

[42]Pyarelal, *Mahatma Gandhi: The Last Phase, Vol. I*, Ahmedabad: Navajivan Publishing House, 1956, p. 252.

arms such as spears, lathis, daggers and other lethal weapons including fire arms came out on the streets and started attacking innocent Hindus with jihadi ferocity. Suhrawardy's police looked the other way as dead bodies of Hindus started piling up on the streets and soon dogs and vultures started feasting on them in many areas of Calcutta. Innocent Hindu women were ravished and killed in large numbers even as Hindu property was looted.

The Congress became a passive spectator to the League-sponsored, unprecedented violence against the Bengali Hindus. The orgy of violence, rape and plunder went on for almost three days in several localities. The chilling description given by Acharya Kripalani about the atrocities against Hindus leaves little doubt that what Calcutta saw was a modern-day jihad:

> The British remained amused spectators. Suhrawardy, the Chief Minister of Bengal, was an efficient, unscrupulous and ruthless person. ... He and his companions saw to it that Muslim hooligans were mobilised and supplied with firearms and other lethal weapons. Arrangements were also made for transporting hooligans from other places. Petrol coupons for hundreds of gallons were issued to the ministers for this purpose. (Rationing of petrol introduced during the war was still in force.) ... The Chief Minister, who held the portfolio of law and order, had systematically transferred the Hindu police officers from 22 out of 24 police stations in Calcutta and replaced them by Muslim officers. The remaining two police stations were under Anglo-Indians. Thus, the stage was set for the 'Great Calcutta Killing'. It started on the 16th morning. A huge procession of thousands of armed men, carrying League flags and raising deafening cries of 'Ladke Lenge Pakistan' ('We will fight and take Pakistan'), started from Howrah towards Calcutta. Their passage through the roads and streets of the city created terror. A huge rally was held under the chairmanship of the Chief Minister and inflammatory speeches were made against the Hindus. (The quarrel could have been, if at all, with the Congress and not

with the Hindu community. But in that case it could not have been given the character of a religious war, jihad.) After the dispersal of the meeting began killing, looting, arson, rape and other unspeakable forms of crime. Life in Calcutta was paralysed within hours. For two days this orgy swept over the city unchecked. ... The Chief Minister installed himself in the police control room, overriding the orders of the officers of his own choice. He also ordered immediate release of rioters wherever they were arrested. Complaints about the Chief Minister's scandalous conduct reached the Governor, but he remained unconcerned, though he belonged to the Labour party of England! On the third day, the Hindus, failing to get any protection from the Government, including the Governor, were compelled to organise resistance in self-defense. After that, started the indiscriminate retaliation (by the Hindus). It was only then that the Governor thought of calling in the military. For two days not a shot had been fired when the Muslim goondas were in the ascendancy.[43]

It was only when the Hindus started retaliating in self-defence that the rampaging Muslim crowds gradually started coming under control. But by then it was estimated that 5,000 men, women and children were killed and almost 15,000 injured. The streets of Calcutta were strewn with dead bodies that lay unattended for days. The manholes were choked with corpses. A British correspondent, Kim Christen, wrote in *The Statesman* (an Anglo-Indian paper then): 'I have a stomach made strong by the experience of war but war was never like this. This is not a riot. It needs a word found in mediaeval history, a fury.'[44]

The naked violence demonstrated by Muslims against the Hindus in Calcutta and other places had its effect on the Congress, which was virtually on its knees. The party agreed to form the interim government at the Centre led by Nehru on the invitation of

---

[43]J.B. Kripalani, *Gandhi: His Life and Thought*, Publications Division of the Ministry of Information and Broadcasting, Govt of India, 1995, p. 254.
[44]Ibid.

the British, who too were pressing the Congress. Later, Nehru who had taken a firm stand against the Muslim League aggression only some time ago, on being directed by the party, himself called up Jinnah inviting him to join the interim government—an invitation that the shrewd Jinnah accepted after holding out for some time knowing well that his prescription was working.

Had the Congress had the courage and was indeed wedded to a fearless ideology based on truthfulness, its provincial governments, which were ruling in eight provinces, should have called for action against the Muslim League leaders who had instigated such violence. It could have also called for action against the League leaders after taking over at the Centre. But instead, it ran to the League to patch up. The Congress thus had lost all right to represent Hindu interests.

The Congress's failure to resist the Calcutta killings only encouraged the jihadi mentality of the Muslims in Bengal. Less than two months later started the rural jihad in Bengal in Noakhali, a place not very far from Calcutta but now in Bangladesh, which at that time as now is known for producing maulanas in its madrassas.

Kripalani again gives a vivid description of the Muslim violence in Noakhali:

> The holocaust started on 10 October, 1946. Organised and well-equipped bands surrounded the Hindu homes. The first victims were the leading Hindus and zamindars. The pattern was more or less uniform. They began by looting and burning the houses and killing the menfolk, raping and taking away the women. Maulanas and Maulvis often accompanied the mob. As soon as the work of the mob was over, there and then the Hindus were forcibly converted. In some villages, regular classes were held to teach them the kalma and ayats from the Koran. During our visit to Dattapara, we found a number of men who had been so converted and were compelled to take beef while in the custody of their captors.[45]

---

[45]J.B. Kripalani, *Gandhi: His Life and Thought*, Publications Division of the Ministry of Information and Broadcasting, Govt of India, 1995, p. 278.

That the Calcutta killings followed by the Noakhali violence were jihad orchestrated by the Muslim League is proved beyond doubt by an explosive, 24-point pamphlet circulated amongst Muslims by Muslim League leader Habibur Rahman. The key calls in the pamphlet were:

1. Every Muslim should be prepared to die for Pakistan and after it was achieved should strive to win entire Bharat for Islam.
2. Hindus should be annihilated and Hindu girls should be abducted and made Muslim.
3. Shops and factories of Hindus should be plundered and the plundered material should be deposited in League local offices. Those Muslims who are pro-India should also be killed.[46]

The pattern of violence against Hindus in Calcutta as well as Noakhali confirmed to this violent pamphlet.

While the state government was sponsoring the Muslim violence, the Bengal Hindu Mahasabha worked wholeheartedly for relief work in disturbed areas and in settlement of Hindu refugees during the Calcutta killings and the Noakhali carnage. Major focus areas of the relief work carried out by the Mahasabha were:

1. Rehabilitation work for those who were unwilling to return to their villages
2. Educational relief such as supplying books, providing funds for examination fees, starting students' home, etc.
3. Agrarian and vocational relief
4. Supply of clothes, blankets and utensils and other necessaries of life
5. Establishment of women's homes.
6. Medical relief in terms of a well-equipped 25-bed hospital for both outdoor and indoor patients, mobile medical units attached to each relief centre, ambulances, etc.

---

[46]Gopal Das Khosla, *Stern Reckoning: A Survey of the Events Leading Up to and Following the Partition of India*, OUP India; Reprint edition, 1990, p. 81, 95, 314.

7. Supplementing other sister organizations with help of cash and kind including individual relief and marriage expenses
8. Legal defence of innocent and poor Hindus
9. Protecting and feeding refugees
10. Zonal settlement for repatriation[47]

The Muslim atrocities in Bengal had a chilling effect in several other areas. While reacting to the Muslim atrocities on Hindus in Bengal, Hanuman Prasad Poddar, of Gita Press (Gorakhpur), a leading protector of Hindu culture and interests, castigated the Congress in strong language in the November 1946 issue of his monthly magazine *Kalyan*. He accused the Congress of betraying Hindus in the worst possible manner in its greed for power: 'Hindu male and female are being wiped out in all respects by the terrorists and the government of the people is busy in its other essential tasks!' He said the people had great hope from the Congress, but it had failed to provide even basic protection to the people (read Hindus) against organized terrorism.

However, the antidote to the Muslim vandalism in Bengal was provided by the Hindus of Bihar when the Muslims of Bihar tried to implement a Direct Action in that province. The Muslims were mercilessly thrashed and killed by Hindu crowds in Munger, Patna, Saran, Bhagalpur and Chhapra. This had an impact on the violent Muslims of Bengal and even the Muslim League for some time. The Muslim violence, which had spread to other parts of the country including in the United Provinces, started coming under control.

This clearly proves that had the Congress taken a strong stand against the Muslim League's violent stance from the beginning, all the bloodshed could have been averted. However, Gandhi did an admirable job of going to Noakhali, where Hindus were almost lynched by Muslims. There were strong indications that his visit did have a sobering impact. Even Suhrawardy, known as the Butcher of Bengal, was willing to listen to Gandhi on many of his suggestions

---

[47] *Short Report of Hindu Mahasabha Relief Activities during Calcutta Killing and Noakhali Carnage*, Sagwan Press, 2018, p. 16.

regarding the riots and the protection to Hindus. The bitter pill that Hindus had given to Muslims in Bihar and other places in the form of a violent response to the Muslim League attacks was also one of the elements responsible for Suhrawardy's changed stance.[48] Perhaps he was working on his next move to capture the whole of Bengal for Pakistan in the name of united Bengali culture.

Reportedly, Gandhi wanted other party leaders to visit Noakhali but none of them took his advice except Kripalani, who says in his book:

> So far (in October) none of the Ministers of the Centre or the State had visited Noakhali. But when Muslim League leaders tried to create 'Direct Action' in Bihar in November, Hindus retaliated extensively in rural Bihar. Congress government gave full protection to Muslims. The police resorted to repeated firings. Chief Minister, Dr Syed Mahmud from the state, Nehru, Patel, Maulana Azad, Dr. Rajendra Prasad and Liaquat Ali Khan rushed to the rescue of the Muslim victims in Bihar within no time.[49]

Muslim leaders, analysts and historians generally blame Nehru's and the Congress's virtual repudiation of the Cabinet Mission Plan in July 1946 and other Congress blunders for the rift between the Congress and the League, Jinnah's subsequent Direct Action decision and ultimately the formation of Pakistan. It is an attempt to twist facts so as to absolve Jinnah and Indian Muslims of the blame for Pakistan or at least bring the blame down by rationalizing the move. They ignore the smear and completely false campaign of Jinnah to project the Congress as a Hindu party in pursuance of his separatist objective which had, in fact, begun in the early 1930s and had been sharpened further by Jinnah and his supporters with the progress of time. They also generally ignored or played down the glaring fact that almost 87 per cent of the Muslim

---

[48]B.N. Jog, *Threat of Islam: Indian Dimensions*, Mumbai (Bombay): Unnati Prakashan, 1994, p. 320, 330.

[49]J.B. Kripalani, *Gandhi: His Life and Thought*, Publications Division of the Ministry of Information and Broadcasting, Govt of India, 1995, p. 284.

votes in the 1945–46 Parliamentary and Provincial Assembly polls went to the Muslim League, thus making it clear that a majority of Indian Muslims wanted Pakistan. Right from Abul Kalam Azad[50] and late Congress leader Rafiq Zakaria to Indian authors such as A.G. Noorani blame Congress leaders and Nehru saying that had they not rejected the contents of the Cabinet Mission Plan and had earlier not provoked Jinnah with their intransigence, Jinnah wouldn't have been forced to the wall and to resort to Direct Action and, subsequently, carve out Pakistan. Noorani, in fact, goes a step further and blames Gandhi's, Nehru's and Sardar Patel's arrogance for forcing Jinnah to demand Pakistan. He says: 'Jinnah was ever a statesman from 1906 right up to 1939. Gandhi, Nehru and Patel's arrogant refusal to meet him halfway drove him to extremes. Even so, in 1946, he was prepared to accept a United India. The Congress trio rejected the very idea of power-sharing with the Muslim League.'[51] Zakaria says, 'To blame Muslims alone for Partition won't be right...though Jinnah demanded Pakistan, it is Nehru and Patel who accepted it.'[52]

This is a complete travesty of truth based on facts and an attempt to absolve Indian Muslims and their leaders of the blame of causing Partition. Even at the Muslim League Council meeting, which was held before Nehru's negation of the Mission Plan, Jinnah reluctantly accepted the Plan, and categorically said: 'Let me tell you that Muslim India will not rest content until we have established full, complete and sovereign Pakistan.'[53] Plus, the Mission Plan allowed the provinces to secede from the Union.

A major proof is the letter of key Muslim League leader Jamaluddin Ahmed to Jinnah dated 29 May 1946 saying that

---

[50]Maulana Abul Kalam Azad, *India Wins Freedom*, Orient BlackSwan, 1988, pp. 163–71.
[51]A.G. Noorani, 'Partition Truths,' *Frontline*, 2 May 2014, https://frontline.thehindu.com/books/partition-truths/article5914973.ece. Accessed on 31 July 2021.
[52]Rafiq Zakaria, *Indian Muslims: Where Have They Gone Wrong?* Popular Prakashan Ltd, 2005, p. 462.
[53]Yuvraj Krishan, *Understanding Partition: India Sundered, Muslims Fragmented*, Mumbai: Bharatiya Vidya Bhavan, 2002, p. 43.

the Cabinet Mission Plan was an opportunity for realizing their objective of Pakistan. He wrote: 'We work the plan to the Group stage and then create a situation to force the hands of the Hindus and the British to concede Pakistan of our conception. After we have made the Constitution of the Groups B and C according to our wishes our position will be stronger.'[54] Clearly, Nehru or no Nehru, the League and its leaders were hell-bent on achieving Pakistan.

This intention became all the more clear as soon as Jinnah's five lieutenants joined the interim government. The idea was to tear the government apart to achieve its objective of Pakistan. And it started from almost day one in the government that lasted for over five months and sealed the fate of United India by leading to Pakistan. The embers of the religious violence unleashed by the Muslim League in Bengal had hardly died down but the League ministers had no qualms about speaking in a language which was decidedly jihadi and an indication of what was in store in the coming days.

The most vocal amongst them was Health Minister Ghazanfar Ali Khan. Speaking at Lahore as a minister of the interim government of the Viceroy, he said: 'If Muhammad Bin Qasim and Mahmud of Ghazni could invade India with armies composed of a few thousand, God willing, a few lakh Muslims will overwhelm crores of Hindus.'[55] Once, he had allegedly asked Hindus to become Muslims to save themselves from annihilation. A week before joining the ministry, he told students of a college in Lahore: 'In the interim Government, all our (Muslim League) activities will be guided by two considerations, that is to convince the Congress that no Government can function smoothly without the cooperation of the Muslims and that the Interim Government is (for the League) one of the fronts of Direct Action.'[56] He virtually said that no settlement with the Congress was

---

[54] Robin James Moore, *Escape from Empire: The Attlee Government and the Indian Problem*, Oxford University Press, 1983, p. 123.

[55] Dhananjay Keer, *Veer Savarkar*, Popular Prakashan Pvt. Ltd; Second edition, 2019, p. 376.

[56] Pyarelal, *Mahatma Gandhi: The Last Phase, Vol. I*, Ahmedabad: Navajivan Publishing House, 1956, p. 283.

possible except on the basis of granting Pakistan. And yet, Khan was allowed to continue in the ministry.[57]

However, what incensed the Congress the most was Jinnah's shrewd decision to allow the Congress to nominate a Muslim in the government in sharp contrast to his earlier demand and then choosing to nominate a Scheduled Caste leader, Jogendra Nath Mandal as his party's nominee in the Cabinet as a counter. Nehru, in fact, wrote to the Viceroy saying that the League's decision to nominate Mandal was an indication enough that the League was joining the Cabinet to foment trouble. Gandhi too concurred with Nehru. Both were correct to the core as Liaquat Ali, who was holding the finance portfolio, started targeting Congress supporters by engineering raids on their finance establishments.[58]

Apart from engineering riots and following obstructionist strategy in the administration, a third weapon used by the Muslim League was to boycott the Constituent Assembly, which was to carry on till free India's government was formed and was, in fact, mandated to frame the new Constitution of free India. To solve the deadlock, the British government invited Jinnah and Nehru to London for a conference. This was in response to the call by Patel and other Congress leaders that the League should either quit the government or join the Constituent Assembly. However, the attempt failed as both the leaders stuck to their positions and the British tilt was clearly towards the Muslim League. The British stand meant that the Constitution couldn't be valid until approved by the League.

The League's Constitutional Direct Action continued. It boycotted the very first meeting of the Constituent Assembly on 9 December 1946 and also the second one on 20 January 1947. It soon became apparent that a Constitution formed without the League's concurrence won't be binding on the Muslims. Not content with just boycott, the League, through a party's working committee resolution, recommended to the Viceroy on 29 January

---

[57] H.V. Seshadri, *The Tragic Story of Partition*, Sahitya Sindhu Prakashan, 2015, p. 176.
[58] Maulana Abul Kalam Azad, *India Wins Freedom*, Orient BlackSwan, 1988, p. 337.

1947 that the Constituent Assembly be dissolved.

The Congress now reacted with uncharacteristic resolution. It wrote to the Viceroy that the League's recommendation of 29 January was tantamount to rejecting the Cabinet Mission plan and was part of its Direct Action. Therefore, the League should not be allowed to continue in the government, and so it must quit. Nehru asked the Viceroy to seek the resignation of the League members in the government. He threatened that any delay in the matter would force the Congress to reconsider its position.[59]

Next, Patel declared that the Congress would quit the interim government if the League was allowed to continue in it. The threat made by Patel was coupled with the worsening law-and-order situation on the Hindu–Muslim communal front that saw around 4,000 riots across undivided India during the period of the interim government. Of these 4,000 riots, around 3,000 occurred in Punjab alone and 321 in the Bombay Presidency. Clearly, the Punjab riots were turning out to be worse than Bengal. This was proved in due course as Punjab turned into a bloody cauldron, with Hindus and Sikhs at the receiving end. The fast-spreading communal tension and anarchy had affected the functioning of the government to such an extent that it compelled Patel to openly admit that almost every Muslim servant in the government was a Pakistani, thus virtually saying that everybody should be his own policemen to protect himself.[60]

This precarious situation impelled Prime Minister Attlee's announcement in the British parliament on 20 February 1947 that Britain had decided to transfer complete power to India by June 1948. He also declared that Louis Mountbatten was being appointed in place of Lord Wavell as the new and last British Viceroy of India to ensure the final transfer of power.

The writing for the protagonists of United India was now on the wall. S.P. Mukherjee wrote a moving letter to Savarkar. He

---

[59]V.P. Menon, *The Transfer of Power in India*, Orient BlackSwan, 1957, p. 337.
[60]Dhananjay Keer, *Veer Savarkar*, Popular Prakashan Pvt. Ltd; Second edition, 2019, p. 380.

bewailed: 'If the Hindus had only listened to your call, they would not have remained slaves in the land of their birth.'[61] Savarkar was equally disturbed, but he didn't lose his equanimity. He sent his good wishes to Akali leader Master Tara Singh, who had launched a giant effort to forge Hindu–Sikh unity. Savarkar expressed the hope that Guru Gobind Singh would steal the hearts of Hindu-Sikh brotherhood and strengthen the fight for India's freedom and integrity. Despite being electorally rejected by the Hindus, at no point did Savarkar abdicate his moral responsibility towards the Hindu masses and United India, thus demonstrating his unwavering commitment to unalloyed nationalism.

When Lord Mountbatten arrived in India on 22 March 1947, he found the country on the brink of a civil war entirely fomented by the Muslim League. Savarkar wired to him appealing him to immediately consult the Hindu Mahasabha president and Master Tara Singh before making any fundamental changes affecting Hindus. Soon after this, he urged the Bengal Hindu Mahasabha and the Bengali Hindus to demand a separate Hindu province in West Bengal and expel the Muslim trespassers from Assam. In addition, he also called for joining the contiguous Hindu-majority districts of Sindh to the Bombay Presidency to prevent them from being swallowed by the Muslim League in case of Partition. At this time, he issued an unorthodox but practical threat that the Muslim minority would be given the same treatment as would be meted out to Hindus in the Muslim-majority areas.[62]

Savarkar was deeply disturbed by the possibility of Assam being swallowed by the Muslim-majority Bengal as Assam was cunningly clubbed with Bengal by the British–Muslim League combine in the Grouping scheme. Assam, at that time, was facing the dual threat of Muslim influx from East Bengal and the Muslim League's Direct Action. So, in April 1947, Savarkar appealed to the Assam chief minister Gopinath Bordoloi and Revenue Minister Vishnu Das not

---

[61] Ibid. 379.
[62] *The Free Hindustan*, 6 June 1947, Bombay (also quoted in Dhananjay Keer, *Veer Savarkar*)

to surrender an inch of land to the Muslims and eject every Muslim trespasser. The duo acknowledged his appeal.

However, Assam was not the only part of the country facing the League's Direct Action. In West Punjab too, Hindus and Sikhs were being targeted with jihadi ferocity. The Sir Malik Khizar Hayat Tiwana coalition ministry in Punjab, with the participation of the Congress and the Akali Dal, was violently targeted by the Muslim League, which encouraged unprovoked attacks against Hindus and Sikhs in order to throttle the government. Incidents of stabbing had also become quite common even in cities such as Delhi and Bombay.

Punjab had started to witness the second part of Jinnah's jihad, notwithstanding his message before Partition calling for peace. But the Congress's inability to admit it due to its false notions of one-sided secularism had resulted in the world not yet recognizing one of the greatest calamities to befall the human race in the past two centuries. The Muslim atrocities on Hindus were reminiscent of medieval vandalism of Muslim invaders such as Alauddin Khilji, Firoz Shah Tughlaq, Muhammad bin Tughlaq and, in the later period, Nadir Shah and Afghan invader, Ahmad Shah Abdali. Nearly 15 lakh people, a vast majority of them Hindus and Sikhs, were killed, thousands of women raped and thousands converted. It was a greater catastrophe than what the Jews had faced, particularly since their women did not suffer so much dishonour. And yet, there is hardly any mention of this calamity in world history and world museums. Significantly, the Hindus and Sikhs did retaliate violently, but it was only after they were overwhelmed by Muslim vandalism.

Unable to deal with the riot situation in which League leaders were busy dubbing all Muslims who didn't agree with the Pakistan scheme as anti-Muslims, a hapless Tiwana resigned. Thus, Jinnah had succeeded in bringing down the coalition government in Punjab despite the Muslim League being in a minority.

Following his visits to these riot-affected areas, Nehru bewailed and painted a pathetic picture of the situation. He said what was happening was not politics but jungle warfare in which human behaviour was worse than the brutes. Hinting at Jinnah and the Muslim League, he said, 'Let people struggle to achieve their political goals but they should do so as human beings and with human dignity.'[63] But such words had no effect on either Jinnah or the League in Punjab. They were bent upon snatching Punjab at gun point.

Sadly enough, to save the situation, the Congress surrendered to the Muslim League violence in Punjab by passing a resolution that called for the division of Punjab. The resolution said the predominantly Muslim part of Punjab may be separated from the non-Muslim part.[64] Though the Congress had not technically consented to Pakistan, it was fast moving in the direction of recognizing Pakistan.

The Muslim League strategy in Punjab based on violence had a ripple effect. The Congress ministry of the North-West Frontier Province, led by Dr Khan Abdul Jabbar Khan, started veering towards the Pakistan scheme being convinced that he and the North-West Frontier Province couldn't remain safe or survive with hostile Muslim neighbours and especially when the Congress-ruled, Hindu-dominated territories were a hundred miles away. On 29 July 1946, he said that the North-West Frontier Province would join Group B comprising the Muslim-majority provinces of Punjab, Sindh and Balochistan. He was unequivocal in his pronouncement: 'If we can ever form a Group, it can only be with Punjab, Sindh and Balochistan...as the Hindu majority provinces are hundreds of miles away.'[65]

Thus, whether by the force of the compelling situation or by religious affinity, Dr Khan, a Congress leader, deserted the party finally. Of course, the two Khan brothers tried to float the scheme of a separate Pakhtoonistan, which the British and the Muslim League didn't allow to succeed. They also boycotted the subsequent

---

[63]B.N. Jog, *Threat of Islam: Indian Dimensions*, Mumbai (Bombay): Unnati Prakashan, 1994, p. 326.
[64]Pyarelal, *Mahatma Gandhi: The Last Phase, Vol. II*, Ahmedabad: Navajivan Publishing House, 1958, p. 11.
[65]Ibid. 13.

plebiscite organized to decide the issue of whether the people of the North-West Frontier Province should join India or Pakistan. The reason they gave was that the Muslim League had not given the Pathans the option of forming an independent nation of Pakhtoonistan or joining Afghanistan.

THE BLOODY LEGACY OF INDIA'S PARTITION

This situation created by the Muslim League violence and the resultant violent retaliation by Hindus, which was almost like a civil war, led to the inevitable—the Congress and its towering leader, Gandhi, ultimately accepting Partition on 1 May 1947 but through the medium of plebiscite in the Muslim-majority areas. Nehru wrote to Mountbatten: 'The Congress Working Committee is prepared to accept in principle the division of the country provided there is guarantee for the right of self-determination to the people in pre-determined regions. We are still committed to the idea of unified, indivisible India but are accepting partition to avoid conflict and coercion.'[66]

The CWC's decision led to a curious development in Bengal which showed the complete lack of understanding on the part of a section of its people (Hindus) to comprehend the communal and violent streak of the jihadi brand of Islam. On the issue of the division of Bengal, a section of its leaders including Sarat Chandra Bose, leader of the Bengal Congress Legislature Party, was willing to go with Pakistan if Bengal wasn't divided again. All this was done in the interest of the preservation of Bengali culture! Bose, in fact, organized a meeting of Hindu and Muslim leaders on 20 May which was attended by Chief Minister Suhrawardy and two provincial ministers (Fazlur Rehman and Mohammed Ali), besides the secretary of the Bengal Provincial Muslim League, Abul Hashim. The meeting pitched for an undivided Bengal.[67]

---

[66]B.N. Jog, *Threat of Islam: Indian Dimensions*, Mumbai (Bombay): Unnati Prakashan, 1994, p. 331.
[67]Pyarelal, *Mahatma Gandhi: The Last Phase, Vol-II*, Ahmedabad: Navajivan Publishing House, 1958, p. 42.

These protagonists of 'united Bengal at any cost' drew inspiration from Gandhi, who had expressed himself against the division of Bengal and Punjab. Gandhi even went to the extent of saying that he won't mind entrusting all power[68] in new India to the Muslim League to avoid Partition.[69]

After the violence demonstrated by Muslims in Bengal and later in Punjab, handing over power to the Muslim League either at the national level or at the Bengal level would have virtually meant annihilation of Hindus, as has happened in both Pakistan and Bangladesh after Independence.

While these suicidal moves were being made by a section of Hindu leaders in Bengal, the Hindu Mahasabha, led by S.P. Mukherjee, took a firm stand in favour of the division of Bengal to save the Bengali Hindus from imminent washout under the Muslim League rule. Mukherjee was of the view that even if India was not partitioned, Bengal should be divided. With a view to dissuade Gandhi, Mukherjee had even visited him and warned him that undivided Bengal under Suhrawardy could entirely go to Pakistan as he couldn't be trusted. Gandhi believed that the idea of sovereign Bengal was an idea floated by vested European interests for their own reasons.[70] Incidentally, both the Hindus of Bengal and the majority in the CWC felt the same way—that divided Bengal was a better prospect for Bengali Hindus. The committee ultimately decided in favour of division of Bengal, thus going against Gandhi's inclinations.

By now the country had gone much beyond acceptance or rejection of the Cabinet Mission Plan. The issue was now about whether Partition should be done on the basis of the Congress principle of self-determination through plebiscite or on the basis of the Muslim League's two-nation theory. Interestingly, Lord Mountbatten too floated another, more divisionary proposal in May,

---

[68]Maulana Abul Kalam Azad, *India Wins Freedom*, Orient BlackSwan, 1988, p. 187.
[69]Ibid. 204.
[70]Pyarelal, *Mahatma Gandhi: The Last Phase, Vol-II*, Ahmedabad: Navajivan Publishing House, 1958, p. 185.

which completely exposed the British's cunning plans, and sent it to London for approval. Under this scheme, the British proposed to grant Independence to all the provinces thus creating several sovereign states out of India. However, this was bluntly opposed by Nehru and Patel and therefore had to be eventually dropped.

Mountbatten held several meetings with Jinnah, in which the latter demanded Pakistan without providing a sound logic. Mountbatten virtually described Jinnah as a 'psychopathic case'[71] in a personal report. He maintained in that report that until he met Jinnah, he couldn't believe that a man so devoid of knowledge of administration and sense of responsibility could hold such a powerful position! In the end, Mountbatten offered Jinnah to choose between the Cabinet Mission Plan and a truncated but unsound Pakistan with its north-eastern regions in the form of East Bengal and neighbouring areas far away from the centre in the north-west, which constitutes today's Pakistan. The proposal, if accepted, meant the grim possibility for Pakistan of depending on India for defence and proving a drag on its financial resources in terms of its administration. Jinnah however remained firm that he wanted Pakistan, come what may.[72]

Gandhi, on the other hand, told Mountbatten that to avoid Partition and ensure peace, Jinnah should be given the option of forming a full Muslim League Cabinet with complete powers to select ministers even if all of these were Muslims and that the Congress would sincerely cooperate with such a government till the measures it took were in the interest of the countrymen as a whole.

Finding Gandhi's proposal too absurd, Nehru, Patel and the CWC put their foot down. Nehru said: 'The Muslim League can have Pakistan if they wish to have but on the condition that they do not take away other parts of India which do not wish to join Pakistan.'

---

[71]R.J. Moore, 'Mountbatten, India, and the Commonwealth,' *Journal of Commonwealth & Comparative Politics*, 19:1, 5–43, 1981, DOI: 10.1080/14662048108447372.

[72]Anita Inder Singh, *The Origins of the Partition of India, 1936–47*, OUP India; New edition, 1991, p. 227.

Savarkar turned to the Congress itself in a desperate bid to make it see reason in what was a moral appeal. On 29 May, he made a fervent plea to the Congress not to betray the electorate by consenting to the Partition scheme. He said, after having won the last election on the promise of keeping India united, the Congress didn't have the right to even consider such a proposal. And if it still persisted then, he said, the elected Congress representatives should resign their posts and seek re-election on the issue of a United India or Pakistan. He even suggested that the Congress should call for a countrywide plebiscite to decide the issue of Partition.[73] However, Savarkar's appeal was a cry in the wilderness particularly when the shadow of impending Partition was looming large.

Interestingly, when Mountbatten came back from London on 31 May after getting the Partition plan ratified, Jinnah demanded from the Viceroy a corridor of 1,000 miles through partitioned India to connect East with West Pakistan. But once again, the Congress, particularly Sardar Patel, opposed it with all its might thus leading to the absurd proposal's instant death. Somehow, the Congress had come to realize the price the nation had to pay for its pacifist politics. The British also prevailed upon Gandhi to drop his rigid stand of retaining the unity of India even at the cost of giving all powers to the Muslim League and agree to Partition.

On 3 June, the Partition plan was announced by the Viceroy on All India Radio (AIR) and by Prime Minister Attlee on BBC London. Mountbatten, in his broadcast, explained how Partition had become inevitable due to rejection of the Cabinet Mission Plan. Attlee's speech had almost the same content. Nehru, Akali Dal leader Baldev Singh and Jinnah also delivered broadcasts on AIR. Nehru, after speaking on Partition, hoped for a bright future for partitioned India. Jinnah, while welcoming the plan, bewailed that the Pakistan of the Muslim League's vision had not been achieved. Singh said he was accepting the scheme though it was difficult to accept.

---

[73]Dhananjay Keer, *Veer Savarkar*, Popular Prakashan Pvt. Ltd; Second edition, 2019, p. 381, 382.

The Partition plan was now in its final stages. Yet, Savarkar continued his efforts to prevent what he saw as political matricide. On the occasion of the Hindu Mahasabha working committee's meeting in Delhi on 7 June, Savarkar sent a message to Bhopatkar urging him to continue the struggle. The crux of the message was that the Muslim provinces seceding from the nation should be treated as revolting provinces and the struggle to re-annexe them and to create Hindu-majority provinces in Bengal and Punjab should continue. He also urged for rejoining the Hindu-majority districts of Sindh with Bombay Presidency and also made the same appeal to the Hindus of Sindh. His words echoed loud and clear: 'They have vivisected our India. We will vivisect their Pakistan.'[74]

It is important to note that Savarkar gave the first warning to the Hindus of Sindh not to become prey in the name of unity in the three articles that he wrote in *Swatantrya* magazine in March 1924.[75] Again, in 1927, Savarkar repeated the warning about Sindh:

> Don't throw Sindh into the jaw of Islamic power and culture. If Sindh is separated, Muslim majority will not hesitate to sacrifice Hindu culture of Sindh by following fanatic ideology. After grabbing all the countries from Arabastan to Baluchistan, the conspiracy of Muslims is to create an Islamic world with the wave of Islamic power and drown Sindh up to Rajputana.[76]

Under Savarkar's direction, the working committee of the Hindu Mahasabha passed a significant resolution that stated that the party was committed to the indivisibility of India and there will be no peace until the revolting Muslim areas were brought back into the Indian Union. In another significant move, the party's working committee demanded a referendum in the Hindu-majority areas of Sindh and in the Chittagong Hill Tracts in East Bengal, as in

---

[74]V.D. Savarkar, *Historic Statement by Savarkar*, G.P.Parchure, 1967.
[75]Balarao Savarkar, *Swatantryaveer Savarkar, Ratnagiri Parva*, p. 40.
[76]48/*Sphut Lekh, Shraddhanand* 21 July1927.

Sylhet district of Assam, on whether they desired to join the Indian Union.[77]

Had the Congress followed Savarkar's strategy, India could have saved Hindu-majority areas in the east and the west, including parts of Sindh—an area, when put together, is almost the size of today's Bihar—approx. 90,000 sq. km. Importantly, no honest observer of India's Independence struggle can deny that the Hindu Mahasabha's Save India campaign, despite the party's lack of electoral strength, had contributed significantly to saving whatever Hindu-majority parts of east and west India it did manage to save.

Meanwhile, on 14 June, at the crucial Congress party's meeting called to ratify the Partition plan, various top leaders starting with Gandhi spoke on the Partition plan. Gandhi urged the acceptance of Partition against his own firm views in the larger interest of peace. He said, 'Sometimes certain decisions howsoever unpalatable had to be taken.'[78] Nehru frankly admitted that the Congress had accepted Partition to save the nation from anarchy and to prevent the sabotage from within. Patel was specific that the Congress had to accept Partition as no other way was left to overcome the obstructionism of British–Muslim combine within the government which was threatening the nation with sabotage. He said the Congress faced a stark choice between one Partition and many Partitions.

The last disposition of the then party president Acharya Kripalani in the nine-hour meeting was full of narration of horrendous incidents during his visits to the riot-affected areas in Punjab, which shook one and all. In one village, he said, he had seen a well into which women with their children, numbering 107, had thrown themselves to save themselves from dishonour. In another place, 50 women were killed by their menfolk to keep their honour intact. Then, he narrated his visit to a place where he saw heaps of bones of 307 persons who had been driven, locked

---

[77] *The Free Hindustan*, 8 June 1947, Bombay (also quoted in Dhananjay Keer, *Veer Savarkar*)
[78] Pyarelal, *Mahatma Gandhi: The Last Phase, Vol. II*, Ahmedabad: Navajivan Publishing House, 1958, p. 253.

up and burnt alive.[79]

He admitted that it was the fear of violence that made the Congress accept Partition. But he added in the same vein that more than the lives lost and of wails of the widows and cries of the orphans, the decision was forced by the spectre of the continuing indignities heaped by people upon each other as a result of violence and retaliation that was reducing 'ourselves to cannibalism'.[80] While justifying his differences with Gandhi on the issue of Partition, he openly admitted in his address that when Gandhi taught non-violence and cooperation, he demonstrated a definite method, but now he (Gandhi) himself was groping in the dark. Kripalani added that Gandhi going to Noakhali and Bihar did ease the situation but had no impact in Punjab. He admitted that there are no definite steps in nonviolent cooperation that lead to the desired goal.[81]

At this meeting, many accused Nehru and Patel of caving in before the Partition demand. Purushottam Das Tandon was the most vociferous in opposing the Congress consent to Partition at the meeting. Speaking in a Savarkar-like, heroic tone, he said that even if the party's working committee had failed protagonists of United India like him, there was yet the All India Congress Committee (AICC) with the strength of millions behind it to prevent the abject surrender to the British–Muslim League combine.[82]

However, both Nehru and Patel resolutely defended themselves by reminding the party that it had passed a resolution as early as 1942 declaring that no province of the country would be forced to remain in the proposed Indian Union against its wishes and therefore it was wrong to blame them now.[83]

---

[79] Ibid. 255.

[80] Ibid.

[81] Pyarelal, *Mahatma Gandhi: The Last Phase, Vol. 1*, Ahmedabad: Navajivan Publishing House, 1956, pp. 251–56.

[82] Dhananjay Keer, *Veer Savarkar*, Popular Prakashan Pvt. Ltd; Second edition, 2019, p. 384.

[83] Anita Inder Singh, *The Origins of the Partition of India*, OUP India; New edition, 1991, p. 230.

Finally, on that fateful day of 14 June, the Congress passed the Partition resolution by 157 votes (29 against; 32 abstained). The following extract of the resolution summed up the sombre atmosphere, where every participant was in pain and in a state of helplessness:

> Geography and the mountains and the seas fashioned India as she is, and no human agency can change that shape or come in the way of her final destiny. Economic circumstances and the insistent demands of international affairs make the unity of India still more necessary. The picture of India we have learnt to cherish will remain in our minds and our hearts. The AICC earnestly trusts that when the present passions have subsided, India's problems will be viewed in their proper perspective and the false doctrine of two nations in India will be discredited and discarded by all.[84]

Even at this juncture, the Congress was not prepared to accept that it was religious fanaticism of the Muslims that was the main cause of Partition.

As the Congress accepted the Partition scheme, even Congress-minded newspapers, such as the *Free Press Journal*, criticized the party with the headline 'Nation's leaders betray country's cause.'[85]

This brings us to the moot question: who actually caused Partition? After examining the story of Partition from all angles, no honest historian can deny that Partition was essentially caused due to the beliefs of Gandhi and Rajaji. Nehru maybe accused of not seeing the Partition threat as serious and only as a bargaining chip by Jinnah to get more concessions for Muslims. Patel may be blamed for remaining silent, perhaps under Gandhi's aura, during the crucial period between 1940 and 1942 when Gandhi, and, even the Congress, gave in to the Pakistan demand in the

---

[84] B.N. Jog, *Threat of Islam: Indian Dimensions*, Mumbai (Bombay): Unnati Prakashan, 1994, p. 343.

[85] Dhananjay Keer, *Veer Savarkar*, Popular Prakashan Pvt. Ltd; Second edition, 2019, p. 385.

name of self-determination.

Also, the Congress being a leader-led party then, as it is now, once Nehru, Gandhi and Patel had accepted Partition as *fait accompli*, there was no one to oppose it in the party. Savarkar had repeatedly pointed out this weakness and asked the people to remember that the Congress party and its leaders were not greater than the nation. Dr Ambedkar also held the same view about the Congress and aired it in no uncertain terms in the Constituent Assembly.

Further, Partition itself was allowed in a reckless manner. Gurdwara Kartarpur Sahib, where Sri Guru Nanak Dev Ji spent the last 18 years of his life, was allowed to go to Pakistan though it is just a few kilometres away from the Punjab border. The Congress committed the same blunder when it came to the Hindu or non-Muslim-majority parts that went to East Pakistan (now Bangladesh).

In an attempt to acquire a secular image for themselves, several nationalists have tried to project Jinnah as secular by using some of his selected statements and actions. By doing so, they have probably committed a greater sin than the Congress. After the examination of the minutest details of the pattern of the anti-Hindu carnage in Bengal and then in Punjab before and after Partition, there is scarcely any doubt left that it was Jinnah who was its main author.

However, the ignominy that the Congress attracted by committing monumental blunders was partially, if not fully, effaced by Patel's manly and skillful actions in unifying the princely states and merging them with the Indian Union and taking armed action against the Muslim States of Hyderabad and Junagadh and compelling them to join the Indian Union. That he did so against the strenuous efforts of Jinnah, who wanted the states to either remain independent or join Pakistan, wherever possible, and the machinations of the British, was truly commendable.

TOWARDS RESURRECTION, RENAISSANCE AND REJUVENATION

On 1 July, Savarkar issued a historic statement foretelling India's future greatness and also suggested a road map to achieving it.

Map 3

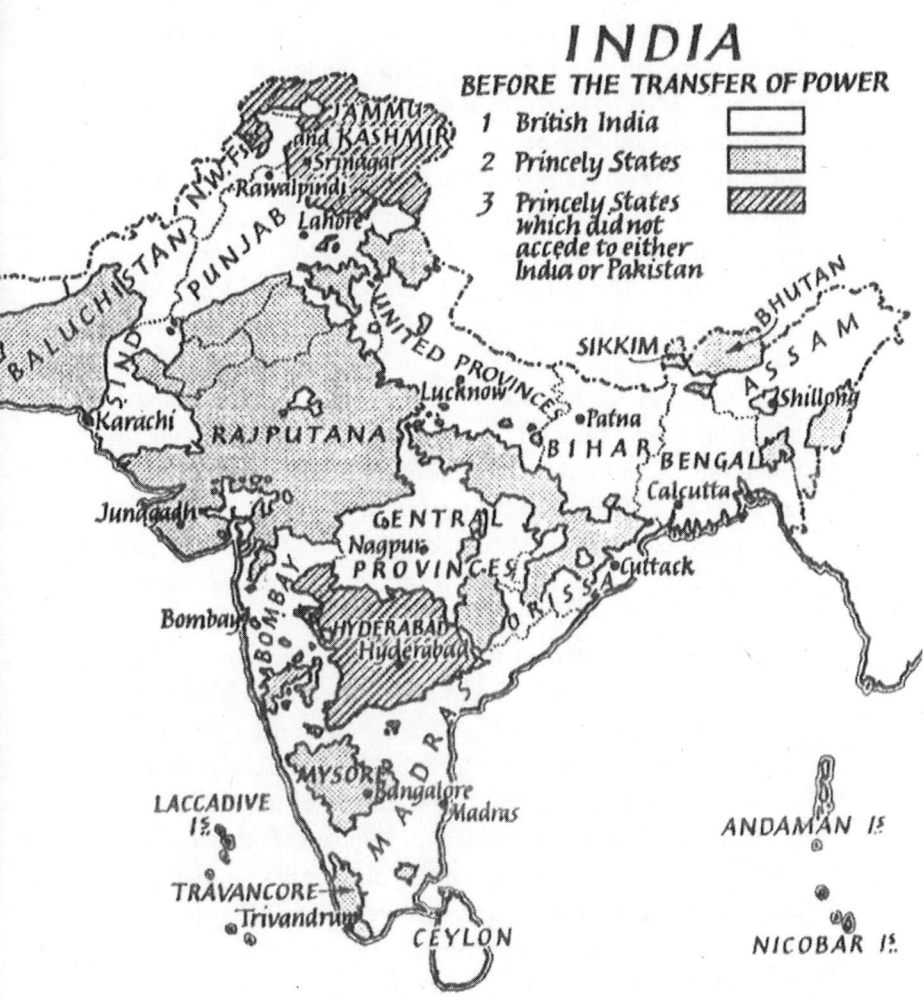

Source: Durga Das, *India: From Curzon to Nehru and After*, New Delhi: Rupa Publications; Eleventh edition, 2020, p. 72.

Several other visionary greats had dreamt about India's rise in future but few of them had suggested a road map. He said:

> My message to Hindudom even on this Black Day in our history is to assure it once more, 'Despair not!—a glorious future awaits the Hindus—if only they do not betray themselves. This is not a mere rodomontade I am indulging in. The detailed observation of the history of Hindus through centuries on centuries points in-controvertibly to the fact that the Hindu Nation is imbued inherently with such an amazing capacity for resurrection, of renaissance, of rejuvenation that the Black Day which finds them completely overwhelmed by anti-Hindu forces is precisely the moment which ushers in the Day of their Deliverance to quote the Pauranic style of the birth of an Avatar. It was in the darkest hour of the night that Shri Krishna was born. It is the indomitable spirit of our inherent vitality that has enabled our national being to prove most immortal in relation to other races or nations—ancient or modern—and invested it with that strength which ultimately demolished and swept away all anti-Hindu forces which raised their head from time to time against us. ... Where are Greeks who accompanied Alexander and his successors right down to the Ganges and were driven back by the triumphant Hindu forces under Chandragupta beyond the ranges of Hindu-Kush? ... Dead, gone and forgotten are also the Huns who overran all Europe, but were smashed in the battlefield by the Hindu sword and surrendered and got converted to Hindudom through the Baptism of our sacrificial fire ...Where are the mighty hordes of the Shakas? Defeated and driven out of Hindusthan...their very identity has become matter of mythological conjecture...
>
> Just take up the map of Hindusthan about 1600 AD. The Moslems ruled over a Hindusthan unchallengeably. Then open out the map of India about 1700 to 1798 AD and what you see? Beating the Moslem Army to a chip in hundreds of battlefields, the Hindu forces are marching triumphantly throughout India [reference to the exploits of Maratha heroes Chhatrapati

Shivaji, Peshwa Bajirao and Senapati Mahadji Shinde besides Sikh, Jat, Bundelkhandi and Assamese heroes like Guru Gobind Singh, Maharaja Suraj Mal, Maharaja Chhatrasal and Lachit Borphukan]... The Moslem Empire which rose like a rocket fell like a stick and on its ruin rose up once more the Hindu Hindustan, resurrected and victorious. It will do good, even to the Moslems, if they realise the import of this historical truth. The fate which overtook them when they had succeeded in converting the whole of Hindustan into an actual and factual Pakistan led by the might of an Aurangzeb cannot but overwhelm the puny Pakistan of today led by Mr Jinnah! If they still want to try again let them try to do their worst.

Nothing has happened in the meanwhile so detrimental to Hindu strength as to make us doubt our fitness to survive in the struggle for existence. The undying spirit of renaissance, of rejuvenation so inherent in our race shall assert itself once more and out of the very womb of the Darkness of this Black Day in our History shall burst out the Golden Dawn of a triumphant Tomorrow,—if only O Hindus, you do not betray yourselves. In this faith let the Hindus rise and renew this vow,—

(1) that we Hindus are a nation by ourselves. (2) that Hindusthan, this Bharat Bhoomi from the Indus to the Seas is our Fatherland and Holy Land, (3) that in spite of the treacherous betrayal by the Congressite pseudo-nationalism in its abetting the crime of vivisection of our Country and our State we Hindus shall continue to resist the revolting Pakistani areas till they are forced to reannexe with our Central and Sovereign Akhand Hindusthani State. (4) That to achieve this consummation we will Hinduise All Politics and Militarise Hindudom.'[86]

Thereafter, the Hindu Mahasabha gave a nationwide call to observe 3 July as anti-Pakistan Day. This received a popular response as people took out processions, hoisted black flags and held

---

[86]V.D. Savarkar, *Historic Statements by Savarkar,* G.P. Parchure, 1967.

demonstrations to condemn the betrayal of the motherland and remember the great martyrs who had sacrificed their lives for it. On the same day, Savarkar delivered a historic and touching speech before a multitude of people in Pune, a city from where vast and brave Maratha armies had less than two centuries earlier gone beyond the river Indus at Attock and captured even Peshawar.

Savarkar told the people of the nation that along with the Congress they too were responsible for the division of their motherland, as they didn't repudiate the leadership at the right time. On this occasion, he warned in a prophetic language that appeasement would never stop and satisfy the aggressor. But his speech also had a silver lining: 'Since you have gathered in thousands to listen to a leader like me who had attained ill-fame owing to his unflagging resistance to the creation of Pakistan, I believe there is still hope for the survival of this Hindu nation.'[87]

While addressing a Hindu convention in Delhi on 8 August, a week before Partition, Savarkar held out one last warning to the nation. He warned the Hindus that in spite of Partition they should never stop their struggle for United India and that if they ceased, there would be many more Pakistans in future.

Hours before the creation of the biggest-ever Islamic nation on the globe at that time, the Hindu Mahasabha exhorted the Hindus not to celebrate 15 August as Independence Day, in view of the untold sufferings that the Partition riots had brought on millions of people across the country. On Independence Day, Savarkar hoisted the tricolour, the flag of United India, and the geruwa (saffron) flag of the Hindu Mahasabha with the kripan (sword) and kundalini. At this delicate hour, Savarkar also demonstrated his flexibility by allowing S.P. Mukherjee to join the first Government of Independent India under Nehru on Nehru's invitation. He showed this magnanimity despite the fact that the Congress had failed to invite Savarkar to India's first Independence Day function in Delhi.

Savarkar's warning that in creation of Pakistan a veritable

---

[87] A.B. Savarkar, *Swatantryaveer Savarkar: Akhand Hindusthan Ladha Parv 1941–1947*, Swatantryaveer Savarkar Rashtriya Smarak, 2020, p. 476.

monster had been let loose came true as the ongoing mass-scale attacks on Hindus and Sikhs of Punjab intensified with Partition and a new wave of violence erupted. Earlier, it was civilian attacks on the Hindu and Sikhs that were taking place in West Punjab. Now the police and the army of the new Islamic country also joined in the attacks, thus proving true Savarkar's prophecy. Millions were uprooted from the land of their birth. Village after village and town after town were littered with corpses of Hindus and Sikhs. It became difficult for them to escape from the jihadi mobs out to pounce on their property and their women.

When Hindus and Sikhs were being butchered in West Punjab after Partition and a helpless Congress government looked on, Savarkar asked the Nehru government or the Congress to hold out a threat that in India the same treatment would be meted out to the minorities. It was a harsh but practical suggestion whose mere mention on the Congress's part could have stopped or curtailed the genocide of Hindus and Sikhs in Punjab in the initial period.

Eventually, the horrendous stories from East Punjab invited retaliation from revengeful Hindus and Sikhs in upper India, particularly West Punjab, where Muslims were mercilessly attacked. Other regions of India too witnessed revenge violence by Hindus against Muslims. But the severity of the violence committed by Hindus and Sikhs was on a much lesser scale than what they faced in West Punjab.

Nehru was shaken by the violence and counter violence, and remarked during a speech in Delhi soon after Independence that he would even resign to fight the Hindu fascists who were demanding a Hindu State and compared them with Hitler and Mussolini.[88]

This remark resulted in a duel between him and Savarkar. Savarkar, who was perhaps the target of Nehru's attack, responded with equal vehemence but with something that had much more logic being based on facts. Savarkar asked what the thousands of Hindus and Sikhs were to do when faced with complete annihilation in the

---

[88] *Selected Works of Jawaharlal Nehru*, Series 2, Vol. 4, p. 152 (Speech Rejection of a Hindu Raj) https://nehruselectedworks.com/. Accessed on 31 July 2021.

face of the total failure of the State to protect them.[89] He recounted the horrors being heaped upon the Hindus and Sikhs in the form of plunder, rape and large-scale massacres by armed Muslims with slogans like '*Has ke liya tha Pakistan, lad ke lenge Hindusthan* (We got Pakistan easily; we shall take India by force).' He remarked that in these circumstances, Hindu and Sikhs, prompted by their instinct of self-preservation and animated by the spirit of pan-Hindu consolidation, had risen to checkmate the Muslim hordes from an invasion of East Punjab and save even Delhi, which he said, would have been otherwise swallowed by the Muslim hordes.

He reminded Nehru: 'If Panditji and his Congress comrades are still safe and secure in their seats, they owe it to this brave fight which the Hindu Sanghantanists and the Sikh forces gave in the nick of time.'[90] On Nehru's threat to resign, Savarkar suggested if the Nehru government gave the reins of power to a Sikh–Hindu Sanghanist coalition, a Cabinet would be formed which would not just be more efficient than the present one but also prove to be absolutely indispensable to face the stark realities. Savarkar dubbed the Hindu hatred of the Congressmen as a stunt to cover up their disastrous failure to protect the life and property of the people and honour of our nation and asserted that only the Hindu Sanghantanist ideology could save the nation and re-establish Akhand Hindustan, from the Indus to the Seas.[91]

Savarkar then asked with what face did Nehru and the Congress vilify the demand of a Hindu Raj when they had surrendered to the Anglo-Muslim conspiracy to create Pakistan by 'cutting our motherland into two halves'[92] instead of fighting the demand. Refuting the Congress's objection to India being made a Hindu State, Savarkar asked Nehru, Gandhi and the Congress, 'Is it not a fact that almost all the States and nations are called after the names of what the League of Nations termed as national majority

---

[89]V.D. Savarkar, *Historic Statements by Savarkar*, G.P. Parchure, 1967.
[90]Ibid.
[91]Ibid.
[92]Ibid.

predominating that State?'[93]

Savarkar's diatribe against Nehru, Gandhi and the Congress as a whole continued. Stressing that Hindu Rashtra meant justice for all, he further asked why the Congress should denounce a Hindu nation in which every citizen would be equal in the eyes of the law. He, in fact, taunted Gandhi and Nehru that after starting their political careers with a theocratic movement in the form of the Khilafat movement, which ended in creating Pakistan on the basis of religion, they should have the least objection to the creation of a just Hindu State.[94] Savarkar reminded them that the culture of the majority of India was the culture of Ram, Krishna, Pratap, Shivaji, Guru Gobind Singh, Kalidas, Vikramaditya, Bhavbhuti and Vivekananda and not of Muhammad Ghori, Mahmud Ghazni, Taimur, Tipu Sultan or Aurangzeb.[95]

He showed Hindus the practical path for the achievement of Akhand Hindustan. His words have indeed been proved prophetic with the arrival of the Modi government, the freeing of Jammu and Kashmir from the hold of Article 370 and facilitating the Ram Temple to fulfill Savarkar's agenda, but at the same time, keeping enough space for that part of religious minorities which wants to remain in the national mainstream and doesn't exhibit fissiparous tendencies.

Clearly, Savarkar's riposte to Nehru was masterly and effectively encapsulated in his vision for India based on very sound logic. Today, in retrospect, when one looks at the struggle waged by the RSS-led nationalist forces since Independence, one cannot deny the importance of Savarkar's statements and speeches. But for the struggle waged by these nationalist forces, India would have been torn apart today by the activities of radical Muslim movements such as the Indian Mujahideen (IM) and the Popular Front of India (PFI).

---

[93]Ibid.
[94]Ibid.
[95]Dhananjay Keer, *Veer Savarkar*, Popular Prakashan Pvt. Ltd; Second edition, 2019, p. 391, 392.

7

NEW PARADIGMS IN NATIONAL SECURITY AND DIPLOMACY

On 15 August 1947, India's freedom struggle culminated in independence for one-seventh of humanity. This long and rather arduous journey, hailed across the world for its remarkable events, also raised pertinent questions regarding the role of freedom fighters in shaping the destiny of a nation. While the non-violent fight waged by the Congress certainly played a role in our struggle for Independence, the importance of the revolutionary movement is often grossly underplayed. These unsung heroes unleashed sustained pressure on the British, who, in turn, relied on the Congress to tackle the revolutionaries as a counterbalance, thus forcing the British on to the negotiating table.

A cursory glance at the connect between the pressure brought by the revolutionaries on the British and the reforms that were introduced as a result—starting from the First War of Independence, i.e., 1857 onwards—proves beyond a shadow of doubt the important role played by these movements in India's independence struggle and finally its liberation from British rule—something the Congress has constantly tried to underemphasize. This chain of events even raises a question mark on the slogan popularized by the Congress: *'De di hame azaadi bina khadga bina dhal* (We ensured liberation [of India] without sword and shield)'.

In fact, there is a historical relation between the revolution as a cause and the reforms that were introduced as a consequence/effect. The First War of Independence (1857) resulted in the Queen's proclamation (1858) that the British crown would rule

India directly through a Secretary of State in place of the East India Company. The Kuka Movement (1872) and the revolt of the legendary revolutionary Vasudev Balwant Phadke (1879) were the main reasons for the British establishing the Congress (1885); they wanted to douse the fire created by the revolutionaries. The reforms brought about by Viceroy Lord Dufferin (1888–92) were also a result of the same. The Bang Bhang Movement (1905–11) for the unification of divided Bengal, in which many a revolutionary fought with bombs, pistols and knives, resulted in the Indian Councils Act (1909) and finally the unification of Bengal (1911). The Montagu–Chelmsford Reforms (1919) were delivered to counter the impact of the Ghadar revolutionary movement in World War I, when scores of revolutionaries from all sections of society, including Lala Har Dayal, Rash Behari Bose and Raja Mahendra Pratap, planned to overthrow the British. Pratap also took the help of some Deobandi Muslim leaders who wanted to overthrow the British, albeit for their own religious interests. The Ghadar Movement was followed by the exploits of Chandra Shekhar Azad, Bhagat Singh, Ram Prasad Bismil and Ashfaqullah Khan, as symbolized by the Kakori Conspiracy (1925) and the legislative bomb attack. This resulted in the Round Table conferences (1930–32). Thereafter, the Cripps Mission (1942) was sent to India following the fall of Rangoon and the rise of Netaji Bose's INA. Finally, the Royal Indian Navy Uprising (1946) at Bombay proved to be the last straw on the camel's back.

A REVOLUTIONARY'S STRATEGY FOR INDEPENDENCE

Perhaps the greatest revolutionary of them all, Savarkar was a great believer in Shadguna Niti, or the six-fold diplomatic policy, which has been in vogue since the time of the Mahabharata and Kautilya to tackle the enemy. It is listed as:

1. Treaty (Sandhi): If the enemy is more powerful than you, preserve your existence by accepting certain conditions until you become stronger.

2. Battle (Vigraha): To attack the enemy as soon as you reinforce yourself.
3. Escape (Yaan): When a powerful enemy strikes and a treaty is not possible, run away to save yourself.
4. Hold (Asan): To remain at the fort or other position with a strategic advantage.
5. Aid (Samshray): Receive support from your enemy's enemy.
6. Deceive (Dwaidhibhav): Pretend to be friendly but continue to do the work for your enemy's destruction from within.[1]

At a very early age, Savarkar insisted that the country would never attain freedom by killing just one or two Britishers, as revealed in his memoirs, *Majhya Aathavani Nashik*, which he wrote as a teenager. He also described the revolutionaries' strategy in a nutshell:

> Secretly collecting weapons in the country, making personal attacks on the evil British officers in India, creating arsenals in and outside the borders of the country and infiltrating the borders as opportunities arise; developing relations with Britain's enemy countries such as Germany and Russia; inculcating patriotism in the army and the police by secretly propagating revolutionary literature, fighting indirect wars, committing petty rebellions from time to time and making it difficult for the enemy to govern the administration of India.[2]

In this way, Savarkar believed, the atmosphere of revolution would gradually be created in society. People would be ready to fight by exercising the art of warfare and, at the end of the day, when Britain would be trapped in a great war; they would grab a golden opportunity to declare the ultimate war in India and make the country independent.[3]

To attain this ultimate objective, Savarkar established the revolutionary secret society called Mitra Mela followed by the

---

[1] *Panchatantra*, Epoch 3, Shloka 7–64.
[2] V.D. Savarkar, *Majhya Aathavani Nashik*, Riya Publication, p. 148.
[3] Ibid.

Abhinav Bharat Society across Maharashtra between 1899 and 1905. Several members of the Society played a key role in the Indian revolutionary movement. In fact, the first successful bomb blast in India was the fruit of the Society's efforts.

Savarkar sent nationalist revolutionaries Pandurang Mahadev Bapat (popularly known as Senapati Bapat), Mirza Abbas and Hemchandra Kanungo Das to Paris from England to study the art of bomb making. A Russian chemical engineer gave Bapat a bomb manual in Russian. Das, who was an expert photographer, took photographs of the manual. Bapat then got the manual translated into English by a female Russian medical student, Miss Annya, at Berlin. Savarkar, who was in London from 1906 to 1909, created several copies of the manual. Thereafter, Bapat, Das and Hotilal Varma, another revolutionary, left England for India with cyclostyled copies of the bomb manual. They reached India in March 1908 and circulated the copies at important centres of the revolutionaries. Bapat met the Bengal revolutionaries Barindra Ghosh (brother of Sri Aurobindo), Prafulla Chakraborty and Narendra Goswami in Calcutta on 7 April 1908. This was followed by Khudiram Bose throwing a bomb in Muzaffarpur on 30 April in an attempt to kill the district magistrate, Kingsford.[4]

Savarkar stressed on physical training such as horse riding, running and handling of arms as well as on intellectual training for revolutionaries. The study circle or 'Sunday meetings' were continued wherever Savarkar went—Nashik, Poona, Bombay, England and even in Andaman. Discussions on political, religious, literary, linguistic and scientific subjects were held at these weekly meetings.

Savarkar tried to convince fellow revolutionaries of Andaman that they should be prepared for the change in their roles and responsibility once India became independent. He said,

> If winning freedom was difficult enough, retaining it after it had been won was more difficult still. And until their minds

---

[4]Dhananjay Keer, *Veer Savarkar*, Popular Prakashan Pvt. Ltd; Second edition, 2019, p. 43.

were trained perfectly, they would never realize this fact of politics and political advancement. No political revolutionary, if he really loved his own country, can afford to be ignorant to trade on the ignorance of his own countrymen. The more they know the practical art of good government, sound administration, and of the management of their country in every walk of public life, the better it is for them and their country when they come into their own.

Everyone who presumes to think of his own country, to dabble in politics, and to aspire to political leadership, must possess full and deep knowledge of subjects like politics, economics and constitutional history. To be wanting in such knowledge is to spell yourself inefficient and unfit for responsible self-government, or for high administrative offices in it. As in religion so in politics, action with knowledge is the key to salvation…you must add knowledge to service and vision to self-sacrifice. Heroism, to do or die, is not enough. It must be illumined by deep learning ripening into wisdom.[5]

Interestingly, in his presidential speech at the Haripura Congress session in 1938, Subhas Chandra Bose raised this point of political training for young leaders. Many years later, in 1956, Dr Ambedkar started the Training School for Entrance to Politics.

The fear that the Indian revolutionaries, including the ones led by Savarkar, had created in the minds of the British rulers was evident in the statement made by the British administrator Sir Herbert Hope Risley on 4 February 1910 while introducing the new Press Bill. It also threw light on the motives, actions and the impact of political assassinations in India and abroad.

He said:

We are at the present moment confronted with a murderous conspiracy, whose aim it is to subvert the Government of the

---

[5]Veer Savarkar, *My Transportation for Life*, Prabhat Prakashan; First edition, 2020, p. 94.

country and to make British rule impossible by establishing general terrorism. Their organization is effective and far reaching; their numbers are believed to be considerable; the leaders work in secret and are blindly obeyed by their youthful followers. The method they favour at present is political assassination; the method of Mazzini in his worst moods. Already they have a long score of murders or attempted murders to their account. As regards the officers of Government, the case is clear. At all costs they must be protected from intimidation and worse. And it is our Indian officials who stand in most need of protection, for they are most exposed to the danger.[6]

In this speech, Sir Herbert mentioned Abhinav Bharat-led assassinations of Sir William Curzon Wyllie in London by Madan Lal Dhingra and of A.M.T. Jackson, collector of Nashik, by Anant Laxman Kanhere.

During his stay in London, Savarkar also established connections with revolutionaries from secret revolutionary parties in Ireland and Egypt, countries under the British empire, and also Russia and in European countries such as Germany. It was through this network of revolutionaries spread across Europe and Asia that he could manage to get secret information.

The revolutionaries of Bengal and Maharashtra drew inspiration from religious philosophies such as the *Bhagavad Gita* and deities such as Durga, Kali, Ram and Krishna as well as from historical heroes such as Shivaji to fight against injustice of the British Raj. Gandhi, on the other hand, brought truth and ahimsa (non-violence) as a political philosophy and method. It was a novel Gandhian contribution to modern Indian politics, although it was never a part of traditional Indian political theory or practice. Gandhi always condemned revolutionary activities as they were opposed to his belief of non-violence. While on a visit to England from South Africa in 1909, Gandhi had criticized revolutionaries

---

[6]Valentine Chirol, *Indian Unrest*, Unistar Books, 2015, p. 337.

as the Maro-Kato (violent) Gang.[7]

Savarkar argued that the ahimsa of the Jains and the Buddhists was opposed to the Gandhian doctrine of ahimsa. According to him, the Jains raised kingdoms, produced heroes and heroines who fought armed battles and Jain commanders-in-chief led Jain armies without being ostracized by the Jain acharyas. This, he said, proves that the ahimsa of the Jains cannot be the ahimsa of the Gandhian School.

Savarkar believed that for saving a saint from being murdered by a violent and armed sinner, ahimsa itself requires that the sinner should be killed then and there if that act alone could save the life of the saint. Such a hinsa (violence) is in itself an act of ahimsa and the Jain scriptures defend it, he said.[8]

Savarkar maintained that Lord Buddha also gave the same ruling when questioned by the leaders of a clan as to whether they should take to armed resistance as soldiers against the armed aggression of another clan. 'Soldiers may fight against armed aggression,' said Bhagwan Buddha, according to Savarkar, 'without committing a sin but if they fight with arms in defence of a righteous cause.'[9]

FATHER OF NATIONAL SECURITY

Early on, Savarkar revealed an unparalleled security and geopolitical vision as evident from his predictions in the first issue of *Talwar*, an organ of the Abhinav Bharat Society, published in 1909. Savarkar had discussed and weighed the possibilities of the outbreak of a war in Europe within four or five years while explaining the complicated affairs arising out of the Kiel Canal issue in 1908[10]. He was of the opinion that the golden opportunity

---

[7]Verinder Grover (ed.), *V.D. Savarkar: Political Thinkers of Modern India—14*, New Delhi: Deep & Deep Publications, 1993, p. 503.
[8]Veer Savarkar, *Hindu Rashtra Darshan*, Prabhat Prakashan, 2020, p. 135
[9]Ibid.
[10]To cope with the mounting traffic and the demands of the Imperial German Navy, between 1907 and 1914, the canal was widened to allow Dreadnought-sized

to create unrest among Indian soldiers of the British army was not to be missed.[11]

In order to achieve this objective, his organization, Abhinav Bharat, tried to propagate the revolution and hatred for the British amongst the Indian soldiers. Hundreds of leaflets were secretly printed by Abhinav Bharat and sent to Punjab, the main recruiting site and camp of the British Indian army. Revolutionaries collected as many addresses as possible of the recruits of the army camps. The leaflets, written in Hindi and Gurumukhi, were delivered to the families of the Jat Sikhs and Dogras in the villages through British postal offices.[12]

From the beginning of the war, revolutionaries including Lala Hardayal, Shyamji Krishna Varma, M.P.T. Acharya, leaders of Abhinav Bharat and the revolutionary parties of Bengal, the US and Japan had an unwritten pact with Germany to provide weapons and finance warfare experts for an armed revolt against the British. There was a detailed plan for Gadar or revolt involving civilians and soldiers in India during the war, but the British foiled the well-planned bid with their accurate intelligence system.

It was a great diplomatic triumph for the armed revolutionaries on the international platform that the 14-point agenda for truce, which the German emperor (Kaiser) King Wilhelm II sent to US President Woodrow Wilson, had an echo of the Indian situation then. Out of these 14 conditions, one was the German demand that the British must give India total Independence.[13]

Savarkar's unparalleled national security vision remained unaffected even after he was sentenced to 50 years of rigorous imprisonment in the Cellular Jail at Andaman. One of the first things that dawned on him was the manner in which Andaman

---

battleships to pass through, thus allowing them to travel between the Baltic Sea and the North Sea without having to go around Denmark.
[11]Dhananjay Keer, *Veer Savarkar*, Popular Prakashan Pvt. Ltd; Second edition, 2019, p. 41.
[12]V.D. Savarkar, *Abhinav Bharat Sangta Bhashane (Samagra Savarkar, Vol. 8)*, Mumbai: Veer Savarkar Prakashan, 1993, p. 34.
[13]Ibid. 40.

could be developed into a strong Indian naval base in the future. He wrote:

> Thus segregated from the rest, I sat there, and it suddenly struck me that the islands were so located in the Bay of Bengal that they constituted the bastion in the naval fortification of India from the East. As such, they had an abiding importance in the future defence of our country. The eastern islands of Andaman and Nicobar are gateways into the Bay of Bengal. If they were not to come under the control of India and if they were not properly guarded and fortified, any foe from the East can easily launch a naval attack and knock straightaway at the door of Calcutta. But under India's control they can be turned into a formidable naval base for the defence of the nation from the East. It can then be equipped with a fleet of aeroplanes and a strong detachment of fighting ships that will guard its waters day and night and hold in bay any attack on the shores of India. The population of the Andamans and the present state of its culture being Indian, the islands themselves must form a political province of India... We should all learn from these mistakes of the past, and profiting by that experience, raise an effective line of fortifications covering in their range Lakhdiv (Lakshadweep) and Maldiv (Maldives) islands in the West, Ceylon in the South, and the Andamans and the Nicobars in the East of India. We must turn this base of defence into a naval fortress, not unlike the formidable Sindhu Durga in the glorious days of Shivaji. Today Singapur constitutes our first line of fortified defence. The Andamans are its natural front line.[14]

It was very disappointing for Savarkar that he was in prison when the actual opportunity of World War I presented itself. Savarkar writes:

> Even in this helpless state of mind and body, I was determined to take full advantage of this rare opportunity in the life-time

---

[14]Veer Savarkar, *My Transportation for Life*, Prabhat Prakashan; First edition, 2020, p. 49.

of a nation to further the cause near my heart in such ways as I could adopt for that purpose... Thinking calmly over all these near and remote consequences of the war, I settled my own line of action, and, at the beginning of it, I resolved to send a long letter on the subject to the Government of India.[15]

In this letter, Savarkar's opponents made several allegations, but the Britishers were not as ignorant as Savarkar's present opponents! Reginald Craddock, the home member to whom Savarkar submitted the petition, wrote to the Governor General in a letter dated 19 December 1913:

> In the case of Savarkar, it is quite impossible to give him any liberty here, and I think he would escape from any Indian jail. So important a leader is he that the European section of the Indian anarchists would plot for his escape which would before long be organized. If he were allowed outside the Cellular Jail in the Andamans, his escape would be certain. His friends could easily charter a steamer to lie off one of the islands and a little money distributed locally would do the rest.[16]

Craddock was right. The armoured German ship named Emden suddenly attacked Madras in 1914 with bombs, and created fear in the British and in the British navy. Emden aimed mainly at attacking the Andaman island and releasing Savarkar and the other revolutionaries present there. It planned to then attack Burma and later join the British Indian army, which was ready to revolt with the support of the revolutionaries and then from there head to India.[17] However, the plan could not become successful as Emden was sabotaged in the mid seas by the British navy.

Several years later during his detainment in Ratnagiri, this security vision for the nation surfaced yet again almost 10 years before

---

[15]Ibid. 185.
[16]Ramesh Chandra Majumdar, *Penal settlements in Andamans*, Gazetteers Unit, Department of Culture, Ministry of Education and Social Welfare, 1975, p. 221.
[17]V.D. Savarkar, *Abhinav Bharat Sangta Bhashane*, p. 39.

World War II. Writing a series of four articles in *Shraddhanand* magazine during February–March 1928, titled 'Don't lose the opportunity of the next war (WW-II)', he urged Indians to take advantage of the impending war for winning India's independence.[18]

The crux of the articles was thus:

> In the previous world war, countries like Armenia, Poland and Lithuania with planned strategies got themselves freed from foreign rules. But India missed the golden opportunity due to lack of strategic awareness. England's difficulty is our opportunity. Indian soldiers fought bravely on European battlefields for Britain but kept themselves aloof from the fight for Indian independence. Sooner or later, the next war would be fought between Britain and Russia. The battlefield would be shifted from Europe to Asia. Unlike Germany's case in the previous war, Russia's hands could reach to India very easily. What Japan would do was not certain then. No sympathizer of Britain would be present in the continent. Indian should not miss this golden opportunity.

It was on the basis of an enlightened security vision rooted in the thinking that in the world arena, an enemy's enemy should be seen as a friend and that there were no permanent friends or permanent enemies on the platform of nations that Savarkar advised Subhas Chandra Bose to use World War II to India's best advantage. In a meeting with Bose in Bombay on 22 June 1940—just three months after Jinnah's March 1940 Pakistan resolution—Savarkar urged him to flee India and join hands with Japan and Germany in organizing an army (which later came to be known as the Azad Hind Fauj or INA) from amongst the Indian soldiers of the British army captured by the Axis Powers in the war.

Several years later in 1952, when Savarkar dissolved his revolutionary organization, Abhinav Bharat Society, Bose's portrait was put on the chair of the chief guest in a meeting. In his speech

---

[18]V.D. Savarkar, *Sphut Lekh (Samagra Savarkar, Vol. 8)*, Mumbai: Veer Savarkar Prakashan, 1994, p. 9.

on the occasion, Savarkar revealed the details of his meeting with Bose on that fateful day:

> I asked Subhas Babu the main question, 'Tell me one thing, in the current world war, what is a person like you doing in India, and leading petty movements like bringing down the statues in Calcutta and getting arrested and going to prison? What is the meaning of this?' ...The true politics is when you dump the enemies in the prison, not yourself. And if a person like you is arrested, then that is what the Government wants. When you were the Congress president, we had a secret meeting. With the same confidence, I wish to make a sincere request to you. When I am propagating militarisation you have been opposing it, as just like the other so-called moderate leaders who believe that I am providing manpower to the British. But I will tell you the fact. I am insisting on Hindus being recruited in the army so that in future these warfare-trained men can revolt against the British and start an armed revolution to gain freedom from the British Rule. During the First World War, we (revolutionaries) reached an understanding with Germany against the British'. I told him about all the efforts we had taken during the First World War.
>
> I further told Netaji, 'See this fresh letter (which was sent secretly to Savarkar through Buddhist monks) by Rash Behari Bose (from Japan). From this, it can be assumed that Japan will blow the war horns within this year. If this happens, then we would get the golden opportunity to attack the British from outside with the help of the German and Japanese weapons and thousands of trained Indian soldiers. At such a time, a leader like you should try and get arrested purposely is a very harmful thing. Just like Rash Behari Bose and other such revolutionary leaders escaped from India and went to Japan or Germany, you should also do the same. There in Germany taking the weapons you get you must openly accept the leadership of the Indian army against the British. As soon as Japan enters the war, with whatever possible means either

through the Bay of Bengal or through Burma, attack the British rule in India from the outside. Without such a brave act, it is impossible to achieve our independence. I see two or three people capable of such bravery. One of them is you. I have high hopes from you!' [19]

Six months later, Netaji fled India and went ahead on the path shown by Savarkar. The revolutionary and founder of the Indian Independence League (later INA), Rash Behari Bose, became the president of the Japan unit of the Hindu Mahasabha in 1938, and Savarkar and Rash Behari were in secret correspondence with each other on the proposal to take the help of Axis powers to free India from British rule.

Savarkar's preparedness to take advantage of Bose's attack on India was exemplary. On 8 July 1943, in a private meeting with S.P. Mukherjee and other leaders at Delhi, Savarkar advised that if Subhas Chandra Bose landed in Bengal with his army, the Bengal Hindu Mahasabha should openly join him and officially disassociate with the Central Hindu Mahasabha as part of a larger strategy.[20] This is exactly the strategy adopted by some of the Wahhabi Muslim groups today in India which profess loyalty to the nation but are actually hand in glove with their brethren in Pakistan.

MILITARIZING HINDUS

Savarkar's national security vision is best reflected in the fact that on one hand, he implored Bose to take the help of Axis powers to overthrow the British, but on the other hand, he called upon Hindus to militarize themselves by taking advantage of World War II and enrolling themselves in the British army. The British, who had by far tried to keep Indians unarmed and unprepared out of fear and distrust, were now keen on encouraging them to join the army to cater to their war needs.

---

[19] V.D. Savarkar, *Abhinav Bharat Sangta Bhashane*, p. 48.
[20] Balarao Savarkar, *Swatantryaveer Savarkar, Akhand Hindusthan Ladha Parv*, 2020, p. 337.

One of the greatest services that Savarkar, Munje and the Hindu Mahasabha rendered to the nation was to convince the British to remove caste distinction between martial and non-martial Hindus in the recruitment of Hindu youth in the British Indian army in the 1930s. In fact, Munje, a votary of militarization of all Hindus, had steadily worked towards the removal of caste distinction in army recruitment even before the arrival of Savarkar on the political scene. This campaign, however, got a major fillip from the British after Savarkar arrived on the political scene. The British desperately needed soldiers to fight for them in World War II and so they grabbed the offer without realizing the long-term consequences it would have on creating a level playing field for Indians, thanks to the visionary Savarkar's secret planning. This was exactly in keeping with the ideals of Chhatrapati Shivaji Maharaj, who turned all Hindus into fighters cutting across caste distinctions in Maharashtra, including the untouchable Mahar caste.

Savarkar's call for militarization of Hindus was backed by robust reasons and rational thinking. He had seen how Muslims were far ahead of Hindus in the army in terms of their numbers vis-à-vis the Hindu–Muslim population ratio. He could also envisage Partition on the horizon, given the Congress's meek response to pan-Islamism and that military strength would decide the final contest between India and Pakistan.

Thanks to the Hindu Mahasabha's militarization campaign, lakhs of Hindu youths joined the British Indian army and, in a span of five years (1939–43), the Hindu strength rose from three-fourth to almost 70 per cent. Alarmed by the increasing Hindu numbers in the army, the Muslim League expressed concern as many as four times between 1941 and 1944. Two of the warnings were from the vice chancellor of the Aligarh Muslim University Sir Ziauddin Ahmad and Pakistan's first prime minister Liaquat Ali Khan, who was then the secretary of the All India Muslim League.[21]

Subsequent developments proved Savarkar right. Of the total

---

[21]Dhananjay Keer, *Veer Savarkar*, Popular Prakashan Pvt. Ltd; Second edition, 2019, p. 259.

Muslim soldiers in the British Indian army, over 90 per cent chose to join the Pakistan army at the time of Partition and, soon after Partition, Pakistan attacked India in 1947 and occupied one-third of Jammu and Kashmir. Had the military balance been against India at the time of Partition as compared to Pakistan, the new Muslim nation could have even tried to swallow Muslim-majority areas on the Indian border in Rajasthan, Gujarat and even West Bengal, where Muslims still outnumber Hindus.

During his militarization campaign, Savarkar went across the country emphasizing his viewpoint that World War II was a golden opportunity for Hindu youths to get arms training and to use it for the nation's advantage as and when the time comes. Savarkar said once you know how to wield the gun, it is in your hands where to turn the barrel to your advantage. The British wanted to keep politics out of the army, but Savarkar emphasized that Indians should carry politics to the army to win the final battle of the nation. Hindu Mahasabha workers joined hands with army recruitment officers and started rifle clubs. Savarkar appealed to the youths of Konkan specially the Bhandari and Kharvi classes, who were traditional sailors, to get their training in the navy and capture positions there. 'Today, it may well appear that these men in the armed forces are mere slaves in the pay of a foreign Government; but there can be no doubt that when the crucial moment comes, they will prove themselves real patriots and staunch Hindus,' he said.[22]

During this phase, Savarkar displayed his unmatched national security vision when he said:

> Formerly youths had to rot in prisons for being in possession of pistols, but today the Britishers are placing rifles, guns, cannons, and machine-guns in your hands. Get fully trained as soldiers and commanders. Get thousands of mechanics trained into technical experts in building shipyards, aeroplanes, guns and ammunition factories.
>
> I ask you to join the Army and wield the guns and turn

---

[22]Ibid.

them to the cause of freedom. I tell you this as plainly as I told the Viceroy himself about it. Do not worry about the bonds and agreements. The reverse of those scraps is blank. You can write new bonds and new agreements on it when the time comes. Mind you, Swaraj will never come to you, although you cover the whole earth with paper resolutions. But if you pass resolutions with rifles on your shoulders, you will attain it.[23]

Savarkar's militarization policy earned him praise from Bose. On 25 June 1944, while delivering a message on Singapore Radio, Bose said,

> When due to misguided political whims and lack of vision, almost all the leaders of the Congress party are decrying all the soldiers in the Indian Army as mercenaries, it is heartening to know that Veer Savarkar is fearlessly exhorting the youth of India to enlist in the Armed Forces. These enlisted youth themselves provide us with trained men from which we draw the soldiers of our Indian National Army.[24]

Rash Behari Bose also paid tribute to Savarkar in his radio talk: 'In saluting you, I have the joy of doing my duty towards one of my elderly comrades-in-arms. In saluting you, I am saluting the symbol of sacrifice itself.'[25] Paying homage to Savarkar's unparalleled sacrifice, untold sufferings and matchless courage, he further said: 'I can see God's divine hand clearly behind your unconditional release. You have once more proved your greatness by propagating the theme that our politics must never depend upon the foreign politics of others. England's enemy must be our friend.' Rash Behari concluded the event with the slogan Vande Mataram.[26]

The Congress, however, perhaps threatened by the public

---

[23]Dhananjay Keer, *Veer Savarkar*, Popular Prakashan Pvt. Ltd; Second edition, 2019, p. 257.
[24]Ibid. 350.
[25]Ibid.
[26]Ibid.

response Savarkar's national security-building campaign was getting, resorted to playing a dirty game. It started projecting Savarkar as a British stooge and lampooned him as 'Recruit Veer'.[27] This was meant to hit at the Hindu Mahasabha's growing popularity owing to its clinical anti-Pakistan campaign. However, Savarkar was unmoved. Like Rana Pratap, for Savarkar too, the nation came first.

The 1946 Royal Indian Navy Revolt, though a brief incident from 18–23 February, has still not got its due place in Indian history. The revolt was the last trigger that sounded the death knell for British rule in India. From the initial flashpoint in Bombay, the revolt spread and found support throughout British India, from Karachi to Calcutta, and ultimately more than 20,000 sailors were involved in 78 ships and shore establishments, which also included a significant number of soldiers who had joined the navy as part of Savarkar's militarization campaign.

On 19 February, just a day after the revolt began, Secretary of State Frederick Pethick-Lawrence made an announcement in the House of Lords about sending a three-man Cabinet deputation to India to resolve the Congress–Muslim League deadlock.[28] As it is, the Labour party held very different views about the Indian problem than its predecessor, the Conservative Party. Two weeks after the revolt, the British prime minister met with the King, and the decision to free India was taken on 5 March 1946.[29]

Even though his militarization campaign saved the nation from future calamities at the hands of Pakistan, Savarkar paid a hefty price politically as the Hindu Mahasabha was severely mauled in the 1945–46 Central Assembly and provincial polls, largely fuelled by the Congress's 'British stooge' campaign. What led to the decimation of the Mahasabha was the Congress's huge machinery which ran the anti-Hindu Mahasabha smear campaign and against

---

[27]Dhananjay Keer, *Veer Savarkar*, Popular Prakashan Pvt. Ltd; Second edition, 2019, p. 258
[28]G.D. Bakshi, *Bose or Gandhi: Who Got India Her Freedom*, K.W. Publishers Pvt. Ltd; First edition, 2019, p. 159.
[29]Ibid. 164.

which the sparse resources of the Saffron party were no match.

However, subsequent history recognized the weight of Savarkar's militarization campaign. The best tribute to this campaign as well as to the role of Indian revolutionaries in getting India freedom was paid by Clement Attlee, the British prime minister, in 1955, in a private conversation with the then acting West Bengal governor P.B. Chakraborty. He remarked: 'The pressure built up by the Azad Hind Fauj, the unwillingness on the part of Indian soldiers returning from World War II to accept British rule and finally the mutiny by Navy soldiers at Bombay Dock in 1946 played a big role in pressing Britain to withdraw.'[30] Attlee further said that the Congress's influence as well as that of Gandhi was 'minimal' in influencing Britain's decision to make India independent.[31]

Several other instances reveal Savarkar's unparalleled national security vision. He became one of the first non-Assamese leaders to warn about the consequences of the East Bengal Muslim migration in Assam and India's North-east frontier. To alter the communal ratio of population in Assam, the Muslim League launched a large-scale, 'three-pronged invasion' of Assam by Muslim immigrants. Muslim League National Guard styling themselves as Khilji Dastas or Khilji columns took illegal possession of vacant government lands in Assam and refused to be evicted.[32]

Savarkar warned that if outsider Muslims (illegal immigrants) are allowed to swamp Assam, India will be faced with a grave problem in the future. He said they would endanger both Assam's cultural identity and also India's North-east frontiers. At that time, the Muslim population in Assam was 10–12 per cent and a large number of them were Muslims of local Assamese origin and not of East Bengal origin.

In November 1941, when Savarkar was on an Assam tour, a few local leaders told him that when they had complained to Nehru

---

[30]This episode was described by Chakraborty himself in a letter to historian R.C. Majumdar which Majumdar quoted in his book *The History of Bengal*.
[31]Ibid.
[32]Pyarelal, *Mahatma Gandhi: The Last Phase, Vol. I*, Ahmedabad: Navajivan Publishing House, 1956, p. 517.

about the infiltration problem, Nehru had trivialized the matter saying 'nature abhors vacuum', meaning that how could people be stopped from occupying vacant space.[33] Savarkar retorted to Nehru's statement with sarcastic humour and said that Pandit Nehru's knowledge about the environment was very poor because he (Nehru) didn't know that nature also abhors poisonous gas.[34] Savarkar supported Congress leaders such as Gopinath Bordoloi, who were fighting a grim battle against Muslim migration in Assam.

Today, the Muslim population in Assam has reached 35 per cent and many of them have turned into radical Wahhabis due to the preaching of the Deoband school in the region. This was not the case when they had migrated. Moreover, the Muslim migration has disturbed the region's equanimity, with various ethnic groups of the North-east such as the Bodos taking up weapons to guard their culture and space. Sometimes, these groups were against each other and sometimes against the Indian State, but the pressure behind their taking up arms was mostly the swamp of Assam and the North-east by illicit migration of East Bengal Muslims. It is only after the BJP came to power in Assam in the 2016 Legislative Elections that the North-east started moving towards the mainstream, casting away fissiparous tendencies, thanks to the Savarkarian approach of the Modi government based on true Nation First.

However, in spite of displaying such a nationalist vision with far-reaching ramifications, Left-oriented historians, in an attempt to subvert true history, insist that Hindutva ideologues (those wedded to Hindu ideals) didn't contribute to the freedom struggle. History stands testimony to the contributions of Vasudev Balwant Phadke, the Chapekar Brothers, Lokmanya Tilak, Aurobindo Ghose, Lala Lajpat Rai, Bhai Parmanand, Lala Hardayal, Pandit Madan Mohan Malaviya, Swami Shraddhanand, B.S. Munje and Rash Behari Bose. All these moderates and extremists were inspired by Hindu

---

[33] Balarao Savarkar, *Swatantryaveer Savarkar, Akhand Hindusthan Ladha Parv*, 2020, p. 115.
[34] Ibid.

nationalism. It is also true that several Indian leaders such as C. Rajagopalachari, B.G. Kher, Yashwantrao Chavan and M.N. Roy, in their young age, drew inspiration from Savarkar's actions and writings, though they followed different paths later. Roy said aptly: 'Savarkar is like a huge banyan tree. We all are just branches of the tree.'[35]

LEADING BY EXAMPLE: TRUE NATION FIRST SPIRIT

Like the banyan tree that protects all creatures under its shade, Savarkar too was magnanimous enough while giving credit of freedom to all. He said:

> No single party can take all credit for liberation of the country—instead concerted efforts of the last 3 generations and of many parties and workers got us our freedom. No doubt the 1857 uprising contributed to it. So did the great patriot Dadabhai Naoroji and Gokhale, who opposed in somewhat gentle manner. The party which was known for its extremist views, also should get the credit. All the thousands of patriots who opposed by non-cooperation struggle also should get their due. I will go farther than this, and will also acknowledge all those, who never took part in any active opposition but prayed for the nation's freedom.[36]

Savarkar had great respect for Sardar Patel, who made stupendous efforts to keep India united after Partition. During this phase, he repeatedly congratulated Sardar Patel for his strong actions. When Sardar Patel survived an accident on 3 April 1949, Savarkar sent him the following message: '...congratulating our nation and yourself on your safety as your life constitutes a national interest. It was your grasp of realities and firm hold on the helm that steered the ship of our newly born Bharatiya State clear of many a rock and shoal.'[37]

---

[35]H.T. Desai, *Shat Pailu Savarkar*, p. 1.
[36]V.D. Savarkar, *Abhinav Bharat Sangta Bhashane*, p. 7.
[37]V.D. Savarkar, *Historic Statements by Savarkar*, G.P. Parchure, 1967.

Savarkar's statement showed his unrelenting belief in unalloyed nationalism or else he wouldn't have praised the same person with such words, rising above personal prejudices in true Nation First spirit. For only five years ago, the same Sardar Patel had by his rhetoric decimated the Hindu Mahasabha in the 1945–46 elections.

Thereafter, Savarkar even congratulated and advised Prime Minister Nehru when he showed toughness on the national security front. In fact, Savarkar's insights on international diplomacy and his security vision were eye-openers. Once when asked whether the US would be infuriated by the meeting between Nehru and his Chinese counterpart, Zhou Enlai, he said enlightened national self-interest should be the only guiding principle for India in diplomacy. He argued that all policies of India at all times be dependent on what is good or detrimental to it. He concluded by asking if the US had taken into consideration India's response while forging defence and foreign relations with Pakistan.[38]

Savarkar was one of India's greatest visionary in matters relating to diplomacy and military planning based on the principle of Nation First. Not since the time of Chhatrapati Shivaji Maharaj, who set new frontiers in diplomacy and taught natives to attack against Muslim aggression rather than defending—as they had mostly done in the previous four centuries of Muslim rule, had India seen such a visionary on security and diplomatic interests.

Savarkar could foresee the impact of scientific progress on defence and diplomacy. In an article published on 15 March 1907, Savarkar, writing on the outcomes of advances in aeronautical science, noted that, while planes were employed in war to a lesser extent up to that point, they were regarded a kind of amusement owing to their limited power. M. Santos-Dumont's experiments in France provided opportunities for change in the global scene that were previously unimaginable. Nations would not have been able to survive if they had just kept their ships at sea. They would also be required to maintain ready-to-fly combat planes. This would

---

[38]Dhananjay Keer, *Veer Savarkar*, Popular Prakashan Pvt. Ltd; Second edition, 2019, p. 489.

also pose a fresh challenge to Britain's sovereignty of the oceans.[39] Giving the same logic, Savarkar warned in 1962 that the Himalayas are no longer invincible.

SECURITY AND DIPLOMATIC VISION AT ITS BEST

It was only for the sake of national interest, Savarkar believed, that nations formed international alliances with other nations on the basis of seemingly avowed aims of freedom or against ideologies such as Nazism or fascism. These 'isms', he said, were of little consequence to them inwardly, as their main aim was to secure national interest. Savarkar insisted that no theoretical and empty slogans of democracy, Nazism or fascism could be the guiding principle to India's foreign policy. When the Congress favoured Britain in the name of democracy in World War II, Savarkar said that both parties were imperialists and were fighting for themselves. His policy was very simple and straightforward: 'Any nation who helps India or is friendly towards her struggle for freedom is our friend and the nation which opposes us or presents a policy inimical to us is our foe.'[40]

History proved him right. The US had first pledged support to protect Korea but when Japan swallowed Korea in 1905, the US was the first nation to recognize the Korean conquest. Another example was the nullification of the 1939 non-aggression pact between Germany and Russia, as Russia joined the Allied powers in World War II following German aggression. His belief that a nation does not have a permanent enemy nor a permanent friend and that an enemy nation's enemy could be India's friend was based on his deep study of history and perhaps Chanakya Niti.

Savarkar could foresee the impact of each move on the chessboard of the war. At the time of the Battle of Stalingrad when Germany attacked Russia, Savarkar said that if Japan failed

---

[39] V.D. Savarkar, *Landonchi Batmipatre*, 1906–10, Mumbai: Veer Savarkar Prakashan, n.d., p. 37.
[40] T.R. Sareen, *Hindu Mahasabha Tryst with United India*, Eastern Book Linkers, 2019, p. 246.

to attack Russia from the eastern side, both Germany and Japan would lose the war and Japan would have to pay for its folly in the long run. What happened was exactly as he had visualized.[41]

Savarkar was also of the opinion that India had secured only three-fourth of its land in 1947 as the rest of United India had gone to Pakistan. Therefore, India cannot be considered fully liberated until the area under Pakistan comes under the Indian flag again. He believed that India won't be able to live in peace till the hostile state of Pakistan remained intact. We see Savarkar's words come alive today when Indian soldiers routinely sacrifice their lives in defending Pakistan's aggression in Jammu and Kashmir.

Savarkar maintained that had India had an iron-willed prime minister or a steel-nerved president after Independence, not just Sikkim, Nepal and Bhutan but even Burma (Myanmar) and far-away Indian semi-colonies such as Mauritius and Dutch Guyana (Surinam), would have joined the Indian union or would have had a strong alliance with it. However, he said after carefully studying the cowardly, emasculating and impotent policies of free India, they had second thoughts and therefore started drifting towards China.[42] On yet another occasion in 1961, when asked what he would do if he gets an opportunity to lead India, Savarkar said he would make India stronger and mightier than even Russia in just two years.[43]

To reinforce this point, Savarkar cited the example of the Soviet Union in a speech:

> That is the reason, that after the Soviet national revolution victory, the practical rulers first started building a strong, modern and well-equipped Red Army and maintaining it. Then they started building factories, schools and agriculture industries as their secondary 5-year plans. (This is) because

---

[41]Dhananjay Keer, *Veer Savarkar*, Popular Prakashan Pvt. Ltd; Second edition, 2019, p. 472.

[42]V.D. Savarkar, *Sphut Lekh (Samagra Savarkar, Vol. 8)*, Mumbai: Veer Savarkar Prakashan, 1994, p. 64.

[43]Pandit Bakhle, *Thus Spake the Prophet*, Mumbai: Swatantryaveer Savarkar Rashtriya Smarak, 1988, p. 2, 3, 5, 7, 8, 11, 23.

even if you build factories, schools and agriculture industries across the countries, how are you going to protect all these from the attack of your strong enemies. ... As is experienced by India that just as a single glittering gold ornament is an inspiration enough for a thief to rob you; similarly [a] nation's unsecured wealth is an inspiration enough for any strong nation to attack you.[44]

Savarkar's national security vision was like an armour for India's protection and it held the potential to give an impetus to India's rise on the global platform. He believed that military strength paves the way for successful international diplomacy because it is the fear of the military alone that brings rival nation(s) or for that matter any nation to the negotiating table. Therefore, he openly said that the talk of world peace without military strength was useless or rather military strength is a prerequisite for ushering in peace. He went a step further and even said that military strength was the only criterion of greatness.

In a speech delivered in 1952, he said: 'It is a great pity that in spite of completing four years of independence, the party in whose hands the Government of this country is vested has not taken a single step in preparing our armed forces in all respects to face any eventuality. It is an unpardonable blunder.'[45] Citing the example of Israel, Savarkar called for compulsory arms training for the Indian youth.

Savarkar made a comparison between the progress made by China and India, though both nations had begun their journey as independent nations at almost the same time. He rightly pointed out that India had criminally wasted six years while China had made rapid and powerful strides outpacing India in defence preparedness and economic development. He even exhorted India to become a nuclear state under Nehru's leadership, a suggestion that his daughter Indira Gandhi accepted as late as in 1975 but

---

[44]V.D. Savarkar, *Abhinav Bharat Sangta Bhashane*, p. 67.

[45]V.D. Savarkar, *Sphut Lekh (Samagra Savarkar, Vol. 8)*, Mumbai: Veer Savarkar Prakashan, 1994, p. 66.

by which time China had further outpaced India in military strength.

It was Savarkar's unwavering belief that military might greatly facilitates economic progress and development. In his view, if you construct roads in the name of development without securing them, then the same roads can be used by the invading army to enslave the nation.[46]

These strong statements unfortunately fell on deaf ears. In 1950, China annexed Tibet even before Prime Minister Nehru could respond. When Members of Parliament (MPs) referred to the melancholy chapter of Tibet, Nehru replied: 'We put up with these things because we would be, without making any difference, merely getting into trouble.'[47]

Savarkar said that the British, while leaving, had given India a chain of buffer states between India and China on one side and Russia on the other side as part of sound geopolitical and security vision. But he lamented that India had wasted the advantage as demonstrated by China's invasion of Tibet which India refused to oppose.

Nehru continued to follow a suicidal policy vis-à-vis China. In fear of China, he refused the US offer to replace China with India as a permanent member in the UN Security Council in 1950 when the US offer was conveyed to him by his sister Vijaya Lakshmi Pandit, India's representative to the UN. The cost of the blunder can be gauged from the fact that even today, China continues to stall India's attempt to secure permanent membership of the UN Security Council.

Thereafter, India started kowtowing to China with homilies such as Panchsheel or the Five Principles of Peaceful Co-existence, based on mutual respect for each other's territorial integrity and sovereignty.

Incidentally, along with Savarkar, the then RSS Sarsanghchalak M.S. Golwalkar and Dr Ambedkar had warned about China. Earlier,

---

[46]V.D. Savarkar, *Abhinav Bharat Sangta Bhashane*, p. 67.

[47]Dhananjay Keer, *Veer Savarkar*, Popular Prakashan Pvt. Ltd; Second edition, 2019, p. 487.

in 1950, Sardar Patel too had expressed his severe differences with Nehru regarding the latter's China strategy.

In 1954, Savarkar issued a stern national message to his countrymen in which he was severely critical of Panchsheel. He said:

> They care not a jot for your Panchsheel because your Panchsheel consists of beads of the rosary while their Panchsheel consists of tanks, submarines, guns, bombers and atom bombs. Today, the nation is run by pen alone. It must be run by the sword. So my message to you, young men, is that: Make the army and the navy and the air force up-to-date. If the other nations prepare hydrogen bombs, you invent oxygen bombs. Thereby, you will make Bharat a strong and prosperous nation and you will be able to live with self-respect.[48]

Savarkar criticized Nehru for going soft on China saying if the Indian prime minister continued to woo China with platitudes such as the Panchsheel even after its open aggression in Tibet, he (Savarkar) wouldn't be surprised if China, emboldened by India's meekness, is tempted to attack India itself to swallow its land.[49]

Exactly eight years after Savarkar's warning about China, he was proved correct when China attacked an unsuspecting India and swallowed a large part of its land even as Nehru continued to chant 'Hindi-Chini Bhai-Bhai' (Indians and Chinese are brothers).

Savarkar continued to guide the nation even after the 1962 debacle. When Indian armed forces were just 20 km away from Lahore in the 1965 war with Pakistan, he exhorted India to capture Lahore. After the war, when Prime Minister Lal Bahadur Shastri was called for peace talks to Tashkent in January 1966, Savarkar feared that under international pressure India would return to Pakistan the territories Indian soldiers had won in the war. And

---

[48]Dhananjay Keer, *Veer Savarkar*, Popular Prakashan Pvt. Ltd; Second edition, 2019, p. 500.
[49]Ibid. 488.

that is exactly what happened. As a result, India invited another war from hostile Pakistan in 1971. After this war, India committed the same mistake under the Shimla Agreement when it refused to settle the Pakistan-occupied Kashmir issue despite holding 93,000 Pakistani soldiers in captivity and even returned the territories it had won in Sindh to Pakistan. Mrs Gandhi, who had shown glimpses of Savarkarian vision, slumped back to the Congress's old pacifism. This led to Pakistan becoming more emboldened and starting the proxy war in Jammu and Kashmir, which continues to claim Indian lives till today.

8

'SAVARKAR-ISM': A VISION RESHAPES INDIA

With India becoming an independent nation, Savarkar, on behalf of the revolutionaries, performed one final duty towards the national revolution. He organized the closing ceremony of one of the several secret organizations he founded/co-founded, the Abhinav Bharat Society, in May 1952 and forbade all revolutionary methods. On this occasion, he appealed to his countrymen to renounce all destructive behaviour and adopt constructive ones:

> As long as the war of independence was going on, all the terrorist activities of sabotaging the government machinery and killing the government officials, looting and damaging government property etc was justified. That was our religion. But now the war is over and we are victorious; now we need to stop these activities and eradicate them from our country. If these methods are allowed to be around, they would turn on us one day and create a bigger problem for us. Hence, our first duty after establishing independence is immersion of all these trends of armed or unarmed revolution and spread the word of law and order amongst the people as now our aim has changed from getting independence to protecting Independence, national development. Now we will follow lawfulness rather than unruliness, not destructive but constructive behaviour. This is our national religion now.[1]

---

[1] V.D. Savarkar, *Abhinav Bharat Sangata Bhashane*, p. 61.

Since the stormy years of armed revolution, Savarakar was crystal clear about how an independent nation will deal with its internal and external affairs:

> Constitution within; Revolution outside!
> Law within; Sword outside!
> Peace within; War outside!

Savarkar appealed to the masses to cooperate with the new government of independent India by attempting to inculcate his unique vision of patriotism. He said:

> No matter which party is in rule on the first day, but that party has to face the havoc and poor conditions as soon as they take over the governance and cannot eradicate it in one day using a magic wand. At such a time, it is our national duty to bear with them and give the new government enough time to take control of the situation and help them in whatever way possible to pacify the situation... I see that the public is unable to bear the extremities and is reacting saying, 'What freedom is this? The British rule was better or the Russian rule would be better:' I feel a chill down my spine (when I hear this) because this is a traitor attitude! This attitude put our motherland through the British rule in the past. There is no greater enemy of our Independence than unruliness. In a way we can accept the unruly governance of our own people, but the foreign rule of the British, Russia or even the Messengers of God is not acceptable. The internal unruliness of a nation is a terrible disease. It may be painful but may not be incurable. But foreign governance is the death of the nation itself. This feeling should be engraved on our people's heart and flow in their veins like blood.[2]

---

[2]Ibid.

IDEAS OF MODERNITY AND REFORM

Savarkar was in favour of a vigilant and healthy democracy. He believed whatever change is to be brought should be done in a democratic way only. He said:

> There will be differences of opinion amongst the parties as well as individuals about what is good for the nation. There is no harm in that. In fact, if these differences are unselfish and inspired by national well-being, they are always beneficial. But after establishing independence, however strong the differences are, they should fit into the ballot boxes only! Just be sure if the base of the ballot box is open or not! This responsibility lies with the people but also on the party which has been constitutionally elected.[3]

Savarkar was very particular about the use of political and social terminologies and understood their far-reaching impact on society. He believed that the wrong usage of words and language, due to ignorance or due to machinations of anti-Hindu forces, have often worked like poison in the development of national mentality. In some cases, even nationalists have erred in not being able to use precise vocabulary.

While speaking on the Nehru government, he emphasized that it is an Indian government and not a government of one political party. He said: 'It's not Congress Rule. It's our rule. Just the operations are handled by the Congress today. This feeling should be clearly emphasised and expressed. Today, the operations are with [the] Congress. Tomorrow some other party may be elected with a majority, as it is the Rule of the Nation!'[4] He discouraged the use of the term 'opposition party' saying:

> We should disown the term borrowed from the British Parliament and instead use the term minority party for opposition party, wherein it would denote the parties that

---

[3]Ibid. 63.
[4]Ibid. 64.

have got lesser votes than the ruling party. This (approach) would not encourage the bad habit of opposing everything that the ruling party proposes and would promote a mutual understanding. The main responsibility of the minority party is to ensure the majority party does not do anything that is not in the well-being of our nation and support wholeheartedly the majority party in anything that is beneficial to the nation.[5]

Savarkar also objected to the use of the word 'Adivasi' to refer to tribal people. He said:

> The term 'Aadivasi'—aadi = since beginning, vasi = inhabitant —stereotypically used by missionaries is politically motivated. Due to this, Bhil, Gond, Naga students studying in (Christian) missionary schools start believing themselves to be older (in antiquity) than Aryans (other castes). They (missionaries) tend to separate (the tribals) from India by seeking autonomy (in their name). They (the Missionaries) say the legend and customs of all these tribes are different and they are the indigenous natives and the rest are outsiders. In reality, there is no basis for this thing. Similar is the case of Dravidian movement.[6]

Savarkar's strong stand in language policy played a key role in India adopting Hindi as the national language and its script as Nagari. This assumes significance in light of the fact that an apt national language and its purity are essential elements of nationalism and also that before Partition, a section of Muslims was trying to push for Hindusthani, a mix of Urdu and Hindi.

On 5 August 1949, Savarkar sent a telegram to the president of the Constituent Assembly stating: 'I am voicing the sense and sentiment of millions of our countrymen when I beseech the Constituent Assembly to adopt Bharat as the name of our nation,

---

[5]Ibid. 64.
[6]Balarao Savarkar, *Swatantryaveer Savarkar Sangata Parv*, p. 214.

Hindi as the national language and Devanagari as the national script.'[7]

Savarkar, a staunch supporter of pure, Sanskritized Hindi, argued that there was a time during the Muslim medieval period when we (Hindus) could not even speak our own language, we could not utter our words. Foreign words, he said, are wounds on our language. He insisted on not using English and Urdu words in our languages, thus retaining the latter's pure and unadulterated form. Few people know that several Sanskritized Hindi words that are part of our vocabulary now were in fact coined by Savarkar, including 'Nagar Palika' for municipality, 'mahapaur' for mayor, 'hutatma' for martyr, 'Doordarshan' for television and 'madhyantar' for interval.

He also revived a few Sanskrit words which were out of use or were in limited usage. These included: 'puraskar' for honorarium/award, 'acharya' for principal, 'prabodhika' for academy, 'vidhigya' for vakil (lawyer), 'chhaya chitra' for photograph and 'visheshank' for special issue. Savarkar argued that difficult words become easy to articulate once they are incorporated into our daily parlance. Thus we can build our repertoire of words through regular use. The impact of Savarkar's language purification drive for Marathi, which was already influenced by Shivaji's great work, can be gauged from the fact that today's Marathi is largely free of several Urdu words which have become part of other Indian languages, particularly Hindi, such as 'kimat/mulya' (price), 'inam/puraskar' (reward) and 'tarikh/dinank' (date). In fact, Article 351 of the Indian Constitution, which provides directives for the development of Hindi language as a medium of expression, supports Savarkar's Sanskrit-based Hindi by advising that: 'by drawing, wherever necessary or desirable, for its vocabulary, primarily on Sanskrit and secondarily on other languages'[8].

Despite his strong views on the subject of language purity, Savarkar was flexible and open to accepting foreign words if there were no synonyms for them in an Indian language. He went even

---

[7]V.D. Savarkar, *Historic Statements by Savarkar*, G.P. Parchure, 1967.

[8]The Constitution of India, Article 351, Directive for development of the Hindi language. http://constitutionofindia.etal.in/article_351/. Accessed on 26 July 2021.

further on this: 'Not only in case of language purification, the heart of all reforms should be that whatever is efficient and beneficial in our culture should not be discarded. And we shouldn't have any hesitation in adopting whatever is good from foreign culture and not found in our culture.'[9]

Savarkar's tireless crusade against untouchability was one of the contributing factors to the enactment of Article 17 of the Constitution which aims to abolish this age-old practice. While speaking on the subject, he drew an apt analogy which pointed to the greatness of Hindu culture as compared to western culture. He said:

> When it was revealed that slavery would be abolished in America, millions of Americans took up arms against the government. After the Civil War, the abolition of slavery was imposed as a condition of surrender. The declaration of abolition of untouchability has not been forced on us; no one has been persuaded to do so as a condition of refuge. It is self-motivated atonement by Hindus for the well-being of the nation. The Constituent Assembly had representatives of all the provinces and of all the castes, and the bill received support from all over the country. On top of that, 'Manu' of this new smriti (code) was a Mahar, 'Maharashtra Kulbhushan' Dr Ambedkar. This is a unique capacity for the reforms inherent in the Hindu race.[10]

In the same article, while welcoming reservations given to the Depressed Classes, Savarkar also recommended that facilities should be given to all needy citizens without any discrimination.

Savarkar can be said to have contributed, albeit indirectly, to the making of the Indian Constitution through the medium of his vision and beliefs and his untiring efforts to propagate them. In fact, the Indian Constitution's definition of Hindu is more or less the one specified by Savarkar in his *Hindutva*, in which he had called Sikhs, Buddhists and Jains as part of the Hindu pantheon. Article

---

[9]V.D. Savarkar, *Bhashashuddhi*, Riya Publication, 2016.
[10]Balarao Savarkar, *Swatantryaveer Savarkar Sangata Parv*, p. 165.

25 (2)(b) of the Constitution specifies that 'the reference to Hindus shall be construed as including a reference to persons professing the Sikh, Jaina or Buddhist religion'[11]. The Hindu Marriage Act of 1955 goes in greater detail to define this 'legal Hindu', by stipulating in Section 2 that the Act applies:

> (a) to any person who is a Hindu by religion in any of its forms and developments, including a Virashaiva, a Lingayat or a follower of the Brahmo, Prarthana or Arya Samaj, (b) to any person who is a Buddhist, Jain or Sikh by religion, and (c) to any other person domiciled in the territories to which this Act extends who is not a Muslim, Christian, Parsi or Jew by religion.[12]

Savarkar was the sternest critic of conversion of Hindus to other faiths through inducements and immoral means. He was of the view that conversion from Hindus was denationalization. To support his argument, the first and foremost example on his list was that of Kashmir. A majority of the Kashmiri Muslims, who were converts from Hinduism, wouldn't have entertained separatist thoughts had they been taken back into Hinduism in the nineteenth century when they wanted to return.

During his active political life, whenever the opportunity presented itself, Savarkar exposed the conversion activity of Christians with full might. In fact, on one occasion he even took on the Pope himself. In 1943, a reckless Vatican openly boasted through its mouthpiece *L'Osservatore Romano* ('The Roman Observer') that India was turning into a fertile ground for conversion. The journal said: 'The Christian light shines already in the subcontinent of India. We hope one day it will blaze forth in full splendour.' Savarkar retaliated with vehemence, and sent

---

[11]Constitution of India, 'Article 25, Freedom of conscience and free profession, practice and propagation of religion'. https://www.constitutionofindia.net/constitution_of_india/fundamental_rights/articles/Article%2025. Accessed on 26 July 2021.
[12]Koenraad Elst, *Who is Hindu: Hindu Revivalist Views of Animism, Buddhism, Sikhism, and Other Offshoots of Hinduism*, Voice of India, 2002, p. 48.

a strong and detailed riposte to the United Press of America, Washington, saying: 'Surely the Vatican could not have chosen a more absurdly ridiculous a moment than this one, when Hitler, Mussolini, Churchill, Roosevelt and other leaders of almost all Christian nations are vowing vengeance against each other (WW-II).'[13] Savarkar reminded the Pope about the reconversion (Shuddhi) movement undertaken by the Hindu Sanghantanists in India and how thousands of converted Christians had come back to their ancient faith, Hinduism, and were getting assimilated both religiously and culturally in the Hindu nation. He also reminded how Lord Macaulay's dream of anglicizing India, both mentally and intellectually, was being shattered. Savarkar's riposte was highly appreciated by the Jewish community, whose spokesperson even issued a statement supporting Savarkar's stand.[14]

Not many are aware that the 'Flag of Indian Independence' raised by Madame Cama on 22 August 1907 at the second Socialist Congress meet in Stuttgart (Germany), was conceptualized by Savarkar. He had also made significant recommendations to the Constituent Assembly regarding the national flag. On 7 July 1947, he sent a telegram to Dr Ambedkar, Dr Rajendra Prasad, Sardar Vallabhbhai Patel and Dr N.B. Khare saying:

> The flag of Hindustan must be bhagwa-ochre coloured. At any rate, no flag which does not bear at least a stripe of bhagwa colour can be recognized by the Hindus as the national flag they can respect. The charkha too must be replaced by a chakra-wheel or any other such symbol signifying progress and strength. All Hindu sanghatanist leaders and organizations should also make a public demand to the same effect.[15]

Significantly, the Constituent Assembly gave a nod to Savarkar's recommendation by having a saffron stripe and a wheel

---

[13]Dhananjay Keer, *Veer Savarkar*, Popular Prakashan Pvt. Ltd; Second edition, 2019, p. 344.
[14]Ibid.
[15]V.D. Savarkar, *Historic Statements by Savarkar*, G.P. Parchure, 1967.

incorporated on the flag, instead of a charkha (spinning wheel). This wheel is recognized as the Ashok Chakra. Savarkar contested this and said it should be Lord Buddha's Dharma Chakra since it was first visualized by Buddha. He said: 'The fact is that this Chakra was not Ashok's discovery nor was Sarnath Ashok's Capital. The Buddha delivered his first sermon at Sarnath and to quote his own words 'set the Wheel of Law in motion—"Dharma Chakra Pravartan".[16] To commemorate this event, Emperor Ashok raised a pillar at Sarnath, Savarkar said, and got the Dharma Chakra carved on it. According to him, this Dharma Chakra appeals to one of the golden epochs of our Hindu history during which Chanakya and Chandragupta Maurya drove the invading armies of Alexander and Seleucus and the Hindu Emperor Ashok, the greatest of his time, ruled over an integrated and strongly centralized Indian nation, right from our strategic frontiers of Hindukush to the southern seas.[17]

AKHAND HINDUSTHAN: UNDERSTANDING SAVARKAR'S VISION

Savarkar's unalloyed nationalism, in which caste, religion and regional pride are secondary to national pride, was passionately attached to the Sindhu River (Indus). His treatise on the rise of the Hindu Civilization on the banks of Sindhu had a description in a moving, poetic language. So, when India was partitioned, he saw the division as fracture of the Hindu culture and dreamt that the Sindhu River would flow again under the Indian flag.

In his speech of 1952, popularly known as 'Sindhu Sukta' among Savarkarites, Savarkar put it very passionately:

> What are you saying? Now forget about Sindhu! Skip her name from the shloka. Otherwise some Tom Dick and Harry will get angry at me, and start hating me! Hence forget about Sindhu! No, no!! Even if the whole world starts hating us, we will not forget the Sindhu; we cannot break, forget or leave our Sindhu. Hindu without Sindhu is like a word without

---

[16]V.D. Savarkar, *Historic Statements by Savarkar*, G.P. Parchure, 1967.
[17]Ibid.

meaning. As long as we have air flowing through our lungs, it is impossible! As long as there is at least one Hindu alive, we can never forget the Sindhu! On the banks of whom (Sindhu) our ancient seers sang their first prayers and on the banks of whom they said their evening prayers, and in respect of whom hundreds of hymns are written.

...Ambitme (Mother of mothers), Naditme (River of rivers), Devitme (Deity of Deities), Sindhu we will never forget you! The Havans (Yagya) done on your banks pleased the Gods and the sweet smell of the offerings pleased them. Drink of your water quenched the thirst of the Gods and the God of Gods, O Sindhu, We will not forget you![18]

In his message to the nation on India's first Republic Day, 26 January 1950, Savarkar appealed for undoing of Partition, drawing an analogy between Partition of 1947 with the one caused by Alexander 2,500 years ago and how the partitioned parts were then won back by Chandragupta Maurya. He said:

Even the painful consciousness of the Partition, which we all so deeply deplore, should not be allowed to instil a sense of defeated mentality in us. If, when all was lost, we have succeeded in liberating three-fourths part of our country, we can surely recover the rest if we are bent on doing so. True, the Partition today is a settled fact. But had not Alexander himself torn off these very parts from our motherland and dubbed it a settled fact? Yet, history tells us how Seleucus handed back to us all those parts of our natural frontiers right up to Hindukush and gave his daughter in marriage to Chandragupta to seal mutual friendship. Verily, we have our own ways to resettle settled facts. Let us first consolidate what we have already got and follow courageously the policy of tit for tat to all outsiders concerned and all will go well with us.[19]

---

[18] V.D. Savarkar, *Abhinav Bharat Sangata Bhashane*, p. 54.
[19] V.D. Savarkar, *Historic Statements by Savarkar*, G.P. Parchure, 1967.

Savarkar and the RSS had advocated the concept of cultural nationalism as opposed to that of territorial nationalism adopted by the Congress. The latter had totally failed with Partition. While giving due credit to the efforts made by Sardar Patel in unifying the rest of India following Partition, one cannot deny the inherent oneness of the Indian subcontinent, which Savarkar referred to as Hindu nationalism and which played a major role in India's evolution. It is significant and inversely true that when and where the cultural, religious or political Hindu identity has weakened, the demand for geographical and political separation from India has cropped up. Significantly, the developments over the past 70 years have fortified Savarkar's words that 'Hindus are themselves a nation in India'.

Until 1947, Pakistan was a nation in search of a State, today it is a State in search of a nation. It was no minor development that a small section of the Pakistani intelligentsia accepted the defeat of the idea of Pakistan in the form of the two-nation theory based on religion-based nationhood with the birth of Bangladesh. The formation of Bangladesh out of Pakistan proved that religious affinity alone can't hold the nation together. Jinnah fought for establishing Urdu as the lingua franca of Indian Muslims, but Bangladesh created from East Pakistan chose its national anthem not in Urdu but in Bangla, and that too written by a Hindu, Rabindranath Tagore, who also penned India's national anthem.

We see separatist demands, howsoever small, based on regional cultural identity emanating from Balochistan, Sindh and even from the Pakhtoons (or Pashtuns). Nawab Akbar Bugti, the famous Baloch leader, before he was killed in 2006, had repeatedly said that Baloch people have been Muslims for the past 1,400 years, but have been Balochis for thousands of years. At the behest of a small section of Punjabi Muslims, who joined hands with local Sikhs and Hindus, Maharaja Ranjit Singh's statue was installed in downtown Lahore a few years ago. This, in turn, fuelled the demand from a very small section of Sindhi Muslims for the installation of a statue of Raja Dahir, the last Hindu king of Sindh before he was enslaved by Muhammad bin Qasim. The Jeay Sindh movement of the late leader of Sindhi nationalism, G.M. Syed, was rooted in Sindhi pride.

These movements might be small in nature, but the fact that they have cropped up and survived in spite of a compelling Islamization drive by Pakistani pan-Islamists for years now, points to the defeat of Jinnah's Muslim nationalism at the hands of Savarkar's geo-cultural nationalism at one level. Nothing captures the state of Pakistan better than a statement by a Muslim from Saudi Arabia: 'In a half a century, the two-nation theory has died a natural death. In Pakistan, it is the four-nation theory that is now in force.'[20]

However, at another level, the fight against Islamic fundamentalism in the form of the ultra-Wahhabi tanzeems (militant organizations) spreading religious hatred continues and poses a threat to India. Nothing exemplifies this better than an incident that one of the authors of this book recounts. In January 2006, one of the authors was present during a speech by a well-known pan-Islamist leader, who is even today a member of the All India Muslim Personal Law Board. The meeting was being held in a public hall in the Paldi area of Ahmedabad. Highlighting the plans of pan-Islamists for India, the leader openly lamented as to why India had still not converted into a Muslim-majority country, despite the religion being in India for 800 years. He said, 'We have to analyse as to what was the shortfall in our strategy that we couldn't convert the Dalits and the exploited Hindus to Islam despite the fact that they were waiting with open arms to accept Islam.'

He continued,

> But when I went to Pakistan recently what I heard was totally different. The Pakistanis told me that Indian Muslims have done very well. On the day of Partition, they (Indian Muslims) were seen as anti-nationals and Pakistanis for having supported the Muslim League and Pakistan. But today, Indian Muslims have a veto over the government which can't take major decisions without their consent.

---

[20]Yuvraj Krishan, *Understanding Partition: India Sundered, Muslims Fragmented*, Mumbai: Bharatiya Vidya Bhavan, 2002, p. 374.

He then delivered the final punch: 'I pondered over what the Pakistanis told me and found truth in it. Today, there are states like Assam, Uttar Pradesh, Kerala and West Bengal, where no party can form a government without Muslim support. We have to create this situation in the entire country and at the national level to ensure that no political party can form a government without the help of Muslim votes.'

This speech exposed the true designs of pan-Islamist Indian Muslims, but common Hindus and even a section of good but naïve Muslims are unaware of it, thanks to the lack of Savarkarian vision.

The lack of intellectual rigour associated with Savarkarian vision also means that the knowledge about Sunni Islamic tanzeems is equally missing in society as well as in the intellectual class, particularly in an age when radical Islam is threatening the universe. The fact that terrorism and ideas of conquering the entire world for Islam come from radical Wahhabi tanzeems and not from moderate Sufi tanzeems (both parts of Sunnism), not just in India but across the world, is still not known to a large part of the Indian population, including the Right-wingers, many of whom paint all Muslims as radicals.

There is little knowledge in society about the fact that the Deoband School, its missionary wing the Tablighi Jamaat and another reform movement called Ahl-e Hadith, which is followed by Lashkar-e-Taiba founder Hafiz Saeed, constitute Wahhabism in South Asia. Wahhabis oppose the worship of Muslim saints at their tombs, as done by Sufis, because they see this exercise as an import from the Hindu practice of guru puja (saint worship). Terrorists invariably come from amongst the Wahhabis but scarcely from amongst the Sufis. But at the same time, only a section of Wahhabis justify or believe in terrorism. A vast section amongst them too is even today moderate, knowing well the price supporters of terrorism have to pay in a world that is uniting against Islamic terrorism.

The lack of knowledge of these inner intricacies of the Muslim community has led to a strange imbalance in the Hindu society, where aggressive Hindus go after the entire Muslim community, thus creating an atmosphere of total mistrust. Savarkar himself was very careful while attacking radical Muslims and Muslim appeasement. He would always treat moderate Muslims with respect, as highlighted by his interactions and free-wheeling dialogue with a section of Lucknow's Shia Muslims in the 1940s.

Interestingly, in one of his statements made just before Partition, Savarkar had advised Muslims to appreciate the importance of history and recognize that they came to India as conquerors, but were ultimately tamed by Hindus. Perhaps he was hinting at the fact that every action has a reaction. Decades of Muslim-appeasement politics have done irreparable damage to Muslims themselves. Today, a large section of the Hindu population sees them as unfaithful to the idea of a truly secular India and as closet pan-Islamists, thus failing to make a distinction between truly secular and pan-Islamist Muslims. The impression is strengthened by the fact that truly liberal Muslims are frowned upon in the Muslim community. Hamid Dalwai, a propagator of reformist Islam who ran a campaign to reform the community by freeing it of religious dogmas and pan-Islamism, died a loner's death in 1977. In his writings, Dalwai had given an in-depth picture of how a number of so-called secular Indian Muslim leaders cutting across lines were actually pan-Islamists masquerading as liberals.

This, however, was not the case with Mughal emperor, Akbar, whom Savarkar viewed as a symbol of Hindu–Muslim unity. He appreciated Akbar's liberality in his book *Hindutva*, in which he says that after years and years of atrocities on Hindus by Muslim invaders, the Hindus 'won a moral victory when Akbar came to the throne.'[21] His views on the Mughal emperor are contrary to the Akbar-bashing practised by right-wing Hindu groups that regard the Mughal king as a closet Islamist. This is a typical example of Indian's lack of sense of history, because actual history is very different.

Akbar's policy of Sulh-i Kul (absolute peace between religions) put a stop to indiscriminate destruction of temples, abduction of

---

[21] V.D. Savarkar, *Hindutva (Samagra Savarkar, Vol. 10)*, Mumbai: Veer Savarkar Prakashan, 1994, p. 32.

Hindu women and imposition of the religious poll tax 'jizya' on Hindus and non-Muslims of the Islamic State. Jiziya had continued for 350 years starting with Qutb al-Din Aibak, Ghurid king Mu'izz ad-Din Muhammad Ghori's nominee left to govern in India from 1192, which marks the beginning of Muslim rule in India. This is the reason why Savarkar appreciated Akbar, which his own followers are unaware about. However, the Mughal emperor's atrocities on the residents of Chittorgarh during his siege of 1567–68 are often held out as a proof of Akbar's jihadi nature. It is true that his conduct at Chittorgarh is a blot on his reign, but it is equally true that Akbar became a liberal and a reformist votary of Hindu–Muslim unity only after he came in touch with known Jain and Vaishnava saints of the country in 1570, two years after the Chittorgarh episode. And Akbar remained steadfastly wedded to liberal ideas till his death in 1605.

In 1679, when the fanatic Mughal emperor Aurangzeb reimposed the jizya religious poll tax on non-Muslims in his empire, Chhatrapati Shivaji, the great Maratha leader and symbol of Hindus' resurgence against Muslim tyranny, wrote a long protest letter to the emperor in which he asked Aurangzeb to emulate his great grandfather Emperor Akbar, whom he described 'as Jagadguru'—an epithet he earned for making Hindus partners in the Mughal empire by treating them with equality.

It is not without reason that Akbar remains a much hated figure in the fanatical Wahhabi (Deoband, Tablighi Jamaat and Ahl-e Hadith madrasas, which are known as Indian schools of Wahhabism) madrassas of South Asia. He tried to reform Islam by removing the jihadi elements and opposed such fanatical maulvis of his time as Shaikh Ahmad Sirhindi, who wanted Muslim persecution on idol-worshipping Hindus to continue. There is evidence to prove that Akbar took strong measures against Sirhindi, which compelled the radical preacher to compromise with Akbar on the surface but continued his radical preaching secretly to save himself from Akbar's ire.

The condition of Hindus before the advent of Akbar was graphically described by historian R.C. Majumdar in *The History* and *Culture of the Indian People (Vol. 6): The Delhi Sultanate* which was published by Bharatiya Vidya Bhavan.[22] He was the editor of the series. One of his accounts citing the memoirs of the medieval Moorish traveller Ibn Battuta is chilling. Describing the celebration of one particular Eid in the court of Sultan Muhammad bin Tughlaq in Delhi, Majumdar, quoting Battuta, vividly narrates how abducted Hindu women belonging to royal Brahmin and poor Hindu families were brought to the Sultan's Darbar, forced to dance and then given away in slavery to the Umraos present on the occasion. Battuta was the Kazi of Delhi then. Battuta says he being the Kazi was again gifted a large number of women slaves by the Sultan but he kept only a few and distributed the rest amongst his servants as he could ill-afford to keep such a large number of women slaves in his harem. This episode clearly shows that before Akbar there was scarcely a Muslim ruler except a handful like Sultan Zain-ul-Abidin of Kashmir who was not a religious tyrant.

Unlike Akbar, who became a genuine convert to liberal ideas, Savarkar believed that Tipu Sultan, the famous medieval ruler of the South, was a religious tyrant who only made a tactical compromise to save his throne by patronizing Hindus in the later phase of his career.[23] The debate on Tipu Sultan is, in fact, unending—while the Left-wingers believe he fought against British rule, the Right-wingers see him as the worst symbol of Muslim atrocity on the Hindus of Malabar and Coorg. The fact is that Tipu Sultan was more fanatic than even Aurangzeb as he also indulged in the dishonour of Hindu women and, unlike Aurangzeb, converted lakhs of Hindus to Islam at the point of sword. But when the Hindu Marathas, the British and the Nizam of Hyderabad united against him and overwhelmed him, he felt a dire need for the support of his Hindu population. At this point, he sought a change of his image to woo Hindus. In order to achieve it, Tipu Sultan started patronizing Brahmins on a large scale.

---

[22]R.C. Majumdar, *The History and Culture of the Indian People (Vol. 6): The Delhi Sultanate*, Bharatiya Vidya Bhavan, 2006, p. 627.
[23]V.D. Savarkar, *Six Glorious Epochs of Indian History*, Mumbai: Bal Savarkar, 1971.

WORSHIPPING VILLAINS; FORGETTING TRUE HEROES

Savarkar also questioned the legacy of Sultan Mahmud Begada, a fanatical medieval Sultan of the Gujarat Sultanate who successfully captured the two forts of Pavagadh and Junagadh. Regarded as a great ruler by a section of the local Gujarat populace, he is remembered every year on Ahmedabad's foundation day along with the city's founder and Begada's great-grandfather, Ahmad Shah, also a religious fanatic. In fact, Begada is the only Muslim ruler in history who demolished both Somnath and the Dwarkadhish Temple at Dwarka. He converted thousands of Hindus at the point of sword. The worst part of this episode is that Gujarat is a major seat of the Vaishnava Baniya community (followers of Dwarkadhish) and several members of the same community eulogize Begada today.

Begada's grandson, Bahadur Shah, is also regarded as a great ruler in local history. But he was the only Muslim ruler whose villainy caused two *jauhars*[24] in the early sixteenth century: the 1532 Jauhar of Raisen Fort in Central India, in which 700 Hindu women including Rani Durgavati immolated themselves and the 1535 Jauhar of Chittorgarh, in which 13,000 Hindu women, led by Rana Sanga's widow Rani Karnavati, killed themselves.[25]

In some history books on Gujarat, Patai Rawal, alias Jai Singh Chauhan (Khichi), the ruler of Pavagadh, whom Begada defeated in 1484 after a siege that lasted 20 months, is depicted as a villain.

However, historian J. Chaube, in his book *History of the Gujarat Kingdom 1458–1537*, writes that after Sultan Begada managed to capture Jai Singh alive, he implored him to accept Islam. However, the Rajput ruler, a descendent of the war hero of Ranthambore, Hammir Dev Chauhan, who died fighting Alauddin Khilji in the fourteenth century, refused to bow down to this demand. He said, 'I can't leave the religion of my ancestors and would instead embrace

---

[24] A practice in which Hindu, particularly Rajput women, immolated themselves by jumping into a fire pit to save themselves from dishonour at the hands of Muslims.
[25] J. Chaube, *History of the Gujarat Kingdom 1458–1537*, Munshiram Manoharlal Publishers, 1975, p. 217, 230, 231.

death.'[26] However, Begada was tempted by the prospect of inducing the entire Hindu population of Jai Singh's kingdom to accept Islam in case he succeeded in converting Jai Singh. And so with this strategy in mind, he gave Jai Singh six months to decide on the issue. During these six months, Jai Singh was kept in great comfort by the Sultan, so that he could be induced to embrace Islam. But after six months, Jai Singh was beheaded when he gave the same reply to Begada on the issue of conversion. So, the question is: who should be regarded as the true hero of Gujarat—Begada or Jai Singh? In Savarkar's estimate, Jai Singh would have been the real hero of Gujarat today.

Unfortunately, even today we celebrate people like Muhammad Iqbal, the poet responsible for the partition of his own motherland, as heroes. Even after 74 years of Partition, Iqbal is freely quoted by poets and intellectuals in different parts of the country. His nazms (verses/poems) are in fact a big draw in mushairas (poetic symposiums) across India. The fact that his shayaris (Urdu poetry) continue to be recited shows how ignorant a section of the Indian population, including the intellectual class, is about their immediate history.

However, when we blame Indian people for their ignorance about the true nature of Iqbal, we also have to blame the makers of Independent India, who never spread awareness about him among the Indian masses. In fact, what they did was exactly the reverse, as evident from the events on the day of Independence itself. Shockingly, Iqbal's 'Saare Jahan Se Achha' was sung on the midnight of 14 August 1947, when India came into being. But Vande Mataram was ignored. The Constituent Assembly adjourned after Mrs Sucheta Kripalani, who later became India's first woman chief minister of Uttar Pradesh, sang Iqbal's 'Saare Jahan Se Achha' and the first verse of 'Jana Gana Mana'.[27]

Yet another aspect of Savarkar's vision that deserves mention

---

[26] J. Chaube, *History of the Gujarat Kingdom 1458–1537*, Munshiram Manoharlal Publishers, 1975, p. 83.

[27] Durga Das, *India from Curzon to Nehru and After*, Rupa & Co., 2002, p. 262.

was changing the names of Indian cities and areas given by fanatic medieval Muslim rulers to impose Islamic culture on Hindus. He dwelt on this while talking about Ahmedabad, whose original name was Karnavati, which was changed to Ahmedabad by Sultan Ahmed Shah, who founded the Ahmed Shahi dynasty. Savarkar said, 'Consequently, now that the day of our triumph has risen, it is our duty to erase away the humiliating and hateful name from the map of Gujarat. Even if the city is to continue as the capital of the state, it should be renamed as "Karnavati".'[28]

Savarkar also called for renaming the Arabian Sea. On Gujarat's coastline was located Dwarka, Shri Krishna's capital, and so the Arabian Sea should either be named 'Ratnakar', as the sea was mentioned in the Puranas, or 'Sindhu Sagar', as the Sindhu river merges with it. Savarkar had also called for renaming the Bay of Bengal as 'Gangasagar', as the holy Ganga merges with it.[29] Interestingly, Savarkar suggested that the new capital of Gujarat should be named after Sardar Patel as 'Vallabh Nagar', in memory of the man whose strong will did much to serve India.[30]

Had Savarkar's vision been followed, the roads in Delhi would not have been named after Muslim invaders such as the Tughlakhs and the Lodhis, who are today also the heroes of Pakistan, India's dreaded enemy, and who committed untold atrocities on Hindus during the Sultanate period. Instead, these roads would have been named after true Muslim heroes such as Ibrahim Khan Gardi, the patriotic Muslim commander who refused to go over to the Muslim coalition under Afghan invader Ahmad Shah Abdali in the Third Battle of Panipat and sacrificed his life fighting for the Marathas; Ashfaqullah Khan, the great revolutionary who went to the gallows fighting the Britishers; Brigadier Mohammad Usman MVC, who died fighting for India against Pakistan in the 1948 Kashmir action; or Ghiyas-ud-Din Zain-ul-Abidin, one of the few truly liberal Muslim rulers of medieval India who ruled Kashmir

---

[28]V.D. Savarkar, *Historic Statements by Savarkar*, G.P. Parchure, 1967.
[29]Ibid.
[30]Ibid.

from 1420 to 1470. Savarkarian vision would also definitely appreciate renaming the roads of the capital after Chandragupta Maurya, Samudragupta, Shalivahana, Rajendra Chola, Ramdev Ray, Bappa Rawal and the emperors of India, instead of those of the invaders. However, a beginning in this direction has been made by the Modi-led government with the renaming of Allahabad as Prayagraj.

The absence of Savarkarian vision has also meant that subjective Left historians, with their agenda of suppressing Hindu pride, held full sway. Further, this pacifist thinking continues to blur India's national vision when it comes to evaluating the true worth of its national heroes such as Guru Gobind Singh, Maharana Pratap and Chhatrapati Shivaji, whom Gandhi described as 'misguided patriots' in 1925.[31] Consequently, Guru Gobind Singh's contribution to national integration should have been known to people across India, but it is limited to only some parts of the country in the north, while in the case of Maharana Pratap and Shivaji, their true and full contribution to the national vision isn't known to even some of their supporters.

This is particularly true in the case of Shivaji, regarded by some as the greatest Indian in over 1,000 years owing to his military might, diplomatic vision and social reform. Described by noted historian Jadunath Sarkar as 'the greatest constructive genius of medieval India' in his book *Shivaji and His Times*[32], Shivaji's achievements are so exemplary that they warrant a complete review of his legacy so as to give him his rightful place in history.[33] However, it is just not Shivaji's contribution that is known to only a handful of people in the country. Few Indians are aware of the contribution of Santaji Ghorpade and Dhanaji Jadhav, two Maratha generals who brought Aurangzeb to his knees in the last two decades of his emperorship in the southern theatre of the Mughal–

---

[31] *Young India*, 9 March 1925.
[32] Jadunath Sarkar, *Shivaji and His Times*, New Delhi: Orient Blackswan Private Limited; Fifth Revised edition (2010).
[33] https://archive.org/details/in.ernet.dli.2015.282812/page/n413/mode/2up, p. 400. Accessed on 31 July 2021.

Maratha War comprising Maharashtra, Karnataka and Tamil Nadu between 1689 and 1707. They defeated the Mughals in a series of battles and terrorized Aurangzeb himself.[34] Ironically, lessons of Maratha aggression on the Mughals during this phase are taught by radical Islamic preachers in Pakistan to their students while preparing them to tackle Hindus in their big but elusive dream of defeating Hindus and Islamizing India.[35] However, these lessons of Maratha resistance to Aurangzeb's religious tyranny and the heroes of this battle are missing from the minds of Indians except in Maharashtra.

Many of Savarkar's ideas on social and religious reform were extremely relevant for India. However, he was ostracized and was considered worthy of condemnation by pan-Islamists and the communists. It is necessary to understand their motives. The first set comprising pan-Islamists dream of converting this nation into an Islamic country, while the second in the form of communists want to ensure that India is never united in pursuance of their elusive dream of turning India into a communist country. Then there is a third set of pseudo-secular parties that crave for Muslim votes and want to curry favour with pan-Islamists and radical communists under the slogan of 'secular India'. The game plan of all the three intertwined forces has always been to keep Hindus divided along caste lines and prevent Muslims from joining the patriotic Hindus by playing the card of Hindu domination to create fear in the minds of Muslims.

Inspired by this vision, several years ago, one of the authors wrote an article on *Daily O*, the digital platform of the *India Today* group, which highlighted the fact that Savarkar's Hindutva was a Hindu protective view and not a Hindu supremacist view.[36] He reiterated that Savarkar's Hindu Rashtra guaranteed equal rights to all and not special rights to Hindus. On reading the article,

---

[34]Jadunath Sarkar, *House of Shivaji*, Sangam Books Ltd, 1979, pp. 226–41.
[35]https://fb.watch/22iwmVqxvt/. Accessed on 26 July 2021.
[36]Uday Mahurkar 'How history distorted Savarkar's ideology,' *Daily* O; 26 May 2015.   https://www.dailyo.in/politics/veer-savarkar-hindutva-conversion-indian-muslims-congress-partition-of-india/story/1/3916.html. Accessed on 6 July 2021.

two Muslims leaders—one belonging to the radical outfit Tablighi Jamaat and another from a Sufi tanzeem—called up the author to tell him that they never knew about this aspect of Savarkar and that if this was true, their differences with Savarkar appeared much narrowed down.

REVISITING THE 'MINORITY' DEFINITION

Savarkar had reasons to believe that India's Pakistan policy was dictated by the sentiment of a set of local pan-Islamist Muslims. India granted most-favoured nation (MFN) status to Pakistan in 1996 despite that country not according the same status to India and trying to dismember India since its birth in 1947. In the 1965 and 1971 wars, India returned Pakistan's land that it had conquered in the Western Sector despite having an upper hand. Till recently, our country never took measures to stop water of the Himalayan rivers originating in India from flowing to Pakistan as a counter measure to Pakistan's unending aggressions.

On the other hand, despite conceding Pakistan on the demand of a vast section of Indian Muslims, India allowed special privileges to religious minorities, especially Indian Muslims, under Article 30 of the Constitution, under which government-aided minority schools are exempted from several provisions which are mandatory for non-minority (read majority) schools, like following the reservation policy for Scheduled Castes and Scheduled Tribes in the recruitment of teachers. A government-aided minority school can keep a maulvi to teach the Koran, but a majority school can't hire a pandit to teach the *Bhagavad Gita*.

The Hindu Religious and Charitable Endowments Department controls many eminent Hindu temples across India, but that is not the case with mosques and churches, which are controlled by the respective communities only. In the case of temples controlled by the government, it takes away the offerings that come at the temples and in turn a part of the same money gets used in the system's well-established minority-appeasement policies.[37] These pro-Muslim policies in the name of secularism have in turn resulted in lowering the self-confidence of Hindus and affected the 'Hinduness' in what is the last and the only land of Hindus in the world.

Independent India's Muslim-centric foreign policy can, in fact, be traced to the Congress's support to the Khilafat movement, which decided to give a total go-by to the Nation First principle. The CWC meeting held in Bombay on 5 October 1921 clearly said: 'When India has attained self-government, Mussulman states should feel assured that her foreign policy will always be guided so as to respect Mussulman religious obligations.'[38]

Further, the pro-Muslim policies at the cost of majority rights that were perpetuated on Independent India had its roots in the 1940 Pakistan Resolution Part-II of the Muslim League which laid down as to how Muslims will be treated in post-partitioned India, when they would be in a big minority. The resolution said, 'In other parts of India where the Mussalmans are in a minority, adequate, effective and mandatory safeguards shall be specially provided in the constitution for them and other minorities for the protection of their religious, cultural, economic, political, administrative and other rights and interests in consultation with them.'[39]

That the policy of Muslim appeasement—an extension of the Khilafat compromise—began as soon as the foundation of new India was laid is clearly evident from the case of AMU, which, from 1939 to 1947, was the centre of the Pakistan movement. It was where all the strategic planning for the much-expected new Muslim state was carried out. Almost the entire apparatus of the institution, from teachers to students, worked towards creating Pakistan over a period of eight years. Would any nation with a patriotic vision allow an organization that was responsible for the

---

[37]'What really happens to your money in Temple Hundi?' http://guruprasad.net/posts/really-happens-money-temple-hundi/. Accessed on 31 July 2021.

[38]P.C. Bamford, *Histories of the Non-Cooperation and Khilafat Movement*, Government of India Press, 1925, p. 39.

[39]Y. Krishnan, *Understanding Partition: Separation Not Liquidation*, Bharatiya Vidya Bhavan, 2002, p. 388.

division of the motherland to continue in the same condition even after Partition? Perhaps not. There are examples in world history where people draw lessons from the past. They never forget such national injuries and reserve remedial measures for them. Sadly, this element is missing amongst Indians, thanks to a vision which is completely lacking in the Savarkarian element.

Not only was the university allowed to function under the same nomenclature, but under pressure from pan-Islamist elements, the Congress government also gave it minority status. This was later challenged in court and remains challenged till this day as the Modi government remains inclined towards correcting the wrong by denying it minority status. The least the nation could have done after Independence was to rename the university after some patriotic Muslims such as Ashfaqullah Khan.

Interestingly, the Aligarh and Deoband schools had opposed each other with great ferocity before Partition on a range of issues relating to Islam and its interpretation. But after Partition, the two schools came together to demand minority status for the AMU in what was clearly a pan-Islamic joint strategy.

The Congress, by continuing in independent India with what the Muslim League had laid down in the form of the second part of its 1940 Pakistan resolution providing special protection to Muslims who were left behind in India after the formation of Pakistan, has harmed the nation no end. The preferential treatment given to Muslims under Article 30 at the cost of Hindu rights even after giving Pakistan to Indian Muslims is, in fact, Part-II of Jinnah's 1940 Pakistan resolution. It is in these pro-minority and anti-Hindu policies of the Congress and other pseudo-secular parties that fantastic demands such as seeking reservation for converted Dalits are rooted.

Distorted logic and information manufactured to portray Muslims as more backward than Hindus—as mentioned in the highly one-sided Sachar Committee Report—was used by the United Progressive Alliance (UPA) government to implement the committee's recommendations for the upliftment of the religious minorities (read Muslims) in what was the latest attempt to appease the Muslim community. However, a well-researched book by two former IPS officers, Ram Kumar Ohri and Jai Prakash Sharma, titled *The Majority Report*, busted the myth about Muslim backwardness and proved that Hindus on the whole are more backward than Muslims when it comes to five globally recognized development parameters.[40] These are: infant mortality, child mortality, life expectancy at birth, degree of urbanization and literacy.

In four of these five parameters, poor Hindus are lagging behind Muslims. And there are at least four well-researched reports produced by different entities which have proved Ohri and Sharma's observations correct. In fact, the Sachar Committee recommendations are a big blow to the Hindus' poorer classes whose rightful share has been snatched away by the recommendations and given away to Muslims and other religious minorities, which are, in fact, ahead of poor Hindus in terms of development. According to Durga Nand Jha, Executive Chairman at the Centre for Policy Analysis, Patna, there are nearly a dozen states and union territories where the income of Muslims is clearly higher than that of Hindus. And at most places where it is lower than Hindus, the main reasons for the shortfall are Muslims' own social reasons and not any slackness on the part of the government.[41]

In his well-researched report titled *India Minority Report*, Jha says:

> The Muslim leaders grumble against backwardness but are unwilling to remove the causes that are constraining the pace of development of the community. This is creating a peculiar situation that can be termed as 'inclusive-exclusive' paradox. It means that the community wants to be inclusive in respect of development while remaining exclusive otherwise.[42]

---

[40]Ram Kumar Ohri and Jai Prakash Sharma, *The Majority Report*, Carried Publication, 2013.
[41]Durga Nand Jha, *India Minority Report: An Enquiry into India's Minority Policy and Analysis of Socio-Economic Status of Muslim Community in India,* Centre for Policy Analysis, 2018.
[42]Ibid.

However, there is a greater argument against Muslim appeasement in India. In the 1945–46 Central Assembly polls before Partition, almost 87 per cent of the total Muslim votes cast went to the Muslim League. However, when Partition happened, over 90 per cent of them stayed back in India. So, logically did they have any right to demand special privileges?

It is not hard to see the damage wreaked by the rulers of this nation by following a pacifist foreign and defence policy, marred by Muslim vote-bank politics, in its formative years, as opposed to Savarkar's national security vision. These doctrines were a combination of self-imposed shackles and perversion of virtues which indeed proved to be strategic blunders.

With its inherent strengths, which are unparalleled in the world, India would perhaps have been far ahead of China and other powerful nations, both militarily and economically. That military strength is a prerequisite to a nation's economic progress in the comity of big nations is as true now as it was when Savarkar expounded this theory nine decades ago.

Thankfully, all these policies have been almost wholly reversed in a span of just six years after the Modi-led BJP government came to power. The impact of the actions taken by the Modi government against Pakistan's provocations including the surgical strike and then the air-strike following the Pulwama attack, is too well known now. There are indications that Pakistan is now backtracking and even China is taking notice of India's new Savarkarian approach.

ISRAEL: A KINDRED SPIRIT

It was this practical approach that was the inspiration behind Savarkar visualizing and predicting the formation of the Jewish State, as early as 1923 in his epic work *Hindutva*, which, he believed, would augur well for India in the future. Today, he has been proved entirely correct when the United Arab Emirates has recognized Israel and even Saudi Arabia, the main seat of opposition to Zionists, is on its way to do the same.

When the independent nation of Israel was born in 1948, Savarkar welcomed it in the following words, which is yet another evidence of his unmatched world vision and profound knowledge of history and religions:

> The whole of Palestine has been, for at least 2,000 years, the national home of the Jewish people. A long line of great prophets and kings, Abraham, David and Moses had endeared the country to them as their Fatherland and Holy Land. It constitutes an event of historical justice and importance. The Arabian Muslims invaded Palestine before they invaded Sindh and just as their fanatical fury exterminated the ancient Egyptians and Persians, they attempted to wipe out with swords the Jewish people too. But they failed in this unholy ambition. In justice, the whole of Palestine ought to have been restored to Jews.[43]

However, after the formation of Israel, it took India 44 years to establish full diplomatic relations with that country, despite the fact that all along, Israel has been keen to help India establish full diplomatic relations. The reason: India's foreign policy, when it affected Muslim sentiments, was always dictated by Muslim vote-bank politics. Interestingly, Jews, like Muslims, have been in India for centuries, but their numbers are minimal as compared to Muslims. And so India allowed Muslim sentiments, rather the pan-Islamic agenda, to dictate its foreign policy on Israel for almost half a century.

Savarkar had, in fact, fought for a pro-Israel Indian foreign policy from the day the Jewish State was born on the basis of a very sound logic rooted in moral and political grounds. He had constantly opposed the Nehru government's Muslim-centric and anti-Israel policy.

Condemning the Indian government's stand against Israel in the United Nations (UN) at that time owing to Muslim pressure at home, Savarkar ridiculed the Nehru government, which had told the UN that India can't stab the unity and integrity of Palestine,

---

[43]V.D. Savarkar, *Historic Statements by Savarkar*, G.P. Parchure, 1967.

thus reminding 'that the same government had stabbed the unity and integrity of our own nation (by allowing Pakistan) the other day'.[44]

Interestingly, India's eagerness to build relations with Islamic nations by keeping Israel at bay to please local Muslim sentiment didn't lead to Pakistan changing its stance towards India. All along Pakistan continued to attack India and India's friendliness with the Gulf nations didn't result in any benefits to it except after the arrival of the Modi government, which is reshaping India's foreign policy in a true Savarkarian mode, keeping national interest supreme.

A TENUOUS RELATIONSHIP WITH THE WORLD

Almost all the allegations levelled by the anti-Savarkar and anti-RSS lobby are wrong, as proved by the plethora of available evidence. The course of unadulterated history has also proved Savarkar right by disproving these unfounded allegations. However, when one honestly evaluates the contribution of a hero, it is necessary to evaluate him critically too. So, was Savarkar flawless? The answer is, no. He did commit a few mistakes.

One of them was his attempt to demonstrate his rational outlook regarding cow worship amongst Hindus. When he said cow was like any other animal and should be seen from a scientific angle only,[45] there was a big hue and cry amongst orthodox Hindus as well as in the echelons of the RSS, which even criticized Savarkar for this view.

Savarkar, of course, had logic to back this statement. He gave due credit to the importance of cow protection but not cow puja. He said during the medieval period, Hindus had lost many battles because the Muslim invaders blunted the Hindu attack by placing cows before the Hindu army in the midst of the battle. As a result, Hindus stopped firing arrows. Savarkar said in such a situation

---

[44]Ibid.

[45]V.D. Savarkar, *Vigyannishth Nbandh (Samagra Savarkar, Vol. 9)*. Mumbai: Veer Savarkar Prakashan, 1994, p. 49.

when one had to choose between the nation and the cow, one should always choose the nation.⁴⁶ There was logic in what he said but the weight of opinion was in favour of the fact that Savarkar shouldn't have raised the question on what was an indivisible part of the Hindu belief system, which considered it as an attack.

Yet another blunder committed by Savarkar was on the eve of Independence when it was decided that India would be partitioned. Expressing extreme fear about a possible clash between the armies of India and Pakistan, Gandhi questioned the need for India to have an army at all. On 7 July 1947, he said:

> Why are the two armies being created? Are they to defend the country against foreign aggression or are they to fight against each other and prove to the world that we are only good at killing each other. Will they rise up and say that they have no need for an army or at least take a pledge that this army will not be used against their Muslim brethren whether they be living in India or Pakistan.⁴⁷

Those who understood the national security angle and the way Muslims had started riots in Calcutta after Jinnah's Direct Action Call and had committed untold atrocities on the Hindus of Kerala in the name of Khilafat just two decades ago, were shocked by Gandhi's statement which almost amounted to having 'No Indian Army'. The echo was particularly deep in Kerala, where Hindus had suffered immensely at the hands of the Moplahs during the 1921 rebellion. The Travancore State, which had played a key role in the rebellion by providing succour to the Hindu victims, was aware of the true face of jihadi Islam and was deeply affected. At this fearful juncture, and after Gandhi's pronouncement, the Dewan of Travancore State, Sir C.P. Ramaswami Iyer, a statesman of high order, said that Travancore would be a free State and would not be part of the upcoming Indian Union. He also gave reasons for doing so.

---

⁴⁶Ibid.
⁴⁷Dhananjay Keer, *Mahatma Gandhi: Political Saint & Unarmed Prophet*, Popular Prakashan; Revised Second Edition,2020 (1973), p. 765.

Incensed at the Muslim appeasement and the Congress's abject surrender before the Muslim League, Savarkar, in a weak moment, supported the Travancore declaration in what was a complete reversal of his own stand of a United India at any cost. Of course, he did it in the name of Hindu protection against Muslim aggression and the Congress's timidity in protecting Hindu rights.

Perhaps Savarkar's stand on Travancore was also driven by the Congress's and Gandhi's stand on the Nizam of Hyderabad, which indicated that the Congress might cave in to the Nizam's demand for either a Kashmir-type accommodation with the upcoming Indian Union or a merger with upcoming Pakistan. In fact, as early as February 1945, Savarkar had warned of the Muslim ambition of 'Pakistan in North and Nizamistan in South'.[48] As a Maratha historian and a leader of the Bhagyanagar (Hyderabad) movement that opposed the atrocities of the Nizam's State against Hindus, Savarkar knew the Nizam inside out. He didn't trust the Congress in the Nizam's case, particularly after Gandhi had himself admitted to this possibility in the event of an anarchy, in the 13 October 1940 edition of *Harijan*. Savarkar perhaps supported Travancore because he saw a Hindu Travancore as a counter to a possible independent or Pakistan-aligned Nizam. However, in spite of these arguments in favour of Savarkar in the Travancore issue, the weight of opinion even amongst his staunchest supporters is that it was an incorrect stand. Fortunately, Travancore reversed its stand in the final tally and joined the Indian Union.

However, Ramaswami Iyer became an ardent admirer of Savarkar and regarded him as a great visionary because of his heroic opposition to Partition and his marked ability to predict the threat to India's security well in advance. Inaugurating a community hall named after Savarkar in Pune in 1958, Iyer said:

> Now a days he who calls himself a Hindu is denounced as a communalist. Savarkar's views are not orthodox and regressive but progressive. His Hindutva isn't based on hatred

---

[48]V.D. Savarkar, *Historic Statements by Savarkar*, G.P. Parchure, 1967, p. 93.

of others. From this viewpoint alone, Savarkar opposed Partition. His object was to preserve the geographical and social unity of the nation. I believe that Savarkarian principles and his way of thinking would bring prosperity to the nation.[49]

Interestingly, Iyer made this statement after a decade of the prime ministership of Pandit Nehru which saw a repeat of pre-Partition type Muslim appeasement by the Congress, which invariably dubbed a devout and assertive Hindu as communal and a communal Muslim as secular. In 1957, just a year before Iyer's observation about Savarkar and Hindu-bashing, Nehru shockingly forged a poll alliance, merely 10 years after Independence, with the Indian Union Muslim League, which had succeeded the All India Muslim League—the very party that had caused Partition, in independent India.

Savarkar excelled in national security in which Gandhi was almost a non-starter with his views based on complete non-violence and brotherhood at any cost. The height of Gandhian pacifism and the danger it posed to India's unity and integrity was quite evident when he started talking about committing suicide, overwhelmed by the bloodshed of World War II, as described by Abul Kalam Azad in his book, *India Wins Freedom*.[50] Azad also revealed in the same book as to how Gandhi advised the British not to retaliate against the German attack in World War II but rely on its moral strength.[51]

Even after Independence, divisive forces have used Gandhian pacifism as a shield. It continues to be milked by pan-Islamists in their pursuit of Islamizing India, as reinforced by the Shaheen Bagh protest of 2019 against the Citizenship (Amendment) Act (CAA) and the National Register of Citizens (NRC). On the surface, the supporters of the Shaheen Bagh agitation saw it as a legitimate

---

[49]Dhananjay Keer, *Veer Savarkar*, Popular Prakashan Pvt. Ltd; Second edition, 2019, p. 509.
[50]Maulana Abul Kalam Azad, *India Wins Freedom*, Orient BlackSwan, 1988. p. 29, https://archive.org/stream/in.ernet.dli.2015.103049/2015.103049.India-Wins-Freedom-An-Autobigraphical-Narrative_djvu.txt. Accessed on 31 July 2021.
[51]Maulana Abul Kalam Azad, *India Wins Freedom*, Orient BlackSwan, 1988.

protest against the CAA because it barred persecuted Muslims of Pakistan, Afghanistan and Bangladesh from migrating to India and allowed only the persecuted minorities of the three nations, namely Hindus, Sikhs, Christians, Buddhists and Jains.

The point here is: why should the Muslims of these three nations, even if they are persecuted, be allowed in India when we have several examples before us of Europe, where in many Christian nations, after having given asylum to persecuted Muslim migrants of Muslim countries, have seen Islamic fanatics rising from amongst them?[52] The broad outline of this subject even found an echo in the UN in December 2020 when Ashish Sharma, First Secretary in India's Permanent Mission to the UN, accused the resolutions of the UN body of being selective while condemning violence against Abrahamic religions, but failing to acknowledge the rising hatred and violence against Hinduism, Buddhism and Sikhism.[53] Speaking on the subject 'Culture of Peace', Sharma said that the culture of peace can't only be for Abrahamic religions. He said while India fully agreed that antisemitism, Islamophobia and anti-Christian acts needed to be condemned, and India also firmly condemned such acts, the UN resolutions on such important issues spoke only of these three Abrahamic religions together. He added that so long as such selectivity existed, the world could never truly foster a culture of peace. He argued if the UN is selective in such matters, the world could end up proving right American political scientist Samuel Huntington's Clash of Civilizations[54].

To reinforce this statement, Sharma recalled incidents such as the destruction of the iconic Bamyan Buddha by fundamentalists

---

[52]Bichara Khader, 'Muslims in Europe: The Construction of a "Problem", *Open Mind BBVA*. https://www.bbvaopenmind.com/en/articles/muslims-in-europe-the-construction-of-a-problem/. Accessed on 31 July 2021.

[53]Scroll Staff, 'India says UN is selective, fails to acknowledge violence against Buddhism, Hinduism, Sikhism,' *Scroll.in*, 3 December 2020, https://scroll.in/latest/980196/india-says-un-is-selective-fails-to-acknowledge-violence-against-buddhism-hinduism-sikhism. Accessed on 31 July 2021.

[54]The Clash of Civilizations is a thesis that people's cultural and religious identities will be the primary source of conflict in the post-Cold War world.

in Afghanistan as well as the terrorist bombing of a gurdwara in the war-torn country in March 2020, where 25 Sikh worshipers were killed. He also made references to the destruction of Hindu and Buddhist temples and minority cleansing of these religions in these countries. Sharma reminded the General Assembly session that India was not just the birthplace of Hinduism, Buddhism, Jainism and Sikhism, but was also the land where the teachings of Islam, Judaism, Christianity and Zoroastrianism had taken strong root and where the Sufi tradition of Islam has flourished. With this Savarkarian initiative of the Modi government at the global level, it won't come as a surprise if Hinduphobia, Sikhphobia and Buddhistphobia are the new terms at the UN in the coming days, just like Islamphobia and Christianphobia.

If Savarkar had visualized the pan-Hindu flag on the global horizon, he had also thought of India as the protector of Hindus and the religions of the Hindu pantheon on the international stage. However, the masterminds of the Shaheen Bagh agitation—the extremist Wahhabi leaders—failed to see the CAA as a realization of one of Savarkar's greatest goals, and instead mischievously depicted it as a move to communally divide and persecute Indian Muslims, even using Gandhi's photo to the hilt, even as the CAA had nothing in it against Muslims living in India.

The aim behind this strategy was to project Prime Minister Modi and Home Minister Amit Shah as divisive, particularly after the severe blow that the Modi government delivered to the dreams of pan-Islamists by first winning the state elections in Assam in 2016 and then in Uttar Pradesh in 2017, freeing Jammu and Kashmir from the clutches of Article 370 and Article 35A and banning triple talaq. Further, with Prime Minister Modi gaining acceptability amongst the Muslim nations of the Gulf and also on the global platform, the idea was to dent this acceptability. In fact, this frustration of pan-Islamists and communists at the arrival of the Modi government in 2014 was visible much earlier when a group of students openly raised slogans on the campus of the Jawaharlal Nehru University in 2016 calling for the dismemberment of India.[55]

Like the pan-Islamists, communists too have milked Gandhian pacifism as much. Communist parties regarded Gandhi as a supporter of capitalists, even describing him as a lackey of British imperialism. He was lampooned because he used Hindu symbolism to convey his public message.[56] However, they started accepting Gandhi partially in 1958 due to political compulsions, something that became more pronounced in the 1970s. And when the Ayodhya Temple agitation of the early '80s began uniting Hindus, communists openly started appropriating Gandhi for the sake of secularism to 'combat communal forces'.[57]

Clearly, the pacifist element in Gandhi's ideology has rare elasticity. It can be hijacked by anyone including anti-national forces. Savarkar rightly maintained that Gandhi's non-violence had little in common with the non-violence of Buddhism and Jainism because both allowed self-defence against unprovoked physical aggression.

Despite his matchless views on national security, Savarkar lagged behind Gandhi when it came to a few other public goals. Gandhi's inclusive model of public service in various fields, especially Dalit welfare woven around bringing social reform from within as against the exclusive model of Savarkar and Dr Ambedkar, who called for dismantling the caste system, left a deep impact on society. In fact, Gandhi's Dalit model, which he called the Harijan Model, has perhaps few parallels when it comes to inclusive social reform. His innovative ways of public service inspired and produced by its example a team of highly

---

[55]India Today Web Desk, 'JNU row: "We will split India" slogan raised by JNUSU members, claims ABVP video', *India Today*, 15 February 2016. https://www.indiatoday.in/india/story/jnu-row-we-will-split-india-slogan-raised-by-jnusu-members-claims-abvp-video-308731-2016-02-15. Accessed on 27 July 2021.

[56]Dr Pingali Gopal, *The Hans India*, 6 May 2021; https://www.thehansindia.com/dr-pingali-gopal. Accessed on 27 July 2021.

[57]Saubhadra Chatterji, 'Gandhi's mass appeal among Indian communists,' *Hindustan Times*; 19 September 2019. https://www.hindustantimes.com/india-news/gandhi-s-mass-appeal-among-indian-communists/story-BHjryLHvBYpcezTySm20DJ.html. Accessed on 27 July 2021.

dedicated social workers who didn't have any political ambition and worked selflessly in various fields for the society's upliftment. Gandhians such as Thakkar Bapa, Vinoba Bhave, Sane Guruji, Shankarlal Banker, Parikshitlal Majmudar, Gokulbhai Bhatt, Jugatram Dave, Mahadev Desai, Nanabhai Bhatt, Ravishankar Maharaj, Usha Mehta, Poornima Pakvasa and Dharampal left a great legacy that still sustains. Gandhi's public service model, in fact, inspired an entire segment in the lower and middle classes, especially in rural areas, the imprint of which is still visible in the form of commendable social work done in distant corners of India.

Gandhi's social work touched diverse fields. It led to innovative but culturally rooted ways to sustain the village economy, which included khadi weaving, natural farming, imparting lessons on cleanliness and hygiene to the poorest and the lowest and teaching inclusive ways of protest to labour unions so that they became promoters of the industry even while fighting for their rights. Gandhi's ideological contribution, which made use of Hindu symbolism, was immense. If he spoke about ushering in sustainable village economy using his idea of Gram Swaraj as a vehicle, he also taught trusteeship to the business class telling them to spare a part of their income for uplifting the poor. His trusteeship principle was rooted in the Mahajan Sanskriti (philanthropist culture) of Hindus which implored the economically well-off sections of society to help the needy. This is what is called corporate social responsibility (CSR) today.

On the other hand, despite his exemplary work against untouchability, Savarkar didn't leave behind any such great legacy. In a way, he can't be blamed for it because his long jail sentence meant that he got only 13 years—when he was in internment in Ratnagiri from 1924 to 1937—to prove his mettle as a social worker. Yet another factor that hindered Savarkar's growth as a social worker and his ideology was the fact that he was unable to get the kind of committed adherents that Gandhi got in the form of several great leaders and workers who continued to take his legacy of true public service forward.

Further, Savarkar's views on the economic model for India was similar to Nehru's ideas being partially rooted in the imported Russian model, with emphasis on nationalization of key industries and even nationalization of farmland for contract farming.[58]

In sharp contrast to Gandhi, Savarkar the rationalist spoke against cow worship as a practice, although he did emphasize the need for cow protection. Therefore, while Gandhi used Hindu symbolism and yet failed to protect Hindu rights against Muslim aggression, Savarkar criticized some of the Hindu ideals and ways while always emphasizing on Hindu protection. Perhaps this was the reason why a majority of Hindus voted for the Congress rather than the Hindu Mahasabha in the final round of elections before Partition, in addition to the astute political game that the Congress played by neutralizing Savarkar's truly nationalist propaganda by symbolic gestures and using Sardar Patel's anti-Pakistan rhetoric against the Hindu Mahasabha.

Savarkar, like many others in Indian history, held promise but his non-populism became an impediment to his acceptability. He was also hamstrung by his attitude and adherence to his beliefs. Burning with anger at the compromises made by the Congress on key national security issues, Savarkar, the blunt speaker not given to populism, used extremely harsh language many a time to criticize his Congress opponents. When Prime Minister Lal Bahadur Shastri died in Tashkent in January 1966, after returning almost everything that Indian soldiers had won from Pakistan in the 1965 Indo-Pak War, Savarkar didn't even pay him homage. On the contrary, he issued a statement criticizing Shastri for the 'Tashkent surrender'.[59] He even said that he didn't feel like paying homage to Shastri for the damage he had done to national interest.[60] Any other leader in Savarkar's place would not have chosen such a delicate occasion to criticize a prime minister who had just passed away.

---

[58]Ibid. 283.
[59]V.D. Savarkar, *Aitihasik Rajkiya Nivedane (Samagra Savarkar, Vol. 8)*, Mumbai: Veer Savarkar Prakashan, 1993, p. 165.
[60]Ibid.

And that too a prime minister who was known for his impeccable integrity. However, to Savarkar, even personal integrity was perhaps secondary to protecting core national interests in true Nation First spirit.

There are several instances in history that point to the difficulty people faced in trying to meet Savarkar without appointment (particularly in his last phase after Independence, when he had grown weak physically), even if he was sitting idle at home. However, he gave a glimpse of his queer behaviour even before Partition, when in 1938, industrialist G.D. Birla, who was driven by the vision to bring patriots of divergent views closer, advised Savarkar to speak positively about Gandhi's work amongst the Harijans in his speeches. Savarkar's response to what was a good suggestion was harsh. He asked Birla to stop donating money to the Hindu Mahasabha's coffers.[61] On another occasion, around the same period, he couldn't spare time for Pandit Madan Mohan Malaviya, who wanted to meet him, as he was occupied with writing his presidential speech in 1937.

Several years later, the aged mother of Mohan Ranade, one of the heroes of the Goa liberation movement, came to see Savarkar, but he didn't meet with her.[62] The old lady became so frustrated that while leaving Savarkar's home, Savarkar Sadan in Bombay, she said it would be better that Savarkar is caged in a glass cupboard and kept for darshan (visit). Savarkar even refused to meet N.C. Chatterjee, the Hindu Mahasabha leader from West Bengal, without appointment. However, when he met Savarkar after proper appointment, Savarkar angrily told him that things would remain depressed on India's military front till Nehru remained prime minister. Chatterjee was surprised by Savarkar's anger on the occasion. On yet another occasion, he sent back then RSS Sarsanghchalak Guruji Golwalkar, who came to meet him because

---

[61]Dhananjay Keer, *Veer Savarkar*, Popular Prakashan Pvt. Ltd; Second edition, 2019, p. 241.
[62]Ibid. 538.

of some urgent work.[63] However, Golwalkar was zealous enough to meet him and succeeded in doing so the next day.

Once after Independence, he refused to meet General (later Field Marshal) K.M. Cariappa for no reason. In fact, two of Cariappa's letters to Savarkar also went unanswered. All this was despite the fact that in an age that was entirely dominated by Nehru, Cariappa had the courage to praise Savarkar's national security vision in his speech during the Hindu Mahasabha's militarization week in Bombay in 1963. Some Savarkar apologists say he didn't meet Cariappa because he wanted to protect him from Nehru's possible ire. It is an explanation that doesn't exactly work in Savarkar's defence, though much later Savarkar publicly praised Cariappa.[64]

This kind of inflexibility on Savarkar's part is justified by his supporters with the defence that after Partition and the way Nehru treated him, making him an accused in Gandhi's assassination—which resulted in public stigma that kept people away from him and his ideology for several decades—putting him in detention on the smallest pretext and his failing health, all had deeply affected his nature. We must appreciate that a man who undergoes a long, depressing incarceration followed by solitary confinement is bound to have some angularities. However, the net impact of Savarkar's attitudinal problems, his strong beliefs and his non-populist approach was that it restricted his growth amongst the masses in a nation which even today can't get over populism. He was too much of a realist for a populist nation like India.

ULTIMATE TRUTH WILL PREVAIL

The emergence of Prime Minister Modi as an unapologetic Hindu who is also fair to the minorities is in a way the realization of the Savarkarian vision—the vision of one who never supported relegating minorities as second-class citizens in the Hindu nation

---

[63] Ibid.
[64] Ibid. 28–41.

and instead saw them as equals with Hindus, but at the same time, strictly forbade the creation of a nation within a nation in the name of religious minoritism.

There are other indications too that point to the dawn of the Savarkar era. For instance, Savarkar was aware of the geopolitical importance of Nepal, and as early as 1928, he wrote: 'Even Nepal itself doesn't know its importance.'[65] He even started his first presidential speech in 1937 by congratulating the king of Nepal. Several years later in 2014, Prime Minister Modi became the first top dignitary to be accorded the privilege of offering special puja inside the Pashupatinath temple in Nepal—a privilege at one time accorded only to the royal family of Nepal. Savarkar was in favour of strengthening connections with Hindu colonies in South-east Asia and Africa emphatically and not in the realm of tokenism. The Modi government is doing just that by bringing Non Resident Indians (NRIs) closer to India through a series of measures and making them a big feature of India's soft power as compared to the token measures of most of the previous governments. What is more, the Modi government has shown every possible sensitivity in dealing with NRI Muslims when they have been under attack while working in Muslim countries. Modi has also added yoga and Ayurveda to this soft power global approach in keeping with Savarkar's dream.

By abrogating Article 370 and Article 35A in Jammu and Kashmir—provisions that went against the core values of our Constitution—on 5 August 2019, the Modi government paid real tribute to Dr S.P. Mukherjee, who was martyred in a Kashmir jail in 1953 while agitating against the imposition of Article 370, as well as Savarkar, who reminded the nation of Mukherjee's motto of 'Ek Vidhan, Ek Nishan, Ek Pradhan (One Constitution, One Flag, One Prime Minister)'. Paying rich tributes to Mukherjee after his death in 1953, Savarkar said:

> Bharat has lost one of the foremost patriots, politicians and a born parliamentarian. May his martyrdom seal the cause of

---

[65] V.D. Savarkar, *Sphut Lekh (Samagra Savarkar, Vol. 8)*, Mumbai: Veer Savarkar Prakashan, 1994, p. 33.

the inseparable and total integration of the whole of Kashmir with Hindusthan Republic. Let us take up the flag and carry on the fight to success. That alone can be the real monument to commemorate the great leader. All Bharat and Hindudom in particular can never be too grateful to his memory who has served them so much and so long.[66]

Savarkar had visualized that a day would come when all religious and social barriers would disappear to make the universe one human world but had averred that till that point Hindus can't let their guard down against religious aggression. A ray of hope in this direction emerged recently when at the behest of the progressive crown prince of Saudi Arabia, Prince Mohammed bin Salman, the school curriculum in the country known for exporting Wahhabi terror till recently, was changed to remove hatred towards non-Islamic religions and include several positive, plural dimensions of Hinduism, Buddhism and even Sikhism and also the Mahabharata and the Ramayana. Obviously, India's new status on the global platform after the arrival of the Modi government and the government's nuanced cultural diplomacy played a role in this.

The late J.D. Joglekar, a scholar on Savarkar, had done a commendable job of propagating Savarkar's thoughts and his personality through his writings. While commenting on Savarkar's death (1966), he concludes one of his masterly write-ups with deep anguish. He says, 'A classic hero passed into eternity. An epoch came to an end. As had often happened before, a prophet died in wilderness.'[67]

However, the great scholar in his agony had forgotten a golden principle of the universe: in accordance with the law of nature, the ultimate truth must always prevail. So what if it takes an unusually long time? Lord Buddha and Buddhism remained on the sidelines for over 200 years after Buddha's Nirvana and surfaced only when Emperor Ashoka embraced Buddhist tenets and donned the role of

---

[66]V.D. Savarkar, *Historic Statements by Savarkar*, G.P. Parchure, 1967.

[67]Commemorative Volume on Veer Savarkar, 1988, p. 41; Article by J.D. Joglekar titled 'Profile of a Prophet'.

a missionary to propagate Buddhism in all directions. None would have thought at that time that over 2,000 years later, Buddhism would be the fourth most widely practiced religion in the world. Like Buddha, the Savarkar era too has arrived in right earnest after remaining on the sidelines for decades.

V.D. SAVARKAR: CALENDAR OF LIFE EVENTS

28 May 1883 – Born in Bhagur, a tiny village in Nasik district of Maharashtra

1892 – Lost his mother Radhabai

1898 – Took an oath before the family deity to conduct armed revolt against British rule

9 September 1898 – Lost his father Damodarpant

1 January 1900 – Founded Mitra Mela, a secret revolutionary society

1 March 1901 – Married Yamuna (Mai)

19 December 1901 – Passed matriculation examination

24 January 1902 – Joined Fergusson College, Pune

May 1904 – Founded Abhinav Bharat, a revolutionary organization

November 1905 – Organized the first public bonfire of foreign clothes in Pune

December 1905 – Passed B.A. examination

June 1906 – Left for London

10 May 1907 – Celebrated Golden Jubilee of the Indian War of Independence 1857 in London

June 1907 – Wrote the book *Joseph Mazzini*, which was later published by Babarao Savarkar

1908 – Wrote *Indian War of Independence 1857*, which was secretly published in Holland

May 1909 – Passed Bar-at-Law examination, but permission to practice was denied

1 July 1909 – Madanlal Dhingra shot dead Curzon Wyllie in London

24 October 1909 – Vijayadashmi celebrated under the Chairmanship of Gandhi at India House, London

13 March 1910 – Arrested on arrival in London from Paris

8 July 1910 – Epic escape through the port hole of S.S. Morea while being taken to India

24 December 1910 – Awarded Transportation for Life

31 January 1911 – Awarded Transportation for Life for the second time, the only person in the history of the British empire to have received it twice

4 July 1911 – Entered the Cellular Jail, Andamans

April 1919 – Yesuvahini, the wife of his elder brother, passed away

21 May 1921 – Both brothers brought back to the Indian mainland

1921–23 – Lodged at Alipore and Ratnagiri jails

6 January 1924 – Released from Yerawada Prison and interned in Ratnagiri on the condition that he would not participate in politics

7 January 1925 – Daughter Prabhat was born

10 January 1925 – A new weekly *Shraddhanand* launched in memory of Swami Shraddhanandji of the Arya Samaj

March 1925 – Dr Keshav Baliram Hedgewar, who was to found the Rashtriya Swayamsevak Sangh (RSS later), met Savarkar

1 March 1927 – Mahatma Gandhi called on Savarkar at Ratnagiri

17 March 1928 – Son Vishwas was born

16 November 1930 – First inter-dining organized as part of his social reform campaign

February 1931 – Instrumental in the establishment of Patit Pavan Mandir open to all Hindus

25 February 1931 – Presided over the Bombay Presidency Untouchability Eradication Conference

26 April 1931 – Was Chairman of the Somvanshi Mahar Parishad in the premises of Patit Pavan Mandir

17 September 1931 – Arranged programmes such as *kirtan* (hymns) by a person belonging to the Bhangi caste, inter-dining of

75 ladies as part of the social reform campaign

22 September 1931 – Prince of Nepal, Hem Bahadur Shamsher Singh called on Savarkar

10 May 1937 – Unconditional release from internment at Ratnagiri

10 December 1937 – Elected as President of the Akhil Bharat Hindu Mahasabha at its 19th session at Karnavati (Ahmedabad) and continued to be re-elected as President for the next seven years

15 April 1938 – Elected as President of the Marathi Sahitya Sammelan

1 February 1939 – Started unarmed resistance against the Nizam of Bhaganagar (Hyderabad)

22 June 1940 – Netaji Subhas Chandra Bose called on Savarkar

25 December 1941 – Bhagalpur struggle

28 March 1942 – The Hindu Mahasabha delegation meets Sir Stafford Cripps

May 1943 – Public felicitations on the occasion of his 61st birth anniversary

14 August 1943 – University of Nagpur conferred Honorary D.Litt. on Savarkar

5 November 1943 – Elected president of the Marathi Natya Sammelan at Sangli

16 March 1945 – Elder brother Babarao passed away

19 April 1945 – Presided over the All India Princely States Hindu Sabha Conference at Baroda (Gujarat)

8 May 1945 – Daughter Prabhat married at Pune

April 1946 – The Bombay government lifted ban on Savarkar's literature

15 August 1947 – Hoisted both Bhagwa and Tricolour flags on Savarkar Sadan to celebrate India's independence

5 February 1948 – Arrested under the Preventive Detention Act after Gandhi's assassination

10 February 1949 – Acquitted in Gandhi Assasination Trial

19 October 1949 – Youngest brother, Dr Narayanrao Savarkar, passed away

December 1949 – Inaugurated the Calcutta (now Kolkata) session of the Akhil Bharat Hindu Mahasabha

4 April 1950 – Was arrested and detained in Belgaum jail on the eve of arrival of Pakistani prime minister Liaquat Ali Khan in Delhi

May 1952 – Public function held at Pune to announce the dissolution of Abhinav Bharat, the revolutionary society, having achieved its aim of freeing India

February 1955 – Presided over the silver jubilee celebrations of Patit Pavan Mandir at Ratnagiri

23 July 1955 – Was the Chief Speaker at the Lokmanya Tilak Centenary Celebrations in Pune

10 November 1957 – Main speaker at the Centenary Celebrations of the Indian War of Independence 1857 held in New Delhi

28 May 1958 – Accorded a civic reception by Greater Bombay Municipal Corporation on the occasion of his diamond jubilee

8 October 1959 – University of Pune conferred honorary D. Litt. at his residence

24 December 1960 – Mrityunjay Divas celebration—a day set down for the release of Savarkar after completing the sentences of two Transportation for Life

15 April 1962 – Sri Prakash, Governor of Bombay, called upon Savarkar at his residence to pay his respects

29 May 1963 – Hospitalized for a fracture in the leg

8 November 1963 – Savarkar's wife Yamuna passed away

September 1965 – Taken seriously ill

1 February 1966 – Takes a decision to fast unto death

26 February 1966 – 10.30 a.m., at the age of 83, Savarkar left his mortal coil

27 February 1966 – Cremation at the electric crematorium, the final salute given by 2,500 uniformed RSS swayamsevaks and millions of admirers across the country

BIBLIOGRAPHY

Acharya Balarao Savarkar, *Swatantryaveer Savarkar: Akhand Hindusthan Ladha Parv 1941–1947*, Swatantryaveer Savarkar Rashtriya Smarak, 2020.
———. *Swatantryaveer Savarkar: Hindu Mahasabha Parv 1937–1940*, Swatantryaveer Savarkar Rashtriya Smarak, 2020.
———. *Swatantryaveer Savarkar: Ratnagiri Parv 1924–1937*, Swatantryaveer Savarkar Rashtriya Smarak, 2020.
———. *Swatantryaveer Savarkar: Sangta Parv 1947–1966*, Swatantryaveer Savarkar Rashtriya Smarak, 2020.
After Partition, The Publication Division, Ministry of Information and Broadcasting, Government of India, 1948.
A.J. Karandikar, *Krantikarak Tilak Ani Tyancha Kaal*, Kaal Prakashan.
Akshay Jog, *Swantantrya Veer Savarkar: Akshep Ani Vastav*, Mrutunjay Prakashan, 2019.
———. *Veer Savarkar: Allegations and Reality*, Krishna Publications, 2019.
Amales Tripathi, *The Extremist Challenge: India between 1890 and 1910*, Orient Longmans, 1967.
Anil Chandra Banerjee, *Indian Constitutional Documents 1757–1939, Volume II*, A. Mukherjee & Co., 1948.
Anilesh Mahajan and Subhash Sharma, *Rashtrawadi Bhagat Singh*.
Balraj Krishna, *Sardar Vallabhbhai Patel: The Man Who Unified India*, HarperCollins India, 2018.
B.G. Kaushik, *The House That Jinnah Built*, Padma Publications Ltd, 1944.
B.N. Jog, *Threat of Islam: Indian Dimensions*, Mumbai (Bombay): Unnati Prakashan, 1994.
Chandrachur Ghose and Anuj Dhar, *Conundrum: Subhas Bose's Life after Death*, Vitasta Publishing Pvt. Ltd, 2019.
Dhananjay Keer, *Lokmanya Tilak: Father of Our Freedom Struggle*, S.B. Kangutkar, 1959.
———. *Veer Savarkar*, Bombay: Popular Prakashan Pvt. Ltd, 1966.
———. *Mahatma Gandhi: Political Saint & Unarmed Prophet*, Popular Prakashan, 1973.
———. *Krutadnya Mi Krutarth Mi*, Mumbai: Popular Prakashan, 2018.
Dr Pattabhi Sitaramayya, *The History of the Indian National Congress Volume II: (1935–1947)*, Padma Publications Ltd, 1947.
Durga Das, *India from Curzon to Nehru and After*, Collins, 1969.

H.T. Desai, *Shatpailu Savarkar*, Prabodhan Goregaon, 1983.

H.V. Seshadri, *The Tragic Story of Partition*, Sahitya Sindhu Prakashan, 2015.

Joya Chatterji, *Bengal Divided Hindu Communalism and Partition, 1932–1947*. Cambridge University Press, 2002.

J. Chaube, *History of Gujarat Kingdom 1458–153*, Munshiram Manoharlal Publishers, 1975.

Koenraad Elst, *Who Is a Hindu? Hindu Revivalist Views of Animism, Buddhism, Sikhism and Other Offshoots of Hinduism*, Voice of India, 2002.

Lal Bahadur, *The Muslim League: Its History, Activities and Achievements*, Agra Book Store, 1954.

Maulana Abul Kalam Azad, *India Wins Freedom: An Autobiographical Narrative*, Orient Longman, 1959.

M.D. Chitkara, *Rashtriya Swayamsevak Sangh: National Upsurge*, APH Publishing Corporation, 2004.

M.G. Ranade, *Rise of the Maratha Power*, Punalekar & Co., 1900.

Mountstuart Elphinstone, *The History of India*, London: John Murray, 1841.

Nathuram Godse, *May It Please Your Honour*, Surya Prakashan, 1989.

N.H. Palkar, *Dr. Hedgewar Charitra*, Bhartiya Vichar Sadhna.

P.C. Bamford, *Histories of the Non-cooperation and Khilafat Movement*, Government of India Press, 1925.

Pyarelal, *Mahatma Gandhi: The Last Phase Vol. I*, Navajivan Publishing House, 1956.

———. *Mahatma Gandhi: The Last Phase Vol. II*, Navajivan Publishing House, 1958.

Ramesh Chandra Majumdar, *Penal Settlement in Andamans*, Publications Division, Government of India, 1975.

Shashi Ahluwalia, *Rajaji and Gandhi*, Alora Publication, 1960.

Sheshrav More, *Congress Ani Gandhijini Akhand Bharat Ka Nakarla?* Rajhans Prakashan; First edition, 2012.

Source Material for a History of the Freedom Movement in India, Vol. II, 1885–1920, Government Central Press, 1958.

Surendranath Sen, *Foreign Biographies of Shivaji*, London, 1927.

Tara Chand, *History of the Freedom Movement in India, Vol. II*, Publications Division, 1967.

T.R. Sareen, *Hindu Mahasabha Tryst with United India*, Eastern Book Linkers, 2019.

V.M. Bhat, *Abhinav Bharat athava Savarkaranchi Krantikari Gupta Sanstha*, G.P. Parchure Prakashan, 1950.

Valentine Chirol, *Indian Unrest*, Macmillan and Co., 1910.

Veena Hardas, *Dharmaveer Dr Balkrushna Shivram Munje Yanche Charitra Part Two*, Lakhey Prakashan, 2013.

Vinayak Damodar Savarkar, *Historic Statements by Savarkar*, G.P. Parchure, 1967.

———. *Six Glorious Epochs of Indian History*, Mumbai: Bal Savarkar, 1971.
———. *Abhinav Bharat Sangta Bhashane (Samagra Savarkar, Vol. 8)*, Mumbai: Veer Savarkar Prakashan, 1993.
———. *Aitihasik Rajkiya Nivedane (Samagra Savarkar, Vol. 8)*, Mumbai: Veer Savarkar Prakashan, 1993.
———. *Hindurashtra Darshan (Samagra Savarkar, Vol. 10)*, Mumbai: Veer Savarkar Prakashan, 1994.
———. *Hindutva (Samagra Savarkar, Vol. 10)*, Mumbai: Veer Savarkar Prakashan, 1994.
———. *Hindutva Che Panchapran (Samagra Savarkar, Vol. 10)*, Mumbai: Veer Savarkar Prakashan, 1994.
———. *Jatyuchhedak Nbandh (Samagra Savarkar, Vol. 9)*, Mumbai: Veer Savarkar Prakashan, 1994.
———. *Mazi Janmthep (Samagra Savarkar, Vol. 2)*, Bombay: Veer Savarkar Prakashan, 1994.
———. *Samajik Bhashane (Samagra Savarkar, Vol. 9)*, Mumbai: Veer Savarkar Prakashan, 1994.
———. *Samajik Bhashane (Samagra Savarkar, Vol. 8)*, Mumbai: Veer Savarkar Prakashan, 1994.
———. *Sphut Lekh (Samagra Savarkar, Vol. 8)*, Mumbai: Veer Savarkar Prakashan, 1994.
———. *Vigyannishth Nbandh (Samagra Savarkar, Vol. 9)*, Mumbai: Veer Savarkar Prakashan, 1994.
———. *Atma Charitra: Mazya Athvani*, Swatantryaveer Savarkar Rashtriya Smarak Trust.
———. *Inside the Enemy Camp*, Swatantryaveer Savarkar Rashtriya Smarak Trust.
———. *My Transportation for Life*, Swatantryaveer Savarkar Rashtriya Smarak Trust.
Yuvraj Krishnan, *Understanding Partition: Separation Not Liquidation*, Bharatiya Vidya Bhavan, 2002.
VSM (Retd) Maj Gen (Dr) GD Bakshi, S.M., *Bose or Gandhi: Who Got India Her Freedom?* K.W. Publishers Pvt. Ltd, 2019.

FREQUENTLY ACCESSED WEBSITES

https://archive.org/
https://www.columbia.edu/
https://www.mkgandhi.org/cwmg.htm
http://savarkar.org/
https://www.savarkarsmarak.com/

INDEX

12-point demand, 20
1763 Battle of Rakshasbhuvan, xl
1942 resolution, xv, 131
1945–46 Central Legislative Assembly elections, xvi
1946 Royal Indian Navy Revolt, 234
1947 Indo-Pak War, x
1962 Indo-China War, xiv

Abhinav Bharat Society, 86, 96, 221, 224, 228, 245
Agrani, xxix
ahimsa, 36, 86, 102, 223, 224
Ahl-e Hadith, 33, 257, 259
Ahmad, Sir Ziauddin, 15, 231
Akali Dal, 102, 120, 180, 200, 205
Akhada movement, 86
Akhand Hindustan Leaders' Conference, 160
Akhand Hindustan Resolution, 137, 138
Ali, Choudhary Rahmat, xviii, 48, 92, 112, 113, 114
Aligarh, xvi, 1, 7, 10, 15, 16, 17, 27, 28, 29, 59, 112, 117, 231, 268
Aligarh College, 10, 15
Aligarh Movement, 1, 15, 17
Aligarh Muslim University, 1, 117, 231
Aligarh School, xvi, 27, 28, 29, 59
Ali, Nawab Amir, 29
All India Congress Committee, 52, 208
All India Muhammadan Educational Conference, 20
All India Muslim League, 20, 92, 187, 231, 275
Al-Mujahid, Prof. Sharif, 163, 164
Ambedkar, Babasaheb, xi, xv, xix, xxii, xxiii, xxix, xxx, 8, 18, 32, 34, 35, 50, 51, 55, 58, 61, 81, 110, 125, 179, 210, 222, 242, 250, 252, 278
Amrita Bazar Patrika, 105, 106
Andaman and Nicobar, xxiii, xxxvii, 226

Aney, M.S., 100
Anglo-Muslim Alliance, xvi, 8
anti-Hindu jizya tax, xxxvii
anti-Pakistan campaign, 234
anti-RSS lobby, 91, 272
anti-Savarkar lobby, xxxiii
Apte, Narayan, xxviii, xxix
Arthashashtra, 6
Article 370, xv, 217, 277, 283
Arya Samaj, 33, 37, 41, 103, 105, 106, 158, 159, 251, 287
Arya Samajists, 122
Asan, 220
Assam, x, xli, 59, 60, 95, 107, 113, 150, 162, 176, 180, 183, 184, 185, 199, 200, 207, 235, 236, 257, 277
Attlee administration, 173
Attlee, Clement, xvii, 173, 235
Attock, 13, 70, 214
Aurobindo, Sri, xli, 221, 236
Axis Powers, 60, 228
Azad, Chandra Shekhar, xxvii, 219
Azad Hind Fauj, xviii, xxvi, 228, 235
Azad, Maulana Abul Kalam, 31, 40, 137, 169, 186, 195, 197, 203, 275

Balakot, xlii
Balochistan, 46, 48, 112, 183, 184, 201, 255
Bang Bhang Movement, 219
Bangladesh, xvii, 20, 191, 203, 210, 255, 276
Bapat, Senapati, 103, 221
BBC London, 205
Bengal, xviii, xxxvi, 8, 11, 12, 14, 40, 41, 45, 47, 53, 55, 58, 59, 60, 70, 105, 106, 107, 110, 111, 113, 114, 118, 123, 126, 134, 146, 147, 148, 150, 152, 156, 162, 176, 180, 183, 184, 185, 187, 188, 189, 191, 192, 193, 194, 196, 198, 199, 202, 203, 204, 206, 210, 219, 221, 223, 225,

226, 230, 232, 235, 236, 257, 263, 281
Bengali Muslims, 187
Bengal Legislative Assembly, 146
Bengal Pact, 40, 41
Besant, Mrs Annie, 34
Betibandi, 83
Bhagalpur, 95, 104, 135, 137, 171, 176, 193, 288
Bhagur, xiv, 286
Bharamputra, 69
Bharat, ix, x, xi, xii, xvi, xxvi, xxvii, xxix, xxxvi, xxxvii, 2, 24, 43, 68, 69, 86, 87, 96, 161, 192, 213, 221, 223, 224, 225, 227, 228, 230, 237, 241, 242, 243, 245, 248, 254, 283, 284, 286, 288, 289
Bharatiya Jana Sangh, 110
Bharatiya Janata Party (BJP), 110, 236, 270
Bharat Khand, 68
Bharatvarsh, 160
Bhopatkar, L.B., xxviii, xxix, 104, 179, 183, 206
Bhulabhai Desai–Liaquat Ali Pact, 163
Birla, G.D., xxxiv, 281
Bismil, Ram Prasad, 219
Bombay province, 44, 46
Bose, Netaji Subhas Chandra, xi, xv, xxvi, xxxv, 58, 62, 140, 176, 178, 219, 222, 228, 229, 230, 288
Bose, Rash Behari, 145, 168, 219, 229, 230, 233, 236
Bose, Sarat Chandra, 140, 178, 202
boycott of British goods, 59
Brahmin, xx, xxv, 61, 260
Brigadier Mohammad Usman MVC, x, 263
British Indian forces, xviii
British Indian government, 17, 130, 143, 146
British–Muslim League combine, 199, 208
Buddhism, 71, 121, 251, 276, 277, 278, 284, 285

Cabinet Mission Plan, 181, 194, 195, 196, 203, 204, 205
Cama, Madame, 158, 252
Canada, 134
Cariappa, K.M., xiii, 282
Cellular Jail, xxiii, xxxi, xxxvii, 171, 225, 227, 287

Central Executive Council, 143
Central Provinces, 11, 57, 58, 106, 110, 178, 184
Chakravarti, 137, 153
Chanakya Niti, 110, 239
Chandavarkar, Sir V.N., 110, 133
Chand, Tara, 15
Chatterjee, N.C., 105, 281
Chatterjee, Ramananda, 133, 134
Chavan, Vamanrao, xxv
Chinese threat, x
Christian communal strategists, 121
Christian Mission, 90
Churchill's statement, 129
Churchill, Winston, 129
Citizenship (Amendment) Act (CAA), 275, 276, 277
Clash of Civilizations, 276
Communal Award, 49, 50, 51, 52, 175
Congress–Khilafat alliance, 33
Congress–League pact, 135
Congress–Muslim alliance, 32
Congress or Conscience, 175
Congress rule, 7, 54, 55
Congress's 'British stooge' campaign, 234
Congress's Khilafat compromise, 36
Congress's pacifist ideology, 65
Congress ticket, 164
Congress Working Committee, 58, 165, 202
Conservative Party, 173, 234
Constituent Assembly, 174, 181, 182, 184, 185, 186, 197, 198, 210, 248, 250, 252, 262
COVID-19, xxi
cow slaughter, xli, 8, 28, 32, 40, 41, 55, 58
cow worship, 80, 272, 280
C.R. Formula, 151, 153
Cripps Mission, 139, 219
Cripps proposal, 131, 133, 136
Cripps, Sir Stafford, 131, 135, 182
C.R. Plan, 151, 152, 154

Dalit emancipation, 61
Dalvi, D.G., 27
Dam, Anang Mohan, 176
Das, Chittaranjan, 40, 41
Das, Durga, 152, 169, 170, 211, 262
Delhi municipal elections, 177
Deliverance Day, 112

Democratic Swarajya Party, 110, 154
Deobandi ulema, 31
Deoband school, 236
Depressed Classes, 50, 125, 169, 250
Desai, Bhulabhai, 140, 163, 164, 165, 166, 178
Desai–Liaquat Pact, 163, 166, 168, 171
Desai, Mahadev, xxii, 279
Dinia, 113
direct action, 170, 187
divide-and-rule theory, 14
Doordarshan, xli, 249
Dufferin, Viceroy Lord, 17, 219
Dwaidhibhav, 220

Ek Vidhan, Ek Nishan, Ek Pradhan, 283
Elphinstone, Mountstuart, 69

Fatherland, 66, 70, 71, 72, 74, 78, 88, 113, 114, 122, 153, 213, 271
father of India's national security, 127
Fergusson College, xxiv, 160, 286
First War of Independence, xxvi, 218
Forward Block, 176

Gaga, Madan Singh, 91, 103, 104
Gandhian cap, 36, 37
Gandhi assassination, x, xi
Gandhi, Devdas, 140
Gandhi, Indira, xxxi, 241
Gandhi–Irwin Pact, 49
Gandhi–Jinnah talks, 156, 157
Gandhi, Mahatma, x, xxii, xxx, 24, 29, 30, 31, 33, 35, 36, 38, 39, 40, 57, 115, 138, 142, 151, 155, 187, 188, 196, 201, 202, 203, 207, 208, 235, 273, 287
Gandhi's release, 140
Ganga-Jamuni tehzeeb, 30
Germany, xviii, 16, 60, 73, 129, 134, 138, 168, 220, 223, 225, 228, 229, 239, 240, 252
Ghadar revolutionary movement, 219
Godse, Nathuram, xxviii, xxix, 104
Goel, Sita Ram, xl, 37
Gogate, Vasudeo Balwant, xxiv
Gokhale, Gopal Krishna, 23, 24, 157
Golwalkar, M.S., xxxii, 242
Gurumukhi, 225

Harijan, 115, 116, 118, 131, 132, 274, 278

Hedgewar, Dr Keshav Baliram, 108, 287
Hindi, xxvii, xli, 47, 54, 57, 66, 67, 68, 71, 72, 89, 100, 141, 225, 243, 248, 249
Hindi-Chini Bhai-Bhai, 243
Hindu-bashing, 275
Hindu–Buddhist front, 145
Hindu civilization, 71, 102
Hindu consolidation, xxxvi, xxxvii, xxxviii, 216
Hindu Dalits, 34
Hindudom, 66, 75, 97, 98, 99, 212, 213, 284
Hindu interests, xxix, xxxvi, 27, 147, 148, 149, 159, 168, 171, 177, 191
Hinduism, 30, 37, 66, 71, 72, 76, 77, 106, 251, 252, 276, 277, 284
Hindu Mahasabha, xiii, xiv, xv, xvii, xix, xxviii, xxix, xxxiii, xxxiv, 26, 33, 37, 41, 44, 63, 76, 87, 89, 90, 91, 92, 94, 95, 98, 99, 100, 103–109, 119, 121, 122, 123, 124, 128, 131–137, 141, 143–151, 153, 154, 157–160, 162, 165, 166, 168, 170, 173, 174, 175, 176, 177, 178, 179, 181, 183, 184, 188, 192, 193, 199, 203, 206, 207, 213, 214, 230, 231, 232, 234, 238, 239, 280, 281, 282, 288, 289
Hindu-majority districts, 199, 206
Hindu–Muslim population, xix, 231
Hindu–Muslim population ratio, xix, 231
Hindu–Muslim problem, 102, 122, 137, 138, 139, 141, 151, 162
Hindu–Muslim relationship, 29
Hindu–Muslim unity, xiii, xxxi, xxxii, xxxv, xxxviii, 14, 25, 28, 29, 30, 31, 34, 35, 37, 41, 42, 50, 55, 56, 87, 89, 94, 102, 113, 115, 126, 127, 138, 155, 161, 180, 258, 259
Hindu nation, xxxvii, 66, 67, 68, 75, 78, 79, 83, 86, 87, 88, 97, 102, 109, 214, 217, 252, 282
Hindu Pad-Padashahi, xxviii
Hindu pantheon, xxxv, xxxvi, xxxviii, 50, 104, 105, 122, 123, 250, 277
Hindu Raj, 7, 141, 215, 216
Hindu Rashtra, xii, xxix, xxxix, 62, 67, 70, 72, 73, 74, 77, 79, 90, 92, 93, 94, 96, 126, 133, 217, 224, 265
Hindu Sanghatanists, 97, 170
Hindu scriptures, 83, 158
Hindu–Sikh unity, 199

Hindustan Socialist Republican Association (HSRA), xxvii
Hindusthan, 70, 71, 72, 73, 75, 87, 91, 98, 99, 109, 125, 138, 154, 157, 161, 171, 175, 176, 179, 212, 213, 214, 216, 230, 236, 253, 284, 290
Hindu Travancore, 274
Hindutva, x, xi, xii, xiii, xxv, xxvii, xxxii, xxxiii, xxxvi, xxxvii, xli, 36, 62, 63, 65, 66, 67, 68, 71, 72, 75, 76, 77, 78, 83, 86, 89, 90, 91, 93, 102, 106, 108, 109, 115, 116, 121, 154, 236, 250, 258, 265, 270, 274
His Holiness Sri Shankaracharya of Puri, 161
Holy Land, 66, 71, 72, 73, 74, 78, 88, 122, 153, 213, 271
Hotson, Sir John Ernest Buttery, xxiv
Hunari and Shakari, 160
Huq, Abul Kasem Fazlul, 53
Hyderabad, xxxiv, xl, 4, 11, 98, 100, 103, 104, 105, 106, 113, 114, 119, 126, 137, 138, 139, 171, 210, 260, 274, 288
Hyderabad Day, 106

idol-worshipping poem, 54
Imam-e-Hind, 47
independence, xviii, xxi, xxix, 11, 25, 48, 49, 75, 94, 98, 113, 120, 128, 130, 133, 138, 151, 161, 174, 218, 228, 230, 241, 245, 247, 288
Independence Day, 214
Independent Labour Party, 110
Indian Council Bill, 21
Indian Liberals, 110
Indian Muslims, xvi, xvii, 31, 47, 48, 55, 56, 71, 94, 100, 118, 131, 154, 163, 168, 178, 194, 195, 255, 256, 257, 266, 268, 277
Indian National Army, xviii, 233
Indian National Congress (INC), xv, 2, 76, 79
Indian Nationalism, 75
Indian Republic, xv, 97
India Wins Freedom, 41, 186, 195, 197, 203, 275
Indo-British Commonwealth, 130, 143
Indus valley civilization, 66
Iqbal, Sir Muhammad, 47, 48, 92, 262
Islamic jihad, 188

Ismail, Mirza, xxxiv, 99
Israel, 241, 270–272
Iyer, Sir C.P. Ramaswami, 133, 273, 274

Jainism, 71, 121, 277, 278
Jallianwala Bagh, 32, 40
Jammu and Kashmir, xlii, 85, 99, 138, 217, 232, 240, 244, 277, 283
Jammu & Kashmir National Conference, 138
janmajaat nahi pothijaat, 80
Japan, xviii, xxvi, 60, 105, 124, 138, 145, 165, 168, 173, 178, 225, 228, 229, 230, 239, 240
Jawaharlal Nehru University, 277
Jayakar, Dr Mukund Ramrao, 44, 45, 100, 140, 173, 183
Jehangir, Sir Cowasji, 110
Jha, Durga Nand, 269
Jhansi-Hamirpur constituency, 54
Jinnah, Mohammed Ali, xviii, xxiii, xxxiii, xxxv, 1, 8, 26, 42, 43, 44, 45, 46, 47, 49, 50, 51, 53, 54, 55, 56, 58, 59, 60, 61, 63, 85, 92, 98, 100, 101, 111, 112, 116, 117, 118, 119, 124, 131, 138, 141, 142, 144, 148, 149, 150, 151, 152, 154, 155, 156, 157, 162, 163, 164, 165, 166, 167, 168, 169, 170, 181, 183, 184, 186, 187, 188, 191, 194, 195, 196, 197, 200, 201, 204, 205, 209, 210, 213, 228, 255, 256, 268, 273
Jinnah-Savarkar meeting, 149
Jinnah's Jihad, 187
Jinnah's Pakistan scheme, xxxv, 118, 167
Joglekar, J.D., 284
Johannesburg, 30
Joshi, Yashwantrao, 104

Kakori Conspiracy, 219
Kashmir, x, xix, xxxv, xxxix, xli, xlii, 85, 95, 99, 100, 107, 112, 126, 138, 139, 217, 232, 240, 244, 251, 260, 263, 274, 277, 283, 284
Kashmiri Muslims, 103, 139, 251
Kautilya, 6, 219
Kelkar, N.C., 110
Khan, Ashfaqullah, x, xxxix, 219, 263, 268
Khan, Azimullah, x
Khan, Dr Khan Abdul Jabbar, 52, 201
Khan, Khan Abdul Ghaffar, 52

Khan, Sikandar Hayat, 53, 56, 116
Khan, Sir Syed Ahmed, 1
Khare, Dr N.B., 165, 252
Khilafat agitation, 31, 32
Khilafat movement, xxxviii, 14, 32, 33, 36, 41, 42, 141, 158, 217, 267
kirpan, 102
Kripalani, Acharya, 126, 178, 189, 207
Krishak Praja Party, 53, 146
Kuka Movement, 219

Labour party, 190, 234
Lahiri, Ashutosh, 91, 176
Lal, Jagat Narain, 137
Lingayats, 122
Linlithgow, Viceroy Lord, 60, 117, 125
local Bengali Hindus, 59
Lord Ram, 47
Lucknow Pact, 26, 27, 29, 43

Madhavrao, Peshwa, xl
Mahabharata war, 68
Mahapour, xli
Mahar, 231, 250, 287
Maharaj, Shivaji, xxiv, 231, 238
Majhya Aathavani Nashik, 220
Malaviya, Madan Mohan, 26, 37, 63, 236, 281
M.A.O. College, 1, 8, 17, 20
Maratha Confederacy, 11, 12
Marathi, xxiv, xli, 57, 249, 288
mass-mobilizing abilities, 63
Mehta, Jamnadas, 110, 154, 160, 161, 176
Menon, V.P., 98, 155, 156, 172, 173, 185, 187, 198
militarization policy, xiii, 233
Mitra Mela, xxxvi, 220, 286
modern-day jihad, 189
Mohani, Maulana Hasrat, 31
Montagu–Chelmsford Reforms, 219
Moplah episode, 35
Morley-Minto Reforms, 21, 22, 23, 24, 25
Mughal–Maratha connection, xxxix
Muhammadan Anglo-Oriental College, 1
Mukherjee, Dr Syama Prasad, xiii, xxviii, 91, 105, 120, 134, 147, 162, 173, 198, 203, 214, 230, 283
Munje, B.S., xv, xxviii, 26, 34, 42, 63, 93, 236
Munje, Dharamvir, xv

Munshi, K.M., 140
Muslim aggression, xxxvii, 63, 107, 137, 171, 175, 238, 274, 280
Muslim-appeasement policies, xiv, xxix
Muslim atrocities, 193, 200
Muslim fanaticism, 36, 58, 161
Muslim League, xiii, xvi, xix, xxxiv, xxxv, 1, 7, 14, 17, 20, 42, 43, 44, 47, 48, 49, 50, 51, 53, 54, 55, 56, 57, 58, 65, 79, 92, 93, 94, 96, 100, 101, 103, 105, 110–113, 117, 118, 119, 120, 122, 123, 124, 131, 132, 133, 137, 141, 142, 144, 146, 147, 148, 149, 150, 151, 152, 154, 155, 156, 158, 159, 162, 163, 165, 166, 167, 168, 169, 170, 172, 173, 177, 180, 181, 182, 183, 184, 185, 187, 188, 191, 192, 193, 194, 195, 196, 197, 199, 200, 201, 202, 203, 204, 205, 208, 231, 234, 235, 256, 267, 268, 270, 274, 275
Muslim League's Lahore resolution, 100, 117
Muslim-majority areas, 53, 137, 151, 152, 155, 181, 199, 202, 232
Muslim-majority Bengal, 184, 199
Muslim-majority states, 26, 53
Muslim State, 92
Muslim victimhood, xvii, xxx, xxxv, 89, 112, 186

Nagari script, 74
Nagar Palika, 249
Naidu, Sarojini, 42
Naoroji, Dadabhai, xvi, 16, 17, 237
Narendra Modi-led government, xv
Nariman, K.F., 160
National Herald, 135
National Register of Citizens (NRC), 275
nation-building plan, 95
Nation First, x, xi, xxi, xxxii, xli, 236, 237, 238, 267, 281
nazarqaid, xxiii, xxv
Nazi holocaust, xxi
Nebuchadnezzar II, 144
Negrosthan, 136
Nehru government, xxix, 215, 216, 247, 271
Nehru, Jawaharlal, xiv, xxviii, xxix, xxxi, xxxii, 50, 54, 58, 60, 100, 110, 113, 134, 139, 152, 153, 169, 170, 177, 178, 185, 186, 187, 190, 191, 194, 195, 196, 197,

198, 200, 202, 204, 205, 207, 208, 209, 210, 211, 214, 215, 216, 217, 235, 236, 238, 241, 242, 243, 247, 262, 271, 275, 277, 280, 281, 282
Nehru, Motilal, 44
Neogy, K.C., 176
Nepal, 96, 98, 171, 240, 283, 288
Noakhali, 146, 191, 192, 193, 194, 208
non-Congress leaders, 110
non-cooperation movement, 31, 37, 41
non-Hindu Indians, 88
non-League Muslim leaders, 167
non-Muslim electorates, 177
non-Vedic faiths, 71
north-west, 92, 204
North-West Frontier Province, 45, 46, 47, 48, 52, 112, 148, 180, 181, 183, 184, 185, 187, 201, 202

one man one vote, 92

Paarshad, xli
Pakistan, x, xv, xvi, xvii, xviii, xix, xx, xxxi, xxxiv, xxxv, xxxviii, xlii, 1, 2, 8, 14, 18, 32, 34, 46, 47, 48, 49, 51, 55, 58, 61, 85, 91, 92, 97, 98, 99, 101, 111, 112, 113, 114, 115, 118, 119, 120, 124, 125, 126, 127, 131, 132, 133, 135, 136, 137, 138, 141, 144, 147, 148, 149, 150, 151, 152, 153, 155, 157, 161, 162, 164, 167, 170, 172, 174, 175, 177, 178, 180, 181, 183, 184, 185, 186, 187, 189, 192, 194, 195, 196, 197, 200, 201, 202, 203, 204, 205, 206, 209, 210, 213, 214, 216, 217, 228, 230, 231, 232, 234, 238, 240, 243, 244, 255, 256, 263, 265, 266, 267, 268, 270, 272, 273, 274, 276, 280
Pakistan-aligned Nizam, 274
Pakistan-occupied Kashmir, 244
Pakistan Resolution, xxxiv, 111, 113, 118, 267
Pal, Niranjan, 40
Pandit, Vijaya Lakshmi, 242
pan-Islamist psyche, xv
pan-Islamists, xv, xxii, xxiii, xxx, xxxviii, 24, 33, 104, 114, 146, 256, 258, 265, 275, 277, 278
pan-Islamist writers, xxv
Paranjpe, S.P., 160, 161
Parmanand, Bhai, 91, 100, 104, 159, 236

Parshuram, Lord, xx
partition, ix, xvii, xviii, xxi, xxii, xxiii, xxviii, 8, 12, 19, 20, 27, 47, 59, 96, 103, 116, 122, 123, 133, 156, 174, 195, 202, 262, 265
Patit Pavan Mandir, xxiii, 86, 287, 289
Phadke, Gopikabai, 158
Phadke, Vasudev Balwant, 18, 219, 236
Pirpur Committee report, 54, 55
plebiscite, 137, 148, 151, 152, 155, 202, 203, 205
population percentage-based representation, 149
Prabhakar, 106
Prasad, Dr Rajendra, 60, 139, 252
Pratap, Maharana, x, xxvi, 64, 73, 75, 98, 102, 132, 264
Princely States, 288
pro-Muslim leanings, 27
pro-Muslim nationalism, 61
pro-Muslim policies, xxxiv, 99, 103, 267
Provincial Assembly, 176, 195
proxy war, 244
pseudo-Gandhians, xxiii
pseudo-secularism, xxxiv, 91
Pulwama attack, xx, 270
Punjab, xiii, xxvi, 15, 45, 47, 48, 53, 56, 60, 101, 110, 112, 116, 123, 126, 148, 149, 150, 152, 156, 162, 169, 180, 183, 184, 198, 200, 201, 203, 206, 207, 208, 210, 215, 216, 225
purification of Marathi, xli

Queen's proclamation, 218
Quit India movement, 142, 152, 164, 177
Quit Kashmir' movement, 100

Rajaji, 14, 58, 113, 137, 138, 148, 151, 152, 153, 154, 209
Rajaji Formula, 151
Rajguru, xxv
Raman, Sir C.V., xxxiv
Ranade, Justice Mahadev Govind, 11, 12
Rangoon, 130, 168, 171, 219
Rani of Nilambur, 34
Rashtriya Swayamsevak Sangh (RSS), xii, xxii, xxxii, 36, 90, 91, 104, 108, 109, 171, 217, 242, 255, 272, 281, 287, 289
Ratnagiri, xxiii, xxiv, xxv, xxvii, xxxi, xxxv, xxxvii, xxxviii, 36, 61, 62, 81, 82, 90, 95,

154, 160, 206, 227, 279, 287, 288, 289
Razvi, Syed Qasim, 103
reconversion, 37, 41, 84, 85, 86, 252
religion-based considerations, 172
Roosevelt, Franklin D., 129, 130, 140
Rotibandi, 82
Round Table Conference, 49, 92
Rowlatt Act, 31
Russia, 19, 73, 134, 220, 223, 228, 239, 240, 242, 246
Russian imperialism, xxvii

Sachar Committee, 268, 269
Samshray, 220
Sandhi, 219
Sanskriti Samvardhan, 80
Sanskriti Sanrakshan, 80
Sanskritized Hindi, 249
Sapru, Sir Tej Bahadur, xxx, 23, 49, 120, 125
Sapta Sindhu, 67, 68
Saraswati, Dayananda, 158
'Sare Jahan se Accha', 47
Sastri, V.S. Srinivasa, 133, 157, 161
Satyarth Prakash, 158, 159
Saurashtra region, 30
Savarkar, Balarao, xxii, xxiv, xxvi, xxvii, xxix, 91, 94, 98, 99, 105, 107, 108, 121, 123, 125, 138, 154, 157, 161, 171, 176, 179, 206, 230, 236, 248, 250
Savarkarian ideology, xv
Savarkarian spirit, x
Savarkar's presidential address, 104
Savarkar vilification campaign, xxxi
Savarkar, Vinayak Damodar, ix, xxiv, 83, 119, 124
Sayajirao Gaekwad III, Maharaja, xxxvii, 96
security-building campaign, 234
self-determination, xv, 51, 115, 116, 118, 131, 133, 134, 137, 141, 142, 148, 154, 172, 174, 183, 186, 202, 203, 210
separatist Muslims, xviii, xxxviii, 4, 21, 99
Seshadri, H.V., 50, 51, 138, 197
Setalvad, Sir M.C., 166
Shadguna Niti, 219
Shastri, Lal Bahadur, 161, 243, 280
Shia Muslims, 89, 258
Shimla Agreement, 244
Shivaji, Chhatrapati, x, xxiv, 39, 70, 95,
102, 132, 175, 212, 231, 238, 259, 264
Shraddhanand, xxx, 32, 33, 37, 39, 62, 84, 206, 228, 236, 287
Shruti-Smriti-Puranoktaas, 80
Shuddhi, 37, 84, 86, 252
Shuddhibandi, 84
Shweta Bharat, 69
Sikhism, 30, 71, 121, 251, 276, 277, 284
Sikh–League coalition, 149
Sikhs, xiii, xxxvi, xxxviii, 32, 50, 56, 75, 102, 103, 104, 120, 122, 123, 125, 150, 162, 169, 198, 200, 215, 216, 225, 250, 255, 276
Simon Commission, 44
Sindh, xxxv, 44, 46, 48, 53, 60, 68, 92, 95, 102, 103, 112, 126, 146, 147, 148, 149, 156, 158, 159, 176, 180, 183, 184, 199, 201, 206, 207, 244, 255, 271
Sindh Muslim League, 158
Sindhubandi, 84
Singh, Bhagat, xxv, xxvi, xxvii, 39, 140, 219
Singh, Guru Gobind, x, xxvi, 39, 73, 75, 102, 132, 199, 213, 217, 264
Singh, Raja Man, 64
Sitaramayya, Dr Pattabhi, 132
Soomro, Allah Bux, 140
South Africa, xxxi, 30, 134, 223
Sparshabandi, 81
Sri Guru Nanak Dev Ji, 210
Suhrawardy, Huseyn Shaheed, 16, 188, 189, 193, 194, 202, 203
Sultan, Tipu, xxxix, 4, 217, 260
Svatva, 75
Swadeshi, xxxvi, 86
Swami Shraddhanand, 32, 33, 37, 39, 62, 236
Swatantrya, 206

Tablighi Jamaat, 37, 257, 259, 266
Tarana-e-Hindi, 47
the Congress, ix, xv, xvi, xvii, xix, xx, xxviii, xxxi, xxxii, xxxiii, xxxv, xxxvii, xxxviii, 2, 6, 7, 8, 16, 22, 23, 25–29, 31–38, 40– 44, 48–63, 65, 79, 91, 92, 94, 95, 96, 99–107, 109, 110, 112, 113, 115–124, 129–133, 135, 137, 139, 141–143, 146–148, 151, 152, 154, 156–159, 161–170, 172–184, 186–191, 193, 194, 196– 198, 200, 201, 202, 203,

204, 205, 207–210, 214–219, 229, 231, 233–235, 239, 244, 247, 255, 267, 268, 274, 275, 280
the Himalayas, 66, 67, 69, 239
the Hurs, 159
the Koran, 8, 9, 32, 159, 191, 266
the *Modern Review*, 134
The Muslim League Council, 187
The New York Times, 128, 136
Thengadi, Dhundiraj, xxv
the North-east, xxxv, 151, 236
Theosophical Society, 30
the *Rig Veda*, 67, 68
Thoughts on Pakistan, xix, 8, 18, 32, 34, 58, 61
Tilak, Satyabhama, 158
two-nation theory, xxxi, 1, 7, 12, 48, 65, 93, 113, 163, 183, 203, 255, 256
Tyabji, Badruddin, 28, 29, 42

ultra-liberals, 110
unalloyed nationalism, x, xx, xxxii, xxxiv, 36, 62, 63, 86, 93, 95, 100, 177, 199, 238, 253
undivided Bengal, 202, 203
undivided British Indian army, xix
undivided India, 141, 163, 198
unification of Bengal, 219
Unionist Party, 53, 169, 180
United India, 96, 97, 120, 125, 128, 133, 144, 145, 152, 154, 162, 167, 172, 174, 177, 181, 182, 186, 195, 196, 198, 199, 205, 208, 214, 239, 240, 274
United Provinces, 113, 114, 180, 184, 193
UN Security Council, 242
Urdu, xxxiv, 47, 54, 57, 60, 99, 100, 248, 249, 255, 262

Uttar Pradesh, 53, 54, 87, 180, 257, 262, 277

Vadodara state, 96
Vallabhbhai Patel, Sardar, xv, xvi, 99, 100, 109, 110, 119, 139, 174, 177, 195, 205, 237, 238, 243, 252, 255, 263, 280
Vande Mataram, xv, 28, 54, 57, 58, 233, 262
Varnas, 80
Vasudhaiva Kutumbakam, xxvii, 89
Vedalankar, Chandragupt, 160
Vedoktabandi, 82
Vidya Mandir, 57
Vigraha, 220
Vikramaditya, 70, 132, 160, 217
Vikram Samvat, 160
Vishwaguru, xi, xxi, xli, 89
Vivekananda, Swami, xli
vivisection of India, 115, 135, 136, 156
vivisection schemes, 161
vote-bank politics, xxi, 270, 271

Wadhwani, Dr Hemandas, 149
Wahhabi Muslim, 230
Wahhabism, 33, 257, 259
Wavell Plan, 167, 168, 169, 170, 171, 172
Wavell, Viceroy Lord, 159, 167
World War I, 31, 219, 223, 226
World War II, xviii, 43, 59, 109, 112, 117, 128, 129, 144, 146, 164, 173, 228, 230, 231, 232, 235, 239, 275

Yaan, 220

Zakaria, Rafiq, 195